Also by Barbara Norman

The Spanish Cookbook
The Russian Cookbook

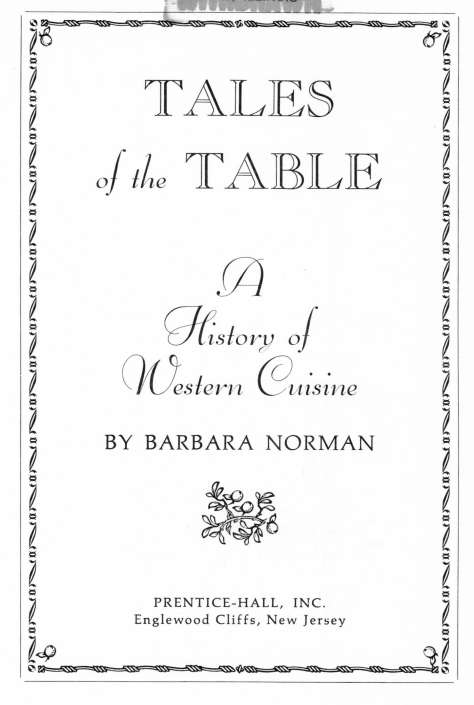

TALES
of the TABLE

A History of Western Cuisine

BY BARBARA NORMAN

PRENTICE-HALL, INC.
Englewood Cliffs, New Jersey

Design by Linda Huber

TALES OF THE TABLE: A History of Western Cuisine
by Barbara Norman

ISBN 0-13-884205-1
Library of Congress Catalog Card Number: 77-170499

Printed in the United States of America T

Prentice-Hall International, Inc., London
Prentice-Hall of Australia, Pty. Ltd., Sydney
Prentice-Hall of Canada, Ltd., Toronto
Prentice-Hall of India, Private Ltd., New Delhi
Prentice-Hall of Japan, Inc., Tokyo

Illustrations pp. 1, 11, 43, 60, 105, 177
courtesy The Metropolitan Museum of Art

All other illustrations courtesy
of the General Collections, Picture Collection,
and Rare Book Division, The New York
Public Library, Astor, Lenox, and Tilden Foundations

Dedicated to everyone
who enjoys reading about
good food almost
as much as eating it.

CONTENTS

I   INTRODUCTION   2

II   MESOPOTAMIA, EGYPT, AND GREECE   12

III   ROME   38

IV   THE DARK AND MIDDLE AGES   58

V   THE AGE OF EXPLORATION   96

VI   THE CLASSICAL CENTURY   126

VII   THE MODERN AGE   142

An Historical Index to Some Common
and Uncommon Foods   178

Menus and Recipes from Every Era   296

Notes   328

Bibliography   331

I

Introduction

Ever since Eve ate the apple, almost every
event in the history of mankind and every important occasion in a man's life has been connected with
food. Good food has been an instrument of diplomacy and government from primitive sacrificial rites to Christmas dinner. Food has
inspired painters, artists, writers, and inventors, led to discoveries,
motivated explorations, precipitated revolutions, and played a role
in the rise and fall of fortunes and kings. And all this has been
faithfully recorded in thousands of ways in thousands of sources:
in cuneiform, hieroglyphics, manuscripts, and printed books; on
baked bricks, papyrus scrolls, stone tablets, vellum, and paper; in
cave drawings, tomb paintings, Renaissance paintings; in songs,
cantatas, plays, diaries, poems, and epigrams, to say nothing of
cookbooks and literature about good eating.

Cooking was not looked down on as unworthy of the attention
of intelligent men in the old days. Just as Chinese poets wrote
cookbooks, Greek and Roman scholars wrote of food, sometimes
in verse. The earliest piece of Western gourmet literature, the
Heduphagetica (*Delicacies of the Table*), was written over 2,300
years ago by a Greek epicure called Archestratus of Gela, who
traveled for the exclusive purpose of finding and noting the most
delectable specialties of each region. Unfortunately only fragments
of the book remain, preserved in the first gastronomical work that
has come down to us reasonably intact, an anthology of writings on
food and eating compiled about A.D. 230 by another Greek writer,
Athenaeus. Called the *Deipnosophists* (roughly translatable as

2

Connoisseurs in the Art of Dining), it is a collection of works of the preceding 500 years and testifies to the extraordinary number of people writing about the pleasures of the table 2,000 odd years ago.

Among the great epicures Athenaeus describes in his anthology is Marcus Gabius (or Gavius) Apicius, one of three famous gourmets bearing the same surname. M. G. Apicius lived during the reigns of Roman emperors Augustus and Tiberius, or sometime between 90 B.C. and A.D. 40. An exceedingly rich man, Apicius devoted his life and most of his fortune to eating well. He would go to any amount of trouble to find a new delicacy. Although his home at Minturnae on the sea south of Rome was blessed with particularly delicious and very large crayfish, when Apicius heard that exceptional ones were to be found on the African coast, he embarked on a long and uncomfortable voyage to investigate. As the ship neared the African shore, Apicius engaged some coastal fishermen to bring him the best local samples. Still on board ship, Apicius inspected the crayfish, which he found no larger or finer than those at home. On being assured there were none better to be had in Africa, he turned back to Italy and his own crayfish without touching land.

Apicius spent so much of his huge fortune on such ventures (some sources say 100 million sesterces and others 60 million), that he was reduced to only 10 million, the equivalent of between a quarter and a half million dollars. That should have been enough to keep a rich man well fed for a lifetime in Imperial Rome, but Apicius was afraid of starving to death and poisoned himself at a final, long, and magnificent banquet.

Apicius is not the earliest epicure recorded in history. Great eaters have been immortalized from early Biblical times to the present, from Belshazzar, who feasted while Babylon fell, to Louis XVIII, whose preoccupation with food sometimes overrode matters of state, and who was more often closeted with his maître d'hôtel than his ministers. Some gourmets are important men remembered today for their gourmandise rather than their accomplishments. Lucullus is renowned as an epicure, not as the great general and fine Latin and Greek scholar he also was. The Prince de Soubise is not remembered for his activities as marshal of France, but for the onion sauce named after him.

With a long and varied roster of gourmets, Rome leads the list of civilizations known for voluptuous eating. There was Marc Anthony, who rewarded his cook with a house for a particularly good supper, and Cleopatra, who is said to have dissolved and drunk a large pearl to win a bet that she could surpass Anthony in lavish feasting. There were Roman emperors like Claudius, who interrupted a solemn session in court to exclaim over the meat pastries he was looking forward to at supper; others like Verus, who wallowed in a carpet of narcissus blossoms at his notorious banquets, where not only was the food the most costly available, but the crystal, gold, silver, and even the handsome serving boys were given away to the guests.

After the Roman era, the jolly monks and princes of the Church continued the tradition of hearty eating and drinking, resisting for centuries all efforts to curb their appetites. The extravagance of medieval clergy can be judged from the scale of their entertainments, at which hundreds or even thousands were feasted for days. The proclamation of Archbishop Cranmer in 1541 limited the higher clergy to a diet in which archbishops had a daily allowance of only six kinds of meat or fish, four second dishes, and a meager dessert of custard, tart, fritters, cheese, and two kinds of fruit, and lower ranks were scaled accordingly. The edict was judged far too austere. Like subsequent rulings, it was ignored, leaving the fame of churchly gourmets untarnished.

Gourmets number a great many artists. As Thackeray said, "every man who has been worth a fig in this world—as poet, painter, or musician—has had a good appetite and good taste." Writers have been inspired by food for 2,500 years, often elevating cooking to a place with the other arts. Anatole France praised *cassoulet* for the foundation that gives it a flavor otherwise found only in the paintings of old Venetian masters; Proust compared the patience and love of a good cook to the "conscience disdaining all fatigue" of Renaissance painters and builders of cathedrals.

Renaissance painters might have liked the comparison; painters have always been inspired to paint food as well as to eat it. The luscious grapes and wines more sparkling than reality of Caravaggio, Rubens, Veronese, Chardin, Renoir, and others betray more than a passing interest in the pleasures of the table. Poets shared their enthusiasm. In the nineteenth century, historian Sébastien

4

Mercier wrote, "the more delicate a poet is in his verse, the greater an eater he is at table . . ." But the most delicate poet would have had difficulty in outeating Haydn, who used to go to his favorite hotel, order a dinner for five on the pretense of expecting guests, and then eat it happily by himself.

Even more has been written about feasts than about gourmets. From early times, the feast, private or public, was the main social entertainment. Starting with Mesopotamian banquets of 1800 B.C., feasts have been described in detail in records of purchases and expenditures, household inventories, menus, and contemporary accounts in diaries, letters, and chronicles. The scale of feasts of the past is almost unbelievable. At the largest, people were fed in the thousands, literally herds of cattle were slaughtered, and as many as 30,000 individual dishes presented on the menu. Medieval feasts sometimes lasted for days or even weeks. The endless eating alternated with jousts or hunts. Courses of food were interspersed with wild practical jokes, outlandish pageants, and pantomimes with ingenious mechanical devices and animated figures. Tightrope walkers teetered across ropes over the heads of guests at the table, ships bobbed on artificial waves in ponds constructed in the dining hall, and dragons yawned to release a chorus of singers. Equally popular were pranks in food such as pies of live larks or live musicians, peaches that spit fireworks, ceilings that opened to shower down perfume and sweets. No trouble was too much, no idea too farfetched for a feast, whether it took filling the Circus canals with wine for Heliogabalus or making an artificial lake of punch for an eighteenth-century naval lord, who had a page boy row about on it to serve his guests.

Feasting was not all for fun. Starting with the early Greek religious rites, public feasts were an instrument for satisfying the public and keeping the poor under control. The triumphal banquets of Roman victors, at which several hundred thousand were fed, built up support and affection for the new strong men, whose political positions, if not their lives, were often in danger on their return to Rome. It was to keep the public happy that kings in the Middle Ages held open house on holidays, and in the seventeenth and eighteenth centuries admitted any decently dressed person to their dining rooms to enjoy the spectacle of royalty eating. Nowhere was rigid feudal ceremony more skillfully combined with popular appeal than in the public meals of French kings, which attracted a steady stream of carriages from Paris to Versailles. But as kings lost absolutism, they gained privacy. Louis XVIII is reported to have shut the door of his dining room after an embarrassing incident. According to the story, he was annoyed at dinner one day to find spinach, one of his favorite vegetables, missing from the menu. When he asked for it, he was told his chief physician had forbidden it. Louis XVIII exclaimed loudly in anger, "What! I'm king of France and I can't eat spinach?" The bodyguards in the adjoining room burst into uncontrollable laughter, and the king's dining-room doors closed for good.

Probably the earliest marketing list is a stone tablet of 1900–1800 B.C. recording items ordered for a two-day feast given by an Assyrian king in the gardens of his palace of Mari. However it is only in the era of the Greeks and Romans that it becomes possible to reconstruct precise menus and recipes. There were Greek and Roman cookbooks; Athenaeus mentions over twenty Greek cookbook authors by name, in addition to writers on cooking terms, on food and medicine, votive offerings, and gastronomy. The earliest cookbook to survive is a Roman one of the third, fourth, or fifth century A.D. Entitled *De Re Coquinaria*, it is also known under the name of that early gourmet Apicius, though he may have had nothing to do with the book at all.

At first glance the recipes seem to be a senseless jumble of incompatible ingredients. If a recipe did not call for asafetida (an evil-smelling herb known colloquially in English as devil's dung), it was apt to call for garum, a Roman sauce whose principal feature was well-rotted fish entrails. The Roman's heavy hand with spices is repelling, and things do not improve much in cookbooks of the Middle Ages and Renaissance, in which food is almost always ground to a pulp and mixed with sugar and a heavy dose of aromatic spices.

Strange birds and animals were served at the table. The Romans, in particular, seem to have eaten everything that moved, from dormice to ostriches and grasshoppers to camels. Medieval cookbooks tell how to prepare hedgehogs, porcupines, foxes, gulls, herons, whales, and a multitude of other beasts, fish, and birds not commonly eaten today. The records of medieval banquets present these birds, fish, and beasts in what appears to be an orderless and bewildering procession, interrupted by sweets and sometimes ending with soup or hard-boiled eggs.

The amounts called for are staggering, though so was the size of the average noble household. Even a century ago, European cookbooks included cake recipes calling for eggs by the dozen, crayfish soups containing hundreds of crayfish, oyster sauces made with oysters by the peck. In the eighteenth century, great chefs daily reduced to a small amount of essence huge pieces of meat that could have fed a large family for a week.

One of the best illustrations of this kind of extravagance is a story the famous literary gourmet Brillat-Savarin tells of the steward of the Prince de Soubise. One day the prince asked his steward to bring him the menu for a small supper party he was giving. The steward presented an elaborate document. The prince burst into indignation at the first item, "fifty hams." Only one ham would appear on the table, the steward calmly explained, adding "The others are no less necessary for my espagnole sauce, my *blonds*, my garnishes, my—" The prince protested that the man was cheating him.

"Ah, monseigneur," replied the artist, barely able to keep his temper, "you underestimate our resourcefulness. Give the order, and I will put these hams that annoy you into a glass vial no larger than my thumb."

Along with the unfamiliar, there are many foods of the past that sound surprisingly like those of today. Many of our recipes and cooking techniques are very old indeed, and our culinary art, like so much of our heritage, comes to us from the Romans and before them, the Greeks, and before them, the Egyptians, Babylonians, and Hebrews. Lentil soup and pease porridge were comforting people on cold nights 2,500 years ago. Wine has been made for close to 4,000 years, beer possibly twice as long. Cheesecake is an old Greek favorite of the fifth century B.C., along with pancakes, poppy-seed rolls, and ham with mustard. The Romans enjoyed chicken croquettes, meatballs, chicken stew with leeks, and salads dressed with vinegar and oil. They had learned to thicken sauces with flour, reduce wine in cooking, and bind sauces with egg yolks. One can imagine sitting down with pleasure to the meal the

7

first-century Roman writer Juvenal proposes in his Eleventh Satire as a contrast to the sumptuous banquets of spendthrifts. The menu consists of milk-fed kid, mountain asparagus picked by Juvenal's overseer's wife, eggs, pullets raised on his farm, and for dessert grapes preserved for six months "but as fresh as when they were gathered," baskets of Syrian pears, Italian bergamots, and dried apples.

The cooking of each epoch generally reflects the characteristics of the epoch itself; it is a good index of the level of civilization. Great eras have almost always produced great food. In common with the other arts, a cuisine can develop only where there is a certain wealth and leisure. Where there is too much wealth and leisure, cooking, like all arts, lapses into a decadence in which cost and elaborate form take precedence over taste and content. When Roman sculpture was losing its virility and strength of line, Roman hosts and their chefs were concentrating on elaborate presentations of foods valued mainly for their rarity or price—the heel of a camel, for example, or a sauce in which precious stones had been dissolved. Again, when classic Renaissance architecture turned to the undulating, elaborately decorated baroque and rococo, chefs prided themselves on building foodstuffs into elaborate reproductions of scenes and figures, never meant to be eaten. When Victorian gimcrackery decked buildings with fringes and icings, cooks prided themselves on garnishes that had no connection with the dish served: cockscombs, kidneys, chicken quenelles, and sweetbreads might be piled on top of a fish, for example.

To trace the history of the Western cuisine is to follow the course of history itself. Cookery has been directly influenced by many major events: the Greek conquest of Egypt, the Roman conquest of Asia Minor, the barbarian invasion that put an end to the Roman Empire, the Crusades that reintroduced spices, the Renaissance, the discoveries of new routes to the Far East that dethroned Italy as center of trade and culinary and artistic inspiration, the French domination of Europe, the discovery of the New World, the rise of the middle class, and the Industrial Revolution.

Cooking has also had its influence on history. As Brillat-Savarin pointed out, "The destiny of nations depends on how they eat." Napoleon, who was indifferent to good food himself, understood its usefulness thoroughly. He assigned the task of diplomacy through gourmandise to two able statesmen and gourmets: his archchancellor, Cambacérès, who believed men are ruled largely by what they eat, and his foreign minister, Talleyrand. Some historians claim Talleyrand's chef rather than his diplomatic skill was responsible for his success at the Congress of Vienna. Napoleon was also well served by his chief steward and palace prefect, the Marquis de Cussy, who had been reduced to working after squandering an enormous fortune (on good living, we assume). It was the marquis who said that, if historians wanted to learn the reasons for statesmen's successes, they should devote more study to the records of the statesmen's kitchens than to their labors in parliament.

The influence of food on history is by no means limited to a role in diplomacy. How much did the eating of fish contribute to England's naval supremacy? The fishing fleets of Elizabethan days were recognized even during those times as one of the best training grounds for the navy that defeated the Spanish Armada. And how much credit for the prosperity of the Hanseatic League, and of Holland itself, should be given the Dutchman who discovered a superior way to pickle herring? To what extent did the demand for spices lead to the discovery of new navigation routes to the Far East and to a subsequent shift in the balance of power in Europe? Such are the questions that occur to anyone taking a cook's eye view of history.

These odd bits and pieces make up the story of the Western cuisine, interwoven with the history of our civilization over the past two or three thousand years. To tell the story is to wander down back corridors of history, and to talk more of oddments, quirks, and curios than great battles. Yet somehow those wanderings give a feeling of being close to the great events, their heroes, victims, and bystanders. Pieced with tidbits and crumbs from the history of the table, the table of history becomes alive and complete.

60984 81800

II

Mesopotamia, Egypt, and Greece

Eating preceded cooking, and the history of
food goes back to a time before the first inscription was carved in stone or baked in brick. At some point
in that distant, unrecorded past, on discovering that grain could be
sown for a larger, more certain harvest and stored against times of
shortage, our nomadic ancestors gave up the constant chase after
game and wild foods. It was then that farming, civilization, and
with it, civilized eating, began for the West, sometime before
9000 B.C. The earliest evidence of a settled, organized farming
community was found at Jarmo in northern Mesopotamia and
dated at about 7000 B.C. Another Mesopotamian site known as
Hassuna, believed to have thrived about 5750 B.C., yielded the remains of grain-storage bins, a bread oven, storage jars, stone hoes,
and the bones of sheep and cattle. From these remains, we know
the inhabitants tilled the soil, baked bread, stored grain for the
winter, and raised animals.

Tell Hassuna is the first Western site known to have had the
basic essentials for cooking, which requires more than knowing
how to build a fire. Without an oven, you cannot bake; without a
pot to put over the fire, you cannot make a stew, sauce, or soup.
It is true that some primitive tribes heated liquid in the hollows of
rocks by dropping in heated stones, and baked food wrapped in
leaves or buried in pits, but no one has advanced the theory that
there was much in the way of cuisine at that primitive stage. Just
as necessary to a cuisine as ovens and pots are a variety of liquids,

12

fats, seasonings, and utensils such as ladles, spoons, and strainers. These essentials made their appearance in a number of early civilizations in Mesopotamia and the Indus River valley, among the early Hebrews, in Persia, and in the Egyptian Empire.

Archaeological evidence being limited to the nonperishable, and food being highly perishable, there is a great deal we do not know. The oldest evidence consists of cave drawings, relics excavated in kitchen middens such as those of Tell Hassuna, and the fossilized remains of peas, lentils, beans, grains of cultivated wheat and barley, and seeds of fruits found in Neolithic pile dwellings in Switzerland.

The picture pieced together of man's earliest food is very incomplete. In early prehistoric times, he hunted, fished, and gathered wild fruits, roots, and nuts, particularly acorns. Acorns were so important in the European diet that Virgil commented it was only when the acorn ran short that agriculture began. Cereals, rapidly harvested, were planted long before the other two Mediterranean staples, grapes and olives. It takes a large measure of security and stability for people to want to plant olives, which bear a full crop only after sixteen or eighteen years, or grapes, which begin to yield in three.

Despite the stereotype of early man gnawing on hunks of meat, an image reinforced by Homerian tales of Greek heroes roasting oxen on great fires, the staple diet of civilizations from ancient Mesopotamia to Renaissance Europe was a kind of porridge. Meat was eaten only on special occasions when animals were sacrificed and the meat shared with the gods by the celebrants. Otherwise the diet of the poor, of country people—and, in the early days of every great civilization, of almost everyone—was cereal.

The recent discovery of thousands of stone tablets at the site of the royal Assyrian palace of Mari yielded an extraordinarily rich mine of information on food. Approximately thirteen hundred of the tablets, some 3,800 years old, are records of foods served at the king's meals and lists for purchases of food and kitchen equipment. Some lists are receipted in the name of Ilukanum, presumed to be the chief chef, the earliest cook named in history. Added to previous archaeological findings, these tablets make it possible to reconstruct Assyrian feasts in some detail. The royal household ate

fresh and smoked fish, grilled, roasted, or broiled mutton, beef, pork, and fowl, especially fattened for the table, lettuce and other fresh and dried vegetables, various kinds of bread, goats' milk and cheese, delicacies such as shrimp and truffles, and molded cakes made with oil, honey, sesame seeds, raisins, and dates (a number of terra-cotta cake molds were found at Mari). The king also had a choice of figs, dates, pistachios, apples, pomegranates, and pears, all of them fresh or dried, for dessert. There was no lack of seasoning; the Assyrians used cumin, coriander, garlic, ginger, fennel, mustard, sesame, and thyme. From the quantities of foodstuffs and kitchen equipment ordered for the palace of Mari, it can be assumed the Assyrians had vast kitchens well equipped with ovens, stoves, and utensils, and staffed with brewers, butchers, pastry chefs, and cooks.

Bas-reliefs from Khorsabad show us how the Assyrians ate in in the eighth century B.C. The poor are pictured crouching around a single plate whose contents are heaped up like a pyramid. Noblemen perch on high chairs, their feet dangling, and eat from low individual tables on which food is placed on big trays. Though not shown in the illustration, archaeological diggings have established that the Assyrians had portable braziers, ornamented pots, plates of stone, alabaster, or bronze, and cups of gold and silver.

The earliest feasts that can be reconstructed in great detail are those of the Egyptians, who outstripped the Assyrians in culinary

14

matters by making leavened bread and beer over 5,000 years ago. The vessels, inscriptions, and paintings in Egyptian tombs contain a wealth of information. Fortunately for our record, the Egyptians believed the dead man would be provided with food in the next world if his tomb paintings showed him seated before a full table. To enliven his afterlife, they often added a series of banquet scenes. The paintings are so painstakingly precise that one Egyptologist was able to identify fifteen kinds of bread and nine kinds of meat in the drawings of a single tomb. From such sources archaeologists have put together a picture of an early Egyptian feast.

The arriving guests were greeted by the children and servants, given garlands and perfumed ointments, and then led into a hall lighted with lamps fueled by castor or olive oil. There the honored guests and masters of the house were seated on high-backed chairs of wood encrusted with turquoise, cornelian, lapis lazuli, silver, and gold. The lesser guests sat on stools, the humble on mats, children on leather cushions. Musicians, dancers, and acrobats assembled to provide entertainment.

Food was placed by servants on stands or low round tables, one for each guest or one for every two guests. At the height of their civilization, the Egyptians had spoons of wood, ivory, and metal, goblets of glass, porcelain, alabaster, rock crystal, bronze, silver, and gold. Their menus included wild game, many kinds of force-fed cattle, poultry served grilled, cooked in sauce, or spit-roasted, and fish, fresh, dried, or salted. Food was seasoned with herbs and the many spices the Egyptians fetched from the Orient on ships sent down the Red Sea. Breads and honey cakes, fruit piled in pyramids, and wine served in jars complete the meal. After dinner there was singing, music, and dances, followed by a new round of tidbits to eat. To remind themselves of the brevity of these earthly joys, the Egyptians liked to bring in the wooden image of a dead person in a coffin.

How elaborate later Egyptian feasts became can be judged from a contemporary historian's description of preparations for a feast given in Alexandria by King Ptolemy Philadelphus of Egypt in the first half of the third century B.C. A pavilion large enough to hold 130 couches was erected inside the citadel walls for the occasion. It was covered with a circular canopy of scarlet edged in white, supported by beams concealed by white-striped tapestries. Between the beams were panels painted by well-known artists. A columned portico surrounded the pavilion on three sides. Inside, the walls were hung with red curtains, interspersed with animal pelts. Though it was winter, the entire floor was strewn with flowers. One hundred marble statues were placed between the supporting columns along with paintings and tapestries with gold-embroidered portraits of kings or mythological subjects. Wood columns shaped like palm trees graced the interior. Persian carpets were spread over the center. One hundred golden couches covered with purple-wool rugs and embroidered throws stood in a circle for the guests. Next to the reclining guests were two hundred three-legged tables made of gold, two beside each couch; each couch also had a silver basin and pitcher for hand washing behind it.

Advanced as the Egyptians were in the art of luxury many centuries before Christ, it was from the Persians that Greece first learned of the delights of the table. The Greeks are generally reputed to have been restrained and balanced in all things, including drinking and eating, while the Romans are pictured as forever wallowing in lusty gastronomical indulgence. Both pictures are inaccurate. Hedonists were Greek, after all, and while the Spartans gave us the word "spartan," the Sybarites gave us "sybaritic," and both were Greek. We overlook the paintings of drunken revels on Greek cups and kraters just as we banish from consciousness the knowledge that Greek columns and statues were once covered with gaudy paint.

In the good old simple days of which Homer wrote, which historians have situated about twelve or thirteen centuries B.C., kings, princes, and chieftains feasted on bread, wine, and broiled meat, the latter always prepared as a sacrifice by one of the heroes himself. After the sacrifice, they would eat and drink copiously for hours; Homer tells us so again and again. "So the whole day long till sundown we sat and feasted on our rich supply of meat washed down by mellow wine," he says as Odysseus and his companions consume a large ram offered to Zeus. When Odysseus arrives at the home of Circe, five pages later, he kills a stag: "So the whole day long till sundown we sat and banqueted on our rich supply of meat washed down by mellow wine." The phrase recurs like the chorus of a ballad, and the feast continues. Odysseus and his men

16

stay with Circe for a whole year, "feasting on meat galore and mellow wine."

The Homerian menu was always the same except for variations in the kind of meat broiled: oxen, goats, sheep, swine, rams, or wild game. The menu for one feast is comprised of three fatted hogs, some choice goats, and a heifer. King Alcinous sacrificed "a dozen sheep, eight white-tusked boars, and a couple of shambling oxen" for the reception of Odysseus. Usually the meat was cut up and roasted on a spit; shish kabob, still featured in Greek tabernas today, is a very old dish indeed.

Preparations for a feast are described in detail in the *Odyssey* and the *Iliad*. Servants sweep and sprinkle the floors, throw purple covers on the chairs, wipe the polished wood tables with sponges, and wash the two-handled cups for the guests and the bowls for mixing wine. Firewood and water are fetched. The swineherd, goatherd, or cowherd drives the live animals for the meal into the courtyard. For a very special occasion, a goldsmith gilds the horns of a heifer selected for sacrifice.

The banquet takes place in the great pillared hall of the palace, where tables are set up for the feast. As yet there is neither dining room nor any permanent arrangement for eating; furniture is moved in when needed. In the *Iliad*, Hephaestus, the god of fire, forges three-legged tables with elaborate handles and a gold wheel on each leg so that the tables will roll in and out of his banqueting hall of themselves for feasts.

Guests arriving from a journey bathe, are rubbed with olive oil, and are given tunics and warm mantles before the meal. Cleanliness is essential, because a feast is a religious act. In the *Iliad*, Hector refuses to make a libation to Zeus with unwashed hands. Before the banquet begins, a maid pours water from a golden jug over a silver basin so that the guests can wash their hands. She then draws the table close to them. Bread is brought in baskets and put next to the guests "together with a choice of dainties."

Before the sacrifice, the feasters pray to the gods while sprinkling white barley meal. Barley was such a necessary part of the ritual that when none was available in the wilderness, Odysseus substituted leaves from an oak tree. The king, his sons, or one of the chiefs performs the sacrifice by slitting the animal's throat, flaying

17

him, and cutting slices from the thighs for the gods. Wrapped in folds of fat, the thighs are put on the fire with the entrails on top. Young men stand by with five-pronged forks to turn the meat. Libations of wine are sprinkled over the entrails and thighs. When the thighs are burnt, the feasters taste the inner parts, then carve the rest of the animal into small pieces, skewer them, and roast them. The best servings, "chines cut the whole length," are awarded the bravest and most honored. Wine is passed by stewards or young noblemen.

After the guests have eaten and drunk their fill, the entertainment begins. No banquet, Homer remarks, is complete without music and dancing. The simplest entertainment was provided by a bard with lyre. In the palace of King Menelaus, there were acrobats turning cartwheels and dancing to the lyre. King Alcinous suggested some outdoor sports after his feast—wrestling, jumping, and running, following which his stewards swept the floor for a dance performance.

The feast always came to an end when the sun went down; there seems to have been a feeling that it was improper to continue after dark. A final bowl of wine was mixed, each guest was served, and each made libations to the gods before leaving. The wines, described as mellow, ruddy, sparkling, or, on a special occasion, ten years old, were always mixed with water.

The first Greeks to indulge at the table were those who first encountered the opulent civilizations of the East. These were the Greeks who founded trading stations or colonies throughout the Mediterranean and Asia Minor beginning in the eighth century B.C. There were Greek cities in the Middle East, in Sicily (where Greeks came in contact with the Phoenicians), in southern Italy, and in Asia Minor. Sybaris was established by Greeks in 720 B.C. in southern Italy, where for 200 years it was famous for banquets, jewels, clothes, and devotion to pleasure. Athenaeus claims that when the Sybarite ruler Smindyrides sailed off to secure a bride, he took along no fewer than 1,000 cooks and fowlers to attend to his table. Culinary inventions in Sybaris were protected by what is believed to be the first patent law, giving the creator exclusive rights to the making and selling for one year. In Sicily, according to Athenaeus, the culinary art had been raised almost to the dignity of a science

18

early in the fifth century B.C. Sicily remained famous for cooking through Roman times, with both Romans and Greeks eagerly hiring Sicilian cooks, particularly ones from the city of Syracuse, gastronomic mecca of the island.

We know from the writings of Hippocrates, the comedies of Aristophanes, as well as a number of sources quoted in Athenaeus, that by the fifth century B.C., dinner on the Greek mainland bore little resemblance to Homerian feasts. Fifth-century guests were "lolling on Milesian rugs" and cushioned beds at banquets in Oriental style. There were perfumes and wreaths for the guests to put on, flute girls and dancing girls to entertain them. To eat, there was fresh, salt, and pickled fish—sturgeon, turbot, and mullet; there were oysters, crabs, mussels, cockles, sea urchins, and eels. Ducks, geese, and chickens were served, stewed thrushes and ring-doves, roast beef, hare grilled on the spit, tripe cooked in honey. Cuttlefish was fried in olive oil and then sprinkled with vinegar as it still is in Spain today. There were delicate hot rolls made with fine wheat flour from Phoenicia, cakes of honey and sesame, and that very ancient favorite, cheesecake. There were also humbler dishes: pease porridge, "beautiful and brown," lentil soup, omelets, sausages, fried kidney beans with barley, chestnuts roasted in the embers. When the meal was over, the drinking began, accompanied by almonds from the island of Euboea, raisins and dried figs from Rhodes, and Phoenician dates.

The Persians were not impressed by the Greek table. When they came in contact with the Greeks during the Medic Wars in the first half of the fifth century B.C., they complained of leaving a Greek dinner hungry because there was nothing worth eating except the cereal. Antiphanes, comic poet of the fifth century, probably echoed Persian sentiments when he wrote of "leaf-chewing Greeks, scant of table."

The Greeks, on the other hand, were much impressed by the Persians. Herodotus wrote of the capture of a Persian fortified camp in which the dazzled Greeks found "tents adorned with gold and silver and couches gilded and silverplated and golden bowls and cups and other drinking vessels" and even "caldrons of gold and silver. . . ." The king of Persia, Herodotus said, had water brought him from the river Choapses; the water was boiled, put in silver jars, and transported by a large number of mule-drawn wagons. The number of animals slaughtered daily in the Persian royal palace was staggering: 1,000 horses, camels, oxen, asses, deer, ostriches, geese, cocks, and other birds and small animals. Most of this was left over for the bodyguard and troops, whose food constituted their pay. The royal table was expensive nonetheless. Herodotus comments that the Greeks who received Xerxes in order to avoid having their towns destroyed would have been destroyed anyway had Xerxes stayed on for a second meal. Darius used to travel about with 12,000 to 15,000 men, and the expense of giving them dinner was imposed on cities in proportion to their population.

It was during his sojourn in Persia that Alexander the Great of Macedonia learned what good eating was, discovering Oriental spices, new fruits such as peaches and apricots, and new luxuries of all kinds. He showed how much he had learned from the vanquished at an elaborate feast he gave to celebrate his own marriage and that of eighty friends after defeating Darius III. For five days the wedding guests ate and drank while reclining on silver couches and enjoying entertainment by jugglers from India, singers, dancers, harpists, flutists, and comedians.

This luxury was instantly imitated in Alexander the Great's native Macedonia. We owe a detailed description of it to an agreement between a Macedonian historian and a disciple of the naturalist Theophrastus to describe to each other by letter any sumptuous banquet attended. One of these "banquet letters" written about 300 B.C., has been preserved for us by Athenaeus. It describes the wedding banquet of a Macedonian named Caranus.

On entering the hall, each guest was given a present of a golden tiara and, on taking his place on a couch, a silver cup. After a glass of wine, the guests were served a bronze platter bearing a loaf of bread, chickens, ducks, ringdoves, and geese; each guest took his portion and distributed it among his personal slaves, who stood behind him. In came a second platter, this time of silver, again with a huge loaf of bread and geese, hare, kid, curiously molded cakes, pigeons, turtledoves, partridges, and other fowl; the dish was disposed of in the same manner. Next, numerous wreaths were brought in with more gold tiaras. The flute girls, singers, and Rhodian sambuca players arrived, all the girls carrying jars of silver and gold with a half pint of perfume for each guest. Servants brought in a gilded silver platter holding a whole roast pig stuffed with thrushes, ducks, warblers, eggs, oysters, and scallops, with pease porridge poured over it. After another interval of drinking, in came another platter with a kid and spoons of gold for the guests. Next, baskets and bread racks of plaited ivory strips were distributed, along with more crowns and more gold and silver perfume jars. There was a pause for entertainment by dancers, clowns, and naked female jugglers who tumbled between swords and breathed fire from their mouths. The guests were then presented with a silver bread rack with Cappadocian loaves and a huge crystal platter inside a silver one filled with all kinds of baked fish. Again they ate what they wanted and turned the rest over to their slaves. Hands were washed, crowns put on again, more gold tiaras and perfume jars distributed. A chorus of one hundred men sang the wedding hymn, dancing girls dressed as nereids and nymphs performed, and, as darkness fell, the white linen curtains draped around the room were drawn back. By a hidden contrivance, a *tableau vivant* was lowered: Cupids, Dianas, Pans, Hermeses and other figures holding lights in silver brackets. Servants brought in huge roast boars skewered with silver spears on square gold-rimmed platters. As was the custom at large Macedonian dinners, a trumpet announced the conclusion of the banquet. Slaves passed the final drink, a clown performed, and the last course was brought in: various kinds of flat cakes in ivory baskets were presented to the guests along with the boxes in which they were packed. Thereupon the guests left with all their gifts, quite sober, the writer of the letter notes, for fear of being robbed of the great wealth they were carrying away.* The writer mocked his friend for being so unfortunate as to live in sober Athens:

> But you, staying in Athens, think it happiness rather to listen to the precepts of Theophrastus, eating wild thyme and rocket seed and your esteemed rolls while you attend the festivals of Lenaea and the Pots! We, however, have carried away a fortune from Caranus's banquet instead of trifling portions, and are now looking for houses or land or slaves to buy.[1]

---

* Their fears were not unfounded; robbers were common on the streets at night in the ancient world. In fact, one Syracusan ruler who wanted to discourage dinner parties did so by dealing harshly with all criminals except footpads. (Plutarch, *Moralia*, "Sayings of Kings," 175. F.)

Of all periods of ancient Greece, the fourth century B.C. is the one for which we have the most complete picture of the table. Much of the information is from contemporary sources, largely because Athenaeus, who lived five or six centuries later, quoted from so many plays, medical writings, travelogues, historical accounts, and cookbooks of the fourth century B.C. that are now lost to us. A period of great refinement in sculpture and architecture, the fourth century was also a period of refinement in food and one of great interest in food on the part of cultivated people. Many of these were men of letters, who had as much feeling for the right seasoning as for the right phrase. Comedy writers of the time refer to food continuously and in great detail; the cook, an early stock comedy character, plays an important role in many of their plays. Most of these comedies we know only from the extracts preserved by Athenaeus; the same is true of the "banquet letters," and of the previously mentioned gourmet tour of Archestratus of Gela.

In addition to the wealth of material provided by Athenaeus, we are fortunate in having a travelogue written by Anacharsis the Younger, whose minute descriptions of his reception in Athens and elsewhere in Greece are filled with gastronomic information. Other fourth-century sources still available today are Aristotle, Plato, Theophrastus, and Xenophon.

By this golden age, cooks had specialized; pastry makers were distinct from cooks of fish and meat. For banquets, cooks were hired in the market along with the requisite assistants and utensils. At least twelve cooks were necessary for an important dinner. Other aides were available in the market: butchers, sausage makers, instructors in the art of carving, fishermen, musicians and entertainers of various sorts, a marketer to buy the food and a "table-maker who will wash the dishes, get the lambs ready, prepare the libations, and do everything else which it is his business to do." [2] (It is interesting that a hired man had taken over what was once the sacred office of the host.) Fourth-century cooks could become rich on selling the leftovers from feasts. One called Moschion, a slave, "was able in the space of two years to buy three apartment houses and practise wanton lust on freeborn boys and the wives of the most eminent citizens." [3]

In the second half of the fourth century B.C., authorities felt it necessary to pass a sumptuary law limiting the number of dinner guests to thirty. Wedding caterers were obliged to register so that inspectors could determine whether anyone hiring a caterer invited more than the legal quota of guests.

Though we have no complete recipes from this period, the writers of comedies have passed on a number of menus and fairly precise descriptions for making some of the dishes; so have Anacharsis and the traveling gourmet, Archestratus of Gela. From these sources we know fourth-century Greeks were cooking with wine, gratinéeing with cheese, making meat broth and gravy meat stews, stuffing birds, meats, fish and fig leaves, and serving combinations such as "browned pork ribs on cakes of finest meal." They made a number of sauces—peppery ones, sour ones, ones with herbs—some gastronomes thought there were altogether too many of them and spoke critically of "sticky sauces with too much cheese and oil." Many vegetables were served, including vegetable garnishes, as in a dish of Byzantine tuna covered with beets mentioned in a play by Antiphanes.

The Greeks and Romans ate a number of bulbous roots, most of which no one could identify with certainty today. The bulbs of a kind of squill, of iris, and of gladiolus seem to have been among them. The latter were added to bread for flavor and weight; asphodel bulbs were roasted in hot ashes and served with salt and oil, or pounded and mixed with figs. Bulbs were also served with pine nuts, rocket, or pepper, or in a highly seasoned sauce.

Cumin from Ethiopia, silphium * from North Africa, capers, mustard, and various herbs were common seasonings. Truffles were much appreciated and even imported from North Africa. The Greeks had also acquired some of the perverse tastes associated with the Romans, such as a predilection for the matrix of a sow that had miscarried, a delicacy served in white sauce or brine and rue.

---

* Silphium has never been positively identified from ancient descriptions of the plant. It appears not to be identical with asafetida, though used in somewhat the same way. Theophrastus described it as a plant with a thick root and celerylike leaf. The roots, he said, can be eaten fresh or cut up in vinegar. Silphium was usually used in sauces and as a seasoning on foods. The best variety came from Cyrene, Africa, whose inhabitants were obliged to deliver silphium to Rome as tribute. The Romans considered the plant so precious that they locked it up with the gold and silver of the public treasury. Neither Greeks nor Romans were successful in cultivating silphium, which became rarer and rarer until it had almost disappeared by the beginning of the Christian era. It is unknown today.

While Homer's heroes ate meat almost exclusively, meat was a minor dish at Greek banquets of the fourth century B.C. Meat was actually scarcer because the growth of agriculture had absorbed pastureland and made it necessary to breed oxen for work rather than food. There was butchers' meat in the market, but many people were afraid to eat a nonsacrificed animal. Fish, which Homer had scorned, now took the place of honor at the banquet table.

Having such an abundance of fish at hand, the Greeks disdained the smaller fry and sought larger and rarer fish, many imported from other parts of the Mediterranean. Great ingenuity was exercised in preparing them. The Greeks had discovered the court bouillon and the advantage of boiling salt-water fish in seawater. They poached fish, baked it, stuffed it, fried it, batter-fried it, and served it with herbs, spices, and sauces such as mulberry or vegetable sauce, or wrapped it in a fig leaf and baked it under the ashes.

The following passage from a fourth-century playwright, Sotades, represents a cook describing his preparation of various fish for a dinner. It illustrates both the ingenuity of Greek cooks and the intense interest in cooking of Greek playwrights (and, presumably, Greek audiences):

> First I took some shrimps; I fried them all to a turn. A huge dogfish is put in my hands; I baked the middle slices, but the rest of the stuff I boiled, after making a mulberry sauce. Here I fetch two very large pieces of grey-fish cut near the head in a big casserole; in it I have added sparingly some herbs, caraway seed, salt, water, and oil. After that I bought a very fine sea-bass. It shall be served boiled in an oily pickle with herbs after I have served the meats roasted on spits. Some fine red mullets I purchased, and some lovely wrasse. These I immediately tossed upon the coals, and to an oily pickle I added some marjoram. Besides these I bought some cuttle-fish and squids. A boiled

⊸§ *Mesopotamia, Egypt and Greece* §⊸

squid stuffed with chopped meat is nice, and so are the tentacles of a cuttle-fish when roasted tender. To these I fitted a fresh sauce of many vegetables, and after them came some boiled dishes for which I made a mayonnaise to give them flavour. To top this I bought a very fat conger eel. I smothered it in a fresher pickle. Some gobies, and some rockfish of course; I snipped off their heads and smeared their bodies in a batter of flour, just a little, and sent them on the same journey as the shrimps. Then a widowed bonito, a very fine creature, I soaked just enough in oil, wrapped it in swaddling-bands of fig-leaves, sprinkled it with marjoram, and hid it like a firebrand in a heap of hot ashes. With it I got some small fry from Phalerum. Half a gill of water poured over this is generous. I then cut up some herbs very fine and abundantly, and even if the jug holds a quart, I empty it all. What remains to be done? Nothing at all. That is my art; I need no written recipes and no memoranda.[4]

A separate chapter could be written on Greek pastries, which were varied and plentiful at banquets. Athens was famous for its pastry. Cakes were made of flour, honey, eggs, and sometimes milk. Some were made in molds; some were layered. They were seasoned with dried figs, walnuts, grape syrup, poppy seed, almonds, filberts, sesame seed, cheese, or wine. They were baked in the oven or on charcoal, or fried; fried cakes soaked in honey were popular in Greece twenty-three centuries ago as they are in parts of the Mediterranean today. Other sweet desserts were pancakes flavored with sesame and curds made with honey.

Such delicacies were not for the poor; they were not for any but the very rich and their guests. As for the others, playwright Antiphanes wrote in the fourth century B.C.: "Our dinner is a barley cake bristling with chaff, cheaply prepared, and perhaps one iris-bulb or a dainty dish of sow-thistle or mushrooms or any other poor thing that the place affords us poor creatures." A century later, Poliochus wrote: "Both of us broke a bit of black barley bread, with chaff mixed in the kneading, twice a day, and had a few figs; sometimes, too, there would be a braised mushroom, and if there were a little dew, we'd catch a snail, or we'd have some native vegetables or a crushed olive, and some wine to drink of dubious quality."

25

The Athenians and Spartans were known as the most frugal of the Greeks. The Athenians were particularly reproached for serving a procession of tidbits. Alexis wrote of wanting to give a feast, but "not in any Attic fashion; and I must not stretch the gentleman on the rack of famine by stingily setting before him each little dish separately. . . ."

The Spartans were ridiculed for their notoriously restricted common table. Over a long period of time, in Sparta as in Crete, all male citizens were required to take their meals in a common mess.* The Spartan common table is said to have been instituted by Lycurgus, a possibly fictitious early king and reputed founder of the constitution. His motive, according to Plutarch, was to eliminate all rivalry for wealth and ensure everyone an equal portion of food and drink. To make certain no one would indulge in luxury at home either, he passed a law that a saw and an ax were the only tools that could be used to make the doors and roofs of Spartan houses. He was certain no one would try to bring gilded couches, silver tables, purple rugs, and furniture inlaid with precious stones into such roughhewn dwellings.

The Spartan mess was a military as well as a social organization; messmates in peace were tentmates in war. Fifteen reclined at each table on couches of oak with a stone or block of wood to support their left elbow. If a vacancy occurred, it was filled by unanimous vote. Absence was excused only if a man was holding a sacrifice at home or was late returning from the hunt. The king also attended the mess; as king, he got a double portion and did not have to contribute. The others furnished a certain amount of barley, eleven to twelve pitchers of wine, plus cheese, figs, and money for meat each month. They were permitted to bring additional food from their fields, barnyards, or hunting expeditions, but could eat it only after consuming their portion of the black broth for which Sparta was notorious. This broth, made of pork meat, blood, salt, and vinegar, led one visitor to remark he understood why Spartans were so willing to die in battle. However, the Spartans are said to have been very fond of it, so fond that the Sicilian tyrant Dionysius

---

* M. H. Jeanmaire states in "La Cryptie lacédémonienne," *Revue des Etudes Grecques*, Vol. XXVI (1913), that he believes women and children may also have had common tables.

was once tempted to try it for himself. He bought a slave who had been a Spartan cook and ordered him to make the broth, sparing no expense. When it was served him, Dionysius spat it out in bewildered disgust. The cook explained that one had to have exercised as much as the Spartans to enjoy it as much as they.*

In the belief that a stringent diet made men daring, healthy, self-reliant, and handsome, the meals were, as we say, spartan. Cooks were allowed to use no seasoning except vinegar and salt, and could make no prepared dish other than the famous black broth. On the other hand, there was plenty to eat. Sparta was well provided with wild hare, fish, and even butchers' meat; its cheese was famous. Cakes and barley bread were plentiful as were the several kinds of wine of which Spartans could drink their fill at the public meal. Gaiety was encouraged. Lycurgus is said to have put a statue of the god of laughter in the hall, but decorum was maintained by the old men, who were listened to with respect and whose talk played a part in the formation of the young.

These spartan ways did not last. Citizens gradually stopped going to the common mess, and on the rare occasions that they went, turned the frugal meal into a feast. From about 300 B.C. on, they used to set up small booths with draped couches in imitation of the Persian royal court. Spartans eventually became as luxury-loving as any Greek.

As for the accusation that Athenians did not eat well, let us let an Athenian of the fourth century B.C., a guest at one of Anacharsis' dinners, answer:

> The Athenians are perpetually reproached with their frugality. Our meals indeed are in general shorter and less sumptuous than those of the Thebans and some other of the Grecian states; but we have begun to follow their example, and presently they will follow ours. Every day we add new refinements to the pleasures of the table and see our ancient simplicity gradually disappear, with all those patriotic virtues which originated in necessity and could not be the growth of all ages. Let our orators remind us as often as they please of the battles of Marathon and Salamis; let strangers admire the monuments that decorate this city; Athens

---

* There are several versions of this story in ancient sources. The one given here is Plutarch's.

possesses a more substantial advantage in my eyes in that abundance which we enjoy here during the whole year; and in that market which daily presents to us the choicest productions of the islands and the continent. I am not afraid to assert it: there is no country in which it is easier to find good cheer, not excepting even Sicily.[5]

Athens, the speaker went on to say, had particularly well-fattened poultry of all kinds, plenty of game including pheasants and partridge, wild rabbits nourished on thyme, rosemary, and other native herbs, wild boar from the forests, roebuck from the isle of Melos, and a huge variety of fish, including the incomparable conger eel from Sicyon. Of the refinement of the Athenian gourmet, he said:

> The vulgar, dazzled by a name, imagine that every part of what is reputed a delicacy is equally delicate: but we, who analyze merit more minutely, prefer the forepart of the *glaucus* [a fish], the head of the barbel and the conger, the breast of the tunny, and the back of the scate, and leave the rest to less difficult tastes.

After he had mentioned the famous eels of Boeotia from Lake Copais and salt fish from the Hellespont, Byzantium, and the Black Sea coast, another guest continued with a description of Greek shellfish, the infinite variety of vegetables brought to the market fresh each day, and the superiority of Athenian fruit, particularly the figs that "find their way even to the table of the king of Persia." Another praised the dazzling white bread and the thousands of kinds of pastry.

Anacharsis gives a vivid description of the dinner itself, held at the house of a rich Athenian. Seven people are invited, all men of course, one of them a "parasite," a Greek and Roman phenomenon described in detail later. An uninvited wit joins them to make a total of nine.

The guests arrive at the house at the appointed hour, when the shadow of the sundial's pointer is twelve feet long. Passing through the small court or portico with its sacrificial altar, they enter the dining room where frankincense and other perfumes are burning.

On the buffet is a display of silver and gilt vessels, some with precious stones.

> Some slaves in waiting now poured water on our hands and placed chaplets on our heads. We drew by lot for the king of the banquet, whose office it is to keep the company within bounds, without checking a proper degree of freedom; to give the signal for circulating bumpers, name the toasts, and see that all the laws of drinking are observed. . . .
>
> After the table had been several times wiped with a sponge, we seated ourselves around it on couches with coverlets of purple. The bill of the supper being brought to Dinias [the host], we set aside the first portion of it for the altar of Diana. . . .
>
> We were first presented with several sorts of shellfish; some as they came out of the sea, others roasted on the ashes or dried in stoves, and most of them seasoned with pepper and cumin. Fresh eggs were served up at the same time, both of common fowls and peahens, the latter of which are in highest estimation; sausages, pigs' feet, a wild boar's liver; a lamb's head, calves' chitterlings, a sow's belly seasoned with cumin, vinegar, and silphium; small birds on which was poured a very hot sauce composed of scraped cheese, oil, vinegar, and silphium.
>
> In the second course, we were presented with whatever was esteemed most exquisite in game, poultry, and particularly fish. The third course consisted of fruit. Among the multitude of dainties that were successively placed on the table, each guest had the liberty of choosing what was most agreeable to the taste of his friends and sending it to them, an attention seldom omitted at ceremonious entertainments.
>
> No sooner had we begun supper than Demochares [who had been chosen king of the banquet], taking a cup, slightly applied it to his lips and handed it round the table, each of us touching the liquor in his turn. This first taste is considered as the symbol and bond of friendship by which the guests are united. Other full cups quickly followed this, regulated by the healths Demochares drank, sometimes to one, sometimes to another, and which the person drank to immediately returned.

The meal was followed by ten-year-old wines, biscuits to dip in wine, and the singing, to the accompaniment of a lyre, of songs such as the following to Bacchus: "The future does not yet exist, the present is no more; life is the only moment we enjoy. Let us love, let us drink, let us sing Bacchus." Anacharsis continues:

We now heard a great noise at the gate, and Callicles, Nicostratus, and other young men made their appearance, bringing with them some dancing girls and female performers on the flute with whom they had supped. Most of the company immediately rose from the table and began to dance; for the Athenians are so passionately fond of this exercise that they consider it as a want of politeness not to join in it whenever circumstances require. Several relishes for the purpose of stimulating the appetite were brought in at the same time such as *cercopes* [an insect resembling a grasshopper] and grasshoppers, sliced radishes pickled in vinegar and mustard, roasted vetches, and olives taken fresh out of the pickle.

This new service, accompanied with a fresh stock of wine and larger goblets than we had hitherto made use of, seemed the prelude to excesses which were fortunately interrupted by an unexpected scene. On the arrival of Callicles, Theotimus had stepped out of the room and now returned, followed by some of those jugglers and buffoons who amuse the populace by their deceptions in the streets and markets of the city.

The table was soon after cleared. We made libations in honor of the good genius and Jupiter Saviour; and after washing our hands in perfumed water, our sleight of hand men began their tricks. One placed a certain number of shells, or little balls, under dice boxes which he caused to vanish or appear at his command with such dexterity as to escape the eye. Another wrote or read, at the same time whirling round with the utmost rapidity. Some there were who vomited flames from their mouths or walked with their heads downward upon their hands, imitating the motions of dancers with their feet. A woman appeared holding twelve brass hoops in her hand with several little rings of the same metal strung on their circumference, and while she danced, successively threw into the air and catched the twelve hoops. Another rushed into the midst of several naked swords. These tricks, some of which interested without pleasing me, were almost all performed to the sound of the flute.

The menu, while not particularly refined, is certainly copious enough, though it should be remembered that not all of it was necessarily meant to be eaten on the spot. It was common for guests to take home leftovers which they handed to their personal slaves, who stood behind them during the meal as at the wedding of Caranus. Normally no one had a chance even to taste all the dishes served. Because there were no individual plates, people ate directly from the serving dishes put nearest them, diving in with their free right hands (the semireclining position, supported on the left elbow, rendered the left hand almost useless). Some Greeks found this system frustrating. In *The Centaur*, playwright Lynceus has a character complain, "While I am eating this, another is eating that; and while he is eating that, I have made away with this. What I want, good sir, is both the one and the other, but my wish is impossible. For I have neither five mouths nor five right hands."

Under the Greek system, greedy eaters faced the problem of getting enough of a good dish before it disappeared. Athenaeus describes gourmets who went into special training to ensure the satisfaction of their appetites. One had finger shields made so he could eat food as hot as his tongue could stand. Another frequently soaked his right hand in hot water in the public baths to accustom it to heat and gargled with very hot water to accustom his throat. Still another devised a protective sheath for his tongue.

Table forks were not to exist for another fifteen centuries or more. Spoons were used only for sauces or liquids, and even then not often; a crust of bread usually served the purpose. The only knife on the table belonged to the carver, who was either part of the household staff or hired in the market for the occasion. All food was cut into small morsels before it was served, as it is today in most of the Orient. Handwashing preceded and followed the meal, and during the meal, the guests wiped their fingers on pieces of bread or pellets of dough which they then threw to the dogs.

When dinner was over, the part of the banquet known as the symposium began. As in the Homerian epoch, this was the time for drinking and entertainment, but everything in a symposium was a bit more elaborate. Incense was burned, the guests perfumed themselves again and donned wreaths of flowers, herbs and tree leaves. Sometimes one person would wear as many as three wreaths, one on his head in the belief it prevented drunkenness, the others around his neck for the pleasant smell. Sometimes wreaths were put on servants, dishes, and vessels too. Wreaths had become so essential that when Xenophon's soldiers held a banquet in a village during the Persian Expedition, for want of flowers, they made crowns of hay. In Plato's *Symposium*, a reveler swaggers in wearing a bushy wreath of ivy and violets with a great array of ribbons.

After the libations and a swallow of unmixed wine, the tables were removed and new tables brought with a dessert course of foods chosen to stimulate thirst and drinking. At the earliest symposiums, dessert consisted of dried fruits, dried legumes, nuts, olives, and cheese. The poor ate onions (as Homer's royal heroes had) or garlic. By the fourth century B.C., dessert was enlarged to constitute a kind of second meal. Eggs, hare, thrushes, and honey cakes and other pastries were typical foods served.

In the sixth century B.C., the Greeks had elaborate dining couches with mattresses, cushions of linen, wool, or leather, and covers of fur or cloth embroidered in vivid colors. By the fourth century they had adopted simple beds with no mattresses and a single cushion to support the diner's elbow. Beds were always placed on only three sides of the table, leaving the fourth free for service.

We do not know when the Greeks adopted beds for eating. We do not even know whether they were seated in Homer's time, for although the heroes he writes about used chairs, he was writing of a period earlier than his own. Using a bed for eating was a very old

custom in Asia Minor, where almost all civilized men had been reclining to eat and drink for centuries. Inferiors were excepted, as
were children and adolescents. Hegesander, historian of the first
half of the second century B.C., records that Macedonian men were
allowed to recline at dinner only after having speared a wild boar
without using a hunting net; until they had performed this feat,
they ate seated. Women were not permitted to recline until the latter days of Rome. Wives were present at family meals, but sat on
high chairs at the foot of the bed. Courtesans were the only women
to lie with the guests, and in most countries, the only women present when guests were invited.

Greek men could not bear the idea of having dinner alone. Because sacrifices, weddings, public festivals, and private invitations
failed to fill every evening, they formed a great number of associa-
tions which held feasts at the house of one of the members or in a
rented hall or at the place of some courtesan of the town. The tradition was a very old one, going back to tribal dinners held to promote the solidarity of the tribe. There were numerous religious fra-
ternities; philosophic cliques held dinner parties, gathering young
men together to dine with them. To some of these parties, and even
to some private suppers, guests brought their own food, the host
supplying only the perfumes, wreaths, incense, and wines. This,
too, was a very old custom. Homer wrote as if it were a normal oc-
currence that when King Menelaus gave a feast to celebrate the
weddings of his son and daughter, his guests had their wives send
bread on ahead, while they themselves arrived driving their own
sheep before them and carrying their own wine.

How common the Greek box supper was can be deduced from
the food baskets often hung from the walls in the drawings of suppers on Greek vases. Box suppers are also mentioned in early Greek
plays. In *The Acharnians* of Aristophanes, a messenger comes to
bring a man an invitation to supper and tell him to bring his pitcher
and supper chest. Again, in the same author's play, *The Wasps*, are
the lines:

> So come along: we'll dine at Philoctemon's.
> Boy! Chrysus! pack our dinner up; and now
> For a rare drinking bout at last.

Though there might be any number of couches in a Greek dining room, food authority Archestratus thought it prudent to limit the number of places to a maximum of three, four, or at most, five "else we should presently have a tentful of freebooters." Freebooting, or party crashing, was an established institution in Greece and Rome. It had begun with the custom of allowing close friends to bring other people to dinner or to come uninvited. Those who often went out uninvited eventually formed the class of parasites, later called shades (a term probably of Roman origin). The same gourmet who had had shields made for his fingers, a dithyrambic poet named Philoxenus, used to make the rounds of his own and other cities with a train of household slaves carrying oil, wine, fish paste, vinegar, and relishes. He would walk into houses, even the houses of strangers, to see what was cooking. If tempted, he would join the feast when it was ready. He once landed at Ephesus in Asia Minor where he found the food shop entirely sold out for a wedding. Unabashed and uninvited, he attended the wedding, delighting the company with a wedding song after dinner.

The word "parasite" originally had a very different meaning. It was the title given Greek citizens holding a sacred post at a temple. These citizens, chosen from the rich and respected, assisted the priests in their rites and sacrifices. In some instances parasites ate their meals at the temple and received part of the sacrifice as a reward. Parasites served for about a year and were unable to refuse the honor. The practice seems to have been abandoned in the sixth century B.C.

The new meaning of the term was probably not general until Alexis wrote a play called *The Parasites* in the middle of the fourth century B.C., but the function existed long before that. The old man who attended feasts uninvited at Odysseus' house was a parasite. In one of his comedies of the sixth century B.C., Epicharmus speaks of a man who has dinner with anyone who asks him, or else comes unasked, makes everyone laugh, lavishes praise on the host, and takes up the host's causes in a quarrel. By the fourth century B.C., parasites were a social institution. Some were kept by rich old women, some did the marketing and errands for their sponsors, others were free-lancers who watched the section of the market where cooks and crockery were for hire and kept close track of weddings and other festivities at which food was likely to be plentiful. In all events, the parasite's primary duty was to amuse. As Philip the jester wails in Xenophon's *Symposium* when his jokes fall flat:

> Since laughter has perished from the world, my business is ruined. For in times past, the reason why I got invitations to dinner was that I might stir up laughter among the guests and make them merry; but now, what will induce anyone to invite me? For I could no more turn serious than I could become immortal; and certainly no one will invite me in the hope of a return invitation as everyone knows that there is not a vestige of tradition of bringing dinner into my house.

In Plautus' play, *The Stichus*, a parasite down on his luck holds a mock auction: "What am I bid for these funny stories? A dinner? Come, come now! Does anyone offer a lunch? . . . who wants . . . an empty parasite who will hold your table crumbs?"

Along with other Greek customs, Rome inherited that of parasites, which was immediately grafted into an age-old system of clients. The client system developed in Rome at least as early as the fifth century B.C. when the republic was weak and its citizens in need of the protection of the more powerful lords. Those who sought that protection became clients, giving service and obedience in exchange. Patrons took their obligations to their clients very seriously in the beginning of the republic, but the patronage system degenerated toward the end of it. Slaves took over the services clients had performed, and clients curried favor by flattery and by attending the levees of great personages and running alongside their litters in the streets. At times clients were repaid with an invitation to a meal where they were happy to be given an inferior menu, to sit on a bench instead of lying on a couch, and to take any abuse, verbal or physical, with good humor. Occasionally they were given a toga or other gift. At one time, dinner invitations were abolished by law and clients granted a daily ration, a "basket of scraps on their patron's doorstep" for which even the nobility queued up, according to the Roman satirist Juvenal. Later there was a money dole. Though parasites (or clients) were stock comedy characters of Greece and Rome, there were famous writers and poets among them, including epigrammatist Martial, who wrote many satirical pieces on the system.

35

III

Rome

When Rome was founded, about 700 B.C.,
the Romans lived as simply as the early Greeks
had and much more simply than the Etruscans they sup-
planted. It was only when Rome spread her conquests to Greece
and other points east that she began to enter the world of gastronomy. By the beginning of our era, when the first Emperor, Augustus, was in midreign, Rome was the Rome of unbridled luxury
and extravagant eating. While the Romans learned much about
food from the Greeks and at first imported Greek chefs, latter-day
rich Romans carried luxury at the table farther, seeking the sensa-
tional, enjoying conspicuous consumption for its own sake, and indulging in greater vulgarity and cruelty.

In the old days, Roman kings worked in their own gardens;
Roman generals like Cincinnatus tilled their own fields. As later
Romans never tired of pointing out, and as Juvenal wrote in one of
his satires, Curius Dentatus, a famous general of the third century
B.C., "gathered his scanty vegetables and cooked them himself on
his little stove." Agriculture was a noble task. Eating, as in early
Greece, was a religious act; so was cooking. The cooking fire was
sacred to the household gods, the lares; the irons supporting the
burning wood were a kind of altar. In the early days, the fire was in
the central room in which the family lived and ate and cooked.
Smoke from the open hearth escaped through a hole in the ceiling,
but only after blackening the walls; this may have given the room
its name of atrium, from *ater*, meaning coal-black.

At the beginning of the republic, the main meal at midday was probably the only one at which hot dishes were served. According to Stoic philosopher Posidonius, early Romans outdid Spartans in spartan living. Even the wealthy trained their sons to drink mainly water, to eat whatever happened to be on hand, and to be satisfied with a choice of pears or walnuts for dinner.

By the late third century B.C., many changes had taken place. The Romans had conquered Sicily and Sardinia, where more indulgent civilizations were established, and had enjoyed friendly relations with opulent Egypt for half a century. They had also made their first contacts with Greece as allies of some of the Greek states, whose internecine wars paved the way to an eventual Roman take-over. The Romans were quick to copy the riches of civilizations they encountered, in cooking as in all else. Some Roman house-holds now had a special room for preparing meals: a kitchen. Dinner was moved toward evening, following the afternoon bath. There were hot dishes twice a day and three or more courses at dinner. Because cooking took more and more time, every wealthy family acquired a slave whose only duty was to cook. For banquets, a professional cook was hired in the marketplace.

The greatest change, however, came after 187 B.C. when the Roman army returned from fighting in Asia Minor with loot, slaves, and new ideas. As historian Titus Livy put it:

> The beginnings of foreign luxury were introduced into the City by the army from Asia. They for the first time imported into Rome couches of bronze, valuable robes for coverlets, tapestries, and other products of the loom, and what at that time was considered luxurious furniture—tables with one pedestal and sideboards. The female players of the lute and the harp and other festal delights of entertainments were made adjuncts to banquets; the banquets themselves, moreover, began to be planned with both greater care and greater expense. At that time the cook, to the ancient Romans the most worthless of slaves, both in their judgment of values and in the use they made of him, began to have value, and what had been merely a necessary service came to be regarded as an art. Yet those things which were then looked upon as remarkable were hardly even the germs of luxury to come.[6]

The war with Persia that ended in 168 B.C. was another boon to the table. It was after that war, according to Pliny, that Romans stopped baking bread at home and acquired specialized bakers (like the first foreign chefs in Rome, the first bakers were Greek). As Roman conquests continued, Roman luxury increased, with money pouring into Roman coffers from war booty, profitable administration, and increasing trade. Thanks to the many wars, slaves were abundant and cheap in Rome in the first two centuries B.C. This enabled the Roman upper classes to build up great estates manned by slave labor, and to maintain enormous and elaborate households while amassing fortunes. Athenaeus claims rich Romans sometimes had as many as ten to twenty thousand slaves, though this may be an exaggeration. Figures are lacking, but scholars generally agree only emperors could have had that many. We know Pliny the Younger had at least five hundred, and Pliny the Elder wrote in the first century B.C. of a rich man who left 4,116 slaves at his death. We also know that while the majority of Greeks had no slaves, even a humble Roman householder went around with a train of eight in attendance.* With no shortage of hands, the complexity of the cuisine was limited only by the imagination.

Where the Athenians were dazzled by a public sacrifice of three hundred oxen, Caesar feasted 260,000 people for several days to celebrate a triumph. Where the Greeks had established a few fish ponds in Boeotia for the reproduction of their beloved eels, the Romans constructed large enclosures for fish outside their private villas on the sea and built aviaries and animal enclosures covering tens of acres where they bred or fattened wild birds and beasts. The Greeks had progressed to a permanent dining room before the Romans, but the latter now had several dining rooms in a single house—some for small dinners, some for large banquets, some for winter, some for summer—in addition to pavilions for outdoor din-

---

* Slaves were considered a necessity not a luxury. Boasting of a trip in which he and a friend reverted to the simple life, Seneca wrote, "My friend Maximus and I have been spending a most happy period of two days, taking with us very few slaves—one carriage-load—and no paraphernalia except what we wore on our persons." Epistle LXXXVII, *Epistulae Morales* (The Loeb Classical Library. London: William Heinemann, 1953).

ing in the midst of game parks or near marble pools. While the Greeks had simplified their beds in the classic period, the Romans made them more and more elaborate and costly; Emperor Heliogabalus had one of solid silver. Both Greeks and Romans sought imported foods, but the latter sought them in greater quantity and farther afield, from Britain to Africa to the Black Sea, and found more elaborate ways of preparing them.

Roman ports were filled with ships loaded with grain, truffles, and 49 varieties of dates from Africa and Egypt, oil, cured meat, and pickled fish from Spain, venison from Gaul, spices carried by camelback and boat from India. Cheese was shipped to Rome from what are now Holland, Belgium, France, Switzerland, Germany, Britain, and various parts of Italy. Cheeses brought from Luna (Spezia) weighed up to a thousand pounds each. Cured hams from Asia Minor and the northernmost parts of the Roman Empire, oysters from Britain, live parrot wrasse and eels from Sicily, sturgeon from Rhodes, turbot from Ravenna, tuna from Byzantium, peacocks from India, flamingos from Persia, parrots from Africa— all poured into Rome.

Plants, fish, and animals were brought from foreign lands to be raised and propagated as well as eaten. In their expeditions, the Romans discovered and brought back the cultivated cherry, the peach, and pheasant from Asia Minor, the almond and walnut from Greece, the pistachio from Syria, the guinea hen from North Africa.

New foods were snatched up eagerly. When first introduced, a single peach brought up to thirty sesterces, a sum that would buy about thirty-five pounds of bread or thirty lamps or thirty plates. New plants were quickly introduced into Roman agriculture. Within a few decades, six kinds of peaches were grown around Rome.

The Romans developed many varieties of plants. Pliny the Elder's *Natural History* lists 15 kinds of olives, 12 of plums, 41 of pears, 29 of figs, 8 of quince, 13 of laurel, and 11 of myrtle. The Romans learned to grow cultivated asparagus where only wild had been known, developing larger and larger stalks for the gourmet.

They imported parrot wrasse from the sea near Rhodes and bred it successfully off the coast near Rome. They fed special diets to sea snails, land snails, and fish to improve their flavor; they established the first oyster beds. Passionately fond of dormice, they devised special hutches in which to fatten them in the dark. Peacocks, flamingos, and guinea hen became common barnyard fowl on the estates of the rich.

Prominent Romans took a passionate interest in food and its preparation. Roman savants wrote recipes, poets like Horace devoted long poems exclusively to eating. Pliny credits a Roman consul with the discovery of a way to enlarge goose liver; the son of a famous orator with the invention of a dish of roasted webbed goose feet stewed with cockscombs, and a wealthy epicure with enlarging sows' livers by feeding the sows figs and giving them quantities of honeyed wine just before slaughter. Roman writers recorded the names of various other gourmet innovators: the man who made the first warrens for dormice, or built the first aviaries, the first game parks, the first oyster beds, or first served peacocks, or first learned how to fatten them, or first presented a whole wild boar to his guests. All these innovators were emperors and aristocrats: knights, consuls, tribunes, aediles, generals.

The first truly extravagant Roman was Lucullus, the brilliant general who defeated Mithradates of Pontus and Tigranes of Armenia, but is best known for his Lucullan life. According to Athenaeus, after his return to Rome from the wars in 63 B.C., Lucullus "celebrated a triumph, rendered an account of his operation in the war, and then, abandoning his earlier sobriety, he went to smash in a career of extravagance. It was he who introduced luxury among the Romans after he had harvested for himself the wealth of the two kings [Mithradates and Tigranes]. . . ." [7]

When a mountain separating his villa from the sea kept fresh tides of seawater from his fish preserve, Lucullus cut a channel through the mountain, though it cost him more to do so than it had to build the villa. In addition to establishing a fish preserve, he built an enormous aviary which he combined with a dining room so that he could "dine luxuriously and see some birds lying cooked on the dish and others fluttering around the windows of their prison." [8]

Horace reported that Lucullus had more than 5,000 purple robes, an object considered particularly precious. Plutarch describes his banquets with purple-covered couches, gem-studded plates, dancing

Cicero's hives and an aviary

girls, and elaborate and varied cooking. Curious to see how Lucullus lived when he did not expect company, Cicero and Pompey, on meeting Lucullus in the forum one day, asked him to do them the favor of letting them join him for dinner on just the food prepared for him alone. To be certain no extra effort would be made, Cicero and Pompey made Lucullus promise to advise his servant in their presence and give no instructions other than to lay two extra places. All Lucullus told his majordomo was that he would have dinner in the Apollo dining room with two guests. He thereby outwitted Pompey and Cicero, for each of his several dining rooms had a predetermined style of dinner and minimum expenditure. The minimum outlay per guest in the Apollo was, as his majordomo knew, 25,000 sesterces, enough to keep a middle-class Roman modestly for a year. Cicero and Pompey would not have fared badly in any case. Once when Lucullus was eating alone, his majordomo thought a dinner costing 10,000 to 12,000 sesterces would be adequate. It was a mistake he was not to make twice.

The main meal, often the only one that amounted to anything, followed the end of the Roman business day, which, in the first century, was over at one P.M. After a visit to the baths, Romans assembled sometime between two and five P.M. for dinner, always a lengthy affair under the empire. A banquet might last all night. Nero, aided by his physician, managed to keep on eating for thirty-six hours at a time. Even a sober scholar like Pliny whiled away an average of three hours at the dinner table, but a great part of that time was spent listening to a slave read edifying works aloud.

As in Greek banquets, the arriving guest removed his shoes, had his feet washed, and put on sandals before taking his position on a couch. He also changed into a lighter, more comfortable toga, brought along from home by his slaves; sometimes Romans changed several times during a meal. At a large banquet, a butler known as the nomenclator announced the guests and showed them to their places. Slaves carried basins and pitchers filled with perfumed water around the room for diners to wash at the beginning of the meal and after each course.

Though they had spoons, Romans ate almost entirely with their fingers, as the Greeks had. Like the Greeks, too, they vomited if they felt like it, and some physicians recommended vomiting during a meal. *Vomunt ut edant, edunt ut vomant*, as Seneca said. Sometimes they also relieved themselves in the dining room, and sometimes they bawled out their slaves or beat them. Some banquets ended in sexual orgies or brawls; others were gay but decorous.

Food was brought in on trays and set on tables in front of the guests. The first course was a kind of hors d'oeuvre served with sweet or honeyed wine: eggs, salads, vegetables such as cabbages, edible thistles, asparagus, leeks in oil and wine, melons, olives, mushrooms, truffles, oysters and other shellfish, snails, and sometimes pâtés, roast fowl, or dormice. This course was followed by from two to seven more, each consisting of several dishes of meat, vegetables, fowl, and fish, all accompanied by hot rolls and a variety of wines. The highlight was usually a stuffed pig, wild boar served whole, or an exotic bird such as a peacock dressed in its feathers and carried in on a silver dish.

The courses seem jumbled to us today as they do in an Oriental meal in which fish may be served with or after meat. Roman dinner menus also seem extraordinarily heavy, but, as in Greece, not all was eaten, nor did everyone partake of every dish. It was not uncommon for the host to invite friends of lesser importance or parasites to feast on the leftovers the following day, if, that is, he could salvage enough from his guests, who habitually handed what was left on the platters to their slaves behind them. Martial ridiculed one of these greedy guests as follows:

> When he has been invited and has hurried off to the grand dinner he has for so many nights and days fished for, he asks thrice for kernels of boar, four times for a hare, and both wings; nor does he blush to tell lies about a fieldfare and to snatch the discoloured beards of oysters. With mouthfuls of cake he stains his napkin; there too are packed preserved grapes and a few grains of pomegranate and the unsightly skin of a scooped out haggis and an oozing fig and a flabby mushroom. And when his napkin is already bursting under his thousand thefts, he secretes in the reeking folds of his gown gnawed vertebrae, and a turtledove shorn of its head already gobbled up. Nor does he think it disgraceful to pick up with a long arm whatever the sweeper and the dogs have left. Nor are eatables sufficient loot for him; he

fills behind his back a flagon with the wine and water. When that greedy fellow has carried these things home up two hundred stairs and anxiously shut himself in his locked garret, the next day—he sells the lot.[9]

Some hosts saved their most delicate foods from predatory hands by serving coarser dishes to men like Martial's garret dweller. There is no lack of references to show that it was a common custom to serve inferior wine and dishes to lesser guests. Juvenal wrote lengthy satirical verses on the subject:

> Just get the size of that crayfish: it marks out a platter
> Reserved for my lord. See the asparagus garnish
> Heaped high around it, the peacocking tail that looks down
> On the other guests as it's brought in, borne aloft
> By some strapping waiter. But *you* get half an egg
> Stuffed with one prawn, dished up in a little saucer
> Like a funeral offering. Himself souses his fish
> With the finest oil, but *your* colourless boiled cabbage
> Will stink of the lamp. . . .[10]

As in Greece, it was when the meal was over that the party began in imperial Rome. The hostess, who took her place on the couch for dinner unlike Greek matrons and Roman women in earlier days, left the room along with older guests who did not feel like reveling. Close friends stayed on as did the parasites, more of whom arrived to sit on a bench and amuse the guests. As in Greece, there was a libation to the gods, food was set aside for them, the tables were cleared, hands washed, garlands distributed, and new foods brought in to excite thirst and revive appetites.

Ancient Romans sang at the table to the accompaniment of a flute. By the second century B.C., their after-dinner entertainment resembled a Greek symposium (the Romans called it *comissatio*) with male and female musicians, singers, dancers, mimes, buffoons, and actors. The kind of entertainment depended on the host's taste. Hadrian had sambuca players, readers, poets, or actors playing tragedies, comedies, or farces at his banquets. Less intellectual Romans amused themselves with dwarfs, idiots, lascivious songs and dances, and, finally, fights between gladiators or wild beasts in adjoining courtyards.

In the famous description of Trimalchio's banquet in the *Satyricon* of Petronius, written in the first century, the eight- or ten-hour meal is divided into several intervals in which guests are entertained by a gesticulating skeleton, acrobats, riddles, a lottery, and the distribution of flasks of perfume through an opening in the ceiling.

Ceilings that opened were one of the special features of dining rooms of rich Romans under the Empire. Along with food and entertainment, dining rooms, their furniture and tableware had become increasingly elaborate. The couches and table were permanently installed, always following the pattern of three sloping couches for three people each, grouped on three sides of a table. This arrangement, known as the triclinium (from the Greek *tri* for three plus *klinion*, dimunitive of *kliné*, couch), was so standard by the end of the republic that triclinia were set up for public feasts. Triclinia of masonry or marble were built in the gardens of villas near altars for libations to the gods, pergolas for shade, pools and fountains for refreshment. Over forty such open-air triclinia were excavated in Pompeii, some with marble tables, carved with heads of lions or panthers.

Inside the house, only the poor made do with a masonry bed. The rich, particularly after the campaign in Asia Minor, had a variety of elaborate beds of exotic or carved woods, often inlaid with bronze, silver, gold, ivory, or tortoise shell. Under the Empire, silver-plated beds became popular for women. When a circular or oval table came into fashion, a U-shaped bed (called a *sigma* or *stibadium*) replaced the three individual beds. If more than nine people were having dinner, other beds and tables had to be brought in to accommodate them unless the dining room was designed for a larger number; Cicero wrote of one room with thirty beds.

The tables of the rich were of ivory, bronze, silver, copper, and gold encrusted with stones. The most sought-after, however, were of citrus wood. Though a small citrus-wood table cost about a million sesterces, Seneca had five hundred of them. Napkins, unknown in Greece, were introduced for the first time in Rome. Some were of linen, some embroidered with gold. Guests often brought their own; they were handy for carrying food home. Tablecloths were a late Roman innovation. The Romans also had a variety of spoons of wood, marble, or silver, including a small pointed one specifically designed for eggs and shellfish. Silver dishes were so common that Martial mocked rich men who failed to give their clients at least three pounds of silverware for the festival of Saturnalia, and Emperor Pescennius Niger found it necessary to forbid soldiers on campaign to drink out of silver cups.

Tablespoons, tablecloths, napkins and even glassware were seen on the table for the last time for many centuries. After glassblowing was discovered in the first century, glass production became an important Roman industry. Romans spent fortunes on opaque cameo glass and incised glass. They spent even more on murrhine ware, which has not been identified with certainty today. Pliny speaks of an ex-consul who had a murrhine cup holding "only" three pints (apparently a small cup for Roman drinkers) that cost him 70,000 sesterces. Elsewhere he speaks of a murrhine dipper costing 300,000 sesterces. Nero outdid everyone by paying a million sesterces for a single murrhine bowl. In addition to murrhine ware, rich Romans indulged in mural paintings, hangings to drape dining-room walls, floor mosaics of marble fragments, bronze doors and grilles, porcelain, crystal, and gold or gem-studded vases, dishes, and cups to display on their sideboards.

The Roman kitchen was equipped with almost everything we have today except for gas or electricity. With an abundant supply of slaves, rich Romans could afford an army of cooks, many of them specialized. The chief chef often made a fortune from presents and wages, bought his freedom and became a rich man. There was a large staff under him, the greatest number, of course, in the emperor's palace: furnace tenders, marketers, sweetmeat makers, tart bakers, cheesecake makers, sausage makers (who also fattened fowl), kitchen aids, and scullions. The dining-room service with its own many specializations (table setters, carvers, drink pourers, tasters for poisoned food, and so on) was a separate department.

The chief chef prided himself on ingenious presentations. In Petronius' satire ridiculing the dinner of a rich parvenu, the chef serves a succession of dishes such as eggs of pastry which when broken, hatch a plump bird covered with yolk, or a roast wild boar which when stabbed by a slave dressed as a hunter, releases a flock of live thrushes. In another instance, a chef proudly pre-

48

sented a pig roasted on one side, boiled on the other, and stuffed with thrushes, pork paunches, egg yolks, and various sauces.

Many of the dishes mentioned in Roman sources sound familiar: meat broth, ham with raisin sauce, duck with turnips, salads with cheese or herb dressing, or just oil and vinegar, jellied salads, seafood croquettes, fish balls, dumplings, stuffed vegetables, fruit compotes, custards, fruit tarts, and candied dates stuffed with nuts, to name just a few. To what extent they tasted like today's recipes we do not know. Almost all Roman formulas call for a great many spices as well as honey, pepper, and asafetida.

Throughout Roman writings about food there are references to a highly valued spice that was indispensable in almost all dishes of the *haute cuisine*. Scholars have concluded (although not beyond a shadow of a doubt) that this spice, variously referred to as laserpitium and *laser*, is identical with asafetida, a condiment still used by some peoples of the Far East and South America but so foul smelling that it is also called devil's dung: * There were three related condiments of which the Romans were excessively fond. Garum was a sauce of decayed entrails of fish and blood the Romans paid dearly for and used constantly. It was called for in many recipes, was eaten with a variety of foods as a condiment or sauce, and was even drunk in a diluted form. It has been likened to a present day Vietnamese condiment of macerated fish called *nuoc-mam*. No precise recipe for garum has come down to us, although we have some incomplete descriptions of the way it was made. Since quantities are not indicated, the result may have been less horrendous than would appear from a list of ingredients, and garum may have been no more offensive than anchovy paste.

Pliny wrote that garum is a "choice liquor . . . consisting of the guts of fish and other parts that would otherwise be considered refuse; these are soaked in salt, so that garum is really liquor from the putrefaction of these matters." Another source explained that the salted fish was exposed to the sun for about two months.

---

* The *Columbia Encyclopedia* defines asafetida as an "ill-smelling gum resin exuded from the stem and root of the genus *Ferula*, an Oriental parsnip." Asafetida is still used in laxatives and expectorants; formerly, a bag of asafetida worn around the neck was believed to ward off diseases.

Garum was manufactured and put in jars in Pompeii, but the best garum came from Carthage and was probably made of mackerel.

Alec (also alex or halec) sometimes referred to the residue from the making of garum. In the first century A.D., alec was made from a tiny, otherwise useless fish called *apua*. This inexpensive fish pickle was bought by the poor and fed to slaves by the rich. Later it was made from anchovies, and still later developed into a luxury condiment manufactured from oysters, the liver of red mullet, shrimp, sea urchins, and other rich ingredients. *Muria* was an inferior garum, often highly spiced. The term was also applied to the brine in which olives or vegetables were pickled for preserving.

Rich Romans sought the rare and unusual whether or not it added to the flavor of the meal. As satirist Juvenal put it, the high price was much of the flavor. Clodius Aesopus, well-known tragic actor, was reported to have eaten a dish valued at 100,000 sesterces and consisting solely of birds remarkable for their song or their imitation of the human voice. Emperor Geta devised meals comprised of all kinds of meats served in alphabetical order. Apicius had a penchant for heel of camel and was the first to discover the delicacy of flamingo tongues. Following Cleopatra's example, Caligula drank costly pearls dissolved in vinegar and served his guests loaves and meats of gold "declaring that a man ought either to be frugal or Caesar." * [11]

Roman Emperors also went in for quantity, though some of the tales of their eating feats are probably exaggerated by their biographers. Maximus the Elder is said to have consumed between forty and sixty pounds of meat and close to seven gallons of wine in one day. To explain his capacity, his biographer points out that Maximus never touched vegetables. L. Aurelius Carinus used to serve 100 pounds of birds, 100 pounds of fish, and 1,000 pounds of meats of various kinds at his banquets, and would swim about among apples, melons, and imported roses strewn over his banqueting halls. Albinus is credited with eating in one morning 300 figs, 100 peaches, 10 melons, 20 pounds of muscat grapes, 10 figpeckers, and and 40 oysters. Vitellius celebrated his arrival in Rome at a dinner where 2,000 select fishes and 7,000 fattened birds were eaten.

---

* It is supposed to be technically impossible to dissolve a pearl; possibly Cleopatra and Caligula crushed the pearls and gave an impression of dissolving them before drinking them down.

◈§ *Rome* §◈

It would be a mistake to assume this was Roman daily fare. Far from it. Even the rich did not feast every day, and the majority of Roman citizens could not afford riotous living or any semblance of it. The minimum property qualification for the equestrian order and also the minimum capital that would yield a "vital minimum" for the existence of a middle-class Roman citizen was 400,000 sesterces, providing an income of 20,000 per year at the rate of 5 percent. When a single fish could cost 8,000 sesterces and a banquet 100,000 or more, 20,000 a year did not go very far. From a record of first-century prices taken from graffiti in the ruins of Pompeii, it is easy to see that the minimum income would have to be severely budgeted to provide the Roman citizen with proper trappings: one sesterce bought a little over a pound of bread, 520 bought a mule, and 5,048, two slaves.[12] For a senator's career, a man had to have one million sesterces at the time of Hadrian.

While the luxury of rich Romans increased, people with small estates, particularly those who lived in the country, continued to live simply. Many philosophers praised the simple life, and many others were forced to live it. Grain or rice, as Gibbon pointed out in *The History of the Decline and Fall of the Roman Empire*, "constituted the ordinary and wholesome food of a civilized people." Farmhands of the mid-second century B.C. were given four *modii* of wheat in winter, and four and a half in summer, according to Cato the Elder. (A *modius* = seven quarts plus.) The slave chain gang, he wrote in *De Agricultura*, should have a daily ration of "four pounds of bread through the winter increasing to five when they begin to work the vines, and dropping back to four when the figs ripen." They were also given wine and a relish of olives dropped by the wind. "Issue them sparingly and make them last as long as possible. When they are used up, issue fish-pickle and vinegar, and a pint of oil a month per person. A *modius* of salt a year per person is sufficient."

The owner of a small estate lived better, though very simply. Horace, who could do justice to a fat thrush or a flaming peacock when invited to dinner in town, writes of life on his farm as follows:

> Only under exceptional circumstances did I ever have anything to eat on a work day except vegetables and a hock of smoked pork. Now and then, when an old friend visited me or

a neighbor came in on a rainy day when work was impossible, we had a good time. We had a meal of a hen or a kid (not of fish bought in the city) and later enjoyed a dessert of a bunch of raisins, nuts, and figs. Then we enjoyed drinking, without any regulation save not to drink to excess." [13]

Martial, who attended great feasts in town as a parasite, invited a friend to a simple dinner at his farm in the following letter:

If you are troubled by the prospect of a cheerless dinner at home, Toranius, you may fare modestly with me. You will not lack, if you are accustomed to an appetizer, cheap Cappadocian lettuces and strong-smelling leeks; a piece of tunny will lie hid in sliced eggs. There will be served—to be handled with scorched fingers—on a blackware dish light green broccoli, which has just left the cool garden, and a sausage lying on white pease-pudding, and pale beans with ruddy bacon. If you wish for what a dessert can give, grapes past their prime shall be offered you, and pears that bear the name of Syrian, and chestnuts which learned Neapolis has grown, roasted in a slow heat; the wine you will make good by drinking it. After all this spread, if—as may be—Bacchus rouses a usual appetite, choice olives which Picenian branches have but lately borne will relieve you, and hot chick-peas and warm lupines. My poor dinner is a small one—who can deny it?—but you will say no word insincere nor hear one, and, wearing your natural face, will recline at ease; nor will your host read a bulky volume, nor will girls from wanton Gades with endless prurience swing lascivious loins in practised writhings; but the pipe of little Condylus shall play something not too solemn nor unlively. Such is our little dinner. . . ." [14]

Even Roman emperors could be frugal. Tacitus indulged only in large quantities of lettuce, which he thought helped him sleep, and in a collection of elaborate and varied glassware. Otherwise he dined in simple country fashion, serving a single cock, a pig's jowl, and some eggs at a banquet, and never eating pheasant except on family birthdays. Didius Julianus was satisfied with a meat-less dinner of cabbage and beans even when it was not a fast day, and if anyone happened to present him with a hare or a suckling pig, he would make it last for three days. Septimus Severus, who came from Africa, was also very sparing in his diet, preferring his native beans. Pertinax was said to be so stingy that before becoming Emperor, "he used to serve at his banquets lettuce and the edible thistle in half portions, and, unless someone made him a present of food, he would serve nine pounds of meat in three courses, no matter how many friends were present. . . ." [15]

Alexander Severus is praised for his restraint by his biographer Lampridius, though it does not seem particularly economical that "his service of plate never exceeded the weight of 200 pounds silver." In any case he needed no more because, when he had a banquet, he used to borrow additional silverplate from his friends along with servants and couch covers. As further proof of his moderation, we are told that he had no gold plate, nor did his servants wear gold-ornamented garments even at public banquets.

Most emperors were not so conservative. In the eyes of Lampridius, Emperor Heliogabalus attains a height unparalleled in Roman gluttony and extravagance. Taking as models the commoner Apicius and gluttonous emperors Otho and Vitellius, Heliogabalus had couches of solid silver made for his banquet halls and bedrooms and covered them with gold coverlets and cushions stuffed with partridge down or rabbit fur. He was the first to use silver urns and casseroles and vessels of chased silver weighing a hundred pounds, some with lewd designs. His was a tireless search for novelty and excess. He would give summer banquets in various hues—green one day, iridescent the next, then blue, changing colors every day. He would have fragrant flowers such as lilies, violets, hyacinths, and narcissus strewn over his porticoes, banqueting rooms, and couches, and then stroll around in them. His banquets never cost less than 100,000 sesterces, and sometimes, everything included, as much as three million.

He ate camels' heels, and cockscombs taken from living birds, the heads of parrots, beards of mullets, and tongues of ostriches. Sometimes he would have meals of only one kind of food: one day nothing but pheasant, another day only fish, and so on. He offered a large prize to anyone inventing a new sauce, but if the sauce failed to please him, punished the inventor by forcing him to eat nothing else until he thought up a better one. Some dishes he invented himself; he was the first to make forcemeat of fish or shellfish.

Given to rather crass amusements at meals, he would have his tamed lions and leopards let loose to leap up on the guests' couches and cause panic. Sometimes he exhibited criminals in a wild beast hunt at lunch. He was fond of giving eunuchs or four-horse chariots as banquet favors, or distributing chances inscribed on spoons which would give one person ten camels, another ten flies, another ten pounds of gold, another ten pounds of lead, or ten bears, or ten dormice and so forth. He once filled the Circus canals with wine for a naval spectacle. On another occasion, he had snow carted to his garden in summer to make an artificial mountain. In a banqueting room with a reversible ceiling, he had such quantities of violets and other flowers released on his guests that some of them smothered to death.

Trick ceilings were very popular. In his famous golden house, Nero had several dining rooms with fretted ceilings of ivory panels which could be tipped to shower flowers on the guests. Emperor Otho installed gold and silver pipes to sprinkle perfume on his guests. At a banquet given for a Roman general in Spain, a statue of victory descended from an opening to the sound of thunder and put a crown on the general's head as he took his place.

No longer were there only six or nine or even thirty guests: 600 used to attend the feasts of Emperor Claudius. In addition to private banquets, there were public ones, customarily given by candidates for public functions, heritors, generals victorious in war, and, last but not least, emperors.

Bread and circuses became the Roman emperor's way of keeping the people happy, or at least quiet. Rulers had to ensure a supply of grain and, when famine threatened, had to obtain it and distribute it to the populace. Any emperor who abandoned this kind of public dole would not have lasted long. Jérôme Carcopino estimates in his *Daily Life in Ancient Rome* that between one third and one half the city's population lived directly or indirectly on charity. When the first Roman emperor, Augustus, found grain had become plentiful again after a period of shortage, he wrote:

> I was strongly inclined to abolish forever the custom of distributing grain to the people at the public expense, because they depend so much on it that agriculture has been neglected. But I did not carry out my purpose, feeling sure that the practice

would one day be renewed by someone ambitious of popular favor.[16]

Under Augustus, not only free grain but money tickets (which were small tablets or round, hollow balls of wood marked with numbers) were sometimes distributed to the people instead of food. The holder was entitled to receive the amount of grain, oil, and other commodities inscribed on the ticket. Nero had the more spectacular habit of throwing presents to the people every day. According to Suetonius, the daily lot included "a thousand birds of every kind each day, various kinds of food, tickets for grain, clothing, gold, silver, precious stones, pearls, paintings, slaves, beasts of burden, even trained wild animals, and finally, ships, blocks of houses, and farms." [17] Vespasian, in an effort to rid himself of a reputation for stinginess, dedicated a new theater, revived old musical entertainments, donated money to actors, and "gave constant dinner parties, too, usually with many sumptuous courses, to help the marketmen." [18]

Probus, who was Emperor toward the end of the third century, held one of the more spectacular distributions. His biographer, Vopiscus, described it in the following passage:

> He gave in the Circus a magnificent wild beast hunt at which all things were to be the spoils of the people . . . great trees, torn up with the roots by the soldiers, were set up on a platform . . . on which earth was then thrown, and in this way, the whole Circus, planted to look like a forest, seemed, thanks to this new verdure, to be putting forth leaves. Then through all the entrances were brought in one thousand ostriches, one thousand stags, and one thousand wild boars, then deer, ibexes, wild sheep, and other grass-eating beasts, as many as could be reared or captured. The populace was then let in and each man seized what he wished.[19]

IV

The Dark
and Middle Ages

The Roman cuisine and the Roman Empire
degenerated together until they disappeared, over-
rich, overripe, and overrun. What remained of Roman
culinary art, including the Apicius manuscript, was preserved by
monks in their monasteries along with other bits and pieces of the
dead civilization while most of Europe returned to the hard, rude
life it had known before the Romans came.

When the Romans conquered Germany, Gaul, Britain, and
Spain at the beginning of our era, they found cooking and other
arts of civilization in a sorry state. For a few centuries, the glory
of Rome spread over most of Western Europe. Everywhere Roman
ideas on the good life, on agriculture, and on cooking followed on
the heels of Roman armies. The Romans are credited with importing into Britain at least twenty-five kinds of plants from apples to
walnuts, and turning France into a wine-drinking country by the
propagation of the vine. Everywhere the conquerors introduced
their kitchen equipment, tableware, couches, and concept of proper
dining. The Gauls, who had been eating grilled pork and raw
apples while sitting on straw, were soon enjoying spicy Roman
dishes while reclining, crowned with wreaths, on divans in halls
strewn with laurel leaves. Britons too, Roman historian Tacitus
wrote, were "little by little seduced into alluring vices."

The glory was not to last; all vanished with the Empire. Many
of the amenities the Romans took for granted such as plates and
napkins were rediscovered only in the fifteenth or sixteenth cen-

tury. The cultivation of herbs, vegetables, and fruit fell into such profound neglect that, if monks had not continued to grow them behind monastery walls while the rest of the countryside was ravaged by wars, some strains of fruits and vegetables might have been entirely lost to us. The extensively equipped Roman kitchen was forgotten, to reappear only when archaeologists started to dig. There was, in fact, no longer any kitchen at all, much less a cuisine, and even a great lord's house was a primitive shelter, a single room where the family and retainers lived, ate, and slept together.

No one gave up food however. People continued to eat and even to feast. Indeed, along with hunting and fighting, feasting was the main pastime of the upper classes in post-Roman Europe.

The long, long stretch of the Dark and Middle Ages is marked by a significant absence of change. The description of Hrothgar's great mead hall in the eighth-century epic *Beowulf* could as well be of the hall of a fifteenth-century English manor house. Through the Middle Ages, the hall served as court of justice for lord and vassals, bedroom for members of his household, and dining room for all. As in *Beowulf*, everyone ate in the hall—lord and lady, guests, knights, servants—everyone. Eating in private was considered a disgrace and a scurvy thing to do. The high table for hosts and honored guests stood at the head of the hall on a raised platform. Benches for the retainers lined the tables down the sides of the hall, and a big fire was built in the middle of the room for both warmth and light. (The hall sometimes burned down if the

Feast at a round table, from the Bayeux Tapestry

fire was too close to the wall.) With no chimney, though there was an opening in the roof, the room must have been thick with smoke. For further warmth, the walls were hung with embroidered curtains; wall pegs allowed warriors to suspend their shields and helmets above their heads, ready for fighting at a moment's notice. After the feast, in *Beowulf* as in the later Middle Ages, the bench boards were spread with covers and bolsters on which the warriors slept. (It was these benches that gave us the word "banquet," from the Italian *banco*).

The Saxon feast is pictured in ancient illustrated manuscripts.

This depiction of the Last Supper from Garucci's *Storia Dell'Arte Christiana* shows Christ and the Apostles reclining around a table, Roman style, a circumstance which is probably more accurate than the usual version.

Many show a tablecloth, whose use had spread with Christianity. Associated with the altar cloth of Christian liturgy, it served to make the table a kind of altar for a meal, which was considered a religious rite, particularly in the agapes or feasts of brotherly love held by the Christian Romans in memory of the Last Supper.* On the table are flat cakes of bread, serving dishes holding fish and meat, a scanty supply of spoons, some sharp knives, and drinking vessels of various sizes and shapes, some of glass, some of silver or gold. Many drinking vessels found in Saxon graves are cone-shaped, their convex bottoms preventing them from standing upright, hence the name "tumbler." Probably attendants presented them full to guests when beckoned and stood by to recover the emptied tumbler, a form of service continued, to the growing disgust of thirsty people at the mercy of surly valets, till after the French Revolution.

Aside from bread, fish, and meat, the Saxons ate milk, butter, cheese, honey, beans, and poultry. Pork was the most common meat because pigs were the easiest animals to keep, since they could fend for themselves in the many forests. Quantity prevailed over quality in the Saxon diet, and cooking was limited to a primitive affair of changing raw food into cooked.

When the meal was over, the tables, mere boards on trestles, were removed, and the drinking began. If there was no more pressing business, drinking occupied the rest of the afternoon, sometimes accompanied by accounts of heroic exploits by minstrels and singing and dancing. Any presentable stranger was welcomed to the table of a lord and even a king, a custom that led to the murder of King Edmund of England in 946 when a bandit exiled by the King entered the royal hall and sat down at the royal table. King Edmund, the only man who recognized the outlaw, rose to oust him and was killed in the struggle.

Though the Saxons were noted for overeating and overdrinking, the advent of the Danes in England probably led to even greater

---

* Early Christian mosaics often picture a tablecloth. They also record the change from a reclining to a sitting position at meals. The earliest depict Jesus and the Apostles lying on divans at the Last Supper. The account of the Last Supper in John 13:23 (RSV) gives corroborating evidence: "One of his disciples, whom Jesus loved, was lying close to the breast of Jesus."

excess. To prevent his subjects from imitating Danish ways, King Edgar ruled in the tenth century that all drinking vessels should be marked at specified intervals, and that anyone drinking beyond one of these marks without pause would be severely punished. The last Danish ruler of England, Hardecanute, who used to feast and drink for three days without interruption, is reputed to have died from downing a huge goblet of wine at one draft.

The year 1066 brought great gastronomical changes to England. William the Conqueror crossed the Channel with complete kitchen equipment and staff in emulation of Charlemagne, the first gourmet of the Dark Ages, who took his chefs on all military campaigns. France had been gastronomically ahead of England ever since Charlemagne encouraged the exchange of recipes among his subjects and the diversification of agriculture. It is therefore not surprising that the Normans should bring a taste for sauces, spices, and wine from France. More refined and less given to excess than the English, the Normans first tried to put an end to overindulgence at meals by proclaiming the table should be set only once a day. Monks of early Norman times deplored the new austerity in their chronicles. They were quickly reassured. In no time at all, the Normans fell into Saxon habits of gluttony, eating five or six times a day and sitting for hours over meals, which began with dinner at nine A.M.

Under the Normans, the high table was sometimes moved to an upper gallery overlooking the hall so the lord could avoid the hungry hangers-on who invaded it. Some of these ruffians became so bold they snatched food away before it reached the tables. To protect the guests and cooks, William the Conqueror's son, William II, introduced ushers of the hall and kitchen. At his grand feast at Westminster, there were no fewer than 300 ushers with rods to escort food and drinks safely to the tables.

Norman manor houses sometimes had an extra building housing the kitchen, but because nobles traveled from one estate to another during the year, the kitchen was more often a temporary structure set up for the duration of the lord's stay. Kitchen equipment was carted from estate to estate along with tapestries, bedding—all the lord's meager furnishings. These were the days of few possessions and many servants, when kitchen pots and pans were listed in

The table of a baron, 13th Century

royal wills and household inventories. The pots, spits, and frying pans of Edward III (1327–1377) were listed among His Majesty's jewels. Even great noblemen did not have plates, but ate from a piece of bread known as a trencher, which was eaten at the end of the meal or collected for the poor.

Robert Grosseteste's *Rules*, a set of instructions for English landowners written about 1240, gives an interesting picture of this migratory life:

> Every year at Michaelmas when you know the measure of all your corn, then arrange your sojourn for the whole of the year, and for how many weeks in each place, according to the seasons of the year, and the advantages of the country in flesh and in fish, and do not in any wise burden by debt or long residence the places where you sojourn, but so arrange your sojourns that the place at your departure shall not remain in debt, but something may remain on the manor, whereby the manor can raise money from increase of stock, and especially cows and sheep, until your stock acquits your wines, robes, wax and all your wardrobe. . . .

Permament kitchens were first built in monasteries, which were less subject to destruction in the constant wars. Medieval kitchens were very large. They had to be, not only because of the huge numbers of people fed in noble households and monasteries, but because the kitchen also served as a slaughterhouse; the kitchen at Canterbury is 45 feet in diameter. Even so, except in enormous establishments, most of the cooking for a large feast had to take place outdoors. Much cooking was done outdoors in any case to avoid the smoke from chimneyless fireplaces.

The Normans introduced more equipment and much larger kitchen staffs with many subdivisions, including cooks, assistant cooks, scullions, pages, fire tenders, sausage makers, waferers, pastry cooks, poulterers, butchers, spice powderers, sauce makers, fish specialists, fruiterers, and so on. The chief cook, known as the *magister coquus*, was an important person and well paid. In a royal house he was of high rank and had extensive possessions. William the Conqueror gave land to several cooks, including the manor of Addington in Surrey, which he awarded to Robert Argyllon for making a kind of stew called dilligrout. The lord of Addington was still presenting a dish of dilligrout to the royal table in memory of the grant at the end of the eighteenth century. Tirel, also known as Taillevent, cook to kings and queens of France, was knighted and given a chapel and a house. The cook of Anne de Beaujeu, regent of France in the fifteenth century, was also ennobled, as was the cook of Henri IV of France a hundred years later. Knighted or not, cooks often dressed like noblemen. The cooks and kitchen esquires of King Charles V of France wore "silk cloaks with fur-lined hoods and pearl buttons" on a state occasion, according to the fourteenth-century chronicler Froissart. Cardinal Wolsey's master cook at Hampton Court in the early sixteenth century dressed in velvet and satin and wore a gold chain. In monasteries, the chief cook was sometimes one of the monks. An example of a cook of unusually high rank is that of Cardinal Otto's brother, who served as his chef early in the thirteenth century.

By the eleventh century, dinner guests in England were assigned places by rank and a man usurping a place of higher rank than his due was removed to the lowest seat where anyone could pelt him with bones. By the twelfth and thirteenth centuries, the elaborate etiquette of feudal society was fully developed in France and England. Young aristocrats became pages at a tender age, and, at fourteen, esquires, serving in various offices now considered menial. The butlers, pantlers, cellarers, ewerers, carvers, and cupbearers in the houses of the great were aristocrats. Young nobles were taught how to wield a carving knife as well as a sword. In royal households, the office of carver was held by earls and marquesses. Another particularly important office was that of sewer, the man in charge of safely conveying meat and sauces to the table and directing most of the other officers. Because the danger of being poisoned was very real and ever present until the seventeenth century, these offices were positions of high trust, not to be left to any commoner.*

Aristocrats ate much the same food in France as in England through the eleventh, twelfth, and thirteenth centuries, in fact, throughout the Middle Ages. Not so the common people. In England they lived on bread, milk, butter, cheese, a few vegetables, some poultry, and a little pork. After William the Conqueror made hunting illegal for commoners, salted pork was the only meat the poor had in winter unless they poached, and poach many did, despite penalties ranging from the loss of an ear to death. The poor in France fared less well, subsisting on bread, wine, boiled milk, hot clabber, and a few of the commoner vegetables such as beans and beets in pottage. A black rye bread often responsible for epidemics of fatal ergotism, brought on by a fungus infecting the grain, was the French peasant's staple food. Nevertheless he was better off than peasants in Italy and Spain, who, in turn, were lucky compared to those in Russia, reduced at times to a diet of tree bark, herbs, and roots in summer and bread made from straw in winter.

In contrast, the rich everywhere in Europe ate a great variety of dishes with meat increasingly predominant on the menu. Aristocrats were surpassed at table only by the clergy. One day in the twelfth century, the prior and monks of Saint Swithun appealed to Henry II to rescind an order their bishop had issued suppressing three of their usual number of courses at dinner. It should be pointed out that a single course in medieval days could comprise fifteen or more dishes. Henry II asked how many courses the aggrieved monks had left. On hearing the answer—ten—he swore a curse on the bishop should he fail to reduce them to the number served the royal table.

---

* No doubt the fear of poison was intensified by the frequency of unintentional poisoning because of food spoilage. Dinner parties were sometimes fatal in the old days, as was the case with Enrique IV of Castile's reconciliation banquet with Isabella in 1474, from which he never recovered.

The quantity of dishes at feasts had no limit. A total of 700 were served at a feast given in 1257 for the kings of Scotland and England.

Sauces made the dish in the Middle Ages even as early as the twelfth century, when they were sold by street criers in Paris. Writing at that time, English scientist Alexander Neckam speaks of garlic sauce for roast pork and, for fish, green "savory" made from sage, dittany, thyme, costmary, garlic, pepper, and salt. Herbs were essential both for flavoring and for medicine; every castle and monastery had both a kitchen garden and a physic garden. *Herb* was an inclusive term covering vegetables such as lettuce, cress, leeks, garlic, and cucumbers, while sorrel and beets were classed as pot vegetables. A proper manor-house garden, Neckam wrote, should contain all of these.

It has been said the rich of the Middle Ages ate no vegetables. That is obviously not true, though there was not nearly the variety the Greeks and Romans had enjoyed, and a vegetable hardly, if ever, appeared on a noble table as a separate dish. As more and more meat was eaten in the later Middle Ages, vegetables, except as accompaniments to meat, were more and more considered fit only for the poor who could not afford meat. The sixteenth-century chronicler William Harrison remarked that while fruits, root vegetables, and herbs were plentiful at the end of the thirteenth and beginning of the fourteenth century, they afterwards fell into such neglect that until 1509 they were fed to the pigs if used at all in England.

Spices, sold exclusively by apothecaries, were in great favor from the twelfth century on (before that, in most of Europe, they were saved for extraordinary occasions). Not only were they put in food in quantities, they were carried around and eaten almost like candy. Thomas à Becket is said to have eaten ginger and cloves by the handful.

Many explanations have been offered for the excessive use of spices in the Middle Ages and Renaissance. One is that heavy flavorings were needed to mask the rotten taste and smell of meats, fresh only if just killed in summer, and in winter, dubiously cured. Another theory is that spices were sought to aid digestion after the heavy, meat-laden meals. Others suggest spices were appreciated as stimulants in the absence of alcohol, tobacco, coffee, and tea. It is undeniable that heavy spicing went out of favor in the later sixteenth and seventeenth centuries when these new stimulants were adopted.

The sacking of Constantinople in 1204 revealed undreamed of luxuries to Western Europe. Dates, figs, almonds, new spices, sherbets, sugar, and sweetmeats were enjoyed in the East by the Crusaders and soon became necessities for all European aristocrats. The crusading spirit and the glimpse of Oriental luxuries led to splendor and parade in noble households. Festive dishes such as peacock or head of boar were brought into the hall preceded by trumpets. The peacock, one of the most fashionable dishes of the thirteenth century, was indispensable at any noble or royal feast, although it is reputed to be tough and tasteless. It was skinned, stuffed with spices and sweet herbs, coated with cumin and egg yolk, roasted, and then dressed in its feathers and tail and served with a lighted taper in its beak. The honor of presenting it was often reserved for the most distinguished lady. She set it before the most distinguished guest or the victor of a tournament, who then displayed his skill in carving and took an oath of valor, known as the oath of the peacock, on the peacock's head.

Great or royal houses and large monasteries were run on a scale that entailed problems of supply of vast proportions in that era of horse-drawn transport and no refrigeration. Prior to Edward I's coronation feast in 1274, orders had to be issued for the advance purchase and transport to London, largely on foot, of 278 bacon hogs, 450 porkers, 440 fat oxen, 430 sheep, 13 fat goats, and 22,600 hens and capons. When Edward III invaded France in the fourteenth century, he was accompanied by 6,000 carts drawn by 24,000 horses. Along with tents, pavilions, and mills for grinding grain, according to chronicler Jean Froissart, the carts carried "several small boats, skilfully made of boiled leather, and large enough to contain three men so as to enable them to fish any lake or pond whatever might be its size. During Lent these boats were of great service to the lords and barons in supplying them with fish." In addition, Edward III's invading army included thirty falconers on horseback with their hawks, sixty pair of hounds, and as many greyhounds.

As governments became stronger and local conditions more stable in the fourteenth century, landowners gave less thought to defense and more to comfort in their dwellings. They moved about less, leaving their more distant estates to tenants and making the ones they stayed in more livable. In earlier days, rich and poor alike lived a rugged outdoor life in which the house was just a shelter for eating and sleeping with few basic comforts and almost no privacy. Rooms were gradually added to the rudimentary arrangement of great hall plus small retiring room for the lord and lady. As rooms were added, the hall lost some of its importance. Kitchens became permanent, whether in a separate building or next to the great hall. Various storage and serving rooms were built on. In addition to the single chamber for lord and lady, there was a ladies' bower and a withdrawing room; by the fifteenth century, a gallery for musicians overlooking the hall was common.

The introduction of the chimney had a great deal to do with the changes in the lord's house. The first chimneys were in the lord's private chamber (now built of stone), while the big hall continued to be heated by an open fire. The lord naturally found his chamber more comfortable than the hall and began building other rooms for functions once carried on in the hall. No doubt the lord's cozy fireplace also contributed to the growing (though much deplored) practice of the lord's dining in private. In his *Rules*, Robert Grosseteste insisted on the importance of eating in the hall where one could see everything and everyone and be seen by all. He warned the landowner to "forbid dinners and suppers out of the hall, in secret and in private rooms, for from this arises waste, and no honour to the lord or lady." Nevertheless, the practice spread. The late-fourteenth-century poem *Piers the Plowman* speaks with disapproval of the rich now eating in a room by themselves, cut off from the poor in the hall. Conflict between old customs and the nobleman's growing desire for comfort and privacy continued through the centuries. As late as the sixteenth century, King Henry VIII found it necessary to issue an ordinance that "Dyning of Noblemen in corners" at court was "to be left." [20]

The chimney brought a change to the cook as well as the lord. Now that it was possible to build a fireplace in the wall, it was possible to build an oven. The profusion of pies, tarts, and so-called "baked meats" (meaning meat pies) on menus and in cookbooks from the late fourteenth century on bears witness to the immediate and widespread popularity of ovens.

Feasts continued to be one of the main diversions of medieval society, and feasts meant entertainment as well as food and drink. Entertainment was essential in an age lacking books and intellectual distractions. It was also useful in restraining bellicose guests. Erasmus' advice on giving a feast included the suggestion that, if it turns rowdy and likely to end in quarrels, the host should bring in a pair of mimes to put on a comic pantomime. In the early Middle Ages, minstrels were often permanently attached to royal and noble households and enjoyed special privileges everywhere. They must have abused those privileges, because by the early fourteenth century, some of their rights were curtailed, and a century and a half later, minstrels were in such disrepute that they were outlawed in England. In place of minstrels, fourteenth-century banquets featured vaudeville between courses: wrestlers, buffoons, jugglers, and sword swallowers. At the wedding banquet of the son of Saint Louis in 1237, two men dressed in scarlet astride bulls blew trum-

A banquet in the 14th Century

pets each time a dish was placed on the royal table, and guests were amused between courses by a man on horseback maneuvering on a tightrope. In medieval French, this dinner entertainment was called the entremets, from the words *entre* ("between") and *mets* ("courses").

In addition to the entremets, fourteenth-century hosts diverted their guests by ending every course with a sotelty (or subtlety), a massive representation in sugar paste of a scene or event. In his *Boke of Nurture* (ca. 1460), John Russell suggested four sotelties suitable for a four-course meal for a lord: a young man piping on a cloud and called spring, a "man of War Red and Angry called Summer," a weary man with a sickle called harvest, and, lastly, gray-haired winter sitting on a hard cold stone. Further entertainment was provided by warners, symbolic devices in pastry that preceded sotelties to the table. These could be almost anything. Phallic symbols in pastry and sugar amused sixteenth-century noblemen at table. The Holy Ghost was depicted in one of the warners for the feast celebrating the installing of Archbishop Warham in office in 1504.

Sotelties, warners, and entremets were extremely elaborate at important feasts. The goings-on at a four-day festival Philippe le Bon, Duke of Burgundy, organized in Lille in 1453 for the crusade against Muhammad II, then besieging Constantinople, include a bobbing ship, an elephant, a chateau with moats filled with orangeade, and a huge pastry containing twenty-eight live musicians. The courses, each consisting of forty-four dishes, were descended by automatic machinery from the ceiling in gold and blue chariots.

This event was rivaled by a *"moult bel entremets"* at the wedding of Charles, Duke of Burgundy, with Margaret of York in the fifteenth century as described in the *Mémoires* of Olivier de la Marche. Among the many entremets at the feast was an act put on by forty people that featured a sixty-foot whale so high it dwarfed the two men on horseback on either side of it. Its eyes were "of the very best mirrors that could be found," and as it marched into the hall to the blare of trumpets and horns, preceded by two richly and strangely dressed giants with batons, it moved its fins and body and tail in such a way that it looked alive. Turning to face the table where Duke Charles sat, the whale opened its mouth to dis-

A state banquet of the 15th Century, with dishes brought in and handed around to the sound of musical instruments.

gorge two sirens with combs and mirrors, who began to sing a song. Twelve knights dressed as Moors emerged from the whale while a drum began to beat in the whale's belly. The knights danced with the sirens and held a "fairly long" tourney before the giants chased everyone back into the whale, which then closed its mouth and exited.

The dishes as well as the entremets increased in number and complexity. Lesser lords imitated greater ones even if doing so meant financial ruin. A series of sumptuary laws were passed, a certain sign of increasing lavishness. The following proclamation by Edward II in the early fourteenth century was as ineffectual as sumptuary laws usually are:

> By the outrageous and excessive multitude of meats and dishes, which the great men of the kingdom used in their castles, and by persons of inferior rank imitating their example, beyond what their stations required, and their circumstance could afford, many great evils had come upon the kingdom, the health of the

King's subjects had been injured, their property consumed, and they had been reduced to poverty; but the King being desirous to put a stop to such excesses, with the advice and consent of his Great Council, had ordained: That the great men of the kingdom should have only two courses of flesh meats served up to their table; each course consisting of only two kinds of flesh meat; except Prelates, Earls, Barons, and the great men of the land, who might have an intermeat of one kind of meat if they pleased. On fish days they should only have two courses of fish, each consisting of two kinds, with an intermeat of one kind of fish if they thought fit. And those who should transgress this Ordinance should be severely punished.[21]

In France sumptuary laws were issued as early as 1294 when Philippe IV regulated dress and table expenditures for various social levels. In fourteenth-century England, Edward III continued to issue sumptuary laws improving on those of Edward II, but with little effect. Under his successor, Richard II, who reigned at the end of the century, the splendor of royal entertainments reached its apex. Richard II fed 10,000 daily in Westminster Hall, and to feed them, kept an army of 2,000 cooks and 300 servitors in his kitchen. He also held feasts and tourneys lasting two to three weeks.

It was Richard II's master cook who is credited with writing, in about 1390, one of the earliest post-Roman cookbooks, *Forme of Cury*, a vellum roll containing 196 recipes.* At almost the same time, another royal cook, the previously mentioned Tirel alias Taillevent, wrote *Le Viandier*. A short time later, a household instruction manual containing menus and recipes was written by an anonymous Parisian bourgeois for his young wife. His book, *Le Ménagier de Paris*, is particularly interesting for the menus included (along with such fascinating miscellany as how to make a powder to kill wolves and foxes and how to tell young ducks from old).

These books, the first large collections of medieval recipes, make it possible to speak in greater detail of what was eaten in the late fourteenth century than at any time before. One of the most striking features is the similarity between the recipes in these late med-

---

* There are earlier manuscripts. Samuel Pegge includes an English one of 1381 in his edition of *Forme of Cury*, and a short French treatise of about 1300 is reprinted in the Jérôme Pichon edition of *Le Viandier*.

ieval cookbooks and in Roman sources, including the Apicius cookbook. The Apicius book was known even in the Dark Ages; copies
have been found that date back to the eighth and ninth centuries,
and the book was mentioned by Saint Odon, abbot of Cluny in the
tenth century. A new manuscript copy was made in Italy in the
fourteenth century. The book's popularity seems to have risen
sharply in the fifteenth when ten known manuscript copies and
three printings were made. That it had a direct influence on medieval cooking is indicated not only by its rise in popularity in the
fifteenth century, but by the equally rapid decline at the end of the
Middle Ages. After 1542, there were no new editions until the eighteenth century.

Although we would probably dislike most medieval dishes because of the heavy-handed use of sugar and spice, the blending of
too many ingredients and too many flavorings, we have to admit
they require a high level of culinary skill. Some of the recipes laid
the foundations for some of the sauces of classic French cooking.
Sauce robert, first described by Rabelais, sprang from the old medieval sauce roebuck of onions and vinegar. Vinaigrette, poivrade,
mustard, and raisin sauces are already recognizable in the Middle
Ages. Many medieval techniques are common to modern cooking:
using the broth in which meat or fowl has cooked as foundation for
a sauce, cooking with wine, thickening with egg yolks, poaching
fish in court bouillon, stuffing fowl and meats, and gratinéing with
cheese. With the advent of the household oven, medieval chefs
also began using butter and flour doughs and baking custard and
pies of many kinds.

Like their Roman predecessors, medieval chefs liked to display
their ingenuity, and the sotelties and warners gave them many op-
portunities to do so. They enjoyed making Lenten dishes look like
their meat-day counterparts and delighted in such tricks as making
two capons of one or sewing the forepart of a capon to the hind
part of a pig and vice versa, then stuffing, roasting, and saucing the
hybrids. Chronicler Froissart objected that he could no longer recog-
nize foods; John Russell complained in his *Boke of Nurture* of
"cooks with theire newe conceytes, choppynge, stampynge, and
gryndynge, making new curies every day to tempt people to en-
danger their lives. . . ."

Because show was so important, coloring was essential. Dishes were colored yellow with saffron, red with sandalwood or alkanet, black with boiled and fried blood, green with crushed herbs, and sky-blue with mulberries. Sky-blue was particularly recommended for midsummer meals. Of all colorings, saffron was the most popular; 46 of the 253 recipes in the fifteenth-century *Noble Boke of Cookery* include saffron.

A typical fourteenth-century dish is mawmenee. To make this, you take a pottle (two quarts) of sweet wine and two pounds of sugar, clarify the sugar with the wine, strain it into an earthenware pot, and add cinnamon. Next you fry pine nuts with dates in grease or oil, mix in powdered ginger, more cinnamon, cloves, sandalwood for color, and let it cook slowly. When it is neither too thick nor too thin, you add boiled, shredded chicken flesh.

Mawmenee is archetypical, but a number of other recipes can be cited that are made almost the same way today in some parts of the world. Take, for example, monchelet, which is like certain current Caucasian dishes except for the powdor fort (a mixture of hot spices) for which cumin or coriander would be substituted. To make monchelet, you cook veal or mutton in good broth, chopped herbs, and wine with minced onions, powdor fort, and saffron. At the end you mix in eggs and verjuice, taking care not to let it boil afterwards.[22]

Though the language seems a bit difficult at first, medieval recipes make amusing reading. To beat eggs is to "swing" them, to boil is to "seethe," to garnish is to 'flourish," to cut into little pieces is to "smite to gobbetts," and to bruise and press together is to "ramme hem up." The language is so much more vivid than ours it makes cooking sound like an active sport, as in the following example:

CHARLET

To mak charlet tak freche porke and sethe it and swing eggs then hewe the pork smalle and boile it in sweet milk and serve it.*[23]

---

* The name "charlet" comes from the Middle English *char* or *chare* (meat) and *let* (milk).

Fourteenth-century cookbooks quickly destroy some misconceptions about medieval food. There are no great roasts, in fact, no roasts whatsoever in our sense of the word. Almost all food is soft and mushy, chopped into little pieces, or pounded to a pulp. Because most meat was probably tough and dry—and in winter, except for fresh game, salted—boiling was the only way to make it edible, particularly in an age when scarcely an adult had an adequate set of teeth. Even if food was fried or roasted, it was usually boiled first and also larded to make it tender. The few recipes that begin by roasting meat usually go on to smite it to gobbetts or ramme hem up or both.

Not only were there no roasts, there was almost no beef. Beef is not even mentioned in *Forme of Cury*. Pork is virtually the only meat, but meat ranks far below the game animals and birds, wild and domestic, that dominated menus of the times. Indeed, the variety of birds, animals, and fish eaten in the Middle Ages is one of the outstanding peculiarities of the cuisine.

In addition to the usual chickens, hens, capons, cocks, ducks, and geese, the poultry yard of a properly run medieval manor had swans, herons, pheasants, cranes, coots, doves, kingfishers, woodcocks, and peacocks. The list of wild birds that appeared on the best tables is almost endless, including such dubious delicacies as bitterns, bustards, curlews, cormorants, and magpies. Some of the salt-water birds may have been popular because they qualified along with fish as Lenten fare; they could hardly have been sought for their flavor. Large salt-water mammals such as whales, seals, and porpoises graced aristocrats' tables until the late sixteenth century; Queen Elizabeth had a porpoise every Friday.

Manor houses kept rabbits in hutches; fattened rabbits, called conies, were part of every feast. Venison was popular; so was the meat of wild animals like badgers, hedgehogs and squirrels. The beaver, whose tail was appreciated by gourmets through the nineteenth century and is still served in some restaurants in Spain, was permitted on fish days. The foods served in sixteenth-century Germany were shocking even to a man of that era. Don Anthony of Guevara, chronicler to Charles V, Holy Roman Emperor, wrote with horror of being served roast horse, cat in jelly, and little lizards in broth.

Ret chere made our oſt to vs euerychon

The Canterbury pilgrims at table

As travel and trade with the Orient increased, exotic foods became common in the houses of the rich. Sugar was poured into aristocratic dishes. Almonds were a first necessity; almond milk was more common than cow's milk in medieval recipes, and most sauces were thickened with pounded almonds. In one fifteenth-century cookbook, 83 out of 258 recipes called for almonds.

From the fourteenth through the sixteenth centuries, spices were one of the costliest household items. More was spent on spices at the abbot of Canterbury's feast in 1309 than on the thirty oxen bought for the occasion. More was spent on spices for the dinners of the lords of the Star Chamber in late sixteenth-century England than on any other item. Cinnamon, ginger, pepper, saffron, galingale,* cloves, mace, nutmeg, and cumin were the most common. In addition chefs had to have on hand two compounds of mixed ground spices for ready use: the previously mentioned *powdor fort*, a combination of pepper, ginger, and other hot spices; and powdor douce, a mixture of sweet spices, often sprinkled on dishes just before serving. In large households, grinding spices was quite literally a full-time job, the sole occupation of the yeoman powder beater. He worked in a separate household office known as the spicery, which kept a number of imported nuts and dried fruits that we would not call spices, and also had charge of the supply of butter, which was served before dinner along with local fruits like plums, grapes, and cherries.

Sauces were supposed to be either sweet or sour and, in either case, very strongly flavored. A typical fifteenth-century sauce was composed of currants, bread, vinegar, cloves, and cinnamon. For the sour ones, more vinegar, sour herbs and most particularly verjuice, was used. Verjuice ** was sometimes made from unripe grapes, as it had been in Rome, sometimes from gooseberries or crab apples. It was dispensed in quantity. In *Le Ménagier*, a case is cited of a household that used six to seven queus or about six hundred gallons of verjuice in one year. Vinegar was poured liberally on game dishes. According to Rabelais, it was used after eating to prevent quinsy.

Herbs were very popular in cooking, probably helping to keep the rampant scurvy of the age from being more of a scourge than it was. Mustard was the favorite, always eaten in England with a pork preparation known as brawn. All cookbooks of the times have several recipes featuring herbs: herb fritters, herb omelets, and similar dishes, all popular on fish days. Flowers, particularly elderflowers, roses, and violets, were treated like herbs.

---

* *Cyperus longus;* galantyn, among the most popular dishes of the Middle Ages, meant any dish containing galingale. Galantine acquired its present meaning of meat, fish, or poultry in aspic in the late eighteenth century.
** Verjuice, called for in so many medieval recipes and still used in parts of the Caucasus, can, like vinegar, be made from a variety of fruits, particularly acidulous berries; it can also be made from certain green herbs. Large amounts were consumed from Roman times through the midnineteenth century. Besides being a common ingredient in stews and sauces, verjuice was made into compotes and ices.

Most vegetables were regarded as useless or harmful, and those eaten generally appeared in soups. Onions were the most used by far. They appear in 29 of the 196 recipes in *Forme of Cury*. Leeks appear five times, cabbage and peas two or three times each, and a number of other vegetables only once: garlic, gourds, lentils, parsnips, spinach, and turnips. When used, vegetables were made into a highly spiced pottage or cooked with meat. However, the more usual additions to meat dishes were currants, prunes, raisins, and dates. Like herb dishes, vegetables were on the menu more often on fish days than meat days. There were "salats" too, consisting largely of herbs, onions, and leeks, dressed with oil, vinegar, and salt. Feasts usually included no vegetable dishes at all. In the detailed list of provisions for the festivities at the Field of the Cloth of Gold in 1520, neither fruit nor vegetable is mentioned.

Fruit was almost entirely limited to delicacies from southern Europe and the East. Fig and raisin pudding, figs with almonds, fig fritters, figs fried in pastry, spit-roasted figs, dates, and almonds—these were the fruits enjoyed by English nobles of the fourteenth century. Locally available cherries, apples, rose hips, quince, and pears play a minor role. Almonds predominate in the dishes we might consider desserts, though there are also cheese pies, curd pies, curd fritters, tarts, custards, and other sweet dishes.

These desserts were not served alone and last as they would be today. Instead, several of them would form part of a course along with dishes of fish, meat, and game. The numerous dishes were not eaten or even tasted by everyone. A man ate what he could reach, what was passed down to him, or what was left over for him. It was the custom for the host, who had the greatest delicacies served himself alone, to pass tidbits on to others at his table or to send them to lower tables as a mark of favor. Robert Grosseteste's Nineteenth Rule for the estate owner enjoins him to "command that your dish be so refilled and heaped up, and especially with the light dishes, that you may courteously give from your dish to all the high table on the right and on the left, and where you shall please, they shall soon have what you yourself had before you." Leftovers from the service of the high table were called the relieve; eating them was the special privilege of higher-ranking men serving the lord.

Though everyone ate in the hall, everyone did not eat the same food. Quite the contrary. From the highest to the lowest, each table had its own menu to fit the rank of the people assigned to it. From the lists of the fifteenth century, the era in which keeping minute household accounts became a passion, we can see which dishes were considered too expensive for any but the lord and his guests and which were lowly enough for the humblest servant. The distinctions are many and minute. The lord's cabbage pottage was thickened with egg yolks; that for lesser people with bread crumbs. Pike was sent to the table whole for the lord, sliced for his inferiors. The lord's bread was to be fresh, other bread at his table one day old, all household bread three days old, and trencher bread four days old. The amounts differed too: in fourteenth-century France, barons at court were served half the quantity put before the Dauphin, knights one quarter, and chaplains and equerries one eighth. For the nightly provision or collation, a baroness had four pots of wine to the chaplain's one.

The distinctions and ceremonies of the fourteenth and fifteenth centuries seem ridiculously complex, but they served the purpose of keeping in place people of widely differing rank who ate together in one hall. Ceremony was observed until the enormous household went out of style and the distinction of rank was maintained by separate dining rooms. Household accounts of the fifteenth century and various manuals of instruction for young nobles in the duties of carver, sewer, and other household offices give a clear picture of the procedure of a meal in the great hall. They also happen to be some of the best sources of information for any social history of the era.

The number of a lord's retainers was the index of his power. Since the retainers held household offices, a great lord never lacked people to staff his complex establishment, which was particularly large in the fourteenth and fifteenth centuries. To name only offices connected with food and drink an important household had a pantry, cellar, butlery, spicery, chaundry, ewery, confectionary and wafery, larder, acatery, squillery, pasty and saucery, and bakehouse. In addition to the staffs for these offices, there were the ushers, marshals, carvers, sewers, cupbearers for milord, cupbearers for milady, etc.

The usher's duty was to receive guests and seat them according to rank and station in the great hall, still a dark, cold place in the fifteenth century. Glass was too expensive to permit making windows in private dwellings. The floor was covered with straw and refuse from previous meals. In England, through the fifteenth century, hawks and falcons had perches across the hall; hunting hounds roamed around collecting bones on the floor. The walls were hung with tapestries rather than the embroidered curtains of the early Middle Ages, and the fireplace was now at the side of the room and equipped with a chimney. Wax candles lighted the high table, while the rest of the hall was lighted only by the fire and smoky torches or cressets as it had been earlier. The usual torch, a rope soaked in pitch, tallow, oil, or rosin, was not only smoky but smelly. Though in some households the high table was in a separate room or on a balcony, it was often still at the head of the hall as it had been in the thirteenth century. Nor had tables changed. The high table might be a permanent one and have a settle instead of a bench, but the lesser orders sat on benches and ate off boards and trestles as before.

Guests washed at a ewery at the lower end of the hall while perfumed water was brought to the high table for the lord. As a precaution, the lord's water was first tasted for poison, and the towel brought for him to wipe his hands on was kissed for the same reason. The pantler, an important officer in charge of all bread, tasted the bread and salt. In the meantime, the sewer, a combination headwaiter and taster, washed with the carver at a sideboard with jugs and basins. It was here they would receive food from the kitchen, taste it, prepare it, and pass it on to the high table.

The tables were spread with fringed cloths, perfumed, and strewn with herbs to give a pleasant odor. In France, flowers sometimes replaced tablecloths. Flowers and herbs were valued for their smell and the protection they were believed to give against diseases. Floors of houses and churches were strewn with herbs, judges in Old Bailey sniffed nosegays while confronting the unwashed criminal, and doctors carried hollow canes filled with dried herbs when visiting the sick.

Large silver salt cellars honored the important tables; on other tables, salt was put in hollowed bread. Couples often shared a trencher of bread or a wood platter and a drinking cup. Pewter, silver, and tin plates came in only under Queen Elizabeth, and earthenware was not common until the seventeenth century. As late as the beginning of the sixteenth century, even the powerful Earl of Northumberland normally ate from a wood trencher and hired pewter by the year for use on special occasions only. Bread trenchers, still in use, had the great advantage of being edible. They must have been very good with all those gravies soaked into them, but by the fifteenth and early sixteenth centuries, it was customary to throw them into the alms bowl for the poor.

The first course, consisting of ten to thirty or more dishes, was carried from the kitchen by valets escorted by two esquires. An officer known as the placer took the platters from the esquires and set them down on the sideboard. There the carver and sewer assumed command, trying every dish for poison. Every pie was opened and dipped into, sample pieces were cut from every bit of meat, morsels of bread were dipped in every sauce and gravy. Final preparations for serving the dishes were then made by the carver, and the dishes were presented to the high table, whence they were sent to the table next in rank, called the rewarde in England.

The carver was one of the most important household officers. Various books were written by aristocrats to instruct knights new to the office in their complex duties. The carver had a great deal to do besides tasting. Every bird, every bit of meat, every vegetable or fruit had to be cut according to strict rules, and only certain parts considered superior were served the high table. The carver had to know the rules for each and execute them with skill and grace. Even the terminology was complicated: the verb "to carve" was different for each animal and often picturesque; rabbits were unlaced, crabs tamed, peacocks disfigured, and hens spoiled.

The carver did a number of things we would expect to have taken care of in the kitchen today. If birds were baked in a pie, he took them out, minced the wings, and stirred them into the gravy so the lord could eat the dish with a spoon (forks were not in use yet). If capons were brought in, he took off their wings and legs, poured on ale or wine, and minced the flesh into a sauce with spices. The matter of sauces was a vital part of his education. He was sup-

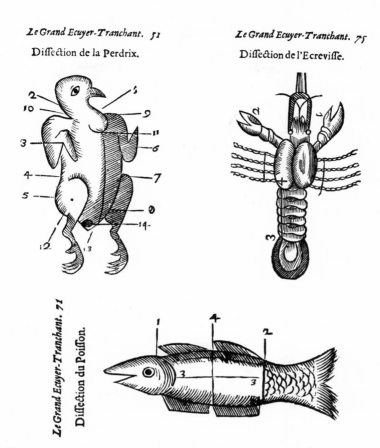

Carving diagrams from *L'Escole Parfaite des Officiers de Bouche*, 1676

posed to know which sauce to put with which meat by memorizing lists: ginger sauce with kid, pig, lamb, and fawn; mustard with brawn, beef, and salt mutton; salt and cinnamon on woodcock and thrush; chawdron (boiled liver, entrails, blood, bread, wine, vinegar, pepper, cloves) for cygnet and swan; butter with mackerel, vinegar with shrimp, and so on ad infinitum.

The powerful Marquess of Villena, who served as carver to the King of Spain, covers the greatest variety of foods in his book on carving, *Arte cisoria*, written in 1423. Much more varied fruits and vegetables were served in Spain in the early fifteenth century than in France and England, for he includes long lists of them with instructions for each. Those eaten raw seem to have been brought into the hall straight from the garden. For example, when Villena

Six of the 12 ways to carve a pear from *L'escole parfaite*. . .

describes in detail how a carver should prepare a carrot for a king, he writes he is first to pare it, then cut it in four lengthwise, and crosswise in two or three lengths.

After covering everything a carver should be familiar with, from carrots to camels to whales, Villena remarks there are a few other foods not in daily use the carver should nevertheless be prepared to deal with should occasion arise. The list that follows is startling. Along with lion meat for bravery, dog meat to reinforce the gums, and crickets against gout, there is "*carne del Ome para las quebraduras de los huesos*"—human flesh for treating broken bones.

But let us return to the hall. As the dishes, tasted, cut, and sauced were presented at the high table, the cupbearer took the lord's great covered cup from the butler and tested its contents while kneeling before handing it to the lord. While the lord drank, his cupbearer held the cover of the cup beneath it to catch any spilled liquor. Milady also had a cupbearer, while various attendants presented drink to the rest of the company on beckon.

The tasting of the second course began at the sideboard while the first was being finished at the table. At the end of the last course, the chaplain brought the alms dish and received all the used trenchers and leftover food the almoner had collected from the tables. Alms dishes were in keeping with the size and standing of the households; one is described as made of silver and weighing twenty-two pounds and three ounces. When the tables were cleared, wafers and a spiced wine known as hippocras were brought in, followed, at the high table, by wine and the spice plate, from which the lord dispensed delicacies, such as comfits of coriander, anise, and fennel, to people he wished to favor. Our term dessert, which comes from the French verb *desservir*, meaning to clear the table, can be traced to this custom of removing everything before the last course. A second handwashing ended the meal, the guests left, and the servitors and attendants sat down to eat.

Even to a great lord of the fifteenth and sixteenth centuries the ritual and crowds became tedious. He escaped by keeping "secret house," meaning that he retired for several short periods during the year to a smaller mansion with fewer household officers. The simplified life he led when keeping secret house was only relatively simple. Among the officers he took along as absolutely indispensable were a chaplain, carver, sewer, two cupbearers, gentlemen waiters, yeomen ushers, yeomen to carry in the dishes, and others of similar rank.

Despite the elaborate ritual, and despite the existence of a number of books on manners (including one by Erasmus), eating must have been rather messy. The fork was not generally accepted in northern Europe until the end of the seventeenth century, and in Italy only in the fifteenth. Spoons were used much less than fingers. Sauces were supposed to be thick enough to cling to food so that morsels could be picked up in the fingers without much being lost. In his sixteenth century *Egloges*, Alexander Barclay paints a sad picture of meals in Henry VII's England: dirty tablecloths, crowded tables, great confusion in the hall, and quarreling servants spilling food on the diners, who were obliged to eat in a hurry to get anything at all. The appearance of an attractive dish, Barclay wrote, led to a scramble among the guests; though the servers were slow in bringing it, they were quick to snatch it away. Nevertheless, he warned, if the dish was a tasty one, it was best not to put one's hand in without a gauntlet because ten knives would already be plunged in the platter. Like Juvenal in Rome, Barclay complained of the contrast between the food served him and that at the lord's table. He resented eating scrawny meat fried in lamp oil while seeing and smelling the dainties served the lord, and equally resented being watched by hungry servants who regretted every mouthful he ate because his leavings were all they would get.

Barclay may have exaggerated, but the need to put such injunctions as "Don't spit across the table" in books on manners written for young noblemen indicates a certain lack of refinement in the age. Erasmus found it necessary to enjoin the young not to lick the dish. Nor were crude manners limited to the young and inexperienced. When King Henry VII finished a meal, his usher knelt down to "make the king's skirts clean" before he rose.[24] In the succeeding reign, the Countess of Worcester stood beside Henry VIII's wife Queen Anne throughout dinner in order to "hold a fine cloth before the queen's face when list to spet or do other wyse at her pleasure."[25] The Marquess of Villena noted it is the carver's duty to

A wild boar carefully delineated into sections for carving

remove the lord's plate so no liquid will fall in his food when he raises his goblet to drink.

The amount of food consumed in large households during a year is altogether extraordinary, though not all of it was eaten by the family, retainers, and servants. The chief household officers in very large establishments had their own staffs of grooms and yeomen and the right to introduce a certain number of people to the hall. The number was determined by the officer's rank: a chamberlain was permitted five, a steward four, the master of horse two, and so on. Furthermore the door was still open to passing strangers in the fifteenth and sixteenth centuries, and it was considered a duty to have leftovers to feed the poor at the gates. Preparing and eating food was consequently an almost uninterrupted process. In the early-sixteenth-century household of the Earl of Northumberland, the cooks were roused at four A.M., and the eating schedule foresaw breakfast from eight to nine, dinner from ten to one, followed by "drinkings" at three, dinner from four to seven, and livery, or nighttime collation, at nine P.M. In his annual budget, the earl anticipated an average of fifty-seven guests at meals daily. Consumption per individual was high. Wealthy Englishmen of the fifteenth and sixteenth centuries thought nothing of eating two or three pounds of meat or fish daily.

Hospitality was on a vast scale. The mayor of London, wrote a German visitor to sixteenth-century England, "is obliged to live so magnificently that Foreigner or Native, without any expence, is free, if he can find a chair empty, to dine at his table, where there is always the greatest plenty." [26]

Feasts became more and more a way for the host to display his wealth and importance. Feasts were also politically useful, both in cementing ties and in impressing foreign dignitaries and heads of state with the power and wealth of a nation, and consequently the advisability of remaining on good terms with it. Cardinal Wolsey, when Lord High Chancellor of England under Henry VIII, kept a suite of 800 people in order to be able to impress foreign ambassadors with the might of England. At a dinner for eight French ambassadors, he served 100 dishes in a single course along with spice plates dressed to represent chessboards with castles, men, and horsed knights in combat. An English expedition to Russia in the sixteenth century came away properly impressed with this land of "barbarians" when the leaders saw the czar eat off gold plates served by 140 men in cloth of gold. [27]

Political considerations led Richard II to give a feast and tourney with sixty knights "to abide all comers" and sixty ladies "fresh apparelled to keep them company" in honor of the Earl of Ostrevant, brother of the French king. The Earl, who was awarded the Order of the Garter during the feast, promised in the warmth of hospitality received never to bear arms against the King of England.

Thousands of people were fed and entertained when public figures received scholastic honors or high posts, or when kings were crowned or married. Six thousand people celebrated the installation of Ralph as abbot of Canterbury in 1309 with a feast at which they consumed, among other items, 9,600 eggs and 500 pounds of almonds. On the occasion of the recitation of his works in Oxford, Giraldus Cambrensis, archdeacon of Brecon in the twelfth century, held a three-day feast, the first day for all the city's poor, the second for all doctors and other academics, and the third for all university students and soldiers from the local garrison.

One of the most famous feasts of this period is one given for the installation of George Neville as Archbishop of York in 1466 or 1467. One thousand cooks and 577 kitchen assistants prepared the following:

> 110 bulls and oxen
> 304 calves
> 1,000 sheep
> 2,304 pigs
> 1,119 venison pasties
> 105 stags, bucks, and roes
> 1,004 rabbits
> 10,029 birds including 104 peacocks, 400 swans, and
>   200 pheasants
> 8,007 jellies, custards, and tarts
> 12 porpoises and seals
> 214 pikes and bream
> *and* "Spices, Sugarred delicates and Wafers,
>   plentie." [28]

Menus for the high table at fifteenth- and sixteenth-century feasts range from thirty dishes in three courses to over sixty in six, divided into three meat courses followed by three fish courses. Even a fast day was no reason not to have a feast, and elaborate menus for fish banquets have been preserved.

One of the great feasts described in *Hall's Chronicle* is the coronation of Queen Anne, wife of Henry VIII, in 1533. To a chorus of trumpets, the Duke of Suffolk, high steward of England, and Lord William Haward entered the dining hall on horseback preceded by sergeants at arms and followed by the sewer (the Earl of Sussex) and the Knights of the Bath bringing in the first course of 28 dishes "besides subtleties and ships made of wax marvelous gorgious to behold." The Earl of Essex carved the Queen's 28 first-course, 24 second-course, and 30 third-course dishes while "the Duke of Suffolk and Lord William rode oftentimes about the hall, cheering the lords, ladies, and the Mayor and his brethern," who dined at their separate tables and were served a lesser number of dishes according to rank. The mayor and his brethern had to be content with only 33 dishes served in two courses.

Pies, especially animated pies, were extremely popular with the aristocracy of Europe in the late fifteenth and sixteenth centuries. Sixteenth-century dinner guests were amused by such antics as having a jester dive over their heads into a big custard in the middle of the table. As late as 1630, a live dwarf was served up in a cold pie for the entertainment of King Charles and Queen Henrietta Maria of England. This was the era of the four-and-twenty blackbirds baked in a pie of the old nursery rhyme, and the late fifteenth-century cookbook *Epulario, or The Italian Banquet*, tells how to make it in a recipe entitled "To make Pies that Birds may be alive in them and flie out when it is cut up." The first step is to make a large, tall, covered pie with a hole in the bottom and to bake it filled with flour. When it is done, the flour is drained out through the hole. Another pie the size of the hole is put inside the larger pie, and through the same hole as many small live birds as space will permit are added just before the dish is sent to the table and set before the guests, where the lid of the great pie will be cut and "all the Birds will flie out, which is to delight and pleasure shew to the company. And because they will not be altogether mocked, you shall cut open the small Pie. . . ."

A taste for this sort of fun continued through most of the seventeenth century; it might be said to have reached its apex at a plan for a banquet in Robert May's *The Accomplish't Cook* (1660). On the table there is to be a ship made of confectionery, equipped with guns charged with real gunpowder and a castle of pie crusts containing live frogs and birds. As the guns go off, the ladies are to be urged to take eggshells filled with perfumed water and throw them at each other while the pies are opened to release the frogs and birds. The frogs are expected to hop about the table to the screams of the ladies. Meanwhile the frightened birds will fly into the light, thereby putting out the candles and leading to great merriment and who knows what else in the dark before the tapers are relighted, the music starts up, and the banquet is brought on. Another amusement May suggests is a pie in which, instead of live birds, you put a snake "which will seem strange to the beholders which cut up the pie at the table." "This," he adds "is only for a Wedding to pass away the time."

Plays and allegories became popular at feasts of the late fifteenth and early sixteenth centuries. At court, interludes and "trick-waggons" were in style. The latter was a big gilt wagon which was wheeled in, filled with men and women dressed as allegorical or

90

classic characters who stepped down and performed. The Elizabethan era favored *tableaux vivants* of classical subjects; even the sotelties bore inscriptions in Latin. Ovid's metaphors in sugar paste produced a splendid effect at the dinner table.

Fountains spouting wine, milk, or liqueurs were popular for public fetes through the seventeenth century, particularly for the passage of a king or queen through a town. Fountains would be installed at the main street corners for these royal visits. Such fetes were not infrequent. Kings were the greatest travelers of the sixteenth century. Taking with them beds, bed curtains, rugs, tapestries, clothing, kitchen equipment, and a train of guards, soldiers, cooks, maîtres d'hôtel, palace attendants, pages, lackeys, coachmen, etc., the kings of France were constantly on the road. Charles IX, according to an Italian traveler of the times, moved about with a train of 8,000 horses and as many people. Starting in the year 1564, that monarch traveled steadily for two years and three months in France making a total of 902 stops, all faithfully recorded in an account of his travels. The Venetian ambassador wrote that during the 45 months he spent in France, he had to travel continuously because the court never stayed in one place more than fifteen days at a time.

Queen Elizabeth was as eager a traveler as Charles IX. Some historians suspect that not a few of the Queen's visits to her more powerful subjects were designed to ruin them under the pretence of doing them honor. A queenly visit was extremely costly. Each of Queen Elizabeth's not infrequent visits to her principal minister, Lord Burghley lasted three to six weeks, during which time she held court and received and entertained foreign ambassadors and dignitaries at the expense of her host, who was out two or three thousand pounds every time she did him this honor.

Lord North recorded in his household book the items consumed during the Queen's two-day visit to his estate at Kirtling in 1577;

> over 10,000 loaves of bread
> 74 hogsheads of beer, 2 tons of ale, 7 hogsheads of
>   wine, 20 gallons of sack, 6 gallons of hippocras
> 12 steers and oxen
> 67 sheep, 7 lambs, 18 calves, 34 pigs
> 4 stags and 16 bucks made into 276 pasties

8 gammons of bacon
220 neats' tongues, feet, and udders
4,828 geese, capons, chickens, pigeons, quail,
    turkeys, swans, cranes, and ducks
559 bitterns, shovelers, pewits, godwits, pulls,
    dotterels, heronsews, cranes, snipe, knots, plover,
    stints, redshanks, tern, partridge, pheasants, and
    curlews
3 kegs of sturgeon
8 dozen crayfish
1 cartload and 2 horseloads of oysters
1 barrel of anchovies
300 red herrings and 18 other fish
430 pounds of butter and 13 pounds of lard
2,522 eggs
1 hogshead of vinegar
6 Holland cheeses, 10 marchpanes, "Grocery ware,
bankett stuff, salletts, rootes, and hearbes." [29]

A life far different from that of the court and the great was the life of the small estate owner who lived largely on what he raised himself, doing without spices and other expensive imports. A sixteenth-century gentleman named Thomas Tusser gives a very full picture of the small estate in his versified advice to husbandmen, a popular book that went into several editions in the mid-sixteenth century. Spices, that costly item in the budgets of great households, he barely mentions except to suggest that with the possible exception of capers, lemons, olives, oranges, rice, and samphire, it was best not to buy anything outside the estate.

The conies in control—detail of a 15th-century engraving

Tusser believed the thrifty husbandman should live on his own produce with care and good cheer, particularly good cheer at Christmas when he would invite the poor of the neighborhood to enjoy with him:

> Good bread and good drink, a good fire in the hall,
> Braun, pudding and souse and good mustard withal.
>
> Beef, mutton and pork, shred pies * of the best,
> Pig, veal, goose, and capon, and turkey well drest,
> Cheese, apples and nuts, joly carols to hear,
> As then in the country, is counted good cheer.[30]

---

* mince pies.

V

❦

The Age
of Exploration

The medieval cuisine and feudal society
were swept away together in the tumultuous
changes of the late sixteenth and seventeenth centuries.
Yet it is surprising how medieval the table remained even in the
late sixteenth century. Indeed, one of the most striking features of
the medieval cuisine is how long it lasted. If there was a trend of
importance during the prolonged Middle Age of cooking, it was
toward more elaborate and richer banquets with more meat and
fewer vegetables, a greater profusion of dishes, and more display
of wealth by the host.

One reason for resistance to change was that medieval views on
food and diet, which had a profound influence on cooking, remained the same through the fourteenth, fifteenth, and early sixteenth centuries. They had been the same, in fact, for 2,000
years. Renaissance physicians clung obstinately to Greek pre-
cepts, distrusting fruit and vegetables as items to be used with
caution and moderation, more as medicine than food. It was
enough for Galen to have condemned a plant for a man of the
Renaissance to shun it.

These physicians were listened to. The spate of books on food
and nutrition of the late Middle Ages found a ready market and
went into edition after edition. The theories therein were hardly
scientific. Men were still divided into four main types as in Greek
medicine—sanguine, phlegmatic, choleric, and melancholic. Foods
were classified as moist or dry, cold or warm, and were forbidden

or recommended to individuals according to the individual's type. All new foods were immediately analyzed and studied for possible harmfulness or benefits within this framework. Many were turned down as "increasing melancholy," a common complaint of the times.

The pronouncements of physician Andrew Boorde in his *Dyetary of Helth* (1542) are typical of midsixteenth century views. He announced that water was bad for Englishmen, that milk was good for melancholy men, old men, and children, that broiled meat was unhealthy, figs aphrodisiac, melon engendered evil humors, and raw cream with strawberries could be fatal. While devoting much attention to herbs, he almost ignored vegetables except for the onion family, and even herbs he treated with caution, suspecting them of carrying the plague.

Fresh fruit was believed to cause fevers. If eaten at all, it was served at the beginning of a meal, so that the warmth of spices and liqueurs to follow would counteract the presumed coldness of the fruit. Through the seventeenth century, physicians continued to recommend aiding the "natural warmth" of the stomach with spices, aromatic wines, and liqueurs. Nutmeg, cinnamon, and ginger were considered aids to digestion as late as 1702.

Among the curious beliefs of the late sixteenth and early seventeenth century was one shared by the Roman élite: that precious stones give precious benefits. It was accepted as fact during the reign of Henri IV of France that a man who ate only gold would become immortal. Various virtues were attributed to various gems by Renaissance savants who believed rubies resist decay and venom, sapphire cures intestinal ulcers, etc. Salves or potions of precious stones were prescribed as well as salves calling for "1¾ oz. of the moss of a dead man's skull or more if you can get it," [31] or a potion of dog's brain, or horse dung.

Belief in the magical power of serpents' tongues and unicorn horns to neutralize poison persisted till the eighteenth century. Sharks' teeth, the substitute used when serpents' tongues were hard to come by, were sometimes attached to the salt cellar by a chain, ready for use. Unicorn horns were believed to be infallible antidotes for poison, but because they had the defect of not existing, the tusk of a narwhal was substituted.

Cooking and medicine were intimately associated as they had been in ancient Greece. The preamble to the earliest English cookbook, *Forme of Cury*, announces the work was undertaken "by the avisement of masters of physic and of philisophy." Andrew Boorde, a doctor himself, noted in his book that "a good coke is halfe a physycyon. For the chefe physycke (the counceyll of a physycyon excepte) dothe come from the kytchyn; wherfore the physycyon and the coke for sycke men muste consult togyther for the preparacion of meate for sycke men." One of the main duties of royal physicians was a daily consultation with the royal chef.

Physicians not only consulted cooks, they tried their hand at cooking and at writing cookbooks, often devising recipes for foods they thought particularly beneficial. Nostradamus, who believed sugar was good for the health, wrote extensively on the making of jams and jellies and the preserving of fruit. Most of the numerous books on food and diet written by fifteenth- and sixteenth century physicians include recipes and menus.

In addition to inflexible medical views, the persistence of feudalism and the rigidity of the class system fostered resistance to change through the early sixteenth century. The table, a faithful mirror of social history, underwent little modification. Change came, however, as the age of exploration opened routes to new wealth and new trade, towns grew, an agricultural population became urban, a stable society became mobile, and a new middle class grown rich on trade acquired power. The old aristocracy found itself unable to afford the old style of living. Lavish feudal hospitality began to disappear in the sixteenth century. Huge, self-sufficient estates became outmoded, and the reduction of household staffs put an end to the great hall with its elaborate medieval table, rigid etiquette, and largess to the poor.

Household ordinances, which give such an illuminating picture of the life of the upper classes in the late Middle Ages, reflect the slow death of feudalism. Originally written to tell landowners and tenants how to run prosperous, self-sufficient estates, by the fifteenth century, the ordinances began to concentrate on defining the duties of the then numerous household officers and correcting the equally numerous abuses in household administration. By the late sixteenth and early seventeenth centuries, the recurrent theme of all ordinances, even of royal households, is to retrench, to limit the soaring expenses, and to eliminate all waste. After citing historical examples of the magnificent scale of previous royal houses, the introduction to Edward IV's household book concludes that "if the king's highness pleases to keep a lesser household than the foresaid great sum shown here, in this book are devised nine other smaller houses, one for a lower prince, one for a duke, a marquess, an earl, a baron, barnette, a knight bacheler and a squyer. Whereof the king may choose such as shall please hym best." [32]

The economy of the king's establishment was a relative one; royal ordinances reflect a curious and sometimes contradictory blend of glory with economy. In announcing that royal household expenses must be reduced, the ordinances of King James I proclaim that "whereas Our-selfe and Our deare Wife the Queen's Majestie have hitherto been served 30 dishes of meat every day, we are now to have only 24 unless we sit abroad in state." [33] Their Majesties' table, even simplified, was not very simple, for royalty was still expected to keep a kind of open house. Louis XIV's table alone occupied a staff of 498 people. In England as in France, the King and Queen each had a complete staff, and so did certain royal relatives; in addition, there were households maintained at court by lords or ministers at their own expense and others subsidized by the king. The multiplicity of staffs made for confusion as well as expense. Spanish courtiers who came to England with Philip in the reign of Queen Mary (1553–1558) said that because all thirteen state councillors and the court favorites lived in the palace of Richmond, each keeping his own cooks in the Queen's kitchens, and because there were eighteen separate kitchens, "such is the hurly-burly that they are a perfect hell." [34]

Matters did not improve with time. As courts became the center of fashion and power in the seventeenth century, royal establishments grew until, under Louis XV, Versailles housed at least 1,500 people and about fifteen complete household staffs. Any significant cut in the royal staff would have undermined the system. As Louis XVI is supposed to have remarked, "If I have officers I do not need, I am sure they need me." [35]

At the same time, great and royal households made a determined effort to reduce the enormous expenditure on food insofar

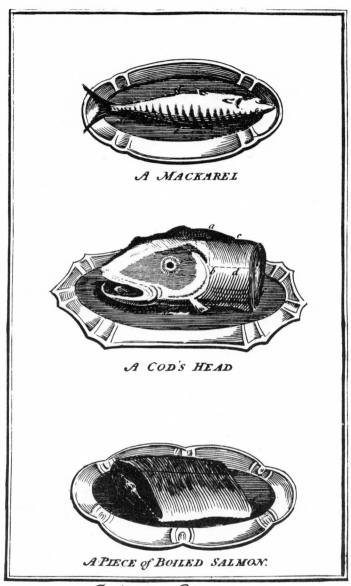

A MACKAREL

A COD'S HEAD

A PIECE of BOILED SALMON.

Rules for Carving. Plate V.

An illustration page from Henderson's *Housekeeper's Instructor, c. 1800*

as possible. Minute savings were carefully noted. Daily accounts were kept of what was spent, and lists were made daily of what was to be served the various household members down to the ounce of bread. Economy is stressed over and over in the household book of the Earl of Northumberland. There are orders one day that no more capons are to be bought except for my lord's men, and that capons must be bought lean, at a specified price, and fattened in the lord's own poultry yard. An instruction soon followed that cranes, herons, and plovers are to be served only at Christmas and principal feasts and only to my lord and his table. Another order limits "Great Byrdes and Bacon Flykes" to the tables of the lord, the master chamberlain, and the stewards.

Household books emphasize that the embezzling that has been going on must come to an end. All leftovers not destined for the poor are allotted to specific household members as part of their pay. As for the rest, according to the ordinance of King Henry VII, "relicts and ragments of meate and drinkes" that had not previously been reaching the poor were to be saved and gathered by the almoners for distribution to the poor at the outer gate "without diminishing, embezzling, or purloining any part thereof."

The pantlers were to be paid only in chippings and cuttings from the paring of loaves or trenchers, the cellar staff in empty pipes, hogsheads, and leftover wine and lees. The kitchen clerk had no wages other than skins from lambs and calves, while the master cook, in addition to his salary, clothing, and food, was entitled to half of "all the fatt arising and comming from the boilers and dripping pannes, broken bones; all neckes, livers, and gizards of poultry and foule, with their feathers; Rabbet and Cony skinnes." [36]

Behind the pomp and parade of the early sixteenth century, the feudal system of vassals and retainers was slowly disintegrating. Retainers no longer needed lords for protection and security, and lords no longer needed to have a large body of knights ready to fight in their households, nor did they need to keep and feed their own artisans. Things could now be repaired or bought in new-grown towns near the lord's estate. The numerous subdivisions of the fourteenth-century household—one department for brewing ale, another for salting a certain kind of meat, and so on—were outmoded once and for all.

When the feudal system broke down, paid domestic servants replaced aristocrats in even the highest household offices. By the end of the fifteenth century, carvers were almost always servants, not noblemen; by the end of the sixteenth century, sewers were no longer noble except on state occasions or in a sovereign's palace. Even the king found difficulty in filling his lower posts with gentlemen. Under Louis XIV, some of the posts, such as that of Senior Cup-Bearer (*premier échanson* or Bouteillier de France) became purely honorary ones with staff and salary but few functions. The last Bouteillier de France under the old monarchy was the Marquis de Lamermary, appointed in 1702.

As always there were many to deplore the changing times. In his *Householde of an Earle*, written in the early seventeenth century, Brathwait clung to the old ways, insisting the chief officers of a great estate must be wellborn men, grave, experienced, capable of buying, selling, and generally managing everything concerning an estate in order to free the lord to do his duty to king and country. Adding he had known earl's sons to serve earls, Brathwait remarked with contempt that of late he had heard some gentlemen whose fathers were nothing better than lawyers and merchants call it a disgrace to serve anyone but a prince.

In an anonymous French work translated by Giles Rose, one of the master cooks in the English royal household in 1682, the author insisted that the office of maître d'hôtel is an honor rather than a service because, though he has a napkin on his shoulder, the maître can also wear his cloak, sword, and hat while serving. The text continues:

> The Exercise of a Master Carver is more noble and commendable . . . [than] everyone will imagine . . . as there are divers distinctions amongst men, so by consequence there is or ought to be in their manner and fashion of eating, as well as living, a great deal of difference: and as it is but reason that all common people should cut their own Meat, it is but just that all Kings, Princes, and great Lords, and Persons of Quality should be exempted from this small pain; not of necessity, but for Honour and Ceremony. . . .[37]

An earlier writer, the anonymous author of *A Health for the Gentlemanly Profession of Serving-Men*, notes that with the cutting down of household staffs for economy, the days of domestic service for men of breeding had passed, and younger sons and poor relations no longer had domestic service to fall back on. In the old days, a quarter of the staff of 100 to 200 in a great household would be of gentle birth, and the posts provided younger sons with an opportunity to acquire polish, experience, and a place in the world.

Gone were the days when Sir Thomas More waited table in the household of Cardinal Morton, and the son and heir of the Earl of Northumberland served Cardinal Wolsey. The difference between lord and servant in that feudal age was one of degree of aristocratic rank, as nicely illustrated in a story of Elizabethan times recounted by Samuel Pepys. According to the story, a young nobleman was waiting on Lord Bedford at table when a letter was delivered to Lord Bedford informing him the earldom of Kent had fallen to his servant. Lord Bedford immediately rose from the table, seated the new Earl of Kent in his own chair, and took a lower place for himself.

Skill in carving was as much a part of a gentleman's education in the seventeenth century as before, but instructions were designed to enable gentlemen to acquit themselves with honor as guests or hosts rather than servants. With what admiration an Italian priest of the seventeenth century wrote in his diary of the expertise of his Milanese host, who held a chicken in midair while slicing up its component parts with a single stroke of the knife so that the wings flew down onto the plate as if alive! Copious diagrams in books on carving contrasted French and Italian methods. Giles Rose's edition of *L'escole parfaite des officiers de bouche* has plates showing no fewer than twelve ways of peeling apples, twelve ways of peeling pears, and eighteen for oranges.

As the feudal system disappeared, society became more receptive to new ideas, experiments, and also new foods. European agriculture underwent a major transformation with an equally major effect on the European cuisine. The change was slow. That tree growing was a subject worth studying only occurred to the French in the sixteenth century, and of the series of books on orchards and gardens that followed, the earliest were far from scientific. Historian Legrand d'Aussy remarked that many of the books were written by scholars in other fields who probably did not know one tree from another. The old absurdities persisted. Liébaut, one of these sixteenth-century sages, recommended writing the word "Raphael" on the plowshare in order to make the soil fertile. The signs of the zodiac governed pruning and grafting. Bizarre graftings to make the same tree bear several kinds of fruit were the special passion of fifteenth and sixteenth-century orchardists just as they had been in Roman times.

Flanders was the first part of northern Europe to cultivate vegetables and fruit extensively; market gardens outside Amsterdam were famous for their salads by the early fifteenth century. Flemish techniques were adopted by France, where, by the midsixteenth century, little lettuces were grown even in winter. True progress, however, was made only in the seventeenth century under Louis XIV's gardener Jean de la Quintinie, who took the all-important step of distinguishing between good and bad varieties, thereby learning to develop earlier and later crops. In the famous gardens he established at Versailles, he was able to provide Louis XIV with fresh asparagus and strawberries all year round. It was thanks to his skill that in Louis XIV's reign tender young spring vegetables were cultivated and sought after as delicacies. Disdaining the large, dried broad beans and peas of the Middle Ages, fashionable Parisians sought the tender young broad beans of spring; young green sugar peas were an expensive dainty much appreciated by ladies at court. Another vegetable that became fashionable was the artichoke, introduced to France from Italy by Catherine de Médicis, who had a passion for artichoke hearts. There are numerous recipes for artichokes and asparagus in seventeenth-century cookbooks, including instructions for preserving them for winter by drying, pickling, or storing underground in fat.

Seafarers brought back new plants from all parts of the world. As William Harrison commented in his *Description of England* (1577–1587), strange herbs, plants, and fruits were brought in daily from the Indies, from America, the Canary Islands, and all parts of the world. Among the "strange fruits" Harrison saw growing in noblemen's orchards were almonds, peaches, figs, and cornel berries. He claims to have seen some tropical plants as well: capers, oranges, and lemons. Among the ordinary fruits first cultivated in England in the sixteenth or early seventeenth centuries are apricots,

gooseberries, muskmelons, raspberries, and strawberries. Lemons, only mentioned twice in the *Oxford English Dictionary* prior to 1500, became very fashionable soon thereafter. Oranges, however, were successfully grown in sixteenth-century European hothouses.

Heidelberg is credited with the first stove-warmed greenhouse. By the seventeenth century, greenhouses, and particularly orangeries, were very fashionable throughout Europe. Louis XIV decorated his porticoes, halls, and antechambers with orange trees for banquets. No expense was spared for the orange, one of the few fruits universally praised by physicians. In a list of dinners for juries and lord treasurers held at the English crown's expense in 1573, oranges appear on nine out of twenty menus. Orange juice was much used in cooking. Recipes for keeping orange and lemon juice all year were included in late sixteenth-century cookbooks; sliced oranges and lemons powdered with sugar were a favorite salad. In the midseventeenth century, oranges and lemons often headed the list of second-course dishes. Pomegranate was another popular southern fruit, in great demand for certain illnesses. In the spring, a single pomegranate would bring a piece of gold.

The list of new vegetables is a long one. In the sixteenth century alone, England began the cultivation of kidney beans, red and white beets, shallots, carrots, chickpeas, lentils, lettuce, chicory, cucumbers, orache, and spinach. Some of these vegetables became instantly popular. The shallot was quickly adopted by epicures as the best possible seasoning for the newly introduced beefsteak. As soon as the cucumber reached England in 1573, recipes for dill pickles flooded English cookbooks. The English rapidly discovered many uses for the carrot, which they made into soup, garnishes, and even puddings and liqueurs. Horseradish, a native English plant long used as medicine, made its way to the table some time after 1597 and became indispensable in numerous sauces in the eighteenth century. Spinach was one of the most appreciated new vegetables. First grown in England about 1568, it was an immediate favorite because it appeared early in the spring when vegetables were scarce and the restrictions of Lent increased the demand for them. Innumerable spinach recipes appeared in English cookbooks of the late sixteenth century. Wealthy families were advised to keep a silver saucepan for preparing them.

Of the many plants brought from America in the sixteenth and seventeenth centuries some, like the tomato and potato, eventually became basic to the Western cuisine; others, like the string bean, remained incidental. Jerusalem artichokes and string beans (only broad beans had been known previously in Europe) reached England in the early seventeenth century. The Jerusalem artichoke was promptly baked in pies with various favorite ingredients of the era—marrow, dates, raisins, ginger, and sack—but the vegetable was so overused that within a dozen years it became unpopular and has remained so ever since. Corn was brought to Europe in the sixteenth century. So was the nasturtium, whose seeds were pickled as a substitute for capers and whose flowers and leaves were put in salads. Various peppers—cayenne, guinea pepper, and others—were introduced to Europe by the Spaniards in the sixteenth century and became very popular for relishes in the early eighteenth.

The potato is sometimes confused in history with the sweet potato, which Sir John Hawkins is credited with bringing to England from Santa Cruz in 1553. This exotic new plant was roasted and made into comfits in the late sixteenth century. When Falstaff says in *The Merry Wives of Windsor* (Act 5, Scene 5), "Let the sky rain potatoes; . . . hail kissing-comfits!" he is talking about sweet potatoes.

The potato proper was introduced later. English nobles planted it in their gardens as a curiosity, and it was considered a great table delicacy in the early seventeenth century, but after a brief period of fashion, became the object of suspicion and contempt. Many believed it poisonous, a prejudice the poor clung to longer than the rich. Consequently, except for Ireland, the potato came into general use only at the end of the eighteenth century, and only after enormous efforts to popularize it on the part of individuals and governments. William Harrison dismissed it summarily in his sixteenth century *Description of England*: "Of the potato and such venerous roots as are brought out of Spaine, Portingale, and the Indies to furnish up our bankets, I speake not." In some areas, planting of potatoes was officially forbidden, as in Burgundy, where the potato was classed as a "poisonous and mischievous root," suspected of causing leprosy and dysentery.

Even when the potato was not feared as poisonous, it was scorned by the English because the Irish ate it, and by the French who insisted on making bread out of it, a use to which the potato does not readily lend itself. Before the Irish took it up, the English gave the potato a try, but their concept of what to do with it was far different from ours, as can be seen from the following typical recipe taken from Thomas Dawson's *The Good Huswife's Jewel*, a cookbook printed about 1587:

> To make a tart that is a courage to man or woman.
> Take two quinces, 3 burre rootes, and a Potaton, and pare your Potaton, and scrape your rootes, and put them in to a quart of wine and let them boil till they be tender, and put in an oz. of dates, and when they be boiled tender drawe them through a

strainer, wine and all, and then put in the yolks of 8 eggs and the brains of 3 or 4 cock sparrows, and strain them into the other and a little rose water and seeth them all with sugar, cinnamon, and ginger, and cloves and mace, and put a little sweet butter and set it upon a chafing dish of coles between 2 platters and so let it boil till it be something bigge.

The tomato was as suspect as the potato. The first identifiable description of the tomato occurs in Italy in 1554 under the name "apples of gold," or *pomi d'oro*. By the end of the sixteenth century, both yellow and red tomatoes were to be found in European gardens, where for one or two hundred years they were grown as exotic ornamentals too dangerous to eat. Tomatoes only came into general use in the middle of the nineteenth century.

The sixteenth century saw the introduction of tea, coffee, and tobacco, the seventeenth, chocolate. Strangely enough, tobacco was greeted as good for the lungs and for respiratory ailments. What aroused a storm of protest on the part of doctors, moralists, and governments was chocolate, tea, and coffee. Tobacco, according to an English botanist named Henry Phillips, was the most esteemed of New World vegetable products. In his book on English navigations and discoveries, Hakluyt remarked that "with the herbe [tobacco] many have bene eased of reumes, etc.," and Harrison commented that tobacco is "greatly used in England against Reumes and some other diseases ingendered in the longes and inward partes, and not without effect." With great perspicacity, Balzac, writing of alcohol, coffee, tea, sugar, and tobacco, said all five had come into such excessive use in so short a time that societies might find themselves inestimably modified by them.

The most important of these new plants in the history of cooking are coffee and tea, which transformed breakfast from one of beer, meat, cheese, and dried herring to one like today's. Tea, which Legrand d'Aussy calls "that insipid and dangerous drink," aroused great controversy in the medical profession. Doctors in England and Holland said new diseases had broken out and others increased in frequency since the introduction of tea drinking. Other people thought tea stimulated the mind. Louis XIV's physician, Lémery, wrote in 1702 that if limited to ten or twelve cups per day, tea refreshed the spirits and cured headaches. In any case, tea and coffee were favored by literary men, happy to find a stimulant that did not stupefy, even in excess. The idea of using coffee or chocolate as a flavoring in food was to come only much later. Indeed, chocolate, a favorite drink of Montezuma's court, though immediately popular in Spain in the sixteenth century, did not come into general use in the rest of Europe until the Spanish sold their monopoly on cacao in the eighteenth century.

The introduction of chocolate, tea, and coffee greatly increased the demand for sugar, which became more and more available through the expanding international trade of the sixteenth century and the planting of sugar cane in the New World in the late seventeenth. Even the lower classes began to insist on sugar, and quantities were consumed by the rich. The new abundance of sugar led to the multiplication of confections, preserves, and jams. Some sixteenth- and seventeenth-century cookbooks were entirely devoted to recipes for candying violets, preserving elder flowers in sugar, and making rose syrups, sugar pastes, and comfits and sugarplums out of the seeds and fruits of every imaginable plant.

Just as sugar outmoded honey, new plants replaced old ones. Celery, brought from Italy at the end of the seventeenth century, drove out the old potherb alexander. The potato, once adopted, drove out the old asphodel, whose bulbs had been eaten since Greek times. The turkey, a new bird imported from North America and Mexico, was an immediately popular substitute for peacock, so popular that peacock, swan, and the whole host of strange birds previously eaten completely disappeared from the table by the eighteenth century. Rice and potatoes largely replaced the dried peas, lentils, and chick-peas that had served as basic starches on the Continent till the seventeenth and eighteenth centuries.

New foods introduced new fashions. The prunes, dates, raisins, currants, and saffron of medieval days continue to appear in some recipes, but are gradually replaced by typically seventeenth-century seasonings and garnishes: mushrooms, truffles, morels, pistachios, capers, cockscombs, lemon and orange juice and peel, anchovies, pomegranate grains, barberries, and, for pastries and sweet syrups, musk and ambergris.

Among the new foods were several essentials of today's *haute cuisine* such as mushrooms, whose reappearance on the table in the sixteenth century alarmed many. Herbalist Gerard, writing in 1597, warned that of "the earthie excrescences called mushrooms . . . fewe of them are good to be eaten and most of them do suffocate and strangle the eater." Nevertheless, mushrooms began to be cultivated in the seventeenth century, and with their cultivation, both the danger and the fear of eating them diminished.

A great advance in this era of scientific endeavor was the introduction of muzzled pigs for truffle hunting. The truffle, without which there can be no true gourmet meal according to Brillat-Savarin, had been in occasional use in France since the late fourteenth century. However, the greatest truffle of all, that of Périgord, only came into favor at the end of the fifteenth century. The truffle was slow to reach England, where it remained an almost unknown curiosity in the seventeenth century; England lagged farther and farther behind the rising culinary superiority of France.

Another gourmet delight, caviar, though brought from Russia by the Hanseatic League in the fifteenth and sixteenth centuries, did not begin to gain favor until the mideighteenth, but *foie gras* was esteemed in France two hundred years before that. Turtle, crab, and lobster became fashionable, and the consumption of that long-neglected bivalve the oyster rose steadily through the late sixteenth and seventeenth centuries. Oysters were eaten by the barrel as a first course or as a kind of collation with wine at almost any time of day. The number of oyster recipes in seventeenth-century cookbooks is most extraordinary; Robert May gives a total of thirty-two in his *Accomplish't Cook*. Oysters were stewed, parboiled, fried, grilled, used in stuffings, and combined with many unlikely ingredients. One of May's oyster recipes calls for onions, white wine, artichoke bottoms, boiled marrow, sliced lemons, gooseberries or grapes, a garnish of grated bread, mace, more lemons and artichokes, and butter poured over all.

Ice, a luxury that had gone out of use at the end of the Roman Empire, was reintroduced in Southern Europe in the sixteenth century. François I's physician, Bruyère-Champier, writing of his trip to Nice with the king, tells of seeing the Italians and Spanish in Nice fetch snow from neighboring mountains to refresh their drinks. Astonished and disapproving, Champier dismissed the custom as thoroughly unhealthy.

Some thirty years later, when Henri III had plates of snow and ice put on his table to cool the wine, it was considered a scandalous and effeminate indulgence. Even the rich did not begin to accept the custom until the seventeenth century, in part, perhaps, because of the longstanding habit of drinking hot water and warm wine during meals. As late as 1702, Lémery warned that Italians and Spaniards had paid with their lives for the pleasure of drinking iced drinks. Nevertheless, by the end of the seventeenth century, there was enough demand for ice to give employment to numbers of professional snow and ice dealers and to make ice houses a necessity for the fashionable. Louis XIV had houses containing 260 cubic yards of ice at Versailles.

When the inquisitive sixteenth century discovered that liquids could be cooled in water in which saltpeter had been dissolved, rich Italians immediately put the discovery to use for cooling water and wine. In 1607, a Neapolitan physician described making ice by putting water in a vessel resting in a mixture of snow and ice with saltpeter and other salts. The germ of the ice-cream maker, and of refrigeration, was born.

Ices were introduced to France by Catherine de Médicis, whose Florentine chefs made a different ice for every day of her wedding celebration. The French court was enchanted with the new dish. After the wedding, numbers of Italians came to France to ply their trades. Some of these were hawkers of liqueurs, lemonades, and orangeades, who added ice to make their drinks more refreshing. One day an Italian called Procope turned the entire lemonade into ice. He was quickly copied by others. By 1676, according to John Beckmann's *History of Inventions*, there were 250 master ice makers in Paris.

The spirit of experimentation that led to the discovery of ice making led to the development of liqueurs. Distilling was known in Europe in the twelfth and thirteenth centuries through Crusaders who had learned of it from the Arabs. However, medieval liqueurs were generally used as medicine and probably also tasted like medicine. Liqueurs were widely served in France only from the end of the sixteenth century when better distilling techniques were introduced by the Italians, notably by the suites of the two Médicis queens, Catherine and Marie. Liqueurs became popular during the reign of Louis XIV, and brandy, the final touch to a great meal for many connoisseurs, was first used in the seventeenth century, but the slow and gradual process of distilling that produces the liqueurs we enjoy today was only discovered two centuries later.

By the midseventeenth century, there was a new cuisine and a series of cookbooks to propagate it. Almost all of them dismiss previous works as "empty and unprofitable" and reflect a new internationalism by including English, French, Italian, Spanish, German, and Dutch recipes. Cookbooks were bought and read eagerly, going into many editions. They were no longer only for professional cooks in great houses; many were addressed to the upper bourgeois. Samuel Pepys wrote in his diary of spending an enjoyable moment reading a book of recipes aloud in company. He himself was an amateur cook, eagerly noting the recipe for a dish of eggs with asparagus butter which Lord Carlingford himself concocted one day on dropping in at Pepys' house at dinner time.

The new cookbooks were serious ones, often including exact proportions. The quantities are startling, but no doubt necessary to feed the large households and hearty appetites of the day. Eggs *quelquechose* in Salmon's *Family-Dictionary* calls for forty eggs, and a cake recipe in Robert May's *Accomplish't Cook* for half a bushel of flour, three pounds of butter, fourteen pounds of currants, two pounds of sugar, and three quarts of cream. An effort was made to introduce some kind of order, often alphabetical, a choice which led to having an oyster recipe follow an ointment for ulcers because most books still combined medical and culinary recipes and often included a parcel of household hints and beauty formulas as well.

By the seventeenth century, France—where native genius combined with superior natural food resources had been encouraged and developed by epicurean kings and queens—had attained acknowledged culinary supremacy in Europe. French cooks were everywhere. William Harrison notes with scorn in his *Description of England* that the cooks of the English nobility "are for the most part musicall-headed Frenchmen and Strangers." The home-trained cook was no longer good enough. There was a cooking school in London as early as 1678, though Italian or French cooks, or cooks trained abroad or at court, were most in demand. Some rich Englishmen sent their chefs to France for training.

A good cook was as important to the new bourgeoisie as to royalty and nobility, perhaps even more important, for a cook could help the bourgeois rise in the world. As Molière said in *Le Misanthrope* (Act II, Scene 5), "He makes his cook his merit, and the world visits his dinners and not him." Being important, the cook was well rewarded both in esteem and money. Richard Burton noted in his *Anatomy of Melancholy*, "Cookery is become an art, a noble science; cooks are gentlemen." Louis XIV's chief cooks had the right to wear swords. In a seventeenth-century household guide called *La Maison Réglée*, the recommended salary for the cook in the house of a bachelor lord is three times as large as the chaplain's.

The new cuisine was not completely new of course; medieval tastes were not stamped out in 150 years. Though Robert May's *Accomplish't Cook*, first printed in 1660, is cited as a product of the new cuisine, it nevertheless includes such a flagrantly medieval recipe as capilotado *françois*, in which a leg of mutton is dressed with a pound of strained almond paste and a pound of sugar, garnished with some roast chickens, pigeons, or capons, and sprinkled with cinnamon and more sugar. Few vegetables other than a handful of primeurs and artichokes, asparagus, and spinach appeared on upper-class tables. On the other hand, the new foods, particularly truffles, mushrooms, morels, and *foie gras*, called for and received a new, more delicate handling.

One of the changes that made this new delicacy possible was the use of butter. Only mentioned four times in the fourteenth century *Forme of Cury* and seven times in the 460 recipes of *Two Fifteenth Century Cookbooks*, butter became common in pastry, on vegetables, and in sauces in the seventeenth century. Butter and flour for thickening began to replace bread and almonds, and the addition of a bit of butter to finish a sauce was introduced for the first time. With the greater use of flour came the creation of béchamel, the all-important basic sauce credited to Louis XIV's maître d'hôtel, the Marquis de Béchamel. The abundance of dishes based on cream and milk was another innovation; there were custards, caramels, and almond creams. All midseventeenth-century cookbooks included *pâté feuilleté* in pastry sections, and confectionery had already become a separate profession. The basic bouillon, the *bouquet garni*, the cream soups—all these belong to a new era of cooking, clearly defined in 1651 in *Le Cuisinier François* by La Varenne, Écuyer de Cuisine of the Marquis d'Uxelles, and inventor of the still-favored *haute cuisine* sauce of mushrooms and onions, *sauce duxelles*.

In the midseventeenth century, the entremet ceased to be an acrobatic stunt or a childish joke in pastry and became a delicate dish such as artichoke *beignets,* new green peas, pomegranate salad, or truffles. Vegetable garnishes became fashionable. For the first time it occasionally, though rarely, occurred to cooks simply to boil and serve vegetables with butter, salt, and pepper, or to present meats with nothing more than their own juice as sauce.

As the old mortrewes and mawmenees went out of style in the sixteenth century, whole large joints of meat appear for the first time, roasted or boiled. Before Queen Elizabeth, it was hew hom smalle and grinde hom well in nine recipes out of ten. By the late sixteenth century, when fresh meat had become available all year thanks to the cultivation of root crops for winter fodder, butchers' meat of all kinds appeared on the best tables. Robert May's cookbook had a separate section of 112 recipes for beef alone.

The greater simplicity of the era is nicely illustrated by the boiled egg. Prior to the midsixteenth century, hardly anyone had thought of simply boiling an egg, though almost everything else that could be done to an egg was tried. In the Middle Ages, eggs used to be emptied at both ends, filled with stuffing, and roasted on a spit, or else baked in the ashes. At last, in the sixteenth century, the cuisine advanced to the point of boiling an egg. The new egg dish was fashionable. Louis XIV used to end his meal with a few hard-boiled eggs after dessert.

However, along with this greater simplicity, there was a new penchant in the seventeenth century for platters heaped with foods, often of many varieties. A favorite that appears in all cookbooks of the epoch was the Spanish olio, which frequently constituted the center platter. The recipe for this dish covers three pages in May's book and calls for beef, mutton, sausage, venison, pork, bacon, carrots, cauliflower, red beets, turnips, onions, cabbages, spinach, sorrel, herbs, barley, cloves, mace, saffron and other seasonings, plus geese and other birds (such as 24 quail, 48 larks, 4 partridges) to make a total of 101 birds, not to speak of other ingredients: bread, marrow, yolks of hard-boiled eggs, chestnuts, pistachios, butter, white wine, strong broth, lemons, and lemon peel.

There were many dishes other than the olio in which chefs competed in mounting the tallest pyramids of food. As late as 1691, Massialot, author of *Le Cuisinier roial y bourgeois*, whose ideas were culinarily in advance of his times, was still loading a single platter with a suckling pig, a turkey, two capons, and a loin of veal. Sometimes the pyramids fell and broke on being brought in. Meats and vegetables, fruits and pastries—all were suitable for building these towers of food. Despite sumptuary laws like a French order of January 1629 that forbade putting more than six pieces on one platter, the penchant for pyramids continued into the eighteenth century. It may have reached its climax in England when Lord Albemarle's pastry cook complained bitterly that milord was not willing to remove the dining room ceiling to accommodate his latest eighteen-foot-high masterpiece.

By the seventeenth century, the drafty old hall was replaced by a new, separate dining room, a comfortable place with carpets on the floor, tapestries and silk hangings on the wall, glass windows, fireplaces, and decoratively carved furniture. Chairs and stools replaced benches; the table was sometimes oblong, oval, or round, or had leaves to accommodate larger numbers.

No longer was there a procession of dishes to a bare board. In addition to a cloth, the table was set with the handsome silver and gold plate that constituted a kind of Renaissance bank account. Venetian glass was even more prized than gold and silver, while porcelain, very expensive and fashionable when it began to be manufactured in Europe in the seventeenth century, appeared on every luxurious table along with gold and silver. Napkins afforded a special opportunity for display; pages were written on how to pleat and fold them in fancy forms such as a pigeon on its nest in a basket or two capons in a pie.

The new comforts were not all limited to the rich. By the midsixteenth century, the middle class were replacing their wooden plates with pewter, and their wooden spoons with silver, pewter, and tin. Half a century later, artisans and farmers had tapestries, silk hangings, a cupboard to display their plate, a wine bowl, a dozen spoons, and a silver salt cellar. Even the poor were discarding the old horn drinking vessels for homemade glass of fern and brimstone. Chimneys had been new enough in the sixteenth century to cause a visitor to England to complain that men once hardened by smoke had grown soft. In the seventeenth century chimneys were taken as a matter of course.

Gradually, individual plates, knives, and spoons were introduced for each person at the table, though this was still the exception rather than the rule in the late sixteenth century. Montaigne remarked with surprise in about 1580 on seeing a spoon per person on the table in Switzerland, and Horace Walpole notes in his letters that the Duke and Duchess of Hamilton continued to eat off the same plate in 1752. Individual soup bowls were not introduced for another hundred years after Montaigne wrote, and even then the French Dauphin's governor, the Duc de Montausier, was thought ridiculous for suggesting soup be served with a big ladle to avoid having each person dip his own spoon in the serving dish. A book of manners of the time of Louis XIV instructed the well-bred to "always wipe your spoon before dipping into a fresh dish, for there are people so fastidiously constituted that they object to eating what you have disarranged with a spoon which you have just taken out of your mouth." [38]

Until the midsixteenth century, there was often only one glass for everyone at the table, and it was noted as a sign of good breeding in books on manners for a man to wipe his mouth on a napkin or the tablecloth before drinking from the glass. By the following century, each had a glass, though he had to signal a lackey to be served drink, and the lackeys had to keep the glasses in careful order on the sideboard. The Marquis de Rouillac, who died in 1662, is remembered as the first to decide he would have his glass and bottle on the table to drink whenever he pleased, and a bell to ring for lackeys if he wanted something. He was considered crazy.

The cuisine of the seventeenth century could hardly have taken form without the introduction of a novelty so revolutionary that it

116

was denounced from the pulpit—the fork. It is startling to think how late the fork came into use. Montaigne, according to his own account, ate with his fingers, and so rapidly he sometimes bit them. Louis XIV ate with his fingers; so did Queen Anne of England. Napoleon is said to have preferred to. Until well into the seventeenth century, except for the effeminate court of Henri III, Frenchmen and Englishmen ate meat with their fingers, tore it with their teeth, and dipped into stews with their fingers or a piece of bread. Henri III was severely criticized by moralists for using the fork. No doubt he had adopted it from culinarily precocious Italy, where an Englishman traveling in 1608 saw and described the instrument, which, he said, was "not used in any other country that I saw in my travels neither doe I thinke that any other nation of Christendome doth use it, but only Italy." [39]

Of course forks had been in existence for centuries. Homer spoke of forks used for grilling meat. Little two-pronged forks for picking up fruit or sweetmeats were listed in medieval inventories of royal jewels. Edward I's wardrobe account mentions a "forcke of chrystal"; Edward II had three forks; Charles V of France had nine of gold and two of silver. Carving forks were used in Spain by 1423, the Tartars used a fork to spear morsels of meat from the communal bowl, and there is one solitary mention of a fork used for eating in the eleventh century by a lady from Constantinople who was married to a Doge of Venice.

Be that as it may, it was only in the midseventeenth century that, despite some of the crowned heads of Europe, the fork began to be used outside Italy, much to the benefit of the cuisine. No longer did food have to be mashed to a pulp or cut up into bits; the fork and knife made the new cuisine of solid meats possible. Nor was it only the cuisine that was transformed. In *Hunger and History*, E. Parmalee Prentice remarks that the use of the fork may mark the period of improving health among Europeans.

The fork was adopted only very slowly and over great opposition. It was considered irreligious. Were the hands the Good Lord gave us no longer good enough to touch His creatures? The fork inspired general ridicule as unmanly and affected. Cooks felt it spoiled the flavor of food. Louis XIV not only did not use it, but was opposed to it, according to the following passage from the correspondence of his sister-in-law, the Princess Palatine:

> The Duc de Bourgogne [Louis XIV's grandson] and his two brothers had been taught the polite innovation of using a fork to eat with. But when they were invited to the King's table at supper, he would have none of it and forbade them to use such an instrument. He would never have had occasion to reproach me in that matter, for I have never in my life used anything to eat with but my knife and my fingers.[40]

The idea that it was not hygienic to have everyone at the table dipping his fingers into a common dish did not occur to anyone. When, in 1658, Louis XIV's first cousin, the Duchesse de Montpensier, expressed disgust that Louis XIV should allow other people to put their fingers in his dish, what concerned her was the sacrilegious familiarity, not the lack of hygiene.

An entirely new method of serving came into being with the new cuisine and the new, intimate dining room. By the reign of Louis XIV, the table was set in advance with dishes of various sizes placed symmetrically on the table. The large middle platter, known as the *grande entrée*, might contain a pair of roast beefs garnished with fried veal cutlets, or an olio, or some other pyramid of mixed meats. At a dinner for twelve, there would be four middle-sized dishes (two *potages*, a partridge *pâté* and a truffled chicken, for example) plus four smaller dishes known as hors d'oeuvres, each containing some delicacy such as braised quail.

When the first course was removed, it was succeeded by the "roast," actually a kind of mixed grill. For this there would be four middle-sized plates, two of grilled meat and two of some composite dish, an entremet which could be a sweet tart or cream or a delicate vegetable dish in a sauce, and four hors d'oeuvres such as truffles in court bouillon, *foie gras*, asparagus salad, and blancmange (also sweet). Dessert, the third and last course, consisted of fresh, dried, and candied fruits, fruit tarts, liquid and dry sweetmeats of various colors, colored jellies, fresh cheeses and clouted creams, marchpanes, syrups, pralines, and in England, bag puddings and trifles, all served at once. It was never expected that each guest would try each dish, of course, and the thrifty host hoped the larger pieces would be left intact to reappear at supper or the following day's dinner.

The number and size of the platters were increased or diminished according to the number and standing of the people eating. A really large dinner, like one served the Marquis de Seignelai in May 1690, would have sixteen *potages* and thirty-two hors d'oeuvres in the first course, sixteen platters of roast, ten small salads, four large and twelve middle-sized entremets, plus twenty-two hors d'oeuvres in the second course, making a total of 112 dishes not counting dessert. That memorable meal required the combined efforts of thirty-six "officers of the kitchen" and numerous aides. There were even larger dinners. At the marriage of Mademoiselle de Blois, illegitimate daughter of Louis XIV, to the Prince de Conti at Versailles, there were three courses of 160 dishes each. When the Duc de Vendôme received the Dauphin on September 6, 1686, he served a total of 486 dishes not including dessert, which alone consisted of 876 dishes of fruits, salads, glasses of dried fruits and compotes, and small dishes of candied fruit.

In England, the order to be discerned in France at the end of the seventeenth century did not exist until the eighteenth, and meals were grosser, with heavy emphasis on meat. In her *Queen-like Closet*, first published in 1670, Hannah Wooley suggests the following menu for a summer family meal in the house of a "gentleman of lesser quality":

THE FIRST COURSE
1. A Boiled Pike or Carp stewed.
2. A very fine Pudding boiled.
3. A chine of Veal, and another of Mutton.
4. A calves Head Pie.
5. A Leg of Mutton rosted whole.
6. A couple of Capons or a Pig or a Piece of roste Beef, or boiled Beef.
7. A Sallad, the best in season.

119

THE SECOND COURSE

1. A Dish of fat Chickens roasted.
2. A cold venison Pasty.
3. A dish of fryed Patties.
4. A Jole of fresh Salmon.
5. A couple of lobsters.
6. A dish of Tarts.
7. A gammon of Bacon or dry'd Tongues.
   then cheese and fruit.

What was suggested in cookbooks and what was actually eaten may not have been quite the same thing. In his diary, Samuel Pepys, who might be called a "gentleman of lesser quality," served nothing so copious even for special guests. When Pepys hired a chef to prepare dinner for company on March 26, 1662, he served, as he carefully noted in his diary, a brace of stewed carps, six roasted chickens, and a jowl of salmon for the first course, a tanzy,* and two neats' tongues and cheese for the second. Elsewhere he writes of dining with his wife on pease porridge and nothing else, and of finding Lord Sandwich "all alone at a little table with one joynt of meat at dinner." Pepys himself sometimes ate bread, butter, and cheese before bedtime instead of having supper.

Bread, butter, and cheese were the staple foods of the poor in seventeenth-century England, particularly bread. In 1670, the soldier's ordinary allowance in the field was two pounds of bread, one pound of meat, or an equal amount of cheese, and one bottle of wine or two of beer. As the Italian professor of medicine Johannis Sala said in *De Alimentis* (1628): "Far the greater part of mankind live on bread alone, and of the rest of our race who have other things, it is the settled practice to eat two to three times as much bread as of anything else." The standard of living was measured by the amount of meat and fish consumed.

For all but the wealthy, there was an acute shortage of meat in the seventeenth century. The poor were far worse off than they had been in the Middle Ages. Even in fourteenth-century Paris, a city of over 200,000 inhabitants, every house had kept poultry, and the

---

* Any dish containing the herb tansy.

fact that a law against keeping pigs in houses was reissued three or four times during the century indicates that pigs were kept too. Grain used to be brought from the fields to Paris at harvest time to be ground in mills attached to bridges on the Seine. Vineyards flourished in the garden of the Louvre in the Middle Ages.

The new overgrown city of the late sixteenth century no longer permitted the half-rural life that had characterized medieval towns. Food had to be brought in from the countryside ready for market. Getting it to town was far from easy, for means of transportation had improved no more than methods of preserving food. Roads were almost impassable after heavy rains or floods. Indeed, it was a problem of transportation that led to the often-recounted suicide of the Prince de Condé's comptroller or *officier de bouche*, Vatel, who killed himself when the fish he had ordered for a reception for Louis XIV at Chantilly failed to arrive.

In general, there was far less food to be had, whether in the country or the city, and there were far more people to be fed. While the population increased, the spread of towns and enclosure of land deprived the peasant of pastures for his animals and fields for his crops. Even poultry, once kept by everyone, became an expensive luxury.

One of the consequences of the meat shortage in England was an increase in the number of fish days in the second half of the sixteenth century. Counteracting the dearth and high price of meat was only one of the motives, however. The other was to develop a navy by encouraging ship building and providing a training ground for sailors. In his *Description of England*, Harrison mentions the introduction of new fish days to increase cattle and maintain the navy which would "otherwise greatlie decaie." Friday and Saturday both became meatless days. In 1595 it was observed that the addition of a third fish day would lead to a saving of 13,500 cattle yearly in London alone. However, even the second day was never strictly observed and was dropped by the end of the century.

Navigation was generally looked upon as the solution to the problems of the age. When Hakluyt said in his *Principall Navigations* that travels will bring more relief to the poor than anyone did by building almshouses, he expressed the sentiment of an age that had seen the Spanish, Portuguese, and then the Dutch grow rich by taking new territories and opening up new trade. England, too, set out to establish herself abroad and on the seas. Thus came the formation in 1600 of the East India Company, which led to a taste for exotic dishes with new flavors. The new sea routes had already decreased Italian influence. As Italian trade languished, culinary discoveries no longer came from that country, but from the Portuguese, Germans, Spaniards, and Dutch. By the end of the century, exotic Oriental dishes were becoming fashionable.

The age of exploration and long sea voyages called for new inventions for storing and preparing food. While cooks studied the chemistry of preserving food and the medical consequences of diet, men of science turned their attention to the kitchen. Typical of the spirit of the Elizabethan age is Sir Hugh Plat, a prolific and popular writer, author of important works on soil improvement, and inventor of such diverse objects as the turnspit used today, the alphabet block, and a reflecting finger ring for gamblers. He also produced a book on candies, preserves, distilling, and home remedies entitled *Delightes for Ladies* (1593/4). Another man of science, Sir Francis Bacon, among his many experiments, tried putting flesh in snow to preserve it, but his work was abandoned before any conclusions were reached. Sanctorious (1561–1636), a professor at Padua who was a friend of Galileo, made experiments in an effort to determine the nutritive value of foods by weighing himself before, during, and after eating.

Among inventors who turned their attention to cooking and preserving in connection with food supply at sea was Denys Papin, a French physician who took refuge in England from religious persecution. In 1681 he published a small booklet on a large and complicated machine he called "A New Digester or Engine for Softening Bones." It was nothing less than the forerunner of the modern pressure cooker. With the hope the new machine might be useful on ships in increasing the production of edible food from a lesser quantity of raw materials, Papin described numerous experiments such as taking an "old male and tame Rabbet, which is ordinarily but a pitiful sort of meat" and cooking it in the machine. Papin reported the machine made it as soft and savory as a young rabbit and turned its juice and bones into a good jelly. Unfortunately the engine was cumbersome, had to be put into a specially built furnace, was difficult to watch while in operation, and, on the whole, rather dangerous. These difficulties remained unsolved, preventing the invention from being put to practical use until some two hundred years later.

VI

❦

The
Classical Century

The *haute cuisine* of the eighteenth century
was a French cuisine, and it was in France that epicurean dinners and suppers became the preferred entertainment of social leaders. In Italy and Spain, according to reports from
travelers, even the upper classes rarely entertained at home, and a
dinner invitation was a rare and formal occasion usually connected
with government or church. England, more hospitable and interested enough in food to produce quantities of cookbooks in multi-
fold editions, never caught up to France in the culinary arts though
London acquired French restaurants and the upper classes acquired
French chefs after the French Revolution.

The French *haute cuisine* came into being in the Regency (1715–
1723) in the intimate suppers of the regent, Philippe d'Orléans,
with his cronies. Eating then assumed that high place in French culture it still occupies in some French circles today. Aristocrats vied
with each other in inventing dishes, or in keeping cooks who invented dishes to immortalize their masters' names. The names de
Berri, Villeroy, Montmorency, Mirepoix, Nesle, Richelieu, and
Talleyrand were perpetuated in garnishes, *vols-au-vent*, cutlets, and
sausages. The Marquise de Pompadour is credited with the creation
of *suprême de poulet à la Bellevue*, the Marquise de Maintenon
with *côtelettes à la papillote. Petites bouchées à la reine* were named
for Queen Marie Leczinska. The kitchen was transformed into
something great lords could be proud of, and kings themselves took
a turn at the stove. Servants were kept out of sight at intimate sup-

pers, where informality of service and delicacy of food were the keyword. Often the table, completely set, was sent up through the floor by pulleys. None of these changes could have taken place under Louis XIV, a glutton interested mainly in quantity, who surrounded himself with clever ministers, but obtuse chefs. (Saint-Simon once remarked that Louis XIV ate so solidly and prodigiously one never got used to it, and the Princess Palatine wrote of often seeing him eat four kinds of soup, a whole pheasant, a partridge, a large plate of salad, two thick slices of ham, a dish of mutton in sauce, and a plateful of pastries, followed by fruit and hard-boiled eggs.)

The little suppers of Louis XV first featured the dishes of Moutier, a chef immortalized in songs of the Regency. He was succeeded by the most famous cook of the century, Vincent de la Chapelle. Sometimes the courtiers themselves took over. At one dinner all the dishes were prepared by the Prince de Beaufremont, the Marquis de Polignac, the Ducs de Gontaut, d'Ayen, de Coigny, and de la Vallière, while the King contributed the *poulets au basilic*. Sometimes the King amused himself by making a sauce or preparing truffles in silver casseroles with the Prince de Dombes. He was not the first king to take casserole in hand. Louis XIII had been an avid amateur cook specializing in egg dishes: *oeufs perdus, oeufs pochés au beurre noir, omelettes* and *beignets;* there is also a record of his making both a quince and an apple tart on one occasion. Nor were the two Louis the only eighteenth-century kings to take a direct interest in cooking. Frederick the Great was inspired by an excellent ragout to write a poem to his maître d'hôtel. Dumas relates that Louis XV's father-in-law, Stanislaus Ier, was so pleased with an onion soup served him at an inn on the way from Lunéville to Paris that he went to the kitchen in his dressing gown and insisted the chef make the dish again before his eyes so he would know how to do it himself.

Good eating was not confined to the court. By the late eighteenth century, Paris had become the gourmet center of the world. Poets, artists, musicians, and the new bourgeoisie were also enjoying the best the world had to eat. In his twelve-volume description of Paris in the 1780's, Louis-Sébastien Mercier speaks of the epicure who knows the provinces only for their fowl or fish, who talks only of turkeys with truffles from Périgord, *pâtés de foie gras* from Toulouse, *pâtés* of fresh tuna from Toulon, terrines of red partridge from Nérac, cooked wild boar's head from Troyes, and of how he is about to rush to the carriage station to meet a particularly magnificent carp he has had sent from Strasbourg. Parisian specialty shops like the Hôtel d'Aligre in the Rue Saint-Honoré sold anything the most demanding gourmet could want. A man lacking a cook could, in fifteen minutes, buy an entire meal of cooked hams and tongues, quail, ortolans in pastry, marinated oysters, mustard pickles, jellies, comfits, dried fruits, wines, and liqueurs.

The impecunious gourmet who could not shop for ready-made dishes had another way of eating well without keeping a staff, according to Mercier. This was to get "a box of white iron that will hold four plates" and an errand boy, then make an arrangement with the cook of a nearby great house to have *la desserte*, or the leftovers. The usual monthly rate, Mercier noted, was 27 francs. At 4:30 P.M., the box is sent over, the scullions put in the dinner's leftovers, intact for the most part or only slightly nibbled on, and the pauper gourmet eats like a king.

In the eighteenth century, great eating extended to prison (for the rich, that is). In her diary entry of April 14, 1772, the Duchess of Northumberland describes a fortress prison near Lyons for people of high rank, none of whom had any hope of being released, but all of whom dined with the governor every day and could spend all the revenue from their estates to have fine wines, fish, and game sent to the prison for them. One prisoner was said to spend three thousand pounds sterling a year on his table. When the French writer Marmontel was imprisoned briefly in the Bastille in 1761, he was surprised to learn that the four-course meal he ate the first day had been meant for his servant. The meal intended for him consisted of an exquisite soup, fillet of beef, a quarter of chicken *au jus*, marinated artichokes, spinach *au jus*, a handsome pear, a bunch of grapes, a bottle of old Burgundy, and coffee. This was poor pickings compared to the fare of Louis XVI and his family when imprisoned by the revolutionaries in the Temple, where a kitchen staff of thirteen prepared and served dinners and suppers of three *potages*, four entrées, three dishes of "roast" or mixed grill, four entremets, a plate of *petits fours*, three compotes, three plates of fruit, bread, a bottle of champagne, a carafe each of Bordeaux, Malvoisie, and Madeira, and coffee.[41]

There is no reason to doubt that Louis XVI enjoyed this meal heartily, perhaps regretting only the slight reduction in the menu since his days of glory. His formidable, compulsive appetite has been the subject of much comment by historians, who agree that the worst misfortune failed to affect it. It was at the end of his first appearance before his judges, after acquiescing to a long list of charges, that Louis XVI noticed the prosecutor held a piece of bread in his hand and asked him for a bit of it. According to the story, when requested to speak up, the king did not hesitate to repeat in a loud voice, "I am asking you for a piece of bread." At last, back at the Temple, he was able to satisfy his appetite with six chops, a big piece of poultry, eggs, and three glasses of wine, after which he went to sleep.

Many factors contributed to the changes in the eighteenth-century cuisine. For one, the agricultural revolution foreshadowed in the previous century was in full sway. Every year brought a new crop, an improvement in poultry raising or cattle breeding, or a new labor-saving device. Agricultural machinery was invented with the encouragement of prizes and grants. Influential men formed societies to further advances in food production. Agricultural improvements became the fashionable preoccupation of great landowners and even kings. Louis XV imported plants from all over the world and established royal nurseries maintained at state expense in every province. He is said to have cultivated plants himself, picking his own salad in a private garden at the Trianon. King George III had his own model farm at Windsor. The Duke of Mantua thought so highly of his gardener that he knighted the man, who thenceforth went about his work wearing a sword.

The kinds and varieties of plants increased astronomically. Coffee bushes, cinnamon and caper trees, melons and pineapples were raised in hothouses; cucumber was grown under glass in 1721 for the first time since the rule of Tiberius. The entirely novel idea of growing vegetables as a field crop instead of limiting them to market gardens occurred for the first time. Cattle breeding was studied; grazing lands were planted; the first veterinary school in France opened in Lyons in 1761.

Even more important to the cuisine than these improvements in food production was the reversal of the medical profession's 2,000-year-old views on fruits and vegetables. The discovery that scurvy could be cured by fruits and vegetables was probably an important factor in forming the new view that, far from breeding disease and fever, they were necessary for health. In 1702, Lémery in his *Traité des aliments*, noted as a mark in favor of fruits and vegetables that "Horses, Beeves, and Elephants live on plants alone and are large, fat, very strong, and rarely out of Order." With the acceptance of luxury vegetables as garnishes and side dishes, the rich began to put heavy spices aside in favor of subtler flavors. The poor were encouraged, though with limited success, to use the commoner vegetables to stretch their meat.

International trade continued to increase, and with it, the introduction of new foods to the European cuisine continued apace. Vermicelli and macaroni became common. Limes, molasses, and rum came from the West Indies, celery, broccoli, and cauliflower from southern Europe. Ginger became one of the most popular spices when it began to be exported in abundance from the West Indies. Vanilla and chocolate were used in European recipes for the first time, sometimes in strange ways, such as sauces for fish. Tapioca, sago, and rennet were added to puddings. Rice was imported in ever greater quantities to offset bad European grain harvests.

However, the greatest change wrought by increased international trade was not in the quantity or variety of imports, but the distribution; for the first time, they began to reach the average person. Tea, sugar, and other commodities that were luxuries at the beginning of the century became commonplace by the end of it. Foreign ways, including customs of eating and drinking, were of great interest to people of the eighteenth century, an interest reflected in the increasing number of exotic dishes that appear in cookbooks meant for use in bourgeois as well as wealthy households: Turkish pilafs, Turkish mutton, Welsh rabbit, shish kabob, and, above all in England, catsups and chutneys.

Still more important than the introduction of new foods, or the acceptance of foods previously known like the potato and tomato, was a complete transformation in the concept of cooking. As explained in *Les Dons de Comus*, one of the first books to expound it, the new cuisine, dating from about 1720, consisted in "decomposing, digesting, and quintessentializing foods to bring out their nourishing juices and delicacy and so blend them that no ingredient dominates and all are discernible; in short, to give food the harmony painters create with color, to make flavors so homogeneous that of their varied tastes only a fine and piquant taste remains, the consonance of all flavors united." [42] The Duc de Nivernais, an eighteenth-century diplomat who had the patience to make his chef repeat a new dish eight days in a row to bring it to perfection, left posterity a little book called *Les petits soupers de la cour* in which he describes the clear sauces, cullises, and essences of the *haute cuisine.*

A recipe of a turn of the century literary gourmet, Grimod de la Reynière, best illustrates the principle of quintessentializing. Entitled "A Roast Without Equal," it calls for an olive stuffed with capers and anchovies inside a figpecker inside an ortolan inside a lark inside a thrush inside a quail wrapped in a vine leaf inside a lapwing inside a fat pullet inside a pheasant inside a wild goose inside a turkey inside a bustard, the whole thing to be cooked in a pot with onions, carrots, ham, celery, lard, spices and herbs, hermetically sealed over a low fire for twenty-four hours. The result Grimod de la Reynière describes as the quintessence of plains, forests, swamps, and the best poultry yard. Dumas later mocked the recipe by adding that at the end one threw away everything but the olive, the apex of quintessence.

The cullis was typical of the new cuisine. It was a kind of essence extracted from an often extraordinary quantity of raw materials, as in the previously cited instance of the fifty hams of the steward of the Prince de Soubise. Most French sauces and composite dishes called for cullis in addition to gravy or meat juice and other preparations the chef was supposed to have on hand, as well as liaisons of cream and egg yolks, the garnishes of truffles, cockscombs, sweetbreads, and other beloved dainties of the eighteenth century. Even a dish of green peas had a cullis of pressed and flavored pea pods added to the cream sauce. The eighteenth century also saw the development of basic white and brown sauces and the introduction of braising.

There was no use for a hodgepodge of aromatic spices in the new style of cooking, though these continued to appear in cookbooks adhering to the old cuisine, particularly in England. Pyramids went out of date. Huge platters of meat were replaced by little dishes that cost ten times as much. Variety was created with an infinite range of sauces and ragouts (spelled "ragoo" in English cookbooks), a kind of sauced garnish such as ragout of asparagus tips cooked in a cullis of veal and ham. Chefs included as many as a hundred sauces in cookbooks and demonstrated their prowess by concocting menus of fifteen principal dishes all of the same kind of meat. Typical eighteenth-century variations for a simple spit-roasted chicken are suggested by Menon in his *Cuisinière bourgeoise: à la reine, à la ravigote*, or with ragouts of cucumbers, pistachios, crayfish, pickles, oysters, cardoons, little onions, truffles, morels, or *foie gras*. Anchovy sauce became a favorite; gourmet Grimod de la Reynière wrote that, if well made, it would make one eat an elephant or one's grandfather.

Good, well-aged wines, so important to a great meal, were a pleasure introduced only in the mideighteenth century. Before that, any wine over eighteen months old was sold cheaper than when young or was used for vinegar. Bruyère-Champier wrote in 1560 of his astonishment in finding a burgundy well preserved after six years. Until the glass bottle came into use in the fifteenth century, aging wine to full maturity was impossible because wines aged in wood improve for only a limited time, then decline in quality if kept in the barrel. Aging began to be considered desirable only when the bottle and cork came into common use after the late seventeenth-century discovery of champagne by a monk known as Dom Perignon. Previously, wine was drunk young, warmed in winter, and usually diluted with water and flavored with sugar and spices or herbs. Drinking pure wine was impolite.

When a recipe for a basic sauce, one to be combined eventually with other sauces and garnishes, called for "twelve ducks, a ham, two bottles of good old Madeira, and six pounds of truffles," [43] some people thought things were getting out of hand. Louis-Sébastien Mercier wrote in about 1785:

> A short time ago it was discovered that it is ignoble to chew like a commoner. A duchess swallows a sirloin reduced to jelly . . . butchers' meat is now good enough only for the common people;

fowl is becoming vulgar; we must have dishes that have neither
the name nor the appearance of what we are eating; and if our
eye is not engaged at first glance, our appetite is not sufficiently
aroused.[44]

There was a revolt in the name of economy—relative economy,
that is—led by English cooks. One of these, Hannah Glasse,
abruptly dismissed one of the more complex French garnishes as
"an odd jumble of trash." For the French cullis requiring a leg of
veal and ham just to mix with another sauce, Mrs. Glasse proposed
a substitute calling for "only" a pound of veal, a little beef, half a
pound of bacon, a pigeon, an old cock "beat all to pieces," truffles,
morels, wine, catsup, herbs, potherbs, and spices. Commenting
archly, "if gentlemen will have French cooks, they must pay for
French tricks," she tells of a cook who used six pounds of butter to
fry twelve eggs "when everybody knows half a pound is enough or
more." [45] Dr. Kitchener, crusty author of *Apicius Redivivus*, proposed several prepared concentrates to substitute for French cullis with the comment that young ladies of the household might do
well to make them and sacrifice some of the time devoted to "Piano
Forte."

Despite an exchange of books, visits, and even cooks, there was
a divergence drawn now and forever between the French and English way of cooking, a divergence as distinct as that marking their
national characters. The difference is notable in menus of the times,
and most particularly in the English (and later American) use of
catsups, chutneys, and other bottled sauces, the idea for which
came from the Far East. More common than the French cullis in
England were gravies made from browned meat, butter, and flour,
often with the addition of pickled walnuts and anchovies, and even
more often "chyan pepper" (cayenne), imported in quantity from
the West Indies and in constant use in England, where it was beginning to supplant the older spices.

In France, Englishmen complained of being served a frivolous
selection of pompously titled tidbits but no real food. Frenchmen
complained that the Englishman's dinner "generally consists of a
piece of half-boiled, or half-roasted meat; and a few cabbage leaves,
boiled in plain water; on which they pour a sauce made of flour and

butter, the usual method of dressing vegetables in England." [46]
More diverting to the French traveler were the English bottled
sauces. A Frenchman crossing England and Scotland in 1784 noted
in his account of a dinner with the Royal Society that each person
seasoned his meat "as he pleased with the different sauces which
were placed on the table in bottles of various shapes." [47] From
eighteenth-century cookbooks we have a good idea of what these
sauces were. As early as 1700, a book by Diana Astry contained
formulas for catsup, spelled "catchope," and calling for vinegar, anchovies, spices, and claret. Later catsups, or catchups, were made
with mushrooms, spices, and ale; others contained walnuts * (tomato catsup was introduced in the early nineteenth century). Elizabeth Raffald gives recipes in *The Experienced English Housekeeper*
(1769) for Indian pickle or "piccalillo" of pickled vegetables flavored with ale, garlic, ginger, and turmeric. From the beginning of
the century, cookbooks contained recipes for melon or cucumber
chutneys known as mangoes, probably because the original Indian
chutney was made with mangoes. Yorkshire and Worcestershire
sauces were invented locally and may have been originally home
recipes. Harvey's sauce was a homemade sauce used by a casual
guest at an English inn run by a Mr. Harvey, who earned a lifetime
annuity by commercializing it. Writing in 1817, Dr. Kitchener
recommended keeping a mahogany sauce box on the table for the
indispensable walnut pickle, mushroom catsup, soy sauce, powdered
mint, pudding catsup, etc. The same box, he pointed out, would be
handy for traveling.

One dish the French liked to copy was the English *pièce de
résistance*, turtle. If English cooks were generally more restrained
than the French, they made up for it when it came to turtle. Its
preparation normally covered three to four pages of an English
cookbook and was of extraordinary complexity and difficulty. One
of the first problems anyone who wanted to try out one of the
recipes would face, aside from finding the turtle, would be getting
it into the kitchen. The recipes do not explain that; they start with
the turtle already in the kitchen, all 100 pounds or more of it, alive.
The nineteenth-century English chef Alexis Soyer offered a recipe

---

* See recipe for walnut catsup, pp. 321.

simplified, he said, so as to be practicable in a private household. The recipe begins as follows:

> Make choice of a good turtle, weighing from 140 to 180 pounds, hang it up by the hind fins securely, cut off the head and let it hang all night, then take it down, lay it upon its back, and with a sharp knife cut out the belly, leaving the fins, but keeping the knife nearly close to the upper shell . . . saw the top shell into four and the bottom one in halves; then put the whole of the turtle, including the head, into a large turbot kettle, and cover them with cold water (or if no kettle large enough blanch it in twice). . . . For a turtle of the above size (which is considered the best, for in comparison with them the smaller ones possess but little green fat), cut up sixty pounds of knuckle of veal, and twenty pounds of beef, with six pounds of lean ham; well butter the bottom of three large stew pans, and put an equal proportion of meat in each with four onions, one carrot . . . place them upon sharp fires, stirring them round occasionally until the bottom of each is covered with a brownish glaze, when fill them up with the water in which you blanched the turtle . . . let them simmer two hours . . . after having passed the stock, fill them up again with water, let them simmer four hours, when pass it and convert it into glaze as directed. . . .[48]

This recipe gives only the basic preparation of the soup. The next step is to make separate dishes out of various parts of the turtle. The flippers, for example, are cooked with mushrooms, artichoke bottoms, cream, egg yolks, and forcemeat balls, and the guts with veal gravy, Madeira, mushroom catsup, shallots, morels, forcemeat balls, lemon, flour, and cayenne pepper, and so on ad infinitum.

A meal in England and one in France differed greatly in the number and kind of dishes. Though English cookbooks contain long, French-style menus for royal entertainments, they also have simple ones, which French cookbooks never did. In *The Ladies' Assistant*, Mrs. Charlotte Mason suggests one-course meals with five dishes for a family of five: pea soup, pickles, hot buttered apple pie, roast beef, and broccoli, for example, all placed on the table at once in positions specified in the menu. Descriptions of meals among country

135

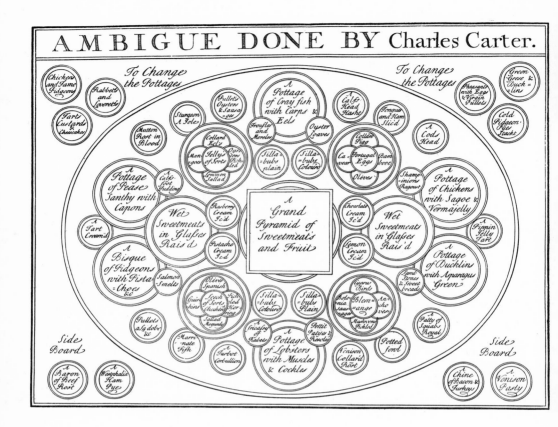

Figure caption (inside illustration): AMBIGUE DONE BY Charles Carter.

gentry taken from letters and diaries of the eighteenth century indicate Mrs. Mason's menus were typical. Take the following excerpt from the letters of Catharine Hutton:

> A little before three, we sat down to dinner, which consisted of 3 boiled chickens at top, a very fine haunch of venison at bottom; ham on one side, a flour pudding on the other, and beans in the middle. After the cloth was removed, we had gooseberries and a remarkably fine dish of apricots.[49]

George III and Queen Charlotte ate far more modestly than Louis XVI, in or out of prison. The Duchess of Northumberland,

136

lady of the bedchamber to the Queen, described the menus usually
served their majesties in 1762:

> Their Majestys constant table at this Time was as follows, a
> soup removed with a large Joynt of Meat and two other Dish
> such as a Pye or a broyl'd fowl and the like. On the side table
> was a large Joynt, for example a large Sirloin of Beef Cold and
> also a Boars Head and a Sallad; 2nd Course always one Roast,
> one of pastry and Spinage and Sweetbreads, Macaron, Scollop
> and Oysters or the like. Their Supper consists of two made
> Dishes usually composed of Poultry as Chickens, smoke Turkey
> a la Bachomel, a Joynt of Cold Mutton, Buttered Eggs Custard
> and constantly Veal and Chicken Broth.[50]

Menus in French cookbooks recommend an unbelievable number of dishes. Menon, in the preface to his *Cuisinière bourgeoise*,
claims to have rewritten an earlier treatise to make it suitable for
people of a *"fortune médiocre."* The shortest of these menus for
the mediocre fortune, designed for a table of ten, has three to four
courses and a total of 25 dishes.

Compositions of food still decorated the eighteenth-century
table, the large *pièces de résistance* sometimes remaining through
the second course to be replaced at dessert by silver or gold spun-
sugar webs over birds nests or fish ponds, transparent puddings,
shimmering jellies. In the late eighteenth century, when Marie
Antoinette was playing dairy maid, elaborate nature studies were in
style. Mercier tells of having seen, on a table twelve feet long, a
river unfreeze, trees turn green, and flowers burst into bloom.
This feat was nothing compared to two earlier eighteenth-century
desserts cited by Horace Walpole as surpassing everything else in
"glorious magnificence and taste." One of these, served at the
table of the Duke of Würtemberg in 1734, was a representation of
Mount Etna which "vomited out real fireworks over the heads of
the company during the whole entertainment." The other was a
dessert offered by the intendant of Gascony on the occasion of the
birth of a Duke of Burgundy. It featured a representation by wax
figures moving by clockwork "of the whole labour of the dauphi-
ness and the happy birth of an heir to the monarchy." [51]

The eighteenth-century table was wide in order to provide space for the display of foods and the elaborate silver. The English, proud of their new mahogany tables, always removed the cloth before dessert. Extra plates and dishes were left on the sideboard with the wine bottles and glasses, still served on beckon by lackeys, a system particularly objectionable to those who did not come to dinner with their own lackeys to stand behind their chairs and tend to their needs, and who were sometimes snubbed by the host's staff. A woman not only depended on a lackey to have a glass of wine, but on the invitation of the gentleman next to her, it being unseemly for her to ask for it herself. She also depended on others to have a chance at the foods she liked. In his rules of etiquette, John Trusler wrote in 1788:

> As eating a great deal is deemed indelicate in a lady (for her character should be rather divine than sensual), it will be ill manners to help her to a large slice of meat at once, or fill her plate too full. When you have served her with meat, she should be asked what kind of vegetables she likes, and the gentleman sitting next the dish that holds those vegetables should be requested to help her.[52]

At least, eighteenth-century guests had begun to pass dishes themselves so that it would no longer happen that a lady invited to dinner, in order not to trouble her neighbors, would eat exclusively and completely a platter of peas for dinner because that was what happened to be within her reach.

VII

~

The
Modern Age

The modern cuisine began with the establishment of the modern restaurant, and the modern
restaurant was an indirect result of the French Revolution.
Before that upheaval, *haute cuisine* was only for the privileged
few. After it, an interest in good food acquired importance in the
lives of merchants, statesmen, and the population at large as never
before. When the Revolution put the privileged few to flight, their
chefs, jobless, opened restaurants in France, England, and America and put their art within the reach of anyone who had the price
of a dinner. Dumas remarks in his *Grand dictionnaire* that for
twelve francs one could eat as well as Tallyrand and better than
Archchancellor Cambacérès. The restaurant was a great step toward
social equality.

The antecedents of restaurants reach back to the beginning of
history. There have always been places serving food and drink to
the public. Greece and Rome had taverns, though they were considered places of ill repute. Inns for travelers date back to the
beginning of trade, though most offered a minimum of bad-quality
food, if any, until the seventeenth century. From Roman days,
whole roasted meats and poultry could be bought in cookshops.
In nineteenth-century England, cookshops would deliver a complete dinner: pudding, roast, gravy, mustard, and seasoning. By
the eighteenth century, in France as well as England, some cookshops served dinners ordered in advance in their premises, or offered a table d'hôte, a set menu, at a fixed hour. A number of
ready-to-eat foods including sauces, pies, and some pastries were

142

sold in the streets in the Middle Ages. As late as the nineteenth century, London workers made their midday meal on pea soup, baked potatoes, and pies of mutton, eel, beef, and kidney, bought from street stalls. In sixteenth-century Paris, people wanting to entertain could rent the sumptuous mansion of some absent proprietor from his concierge for the day and have food delivered there. All this, however, has little in common with the modern restaurant.

England showed France the way in the restaurant business with its ale houses, taverns, and beefsteak houses. In his *London Journal*, Boswell praised the beefsteak house as an excellent and reasonable place to eat, a large, warm, comfortable room in which you sat down in any empty place, ate food "well and cleverly dressed," and chatted or not as you pleased. English taverns were respectable places where people of similar interests or occupations used to meet regularly. Samuel Johnson and his circle made them famous, and Johnson cited them as a sign of England's superiority to France. He once remarked to Boswell, "Sir, there is nothing which has yet been contrived by man by which so much happiness is produced as by a good tavern or inn." The indefatigable diarist Samuel Pepys noted the names of many public houses at which he ate. Indeed, the custom of eating out was common among the English upper classes before the French took it up, though in the days of Louis XIV, Parisian men also used to meet at cookshops or public tables d'hôte.

There was a wide range of tables d'hôte, from the back-alley, grimy basement with its steam of boiling beef like the one Smollett described in London in 1740 where coachmen and unemployed footmen ate beef shins, sausages, and tripe at dirty tables, to the agreeably hospitable Parisian ones whose disappearance was lamented by Grimod de la Reynière. They closed in 1790, he wrote in his *Almanach*, when the people who used to frequent them and exchange intelligent conversation no longer dared voice an opinion in public, and the new rude crop of citizens spawned by the revolution turned the orderly table into a rout and pillage. These places, where men had enjoyed eating in good company without sacrificing the half day required by a dinner invitation, would never be restored, he noted, adding: "One will continue to go eat in sad isolation at the *restaurateurs,* where each, seated at his little table and separated from the others, consumes his portion in silence without concerning himself with what his neighbor says or does."

It is generally agreed that the first French restaurant, in the sense of a place in which a selection of food could be ordered at the hour one chose, was opened in Paris in the mideighteenth century by a soup vendor named Boulanger. Boulanger put a sign over his door reading: *Venite ad me omnes qui stomacho laboratis et ego restaurabo vos.** The modern word "restaurant" is believed to be derived from that sign or from the term *"restaurant"* itself, which then meant a fortifying soup. Soup, or rather a variety of hot soups, formed the main part of Boulanger's menu, though he also offered fowl and fresh eggs. Over the protests of the *traiteurs* (the Parisian guild dealing in ready-to-eat cooked meats) Boulanger was allowed to continue his trade and was soon copied by others.

Boulanger's place was a simple one with bare marble-topped tables. The first elegant restaurant was opened in Paris about 1765 by the ex-steward of the Count of Provence, one Antoine Beauvilliers, who was inspired by the English fashion of dining out in taverns; in fact, he called his new restaurant La Grande Taverne de Londres. Closed during the Revolution, La Grande Taverne reopened afterward along with a rash of luxury restaurants under the aegis of unemployed chefs and stewards of the banished aristocracy. By the end of 1789 there were a hundred restaurants in Paris. By 1804 there were five or six hundred, by 1850 over a thousand. Some were world-famous, establishing once and for all the universal supremacy of the French culinary genius; others were humble places catering to the lower classes.

Through the troubled times that followed, restaurants were filled with people, people short of food at home, people fearing a devalued currency would become even more worthless or simply seizing a moment of pleasure while they could. The sudden popularity of restaurants can also be traced to a rage for English fashions that swept over Revolutionary France. Grimod de la Reynière offers the additional explanation that the new social leaders, legisla-

---

* "Come all ye whose stomachs suffer and I will restore you." (Various versions of the Latin text are given by various sources. The version quoted is taken from Pierre Jean Baptiste Legrand d'Aussy, *Histoire de la vie privée des Français*, Vol. II.)

tors as yet without houses in Paris, and *nouveaux riches* too
embarrassed to display their sudden wealth or uncertain how to go
about it properly, flocked to the new restaurants and thereby set
the trend.

Whatever the reasons, the establishment of restaurants was of
great importance in the development of the French cuisine, partly
because they spread a taste for good food among more people,
partly because they were a stimulus to cooks. As Brillat-Savarin
wrote, "As soon as experience showed that a single well-cooked
dish was enough to make the inventor's fortune, the powerful
motive of self-interest kindled every imagination and set all the
cooks to work." Restaurants provided an ideal vehicle; it was only
in restaurants that the heights of great cuisine, impracticable in
the more modest private kitchens of the post-revolutionary era,
could be reached.

The workers eagerly adopted restaurants. According to Mercier,
who was an eyewitness of the Revolution, "As soon as the ordinary
worker began earning 200 écus a day with the new paper money,
he became accustomed to eating at the restaurateur, spurning the
cabbage with lard for *poularde au cresson*, refusing the pewter pint
for the sealed bottle, and insisting on his cup of coffee and glass
of liqueur." [53] The wine cellars of aristocrats who had fled abroad
were on sale; the barber's apprentice could now drink the best
Madeira. With their paper fortunes, the *nouveaux riches* outdid
the old monks in gourmandise. After the executioners, Mercier
wrote, the busiest people in Paris were the scullions.

The *nouveaux riches* brought the elegant supper back into style
and goaded their cooks into redoubling their refinements. They
took pride in serving the first fruits of all seasons and the whitest
bread while the populace died of famine. Cookbooks did not hesitate to recommend such extravagant dishes as one in which twelve
ducks are roasted on the spit to provide duck juices to season
fifteen poached eggs. According to Edmond and Jules Goncourt,
all the luxury tradesmen who had been ruined by the Revolution
decided to base their fortunes on something eternal and unchang-
ing—the appetite of their fellow citizens. Every street had its
traiteur selling food ready to eat: sausages stuffed with truffles,
Bayonne hams, truffles cooked in champagne, green oysters, and

145

other delicacies. Hunting was open to all; everyone ate venison, partridge, woodcock. The pastry maker sent announcements advertising his ramekins and meringues to the depths of prisons, where they were eagerly received. Mercier wrote, "Never has such a propensity for gourmandise been seen as in those days of calamity and horror. I can testify to it from the six prisons into which I was plunged."

Restaurant owners, caterers, and speculators took over the great private mansions. Nor were the leaders of the Revolution indifferent to the charms of the table. Danton spent fortunes on his dinners; Barras, while in the Directory, had his button mushrooms transported express from Bouches-du-Rhône. Murat's chief chef, Laguipière, was one of the most famous of the century.

A restaurant such as that of Beauvilliers offered an average of 200 diners a bill of fare it would take half an hour to read: 13 soups, 22 hors d'oeuvres, 11 fish, meat and fowl pastries, 23 fish dishes, 15 roasts, 32 dishes of poultry and game, 50 meat dishes, 41 side dishes, 39 desserts, 64 wines and liqueurs, plus coffee and ices. It also had a catering service complete with linens and silver.

However, it was during the Empire that the reputation of Parisian restaurants rose so high that the French cuisine became universal. At the top were the greatest restaurants, founded by the greatest chefs: Beauvilliers; Véry; Méot, former chief chef for the Prince de Condé; Robert, former chef to the Archbishop of Aix, and others. Baleine's Rocher de Cancale was cited by many as the best restaurant of all. The Café de Paris, where Balzac and Dumas were habitués, first opened in 1822.

Under the Restoration there were more and more restaurants offering more luxurious interiors and lower prices in an all-too-successful attempt to oust the old established places; some of the greatest were forced to close. An article written in 1846 noted sadly that splendid interiors and uniform seasonings with brown or white sauce under fancy names had become all too common, along with less-fresh fish and game, and inferior wines. On the other hand, there was a good *cuisine bourgeoise* to be had in the cheaper restaurants, and that, like the very establishment of restaurants, was a step in bringing good eating within the reach of more people.

146

In London, where restaurants had been born, they declined in midcentury in favor of private clubs. The formation of clubs seems to have been spurred by the end of the war with France when many English officers, used to the economy and companionship of officers' messes, sought a way to replace the mess and stretch their meager personal resources. They formed the Army and Navy Clubs, The United Service Club, and others. The advantages were obvious to members of the church, the university, and the bar, who quickly formed their own clubs. By 1856 there were about 30 English clubs, some of which were well known for excellent food that cost no more than a mediocre meal in a tavern. The most famous were the Reform Club, whose kitchens were run by Alexis Soyer, one of the best known English chefs of the nineteenth century, and the Crockford Club under Louis Eustache Ude, former chef to Louis XVI.

By 1890, French and English restaurants had deteriorated to the point that the lamentations of gourmets strike a contemporary note. To quote Theodore Child, writing in 1890:

> In modern Paris, formerly the mecca of gourmands, it is becoming most difficult to dine, and everywhere, even in the best restaurants—we will say no more about private houses—we see the disastrous consequences of the absence of criticism. . . . The hurry and unrest of contemporary life do not conduce to the appreciation of fine cooking, nor is fine cooking possible where it is necessary to prepare food in very large quantities.[54]

Despite the decline, a man who wanted to eat well would still seek out the best restaurant in Paris, and Child conceded that there (and only there) he could still hope to find "in almost satisfactory conditions the best of the cook's art." What one wit said in the eighteenth century was just as true in the nineteenth: though the English have sixty religions, they have only one sauce. There was roast beef and there was turtle; that was the extent of British gastronomy. Aside from the upper class, for whom great emigré chefs from France kept the *ancien régime* cuisine alive, nineteenth-century England continued to subsist on overcooked vegetables and tasteless meats, doused with the peculiarly English collection of bottled sauces, cayenne peppers, curry powders, and ginger.

Thackeray began his delightful essays on dinners with the observation that a Londoner would have little occasion to gather worthy material on the subject.

> A man in London has not, for the most part, the opportunity to make these experiments. You are a family man, let us presume, and you live in that metropolis for half a century. You have on Sunday, say, a leg of mutton and potatoes for dinner. On Monday you have cold mutton and potatoes. On Tuesday, hashed mutton and potatoes; the hashed mutton being flavoured with little damp triangular pieces of toast, which always surround that charming dish. Well, on Wednesday, the mutton ended, you have beef: the beef undergoes the same alternations of cookery and disappears. Your life presents a succession of joints, varied every now and then by a bit of fish and some poultry. You drink three glasses of a brandyfied liquor called sherry at dinner; your excellent lady imbibes one. When she has had her glass of port after dinner, she goes upstairs with the children, and you fall asleep in your armchair. Some of the most pure and precious enjoyments of life are unknown to you. . . .[55]

France, on the other hand, was the gourmet's paradise. Never had food been so important. Where society had once gathered without eating, the serving of dinners had become obligatory. More than ever before, the newly rich made their places in society alongside the wellborn through their cooks, or, as Brillat-Savarin put it, "the cooks fought the genealogists." The Goncourts commented in 1861 that in Paris an open salon, dinners, and ices excused everything; a good cook ensured the company of the best society. The gourmandise of these newly rich is the origin of the many nineteenth-century dishes called *à la financière*, always costly concoctions and usually comprised of cockscombs, mushrooms, truffles, quenelles, kidneys, and *foie gras*.

Gourmandise not only overflowed in the streets, shops, houses, and restaurants of post-Revolutionary Paris, it inundated literature. The nineteenth century was the era of literary and artistic gourmandise, the epoch of Berchoux's long poem on gastronomy, the famous *Physiology of Taste* of Brillat-Savarin for which Balzac composed an appendix, the writings of Charles Monselet and Maurice Sailland. It was the era of Thackeray's essays on gourmandizing and his "Ballad of Bouillabaisse," of Sydney Smith's poem on dressing salad, Charles Lamb's "Dissertation upon Roast Pig," Baudelaire's perceptive pages on cooking. It was the era when Alexandre Dumas remarked with satisfaction, "I see with pleasure that my culinary reputation is increasing and soon promises to efface my literary reputation." [56] Dumas capped his output of 500 literary works with his *Grand dictionnaire de la cuisine*. Léon Daudet wrote a little book for gourmets entitled *À boire et à manger*. Chekhov, Gogol, and Turgenev filled their prose with details of succulent meals.

The *Almanach des gourmands*, founded in 1803 by one of the the most enterprising literary gourmets, Grimod de la Reynière, and published annually with continuing success for eight years thereafter, guided the eager Parisian in the art of eating with its lists of shops and specialties, restaurants, notes on changing customs and manners, the latest menus, and information on seasonal specialties. Through his listings, his criticisms, and the much publicized jury he formed to test new dishes, products, and restaurants, Grimod de la Reynière did much to raise the standards of French food and guide the new society in the delicate art of appreciating good food. His *Manuel des amphitryons*, published in 1808, was designed to introduce the new upper classes to an elegant table and teach them how to establish and maintain one. (It is interesting to note that nineteenth-century books on food no longer refer to the *seigneur*, but the *amphitryon*, a title to which anyone wielding a fork could aspire; nor do books speak of the *noble*; now it is *l'homme opulent*, "the man of means.")

Grimod de la Reynière came by his interest in food naturally. His father, a *fermier-général*, is said to have choked in 1754 while trying to swallow a piece of *pâté* too hastily. He himself became a professional gastronome after studying literature and practicing law. Spurned by a famous actress, he turned to the pleasures of the table where, he pointed out, "the most stupid goose wins over the most amiable woman." He considered five hours "a reasonable latitude for a numerous dinner and a refined meal," quoting another famous gourmand, "the pleasures of good eating are those one knows earliest, leaves last, and can taste the most often. What can you say for the others?" [57]

Grimod de la Reynière was succeeded by other writers on food. Baron Ildefonse-Léon Brisse specialized in articles on gastronomy, edited a gastronomic journal, and wrote two cookbooks. He practiced what he preached so well he had to reserve two seats in the coach from Paris to his country house. Charles Monselet, author of plays, novels and histories, edited an *Almanach des gourmands* dedicated to Grimod de la Reynière, collaborated with Dumas and others on *La Cuisinière poétique,* and founded a magazine called *Le Gourmet* in 1858. Maurice Sailland, better known under his pseudonym Cournonsky, wrote 28 works on food in collaboration with Marcel Rouff; he also founded the Académie des Gastronomes, one of the burgeoning gastronomic societies that counted among their members Rodin, Claude Monet, Toulouse-Lautrec, and Georges Clemenceau.

Of all the statesmen who appreciated food in the nineteenth century, Talleyrand indisputably occupies first place, and it is to him that we are largely indebted for the refinement and elegance of the new cuisine. Giving primary importance to dinners in his diplomatic maneuvers, Talleyrand established a table famous throughout Europe, first under Bouché, to whom Carême dedicated one of his books, and then under the great chef Carême himself. At eight every morning, Talleyrand would spend an hour with his chef discussing the dinner menu, a weighty and lengthy subject, for he gave dinners with as many as 48 entrées or principal dishes. Nor did the discussion of the dinner end there. Frances, Lady Shelley described a meal at Talleyrand's house in Paris in her diary as follows: "During the whole repast, the general conversation was upon eating. Every dish was discussed, and the antiquities of every bottle of wine supplied the most eloquent annotations. Talleyrand himself analyzed the dinner with as much interest and seriousness as if he had been discussing some political question of importance." [58] It was for Talleyrand that Carême reserved his highest praise, calling his house the sanctuary of the French cuisine and saying of its master:

> *C'est que M. de Talleyrand entend le génie du cuisinier; c'est qu'il le respecte, et qu'il est le juge le plus compétent des progrès delicats, et que sa dépense est sage et grande tout à la fois.* * [59]

---

* "M. de Talleyrand understands the genius of a cook, he respects it, he is the most competent judge of subtle improvements, and his expenditures are wise and great at the same time."

Napoleon, himself indifferent to food except to satisfy his appetite, preferring to gobble it in fifteen minutes whenever hunger overtook him rather than have regular meals, relied on Talleyrand and on Cambacérès, Archchancellor of the Empire, to take care of foreign relations at the dinner table as well as the conference table. Carême dismisses Cambacérès as a man so stingy he locked up gifts of food until they rotted and kept lists of leftovers from his banquets to serve up the following day. Whether these accusations are true or not, Cambacérès kept a luxurious and serious table where he himself is said to have eaten with passionate absorption. His concern with food was so intense that the following anecdote is told of him. Cambacérès was closeted with Napoleon beyond the dinner hour in discussion of the fate of the unfortunate Duc d'Enghien, who was subsequently executed. Becoming more and more restive, Cambacérès finally wrote a note which he gave an usher to deliver. His suspicions aroused, Napoleon intercepted the note and read it. It was addressed to Cambacérès' chef and read as follows: "*Gardez les entremets—les rôtis sont perdus.*" * [60]

Literary gourmets of the nineteenth century collected and circulated a large number of amusing anecdotes about the great eaters of the times. Many of the stories were apocryphal, often more than one version has been preserved, and many are attributed to more than one individual; still, there is probably a basis of truth. One version of a story about Brillat-Savarin's aunt, a worthy gourmet in her own right, is that she died in bed at the venerable age of 97 while finishing a rich dinner. Sensing death was imminent, she is said to have whispered, "I feel the end approaching. Quick, bring me my dessert, coffee, and liqueur." [61]

In a story told by Dumas about Grimod de la Reynière, he is said to have arrived late one day at a village inn where he was informed there was unfortunately nothing left to eat. Grimod de la Reynière pointed to seven turkeys roasting on a spit before the fire but was told they had all been ordered by the gentleman upstairs. He must have a large party, commented the hungry traveler. No, the innkeeper replied, the gentleman is all alone. Declaring he would like to meet a man who would order seven turkeys for himself alone, Grimod de la Reynière proceeded upstairs to find the

---

* "Save the entremets, the roasts are ruined."

man in question was his son. When the old gourmet expressed his astonishment, his son explained he had ordered seven turkeys so he could eat only the oysters, the sole part, according to his father's teachings, worthy of esteem in an untruffled turkey.

The capacity of men of the nineteenth century for eating and drinking gave rise to many stories, some probably apocryphal. General Bisson, who was issued triple rations in the field by Napoleon, is said to have consumed eight bottles of wine for breakfast every day. On one occasion, summoned to Malmaison by Napoleon, the general was kept waiting in an antechamber from four to ten P.M., suffering increasing hunger. From time to time a lackey would enter and deposit a roast chicken on the table. Every fifteen minutes or so he would remove it and replace it with another. (Because Napoleon did not like to wait and had no fixed hours for eating, his chef had a roast chicken ready every fifteen minutes.) After observing the arrival and departure of several chickens, General Bisson succumbed and ate one. Though surprised on bringing the next to find the previous one gone, the servant continued to bring a chicken every fifteen minutes. That evening the chamberlain informed Napoleon that three of the chickens brought to his table had mysteriously disappeared. It was no mystery to Napoleon, who immediately identified General Bisson as the guilty one, adding that the general would need an entire steer to make a few sandwiches.

The Vicomte de Vieil-Castel was another sturdy gourmand, famed for a 500-franc bet in which he undertook to consume that amount in food and liquor single-handed within two hours. He won the wager by eating the following meal before a group of fashionable Parisians: [62]

Item	Francs
24 dozen Ostend oysters	30
swallow's nest soup	150
a beefsteak	2
a fish from Lake Geneva	40
a pheasant stuffed with truffles	40
a salmis of ortolans	50
a dish of asparagus	15
a plate of young peas	12

a pineapple	24
a dish of strawberries	20
1 bottle of Johannisberg	24
2 bottles of Bordeaux	50
½ bottle of Constance	40
½ bottle choice sherry	50
coffee and liqueurs	1,50

Total: 548,50

Some of the most delightful stories are about Louis XVIII who, unlike his predecessor Napoleon, was a fine epicure and also an amateur cook. Louis XVIII used to keep statesmen waiting while closeted with his grand maître d'hôtel, the Duc d'Escars, in a discussion of menus and recipes, a number of which the king is credited with creating. One of his creations, a truffled puree of ortolans, the king would make only in the presence of the duke in

A grand dinner at St-Cloud for the Emperor of Austria

order to keep the recipe secret. The dish was the duke's undoing. One night after he and the king had made and eaten it together, the duke was awakened by a terrible, indeed mortal attack of indigestion. In the fear that the king might suffer the same fate, the dying duke sent an attendant to rouse and warn him.

"You say the duke is dying?" Louis XVIII is said to have exclaimed. "Dying of my truffles *à la purée*? I was right then. I always said I had the better stomach of the two!" [63]

As recounted by Carême, one of the chefs, in his *Maître d'hôtel français*, Louis XVIII's banquets and military suppers following the Restoration form a rare culinary document. Carême was in charge of much of the cold entrées and sweet entremets at a dinner for twelve hundred held in the Grande Galerie du Louvre in February, 1815. One hundred cooks worked in a kitchen architects installed in the royal audience hall of the Louvre with an oven fifty feet long and six feet wide. This meal was surpassed a year later by a buffet for 3,000 at the Odéon, which was still nothing compared to the great military dinner for 10,000 men at tables stretched under a vast tent extending from the Étoile to the Place Louis XV (Concorde). The cooks, who included Carême, prepared 6 oxen, 75 calves, 250 sheep, 8,000 turkeys, 2,000 chickens, 1,000 pullets, 1,000 partridges, 500 hams, 500 stuffed tongues and sausages, 1,000 *pâtés*, 1,000 biscuits and babas, 1,000 carp, and 10,000 pike. Carême concluded his account of the event, "*Jamais travaux ne furent plus pénibles pour les cuisiniers.*" *

The school of quintessential cooking of the latter part of the eighteenth century in France laid the foundations of the *haute cuisine* that came into full glory in the early nineteenth, and it was to the famous French chef Carême that the glory is in great part due. Carême, whose father turned him out at age eleven rather than watch him starve, rose from the lowest scullion to become chef to two heads of state, the Prince Regent of England and Emperor Alexander of Russia.

In a book on her travels in France in 1828–1830, Lady Morgan wrote lyrically of a dinner prepared by him at the chateau of Baron Rothschild, who had hired Carême "at a salary beyond what

---

* "Never was work more agonizing for the cooks."

any sovereign in Europe might be able to pay, even though assisted by Monsieur Rothschild; without whose aid so many sovereigns would scarcely have been able to keep cooks at all. . . ."

> The dining-room stood apart from the house, in the midst of orange trees. It was an elegant oblong pavilion, of Grecian marble, refreshed by fountains . . . and the table, covered with the beautiful and picturesque dessert, emitted no odour that was not in perfect conformity with the freshness of the scene and fervour of the season. No burnished gold reflected the glaring sunset; no brilliant silver dazzled the eyes. Porcelain, beyond the price of all precious metals, by its beauty and its fragility—every plate a picture—consorted with the general character of sumptuous simplicity which reigned over the whole. . . .
>
> To do justice to the science and research of a dinner so served, would require a knowledge of the art equal to that which produced it. Its character, however, was that it was in season, that it was up to its time, that it was in the spirit of the age, that there was no *perruque* in its composition, no trace of the wisdom of our ancestors in a single dish; no high-spiced sauces, no dark-brown gravies, no flavour of cayenne and allspice, no tincture of catsup and walnut pickle. . . . Every meat presented its own natural aroma; every vegetable its own shade of verdure. The mayonase was fried in ice, (like Ninon's description of Sévigné's heart,) and the tempered chill of the plombière (which held the place of the eternal fondu and soufflets of our English tables) anticipated the stronger shock, and broke it, of the exquisite avalanche, which, with the hue and odour of fresh gathered nectarines, satisfied every sense, and dissipated every coarser flavour.[64]

The "sumptuous simplicity" of Carême's cuisine was more sumptuous than simple, and behind his praise of the greater simplicity, elegance, and logic of the new era, one senses his regret for the lavish splendor of the *ancien régime*, a regret shared by French chefs through the Empire and Restoration. It was with nostalgia that Carême wrote in his *Maître d'hôtel français* that the modern cuisine had its origins in the beginning of "our all-too famous and unfortunate revolution." It is hardly surprising that chefs should regret the day when great houses provided the chief chef with an assistant pastry cook, an assistant roasting cook, a general assistant

155

and one or two apprentices, when the price of food was not counted and the means of the host were unlimited. When you consider all that, Carême observes, you see what we have lost.

In post-Revolutionary restaurants and catering establishments, cooks directed their efforts to inventing novelties and seeking greater refinements to lure the public. In post-Revolutionary private houses, cooks developed a healthier and simpler cuisine out of necessity. Often having no assistant other than a kitchen maid, chefs were forced to simplify. The *velouté* that used to take two days was made in half a day; the essence that called for twenty hams was distilled from only six ounces with the aid of a new understanding of chemistry. (Chemistry was fashionable; mid-century recipes for beef stock are filled with discussions of the recent discoveries of the German chemist Liebig and talk of "osmazone," a name given to the extractable substance of bouillon.) Menus became shorter and simpler, composed of fewer, more carefully selected, and smaller dishes. No longer was the table covered with a profusion of huge platters. The cullis evolved into today's basic sauces, smoother and subtler. Sautéing, hailed by Grimod de la Reynière as the great culinary innovation of the nineteenth century, was added to braising. Garnishes became more harmonious. Instead of sweetbreads, cockscombs, and kidneys, fish was accompanied by truffles, quenelles, and shellfish. Vegetables at last truly came into their own; Grimod de la Reynière commented that a dish of spinach could make the reputation of a cook, and that a chef able to produce an exquisite dish of cardoons could call himself the first artist of Europe. Instead of two or three great chefs there was a host of capable ones. There was a greater variety of dishes, more inventiveness; more foreign recipes were adopted to the national cuisine. Wines were included on the menu and served in regulated order for the first time, and offering liqueurs with coffee became mandatory.

New meals were introduced to simplify entertaining. The *ambigu*, an eighteenth-century innovation in which all courses were put on the table at once, changed from a meal without fixed hours into a lunch when the dinner hour was advanced from two to six P.M. to suit the schedule of the Constituent Assembly. (Here was yet another important change in eating habits traceable to the French

156

"There are five branches of art: painting, sculpture, poetry, music, and architecture, the main branch of which is pastry-making." Carême's philosophy, and one of the designs from his book on pastry-making—"Rotunde en Ruine #2."

Revolution. Grimod de la Reynière complained, "Three or four hundred bad lawyers from the provinces suddenly changed our most sacred customs and habits.") Picnics became popular at the end of the eighteenth century. The tea was adopted in France, and the ball supper of sandwiches, *pâtés*, and aspics replaced the old elaborate spreads.

After Carême's long sway came a new trend opposed to the excesses he had practiced. Whatever he said about simplifying, Carême had sought complication, particularly in pastry, which he called the ornament of the *haute cuisine*. Pastry, he wrote, was the principal branch of architecture. To acquire the knowledge of architecture he felt he needed, Carême, who was illiterate, taught himself to read and to draw, spending hours daily for ten years in the Print Room of the Bibliothèque Impériale of Paris, copying, then drawing, then carrying out in pastry, monumental pieces such as an octagonal Indian pavilion with orange roofs and a tri-tiered base, fluted sides and innumerable ornaments, or a scene of a waterfall, fountain, and broken Grecian arches and columns in the neoclassic tradition of Romantic landscape painters. Carême himself drew the 110 designs in his book *Le Pâtissier pittoresque*, and a gastronomic writer of the late nineteenth century noted his structures should still be on view in the Tuileries storerooms if not burned during the siege of Paris in 1871.

After Carême, chefs were no longer concerned with restoring the splendor of the past. Writers hailed the new period as the apex of French *cuisine bourgeoise*. Perfection was to be found among the upper bourgeoisie in whose houses a single female cook prepared a limited number of dishes of great quality. The *pot-au-feu* became the basic Parisian dish. This was the era of sole *à la bonne femme*, of herring *nach hausfrauen Art, poulet grand'mère, sole ménagère*, and *soupe à la paysanne*. The *garniture bourgeoise* of carrots, onions, and bacon partly replaced the gaudy mixture called *à la financière*.

The midnineteenth century was also the time when the old "French service," in which the display of food on the table added to the magnificence of the meal, began to yield to the "Russian service," in which dishes were passed, already cut up, and there was

Some modest pastry designs from *Le Grand Livre des Pâtis-siers et des Confiseurs*.

enough of each dish for each guest. Carême, who had observed the Russian method as chef to Emperor Alexander, admitted it was advantageous for the food, but clung to the French way as "more elegant and sumptuous." Opinions were divided. Kirwan, an English literary gourmet, wrote in 1864 that he could not see why the English, who had been civilized for five centuries, should copy the Russians, who were as yet scarcely half-civilized. He added that the passing of dishes prolonged dinner to four hours instead of the usual two and a half or three. Despite objections, by 1900, the Russian service was standard; once again nineteenth-century practicality had won over eighteenth-century magnificence.

Amateur cooks abounded because great eaters no longer necessarily had great means. Even as early as 1803, Grimod de la Reynière found it prudent to observe that it was as rude to arrive early for dinner as late, particularly in a bourgeois household where the hostess would be busy cooking herself. One of the most famous amateur cooks was Alexandre Dumas. Regretting the wonderful suppers he used to enjoy, in 1844 he started giving weekly suppers he prepared himself. An English traveler in France describes Dumas putting aside his knife and fork in the middle of dinner at the Café de Paris to go to the kitchen to learn the recipe, and Dumas at home in a large apron working with the assistance of a cook and kitchen maid. He tells of lunches at Dumas' that lasted from 11:30 A.M. till at least 4:30 P.M. Even when Dumas was in debt, fresh contingents of guests kept arriving and Dumas kept sending to the butcher for fresh supplies while summonses continued to rain and wine flowed.

By the mideighteenth century, cookbooks, once meant for carvers, maître d'hôtels, or chefs of great establishments, and then for ladies running large households, were written for the servants themselves. The prefaces of English cookbooks are addressed to inferiors, clearly so labeled. In her *Art of Cookery Made Plain and Easy* (1747), Hannah Glasse announces her intention to instruct the "lower sort." Elizabeth Raffald wrote in her third edition of *The Experienced English Housekeeper* (1773) "It has been my chiefest care to write in as plain a stile as possible, so as to be understood by the weakest capacity." *The House-keeper's Pocket Book and Compleat Family Cook* (ca. 1785) hoped to give instructions "in so plain

French Service

Russian Service

and full a manner that the most illiterate and ignorant person, who can but read, will know how to do everything in cookery well."

The nineteenth century saw the introduction of the cookbook for the amateur and lover of good food: Baron Brisse's *366 Menus* (1868) and *La petite cuisine* (1870) and Dumas' *Grand dictionnaire de la cuisine* (1869). By the midnineteenth century, there was a distinct division between books for household use and those for professional chefs, just as there was a distinct division between household cooking and the *haute cuisine* limited to royal households or restaurants, where recipes calling for a spoonful each of an essence, a *fond*, a stock, a meat glaze, etc., could be carried out with some semblance of practicality.

Probably no new dishes have been invented since the first quarter of the nineteenth century, only variations under new names. The cuisine, however, underwent rapid changes, brought about by the culmination of the industrial revolution. Chefs entered into the spirit of the age. Alexis Soyer designed a portable camp stove, a teapot with a special repository for tea, and a miniature kitchen for use in the navy. He also concerned himself with food for the poor. In his six-penny book entitled *Soyer's Charitable Cookery*, he devised recipes for the poor using the peelings and ends of vegetables (which he claimed had more flavor than the insides). He helped organize a soup kitchen in London and another, during the famine of 1847, in Dublin. It was under Soyer's supervision that the first attempt to roast a whole ox by gas was made at the annual meeting of the Royal Agricultural Society in Exeter in 1850. Gas was then just coming into use for cooking. Despite scoffing crowds, Soyer set up in the open air a few unmortared bricks, a few sheets of iron to enclose a space about six feet by three, and 216 gas jets. With this makeshift grill, he began roasting his baron of beef *à la Magna Charta*, a baron and saddleback of beef weighing 535 pounds. When the beef was done after eight hours of roasting, eight men carried it through the main streets of Exeter in a triumphal march, accompanied by a band playing "The Roast Beef of Old England" and followed by the once-incredulous crowd. At the end of its march, the beef was placed under a seventeen-foot-high triumphal arch designed by Soyer and composed entirely of farm

162

The frontispiece from *The Improved Housewife*, by A. C. Webster, 1854

produce, such as swans, turkeys, and apples, and surmounted by farming implements.

When you consider that the first hot plate and the first oven heated by hot air only came into use in the late eighteenth century, you realize how rapidly changes have taken place since. Before then, all ovens were heated by burning wood or coal inside them, then raking out the fuel before putting the food in to bake. By 1870, gas stoves were common in England. Electricity was long regarded as very dangerous, coming into use only in the 1930's, though it had an immediate fascination for the public. In 1782, a German traveler in England called it the puppet show of the English and remarked that everyone understanding it at all was certain of being noticed and successful. Great things were expected of the new discovery. In the belief that the sense of taste depends largely on electricity, hope was expressed in the midnineteenth century that "electrogalvanic" plates and utensils might be devised to give the plainest foods, such as rice pudding, the taste of roast beef.

At the beginning of the nineteenth century, transportation and preservation of food was virtually unchanged since Roman days. Chefs had to be capable of great organization and foresight, particularly when in charge of banquets of state held far from the markets of the capitals. Carême's preparations for a series of banquets during Czar Alexander I's review of his troops in a field station in 1815 began with his sending out a butcher with herds of animals to be slaughtered on the spot.

One of the high points of the effort to bring fish fresh from the sea was the plan of an eighteenth-century inventor to build carriages ventilated by fresh air and drawn by a pair of horses traveling six miles per hour with a change of horse every twelve miles. The plan was never put into effect. Scotch salmon, pickled first if the weather was hot, was brought to London on horseback. Poultry and cattle were driven to London on foot at great loss of both flavor and bulk. Graziers estimated cattle driven along the road lost an average of twenty pounds per animal in a hundred miles, while sheep lost eight pounds and pigs ten.

Tainted food was common; even pickled herring rotted en route. Daniel Defoe, in his *Tour Thro the Whole Island of Great Britain* (1724–1727), speaks of loads of "stinking fish" carted by road from

164

the coast. In his book on manners of 1788, John Trusler found it necessary to warn the guest who would be polite to avoid "smelling to the meat whilst on the fork, before you put it in your mouth." Cookbooks continued to give recipes for keeping meats sweet or "making them fresh when they stink." These recipes were concerned only with removing bad smell and taste; that rotten food was unhealthy was not a consideration, though serious or fatal food poisoning had been common for centuries. Some of our ancestors preferred food rotten. George II (reigned 1727–1760) liked his oysters "stale and strong of flavour," [65] and Macaulay wrote of Samuel Johnson: "Whenever he was so fortunate as to have near him a hare that had been kept too long, or a meat pie made with rancid butter, he gorged himself with such violence that his veins swelled and the moisture broke out on his forehead." [66] The Duc de Vendôme preferred fish "stale to fresh and stinking to stale, a perversity of taste which ultimately killed him." [67]

In the nineteenth century, steamships, railways, artificially manufactured ice, and, lastly, mechanical refrigeration made it possible to keep fresh food fresh. With the introduction of the steamship, fish was brought to port packed in ice in 1820. It was an expensive way of carrying fish, limited at first to the luxury market and the seacoast, but when ice became cheaper and inland railroads were built, fresh fish appeared in inland markets and the sale of salted and pickled fish declined. Ice was in great demand. Before the invention of the ice-manufacturing machine about 1850, ice was exported in thousands of tons from America, where farmers' fields were flooded artificially in winter to produce it.

The earliest solution to preserving meat in transport was seen in an invention of Nicolas Appert of about 1800—canning. Canned meat was expensive, but well worth the price for shipboard stores according to Captain Basil Hall, who wrote in the seventh (1842) edition of the *Encyclopaedia Britannica* under the title "Food":

> You must, on examining the lists of prices, bear in mind that meat thus preserved *eats* nothing, nor *drinks*—is not apt to get the rot, or to die—does not tumble overboard, nor get its legs broken or its flesh worn off its bones by knocking about the decks of a ship in bad weather—it takes no care in the keeping —it is always ready, may be eaten cold or hot, and thus enables

you to toss into a boat in a minute as many days *cooked* provisions as you choose—it is not exposed to the vicissitudes of markets nor is it scourged up to a monstrous price as at St. Helena, because there is no alternative. Besides these advantages, it enables one to indulge in a number of luxuries which no care or expense *could* procure.

Gourmets welcomed Appert's invention. Grimod de la Reynière's Almanach hailed Appert "that clever artist to whom we owe the pleasure of eating little green peas in the month of February, gooseberries and apricots in March. . . ." and praised him for having reversed the seasons to the profit of gourmandise. It was, in fact, for the gourmet trade that Appert had built his factory near Paris on land where he grew his own vegetables. The trade proved insufficient to support the factory. Appert then sought to sell his bottled goods, bouillon tablets, and preserved milk to the French navy and explorers going to the Far North. Until he was awarded a prize in 1810 for having invented the best method of preserving food for transport, he met much more opposition than encouragement, and was reduced to going from port to port with letters of recommendation in the hopes of getting naval contracts.

Canned foods were a luxury. Noting that "doubtless a sumptuous banquet might be made out of a selection from these viands . . . almost 20 kinds of soup broth and meat essences; 12–15 kinds of fish; poultry, game, and venison, etc., milk and cream, nearly all the fruits and vegetables ordinarily eaten. . . ." a midnineteenth century commentator added it would be "a rather costly one." [68]

While Appert correctly believed food was preserved by the exclusion of air in a sealed container heated to a certain temperature, the scientific explanation of food spoilage in general and botulismus toxin in particular was discovered only about 1860. Prior to that, a scandal of 1851 in which thousands of cans bought by the British Admiralty were found to be tainted was a temporary setback to the growing canning industry. It was later learned that the problem had been the use of larger-than-normal containers, whose contents were not sufficiently heated by the usual process.

Canning of meat fell off rapidly as refrigeration was developed at the end of the nineteenth century. The first shipment of refrigerated meat was sent from Australia to England in 1880. By chance it froze en route, becoming the first frozen as well as the first refrigerated meat to travel so far. Freezing meat became a standard practice thereafter, and gradually led to experiments in freezing vegetables and fruits. It is always startling to reflect how recent these innovations are, to remember that ice only fully replaced salt for preserving in the twentieth century, that modern refrigeration came into widespread use only after World War I, and that the first package of retail frozen food appeared in a store in 1929.

For the cuisine, modernization brought loss and gain. Gourmets such as Theodore Child could write in 1890, "In these days of progress, science, gas-stoves, sophistication, and democracy, the gourmet's dream is to taste real meat cooked with real fire, and to drink wine made with real grapes." Others deplored the tempo of modern living, when inns where travelers used to stop to rest for a day on their way from Paris to London were neglected now that the trip could be accomplished in a day. Social historian Alfred Franklin wrote, also around 1890, that our ancestors did not know the active, disquiet, busy life which fatigues us and makes us anemic and nervous.

Meals shortened and menus shrank, even for gala banquets of royalty. More people ate decently, but hardly anyone ate magnificently. Gone were the days when excess was the norm for anyone who could afford it. In 1927, something happened that would have been unthinkable in 1900: a French gastronomic society was formed called Le Plat Unique and devoted to one-dish meals. It is interesting to compare the menu of a lunch for the Prince Regent and forty guests at Brighton, England, in 1817, in which a mere listing of the 124 distinct dishes occupies three pages of double columns, with the following menu for King George VI's lunch at Windsor Castle in honor of French President Lebrun in 1939: [69]

Homard Bagration; sauce verte
Poulard poêlée Mascotte; Haricots verts nouveaux au beurre
Pommes fondantes
Mousse de jambon à la gelée; Salade princesse
Bombe glacée Victoria; Bonbonnière de petits fours
Dessert

167

Our modern ideas on diet and hygiene, which have led to the standardized modern meal consisting mainly of a principal dish of meat and vegetables, is extraordinarily recent. Despite the centuries doctors had spent studying the relation of food to health, they knew almost nothing about it before 1900. Vitamins had not been discovered; no one had any idea schoolchildren needed vegetables and fruit; experiments on nutrition led only to useless graphs affirming it takes three hours and thirty minutes to digest boiled beef as compared to one hour and thirty minutes for broiled trout. In the nineteenth century, it was still possible to write, as Brillat-Savarin did, that races fed on fish rather than flesh are "less courageous and are pale."

Food adulteration, practiced in the first half of the nineteenth century on an almost incredible scale, came under control only in the midcentury. Until then, cookbooks blithely recommended using copper pennies to keep pickles green in boiling, and poisons were commonly added to dissimulate foods: sulphuric acid to make vinegar more acid, poisonous cherry laurel for imitation almond flavor, carbonate of copper in spurious green tea, and red lead to color Gloucester cheese. That eating diseased animals could cause disease in people was a novel concept in the 1860's. After centuries of sumptuary laws to control the quantity and luxury of foods, came the modern era with laws to control the hygiene of their contents. The old system of *la desserte*, which enabled the bachelor gourmet to live well on leftovers from the rich man's table, went out of style, the great Parisian Marché aux Arlequins, where scraps and bits of food bought from restaurant scullions were sold, disappeared in the early twentieth century.

Calorie counting, which has had such a violent effect on cuisine, is a recent pastime. Ideas on food combustion as the source of body heat and energy were foreshadowed in the early nineteenth century, but the concept was still so primitive that a number of educated people believed death sometimes resulted from spontaneous combustion. It was only after a series of strenuous experiments, in which scientists climbed mountains to study the relation of energy expended to the intake of food, that the calorie was established as a system of measurement in the late nineteenth century. Moderation in eating had been urged by one or two luminaries of the six-teenth century; in the twentieth, it became one of the primary con-cerns of almost everyone, doubtless to the improvement of the general health, but certainly to the detriment of the table.

By the nineteenth century, the New World was to be reckoned with, even culinarily. It is common, at least in Europe, to consider the United States a sort of culinary wasteland dotted with hot-dog stands and Coca-Cola signs. An American usually has to think hard if asked to name a "truly American" dish, and feels intimidated or ashamed about what appears to be a lapse in American culture. However, since the Western cuisine was largely set in Europe by the time America was settled, it is not surprising that there are few original dishes from the Americas—by that time, there were almost no new dishes being created anywhere. For the same reason, the few that might be called "truly American" are regional ones from the early colonies of the Eastern seaboard: chowder (from the *chaudière* of French settlers), lobster Newburg, planked shad, Boston baked beans, succotash, spoon bread, Maryland fried chicken, hominy grits, scrapple, maple syrup, buckwheat cakes, and the New England clambake. A notable exception is New Orleans, where the happy mixture of French skill, exotic produce, and West Indian and Negro cooking blended to form an entirely distinct cuisine that deserves to be better known abroad.

Most New England dishes are adopted from American Indian ones using native foods: pumpkins, beans, oysters, turkey, and corn. West Indian, Mexican, and South American cuisine offer a multitude of regional dishes based on a blend of native and Euro-pean foods. Mexico had a highly developed cuisine at the time of the conquest, as can be judged from the following eyewitness de-scription written by one of Cortes' men, Bernal Diaz:

> For each meal his servants prepared him more than thirty dishes cooked in their native style, which they put over small earthenware braziers to prevent them from getting cold. They cooked more than 300 plates of the food the great Montezuma was going to eat, and more than a thousand more for the guard.

I have heard that they used to cook him the flesh of young boys. But as he had such a variety of dishes, made of so many different ingredients, we could not tell whether a dish was of human flesh or anything else, since every day they cooked fowls, turkeys, pheasants, local partridges, quail, tame and wild duck, venison, wild boar, marsh birds, pigeons, hares, and rabbits, also many other kinds of birds and beasts native to their country, so numerous that I cannot quickly name them all. . . .

Let us now turn to the way his meals were served. . . . If it was cold, they built a large fire of live coals made by burning the bark of a tree which gave off no smoke. The smell of the bark from which they made these coals was very sweet. . . . He would sit on a soft low stool which was richly worked. His table, which was also low and decorated in the same way, was covered with white tablecloths and rather long napkins of the same material. Then four very clean and beautiful girls brought water for his hands in one of those deep basins that they call xicales. They held other like plates beneath it to catch the water, and brought him towels. Two other women brought him maize-cakes . . . two more very handsome women served Montezuma when he was at table with maize-cakes kneaded with eggs and other nourishing ingredients. These maize-cakes were very white, and were brought in on plates covered with clean napkins. They brought him a different kind of bread also, in a long ball kneaded with other kinds of nourishing food, and *pachol* cake, as they call it in that country, which is a kind of wafer. . . .[70]

The United States was not without its culinary delights in the early days. Taverns on the Schuylkill River outside Philadelphia were famous in the eighteenth century for catfish and waffle suppers and planked shad. Other regions were known for turtle feasts, or turtle frolics, as they were called, for which sea captains returning from the West Indies were expected to bring home a turtle and a barrel of limes for the accompanying punch. A traveling clergyman named Burnaby wrote in 1759 that there were turtle feasts at several taverns on the East River near New York once or twice a week with thirty or forty ladies and gentlemen meeting, dining, and drinking tea until evening when they returned to New York in Italian chaises.

One of the most famous American nineteenth-century gourmets, Sam Ward, could hold his own with gourmets anywhere in the world. Ward did his own marketing, bought his own wines, imported his own coffee and tea from Brazil and China. He is sometimes credited with having introduced good eating to Americans, and he was the first to transact important affairs at the dinner table. His Washington dinners became famous. Statesmen consulted him on the important subject of food, as William M. Evarts, Secretary of State under President Hayes, did in the following letter of September 2, 1880:

> I telegraphed you this afternoon about the materials for my Friday dinner. . . . I never feel safe unless I have everything in

The table spread for William Cullen Bryant's reception by Governor Tilden, February 8, 1875.

the kitchen by Thursday. Soup, chicken, halibut, oysters on the shell, filets of beef (two for each diner), Muscovy duck (two for each diner), all seem among the possibilities. But the turtle soup, oysters, halibut or some equivalent fish, and the filets are all that is essential. . . .[71]

The following menu of one of Sam Ward's dinners might be useful to any American challenged on the plane of cuisine:

dinner for Mr. O'Connor

Little Neck Clams
Montrachet
Potage tortue verte à l'anglaise
Potage crème d'artichauts
Amontillado
Whitebait, Filets de bass, sauce crevettes
Rauenthaler
Concombres
Timbales à la milanaise
Filet de boeuf au madère
Pommery sec
Selle d'agneau de Central Park, sauce menthe
Moët et Chandon Grand Crémant Impérial, Magnums
Petits pois, Tomates farcies, Pommes croquettes
Côtelettes de ris de veau à la parisienne
Cèpes à la bordelaise
Asperge froide en mayonnaise

———

Sorbet au marasquin

———

Pluvier rôti au cresson

———

Chateau Margaux
Salade de laitue
Fromage varié
OLD MADEIRA   CHARLESTON AND SAVANNAH
Bombe de glace   Fraises   Pêches   Gateaux
Raisins de serre
Café
COGNAC ET LIQUEURS [72]

By the First World War, any cuisine of pretensions was basically French, as in the menu given above. The techniques and recipes were established internationally, and they have changed little in the hands of great chefs since except to become simpler and less rich.

The king of chefs and chef of kings, Auguste Escoffier, can be credited with bringing true simplicity to *haute cuisine*. He was the most bemedaled chef of any epoch, awarded the ribbon and rosette of the Legion of Honor, the Commemorative Medal, Croix d'Officier du Mérite Agricole, Médaille d'Or de la Mutualité Française, Médaille de la Reconnaissance Française, Croix de Chevalier de la Couronne d'Italie, and the Croix de Chevalier de l'Ordre du Danneborg. His was the last age of great chefs and great restaurants. He scorned gas and electricity in the belief that only natural heat from wood and coke could roast or grill properly, and he dismissed all but iron and copper pans. The new aluminum he recognized as convenient but unsuitable for the best cooking. He shortened menus and simplified dishes in recognition that "a too-active life does not permit us to devote to the pleasures of the table the long hours our fathers did," and that where time is limited, the menu must be also. He foresaw a continued decrease in the size of meals as "one of the inevitable necessities of the future."

In a desire to recapture the golden age, one of the great twentieth-century chefs, Prosper Montagné, was persuaded in 1920 by a group of gourmet investors to start a restaurant which was to be the essence of perfection. It was the essence of perfection, and it was a total financial failure. Gourmets from all over the world came to Montagné in Paris, but the meals were so memorable that the memory seemed to suffice for most people, who did not go again for a long time if ever. In seven years, Prosper Montagné had lost all his savings and was reduced to selling his collection of cookbooks.

In addition to the expense of the best ingredients and a proper staff, the difficulty of obtaining either, the lack of dedication on the part of the personnel and lack of appreciation and criticism on the part of the clientele, great restaurants today face general disinterest in *haute cuisine* food. The late Alexandre Dumaine, whose Côte d'Or in Saulieu was—and still is—world famous for great food, once remarked sadly that more and more of his customers asked for grilled meat. On the other hand, anyone looking for truly *haute cuisine* food, will find few restaurants in the world that produce it.

What was lost in great cooking, has been gained in good bourgeois cooking at home. While there are few great professional chefs today, or at least few who work under conditions that give scope to their abilities, there is an ever-increasing number of amateur cooks. The development of amateur cooking was inevitable if there was to be any food worth eating at all. Food, always the subject of passionate and unabashed interest among the French, has only lately become so elsewhere. As recently as 1951, Elizabeth David wrote in her introduction to *French Country Cooking*, "Rationing, the disappearance of servants, and the bad and expensive meals served in restaurants, have led Englishwomen to take a far greater interest in food than was formerly considered polite. . . ."

Today, interest in food is open and avid. Never have there been so many cookbooks and books on food; never have there been so many gourmet stores; never have such exotic items been available in supermarkets and the shops of the most provincial town; never have people traveled so much or been so receptive to foreign ideas.

To some degree, the proliferation of books on good food can be traced to the increased difficulties of eating well. It is a curious fact that people enjoy reading about good food when they have trouble getting it. There was a boom in the selling and reading of cookbooks during the siege of Paris of 1871 when even experienced chefs were avidly reading recipes while trying to disguise the cats and rats they were reduced to cooking. Nonetheless, literature on food proves the interest in food is still alive, and so long as it is, it can be hoped that there will be an ever-increasing number of amateurs willing to follow in the footsteps of kings, statesmen, courtiers, and artists in taking a place at the stove.

The future of cookery has been debated from ancient times. The question of whether it should be abandoned if a substitute could be found has been discussed for nearly two thousand years. Plato, who kept cooks out of his ideal republic, was for abandoning cookery. Plutarch, in his "Dinner of the Seven Wise Men," presented the other side. In reply to Solon's question whether it would not be the greatest good to require no food at all, Cleobulus replies it would not, "for when the table is done away with, there go with it all these other things: the altar fire on the hearth, the hearth itself, wine bowls, all entertainment and hospitality—the most humane and first acts of communion between man and man. . . ." Seventeen centuries later, Charles Monselet echoed these views when he wrote that "the most charming hours of our life are all connected—by a more or less tangible hyphen—with a memory of the table," and Anatole France predicted the glory of great French cooking would transcend all other glories when the world grew wise enough to put the spit above the sword.

To abandon hope for the future of good food would be to abandon hope for the future of civilized man. But this is a history. The future is yet to be written.

AN HISTORICAL
INDEX to SOME COMMON
and UNCOMMON FOODS

∾∾∾

ACORN

Though we no longer think of the acorn as something to eat, it was one of the earliest foods in Europe. Great stores of acorns were found buried in the sites of prehistoric villages in northern Italy and Switzerland. Primitive man found it a very convenient food. It was plentiful, nourishing, kept well when stored for winter, and could be ground into flour. North American Indians made acorns into porridge when corn was scarce, and Mexicans made it into bread. In his excursions across the mountains of California, John Muir often carried the hard, dry acorn cakes Pacific Coast Indians still eat today.

Long after man had better things to eat, the acorn was important food for pigs and wild animals. The Roman poet Horace, though he wrote with contempt of luxurious eating, was enough of a gourmet to recommend wild boar from Umbria rather than elsewhere because in Umbria the boars fed on acorns.

The early Greeks thought acorns dispelled headaches. They used them, chopped, as seasoning. The Romans ate them too, usually grilled, and during wars and famine made them into bread. Acorns are still resorted to in times of shortage. As recently as World War II, they were used in Europe in making ersatz coffee.

ALMOND

Native to the eastern Mediterranean, the almond was barely known in Rome in the second century B.C., when it was called

Greek nut after the country of its origin. In Egypt it was unknown before the Roman era. Almond trees spread rapidly through southern Europe under the Roman Empire, and by the Middle Ages, the almond was of great importance in cooking, even in the north. Though almonds must have been an expensive import in England, there, as elsewhere in Europe, almond milk was used more than cow's milk in recipes, and pounded almonds thickened most sauces instead of flour or starch. The almond was essential in early confectionery; recipes for marchpane and other almond pastries abound in cookbooks from medieval times. The use of the almond only declined in the seventeenth century, though almonds underwent a period of disfavor earlier in England at the time of the Reformation when they were branded Popish because Catholics substituted almond milk for cow's milk on fast days.

AMBERGRIS

Though ambergris has been in use for hundreds of years, no one is sure what it is. It is generally thought to be an intestinal secretion of the sperm whale. Still added to perfumes as a fixative, it was once valued as an aphrodisiac, tonic, and flavoring. Cardinal Richelieu is said to have eaten ambergris in chocolate lozenges. A common ingredient in sweets, syrups, and sauces of the seventeenth century, ambergris was out of fashion two centuries later when Brillat-Savarin recommended drinking it in chocolate as a restorative after nights of excess.

APPLE

Apple seeds found in the site of pile dwellings of 10,000 years ago in Switzerland prove the apple to be one of the oldest known European fruit trees. The ancient Hebrews ate apples; so did the ancient Egyptians. Apples were one of the favorite fruits of the Greeks, who had several varieties and used them raw, dried, and cooked in steam or pastry. Alexander the Great is said to have been so fond of them that he filled his ships with the exceptional apples he found in Babylonia.

The Roman agricultural expert Columella named eleven kinds of apples known in his day, the first century A.D. The Romans made apple cider, apple vinegar, and a kind of jam of apples boiled with wine and water. It was the Romans who brought the apple to England, and the English who brought it to America. Despite the expression "as American as apple pie," the apple is not native to the United States and was unknown there until the English carried seedlings to the East Coast. The apple spread westward with, or sometimes in advance of, the early settlers. Seedlings were planted by itinerant trappers or peddlers, the most prominent being John Chapman, known as Johnny Appleseed for his extensive planting of apple seedlings in Ohio and Indiana.

By 1877, there were fifteen hundred named varieties of apples; by 1969, over seven thousand had been identified in the United States alone, though only a handful are important as crops.

APRICOT

Like the apple, the apricot was brought to the Americas by early European settlers, in this case, the Spanish. According to one Egyptologist, the apricot is depicted in Priest Thy's tomb at Saqqâra, believed to have been built between 3100 and 2890 B.C. It was introduced to Greece in the time of Alexander the Great. The Romans first discovered it in the Middle East. Outside Greece, Italy, and Spain, the apricot was not widely known in Europe until the fourteenth, fifteenth, and, in some countries, sixteenth century.

ARTICHOKE

Because there is a great deal of uncertainty about the identification of plants referred to by ancient writers, it is not clear whether what some classical scholars have identified as the artichoke is actually the globe artichoke we know. John Beckmann, an eighteenth century German scientist, made a very thorough study of the subject in his *History of Inventions and Discoveries*. He concluded that what the Romans and Greeks ate is not our globe artichoke, but the pulpy bottom, young shoots, and tender stalks of related plants of the thistle family.

The plant with the edible stalk has sometimes been identified as a cardoon (see CARDOON). Greek naturalist Theophrastus speaks of another plant with an erect stem, also edible, and a fruit vessel which, after the downy prickles have been removed, resembles the fruit of a palm tree and is likewise fit to eat. It is this plant that some classical commentators have identified, rightly or wrongly, as the globe artichoke.

According to Beckmann, the globe artichoke was brought to Italy from the Levant in the fifteenth century, at which time it was considered a new vegetable. Hermolaus Barbarus, who died in 1494, wrote that the plant was first seen in Venice in 1473. In 1466, a member of the Strozza family brought the first artichokes to Florence from Naples. There Catherine de Médicis conceived a passion for the vegetable, which she made fashionable in France after her marriage to the future Henri II in 1533. From France artichokes traveled to England and became the most esteemed European vegetable from the late sixteenth century on. Chapters were devoted to them in seventeenth-century cookbooks, which featured dishes like artichoke pies.

Jerusalem artichokes, not to be confused with globe artichokes, originated in the Americas and were brought to Europe in the early seventeenth century.

ASPARAGUS

At the time Theophrastus (371–287 B.C.) wrote his book on plants, only wild asparagus was eaten; a century later, Cato spoke of asparagus cultivated in gardens. Cultivated asparagus remained rare enough to be reserved for the rich in first-century Rome according to Pliny the Elder, who noted that the best came from Ravenna and weighed up to a third of a pound apiece.

With the eclipse of the Roman Empire, asparagus went out of fashion along with most vegetables and only came back into favor four centuries ago. It was introduced to the English vegetable garden in the sixteenth or seventeenth century and became very fashionable in the seventeenth when Louis XIV's gardener, Jean de la Quintinie, established asparagus beds that provided the king with fresh asparagus all year. Along with artichokes, it was the most sought-after vegetable of the time.

Today there are over forty known varieties of this plant, which belongs to the lily family.

BANANA

Botanically a berry, the banana is an old fruit, wild in Asia. By the sixteenth century, its cultivation had spread to the Pacific islands, the west coast of Africa (banana is an African name), and the Canary Islands, from which it was taken to America by the Spaniards.

Mentioned in ancient times by Greeks, Romans, and Arabs, it became known in England only after being transplanted to America. Eighteenth-century English cookbooks mention boiled banana dumplings, banana tarts, and marmalade. Nevertheless the banana, now basic to Central America's economy, was not eaten in quantity until very recently. It appeared in United States markets only in the nineteenth century and was not fully accepted until the twentieth.

There are about a hundred varieties of bananas, many of which, like the starchy plantain used in tropical cooking, seldom reach North American or European markets.

BEAN

If pale beans bubble for you in a red earthenware pot
You can oft decline the dinners of sumptuous hosts.
—Martial, *Epigrams*, Book XIII

The word "bean" was once always understood to mean the broad or fava bean, long cultivated in Europe and eaten in Mesopotamia in 2000 B.C. This was, in fact, the only bean in Europe until about the sixteenth century except for the soya bean of the East, which was known to Europeans before the discovery of America.

When the Spanish reached the Americas, they found the Indians of Peru and Mexico cultivating a variety of beans: lima beans, scarlet runners, string beans, and kidney beans. Some of these became favorites in Europe. For some reason, Europeans never adopted the lima bean, and Americans never took to the broad bean.

BEEF

When mighty roast beef was the Englishman's food,
It ennobled our hearts and enriched our blood,
Our soldiers were brave and our courtiers good.
Oh! The roast beef of old England!
—Richard Leveridge (1670–1758),
"The Roast Beef of Old England."

Beef

The raising of beef for food is very recent, but the eating of it very old. Egyptians of the thirteenth and twelfth centuries B.C. ate a great deal of meat, beef in particular (though cow meat was proscribed). Egyptian tombs of over 4,000 years ago depict the force-feeding of oxen and calves with bread and roast duck.

Beef is the earliest meat eaten in Greece, where it was consumed in quantities in pre-Hellenic days. Homer's heroes subsist almost exclusively on wine, bread, and meat sacrificed to the gods, and the meat is more often beef than anything else. Anacharsis in his fourth century B.C. travelogue tells of 300 oxen being led to the altar for a single public feast in Athens. Yet Columella, writing in first-century Rome, said the ancients considered it a capital crime to kill an ox, just as serious an offense as killing a fellow citizen. From that, among other sources, we know there were serious taboos on killing cattle for a period of time between Homeric days and the first century B.C. The interdiction had come with the development of agriculture. As farming took up more and more land, natural pasture for cattle disappeared, and the limited number of oxen, bulls, and cows that could be fed were essential for farm labor.

The interdiction did not last long. By the first century B.C., Virgil had occasion in his *Georgics II* to deplore the eating of beef and regret the times:

> Ere godless men, restrained from blood in vain,
> Began to feast on flesh of bullocks slain.*

Beef and other butchers' meat was rare on Roman menus during the Republic and the early days of the Empire. When Petronius

---

* *Georgics* II, 537.

183

wrote his first-century satire of a *nouveau riche*'s dinner, he put beefsteak on the menu, but it is a dish hardly mentioned in the many descriptions of meals and banquets in Roman writings of the time. Beef was probably more common in Rome in the third century, for when the populace petitioned Alexander Severus to reduce prices, beef and pork headed the list of items considered too expensive.

In the royal kitchens of the thirteenth century, whole oxen were roasted again as they had been in Homerian days. Medieval farmers probably ate beef too, at least in the fall, when lack of storable winter fodder made it necessary to slaughter livestock too old to work anymore or too weak to survive the winter. The meat of these animals was hardly choice, so it is not surprising that beef was conspicuously absent from cookbooks of late medieval times when it was considered fit only for peasants. A great deal of the meat sold was tainted.

Beef came into favor again in the late sixteenth century. About that time, the introduction of clover, hay crops, and turnips made it possible to keep cattle over the winter and eat fresh-killed meat all year. A century later, breeding and raising cattle for food became a matter for study, and the quality of meat improved markedly. Problems remained, however. The difficulty of providing cities with fresh meat increased as the population grew and pastureland could be found only at a greater and greater distance from urban centers. Beef was brought in on the hoof, and the meat of the tired animals was coarse and inferior after their long journeys. After slaughter, meat had to be sold quickly or salted, for there was no refrigeration until 1880.

Despite these difficulties, the nineteenth century was the century of great English beef. As Alexandre Dumas wrote in his *Grand Dictionnaire*, "Nothing can compare with the quarters of beef roasted whole that are wheeled about on the miniature railways that separate customers in English taverns. There is nothing so appetizing as those hunks of beef, marbled with fat and weighing up to 100 pounds, that one cuts one's self to one's liking." *

---

* Larger roasts have been recorded. The Duchess of Northumberland described a 360 pound "double baron cold" served at an eighteenth-century feast. The beef cooked in the first public exhibition of roasting by gas weighed 535 pounds.

Although there were no cattle when the first settlers came, the United States can now claim supremacy in beef. It produces two and a half times as much as any other country. The excellent natural grazing lands of America quickly proved inadequate in the face of an ever-increasing demand for butchers' meat, a demand only fulfilled by the revolution in methods of feeding cattle during World War II. That change enabled the United States to become the world's chief producer of beef.* Determined to feed soldiers more meat than the average per-capita consumption, the government succeeded in cutting the time the cattle spent on feeder farms to half the usual six or seven months by stimulating the animals' appetites with corn or meal cake. Unfortunately, no matter how quickly cattle can be fattened now, a thousand-pound prime steer yields only an average of fourteen pounds of fillet. There are still problems to be solved.

BEER

Beer is one of the oldest beverages in the world and still one of the most popular. It accounts for 49 percent of all alcohol drunk in the U. S. A. and 84.3 percent in the United Kingdom. It can be made from most cereals, and the first beer probably dates from the time cereals were first cultivated. Records of beer making have been found in early agricultural societies from pre-Roman Gaul to prehistoric Egypt to Incan Peru. There is some evidence that beer was brewed in Mesopotamia by 6000 B.C. The Babylonians used to make beer by cutting underbaked barley bread into pieces and soaking it in water, a process much like the Russian way of making kvass today. Babylonian beer was sometimes flavored with honey, herbs, or dates; in later times, also with hops. In northern Europe, beer, usually flavored with honey, preceded grape wine and was the common drink of Gaul and Germany at the time of the Roman invasion.

Although Caesar imported vines to Gaul, beer remained the favorite beverage there until Charlemagne. Beer continued to be more popular than wine in northern Europe and was drunk for breakfast instead of coffee or tea until the midseventeenth and

---

* Though heavy beef eaters, the inhabitants of the U.S. are outstripped by Argentinians in consumption per capita.

early eighteenth centuries, when these new beverages came into general use. Every English household used to make its own beer. The theory has been advanced that it was a shortage of beer that drove the Mayflower to land at Plymouth. The following quotation is cited in evidence: "For we could not now take time for further search or consideration; our victuals being much spent, especially our beer." [73]

BIRDS

(see also *CHICKEN, GOOSE, PARTRIDGE, PEACOCK, SWAN, TURKEY*)

Pheasants snared in Colchis, in Africa game-birds,
These are the rarities that have to be chased,
White goose and duckling,
Gaudy in their gay plumes,
Are left to the populace, not to our taste.
—Petronius, *The Satyricon*, No. 93.

The Egyptians of the Old Kingdom raised and ate many kinds of poultry. Though chicken was unknown to them, they had domesticated pigeons, geese, ducks, and cranes, which were force-fed on pellets of dough. The Greeks raised the same birds with the addition, from the sixth century B.C., of chicken, pheasant, and guinea fowl. But while they had a variety of poultry, it was not available in quantity.

From Greek days through the nineteenth century, wild birds were eaten in much greater variety than today. In part this is because game was once so abundant and hunting so popular, but it is also because there was little domesticated fowl.

The Greeks and Romans were fond of small birds. Flocks of thrushes were served as appetizers at Greek dinners of the fourth century B.C. Blackbirds, figpeckers, finches, jays, jackdaws, ring-doves, sparrows, and starlings were also popular tidbits before banquets. Smoked birds were appreciated too: smoked coot and

quail are mentioned by Greek writers of the time. The Romans ate almost every bird they could catch. According to Alexandre Dumas, a dish of a hundred small birds, ortolans, titlarks, robins, swallows, and others was traditional in ceremonial Roman banquets.

When snobbism and a penchant for ostentatious spending overcame all good sense, the Romans used to serve only the tongues of songbirds, and, in the end, the tongues of thousands of birds that had all been taught to say a few words. Heliogabalus, one of the Roman emperors of the third century, tried to better this by serving 600 ostrich brains at a single banquet.

By the first century, exotic birds imported from Africa and Asia, such as ostriches, flamingoes, peacocks, and parrots, were very fashionable in Rome, a fashion begun in Greece where parrots and peacocks had been eaten on rare occasions centuries earlier. Guinea fowl were introduced from Africa. The pheasant, called *phasianus* by the Romans after the river Phasis in Asia Minor, where they discovered the bird, joined the barnyard in the first century B.C. The flamingo was first served by the intrepid gourmet Apicius, the man who also discovered that flamingo tongue is a great delicacy. The peacock made its debut on a Roman table in the first century B.C. A well-run country villa of the first century had in its poultry yard guinea hens, cranes, partridges, peacocks, and flamingos, in addition to such run-of-the-mill barnyard fowl as hens, geese, and ducks; in its dovecotes, ring- and turtledoves.

The more unusual birds were raised only for and by the rich, who fattened them in confined spaces, often in darkness, while feeding or force-feeding them with figs, dates, or cereals soaked in fragrant wine or honey water. Cranes and swans sometimes had their eyes stitched closed for fattening. Squabs were force-fed with boiled and toasted beans which, according to Cato, you were supposed to blow from your mouth into that of the squab. Fattened fowl were early subjected to Roman sumptuary laws. In 275 B.C. it was forbidden to serve poultry other than a single pullet, and the pullet was not to be fattened. The Romans managed a technical evasion of the rule against fattening by giving the birds food soaked in milk; this may have been the first milk-fed poultry.

To have birds on hand and fatten them for the table, the Romans built aviaries in which they kept birds by the thousands.

Varro, writing in the first century B.C., described in detail the construction of one of these aviaries, which were larger than whole villas of earlier days. Varro suggested 5,000 birds as a good round number for an aviary. The aviary itself, he wrote, should be "a large domed building or peristyle covered with tiles or netting in which several thousand fieldfares and blackbirds can be enclosed, though some breeders add, besides, other birds which when fattened bring a high price, such as ortolans and quails. Into this building water should be conducted through narrow channels which can be easily cleaned . . . and the superfluous dripwater from these should run out through a pipe so that the birds may not be troubled by mud. It should have a low narrow door. . . . The windows should be few, and so arranged that trees and birds outside cannot be seen, for the sight of these, and the longing for them, makes the imprisoned birds grow thin. . . ." [74] The aviary also had to have heavy plastering to keep mice and vermin out, plenty

(*Below and right*) A table for the service of birds, from Charles Carter's *Complete Practical Cook*, London, 1730— and table diagrams for service of same.

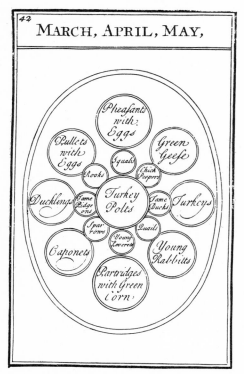

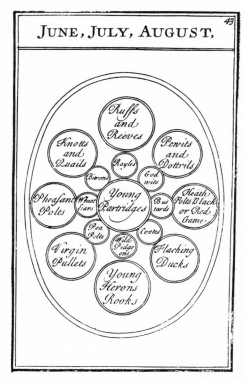

A TABLE OF FOWL

Moſt Proper and in Seaſon for the Four Quarters of the Year.

March, April, May.	June, July, Auguſt.	Sept.[br], Octo.[br], Novem.[br]	Decem.[br], January, Feb.[ry]
Turkeys with Eggs	Ruſſ Reeves Godwits	Wild Ducks	Chickens
Pheaſants with Eggs	Knotts Quails Rayls	Teals	Woodcocks
Partridges w.th green Corn	Pewets Dottrells	Wild Geeſe	Snipes
Pullets with Eggs	Pheaſant Polts	Barganders	Larks
Green Geeſe	Young Partridges	Brandgeeſe	Plovers
Young Ducklins	Heath Polts, Black or	Widgeons	Curlens
Tame Pidgeons	Red Game	Shrilldraks	Redshanks
Squab Pidgeons	Turkey Caponetts	Cackle Ducks	Sea Pheaſants
Young Rabbets	Flacking Ducks	Cygnets	Sea Parrots
Young Leverets	Wheat Ears	Pheaſants	Shuflers
Caponetts	Virgin Pullets	Partridges	Divers
Chicken Peepers	Young Herons	Grouse	Ox Eyes
Young Turkeys	Young Bitterns	Hares	Pea Cocks & Hens
Tame Ducks	Young Bustards	Rabbets	Bustards
Young Rooks	Pea Polts	Ortelans	Turkeys
Young Sparrows	Wild Pidgeons	Wild Pidgeons	Geeſe
	Young Coots	Capons	Blackbirds
		Pullets	Feldefares, Thruſhes.

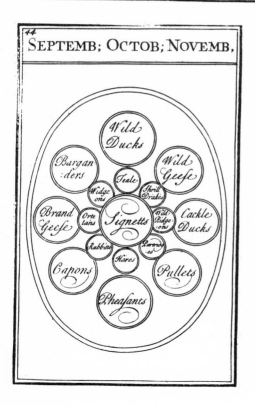

SEPTEMB; OCTOB; NOVEMB,

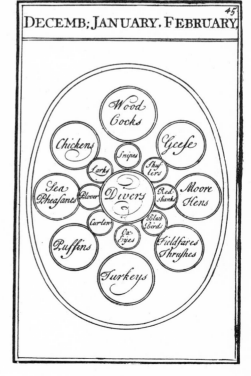

DECEMB; JANUARY. FEBRUARY

of light, and perches and places for food. The birds were fed cumin, baked barley, wheat, millet, beans, vetches, and meal soaked in honey water or fragrant wine. Varro's own aviary was a columned one with a platform for dining set up over the duck pond with benches for guests and a revolving table from which they were served food and drink.

Many Romans built aviaries to supply their own tables, but others built them for profit. Varro pointed out that 5,000 fieldfares raised in a single aviary brought 60,000 sesterces in one year. There was a steady market to supply the large banquets given in Rome almost daily, and several thousand might be sold at once if there was a public feast.

Through the sixteenth, seventeenth, eighteenth, and to some extent, nineteenth centuries, people ate albatross, swans, cranes, bustards, blackbirds, storks, heronsews, magpies, shovelers, bitterns, brewes, falcons, egrets, herons, sandpipers, cormorants, gulls, sparrows, starlings, and fifty-odd other birds. Blackbirds were considered fit for a king, while seagulls and coots were Lenten fare. Pierre Belon, sixteenth-century French naturalist, recommended roast or boiled vulture. Cookbook authors warned that some of these birds were evil tasting and possibly even harmful, but gave recipes for them nevertheless, recipes designed to disguise strong and unpleasant flavors with equally strong and presumably pleasant ones such as saffron and ambergris. If worst came to worst and the birds proved not only evil tasting and possibly harmful but spoiled, instructions were to be found in every early cookbook for taking away, as one of them put it, "the corruption, savour, and stink." [75]

Many birds now scarce were then plentiful. The custom of eating game all year round regardless of season led to the virtual elimination of certain species. Among these are herons, hunted by the fashionable with falcons in the sixteenth and seventeenth centuries; bustards, hunted with greyhounds; and the ortolans Escoffier liked to prepare. Every year, twenty or thirty thousand larks used to be caught migrating through England and sent to the London market for the traditional British steak, oyster, kidney, and lark pie. (Lark by itself was considered very delicate but not very satisfying; Dumas remarked that it was very good to eat, but only after a

190

substantial dinner.) The ortolan, a European bunting, was once plentiful, but is now rare. A number of birds our ancestors ate are now protected by law because of their scarcity: storks, for example, and most songbirds such as thrushes.

Game farming was an American and British innovation of the twentieth century. In the U. S. it is the only way to have game birds on the market because selling of wild birds is subject to such severe restrictions. Even domestically raised game birds are strictly controlled by state laws. While any kind can be sold in thirty states, in three, only pheasants can be raised for sale, in one, only exotic birds.

BOAR

The boar's head in hand bring I,
With garlands gay and rosemary;
I pray you all sing merrily
Qui estis in convivio.
    —Old English Christmas carol

Wild boar was eaten in Greece as early as the fifth century B.C., but Pliny the Elder tells us in his *Natural History* that the first Roman to serve a whole boar at a banquet was P. Servilius Rullus in 63 B.C. In Pliny's time, over a century later, rich Romans had begun to keep and fatten wild boar in their private game parks, and thought nothing of serving two or three of them as a first course.

Boar's head made its appearance as a gala dish in England about the fourteenth century and stayed in high favor until the civil wars of the midsixteenth. At medieval feasts, it was preceded by trumpets and followed by a train of ladies and gentlemen. The tradition of serving boar's head at Christmas to the accompaniment of carols was carried over to the twentieth century at Queen's College in Oxford.

BREAD

Open thine eyes, and thou shalt be satisfied with bread.
    —Proverbs, 20:13

Before man made bread, he made cakes of meal, which anthropologists tell us were simply cereals soaked, pressed into cakes,

191

and dried in the sun or on hot stones. Remains of these small, unleavened cakes have been found in Stone Age dwellings.

Exactly when the first bread was baked has never been established, but it was at least 5,000 years ago. Not only has the knowledge of how the bread was made come down to us, but even some of the loaves themselves. Well-preserved loaves have been found in Egyptian pyramids sealed about 3000 B.C. Loaves of bread were also found in the ruins of ovens of first-century Pompeii, and one loaf of the same era, stamped with a consular seal, was discovered in the ashes of Herculaneum.

The Egyptians were the first to leaven bread by letting the dough ferment, and also the first to use yeast, which they got from their beer brewers. Bread making has undergone little fundamental change since. The Egyptians did not understand how the leavening process worked; in fact, no one did until Pasteur analyzed fermentation in 1857. Whether they understood the process or not, the Egyptians knew how to make it work. In the earliest days, they put flour-and-water dough in a warm place until bubbles formed and the dough rose; then they kneaded it and baked it. Eventually they learned to save a bit of risen dough from one batch of bread to the next as a starter, as our grandmothers did.

The Egyptians made a variety of breads and cakes. The first were baked in heated molds, but by the New Empire (1567–1085 B.C.), there were ovens in which several loaves could be baked at once. For the rich, bread was made from wheat flour; for the not-so-rich, from barley; and for the poor, from durra. Skilled professional bakers produced pastries in the shapes of animals and birds. Bread, at least of the poorer variety, must have been common because there is a record of Egyptian laborers of about 3000 B.C. receiving as pay for a day's work two jugs of beer and four loaves of bread.

Bread was a luxury in ancient Greece and Rome and a staple food only in settled towns. The Roman diet consisted mainly of a gruel known as *puls*. The normal Greek meal was composed of a cooked cereal called *sitos* with a little olive oil on top (used as we use butter) and accompanied by diluted wine. If available, something might be added as a side dish: figs or olives or dates, an onion or a turnip, a dried or pickled vegetable, or, more exceptionally, salt fish or pork. The porridge might also be seasoned with a gravy according to a recipe given in Anacharsis' travelogue of the fourth century B.C.:

> Take some peeled barley. Pound it in a mortar and put the flour in a vessel. Pour oil on it. Keep stirring this mixture whilst it heats gently on the fire. Feed it now and then with pullet, kid, or lamb gravy, taking special care not to let it boil over, and when stewed to the exact point of perfection, serve it up.[76]

Porridge continued to be a staple food in many countries up to the present. Frumenty—hulled wheat, boiled in milk and seasoned —was an English national dish for centuries. Porridge was served at the French royal table as late as the seventeenth century. *Far*, of buckwheat or spelt, is still made in Brittany, and a cornmeal mush is a staple in parts of Italy and Romania. A buckwheat porridge called *kasha* is an important food in Russia.

Though porridge was the common man's food in early Greece, there were skilled bakers for the rich in towns. Poppy-seed bread is referred to in Greek literature as early as the seventh century B.C., and by the fifth century B.C., writers were mentioning an enormous variety of hot rolls, cakes, and breads, leavened and unleavened, made with rice, barley, whole wheat, or pulse, and baked with suet, lard, cheese, honey, milk, or oil. Some breads were made in ovens, some on a griddle; some were roasted on the coals, some baked in the ashes, and others on a spit. Breads were sometimes shaped like mushrooms or flowers, sprinkled with anise or sesame seed, or flavored with cumin or pepper. Some contained almonds or hazelnuts; some were of several layers. Athens was famous in the fourth century B.C. for a special kind of bread baked on a brazier, then folded, and dipped in sweet wine; this was served during banquets and said to revive sated appetites. Delicate white breads, which were a luxury in Europe as late as the eighteenth century, were appreciated in Athens two thousand years earlier.

In early Roman times, flour was ground and bread baked in the household. There were no bakeries in Rome until some time after the middle of the second century B.C., when the city had been in existence for nearly six hundred years. The first professional bakers in Rome were Greeks, from whom the Romans learned the art. They arrived at quite scientific proportions for mixing bread. Pliny's calculation that bread should be one-third heavier than the meal used in baking it coincided with the proportions of meal to bread in Germany in the 1700's. By 100 B.C., there were 258 bakeries in Rome. Emperor Trajan established a school for bakers in the first century A.D., and the art of bread making spread from Rome through the Roman Empire.

Roman bakers formed corporations around the beginning of the Christian era. As bakers became more and more important to Roman emperors, who depended on them for a supply of bread to distribute to the populace, bakers' corporations acquired both more privileges and more restrictions. They were freed from certain obligations; they were granted buildings and raw materials. On the other hand, their property belonged to the collectivity, their children were obliged to become bakers, and they could neither leave the corporation nor marry outside it. The price, quality, and distribution of bread, including the amount to be supplied the state for the public dole, was strictly controlled.

These same corporations survived from Roman days through the Middle Ages; they are the oldest medieval town guilds.

Bakers and millers have long been viewed by governments and people with the suspicion reflected in the old refrain of the jolly miller of River Dee, "I care for nobody, no not I if nobody cares for me." For centuries, bakers and millers were subject to severe punishment for breaking the rules of the trade. The early Persians once passed a law decreeing that any baker giving short weight or adding straw to his bread was to be baked in his own oven. In fourteenth-century London, bakers who did not observe regulations were exposed in the stocks or drawn through the streets with loaves or a whetstone hung from their necks. Nevertheless, because there was always a good profit to be made in falsifying and shortchanging bread, there was a great deal of cheating on the part of bakers, inspectors, and, in at least one case, rulers. Procopius in his *Secret History* tells how the sixth-century Byzantine Emperor Justinian stooped to having loaves made undersized and stuffed with ashes in order to reap a large private profit.

Cheating was profitable because bread was the essential (and often the only) food of the people for centuries. People had to be able to buy nourishing bread or starve. In Cato's days, agricultural workers lived on three pounds of bread a day. Socrates lived in the strictest sense on bread and water except when invited out to dinner. Indeed, the biblical phrase "our daily bread" meant quite literally "our daily food." As E. Parmalee Prentice put it in *Hunger and History*, the bread and wine of the Lord's Supper is not just a symbolic meal: "We can look upon it as the food set before men at any ordinary meal of the ancient world."

Bread was important in the Middle Ages and early Renaissance not only as food but as part of the tableware. Plates, glasses, and such largely disappeared with the Roman Empire, and a slice of bread known as a trencher was used as a plate through much of Europe from the time of Charlemagne through the beginning of the seventeenth century. The stale hard bread, softened by the sauces and juices of the food put on it, was eaten at the end of the meal. In richer households of the fifteenth and sixteenth centuries, trenchers were passed on to servants or the poor.

Almost all bread was stale and hard. The phrase "to break bread" is a literal one. In *La Vie rurale dans l'ancienne France*, Albert Babeau wrote that boys going to boarding school in the province of Dauphiné used to take with them a six months' supply of bread, which they had to break with hammers and soak before eating. Babeau wrote of loaves weighing twenty to thirty pounds that kept for a month in winter in Auvergne.

In early times (and later in periods of shortage and famine) bread was made of whatever was available and could be ground into a kind of flour: barley, millet, oats, buckwheat, rice, vetches, beans, peas, lupines, lentils, panic, tree bark, and acorns. New foods used to be judged partly according to how satisfactorily they could be converted into bread. That the potato made inferior bread was one of the main reasons it took two centuries to become generally accepted in Europe after it was introduced from America.

The obsession with white bread has always existed, but the demand increased suddenly in the eighteenth century when the poor began to expect bread as white as that of the rich. To meet the new demand, bakers resorted to additives to bleach and lighten loaves, rendering them inferior if not poisonous in the process.

Bread is still a vital part of our diet. Despite a marked decrease in consumption, even today, the world, with the exclusion of China and the U. S. S. R., obtains about half its calorie intake from cereals, and the baking industry ranks seventh among all manufacturing industries in the U. S. A.

BUTTER

The date when butter entered our cuisine is much disputed by experts. Butter was known in the Middle East, Egypt, and parts of northern Europe before the Greeks and Romans learned of it, though it was probably not prepared the same way ours is today. A substance mentioned in the Old Testament has been called butter by many translators. According to John Beckmann in his *History of Inventions and Discoveries*, "those best acquainted with Biblical criticism unanimously agree that the word *chamea* signified milk or cream or sour thick milk, and at any rate does not mean butter." In support of his theory, he notes that *chamea* was drunk and used to wash feet, and was also lightly intoxicating. Whether it was butter or not, it must have been more liquid than ours. Classical writers always speak of butter as a fluid; while we cut, knead, and spread butter, the ancients poured it out like oil.

According to Beckmann, the earliest (though still dubious) reference to butter is to be found in the works of Herodotus, a historian of the fifth century B.C. Writing of the Scythians, who lived north of the Black Sea, Herodotus described their slaves shaking deep wooden buckets of freshly drawn milk and skimming off the valued substance on the surface. Hippocrates, a contemporary of Herodotus, corroborates this description of Scythian butter making; he also tells of Thracians and various northern peoples obtaining a kind of butter from milk. Athenaeus quotes the early fourth-century B.C. poet Anaxandrides as ridiculing the guests at a wedding feast for the daughter of the king of Thrace as "your butter-eating gentry, with unkempt hair."

About four centuries later, geographer Strabo spoke of butter in connection with the Iberians of northwest Spain and the Ethiopians. Pliny, writing about the same time, called butter the most luxurious food of barbarous peoples, noting that among them the use of butter marked a man as rich. Again, his description of it does not sound quite like what we call butter today, and he further notes that the ranker it smells the more it is valued.

It appears likely that the Greeks learned of butter from the Scythians and Thracians, while the Romans learned of it from both the Greeks and the northern nations. Butter early played a role in religious ceremonies and was used in medicine. Hippocrates and Galen recommended it as an unguent. The Greek physician Dioscorides not only prescribed butter for eye inflammations, but pointed out that fresh butter could be melted and poured over porridges and vegetables instead of oil, and could substitute for other fats in pastries. Pliny also saw the usefulness of butter in cooking. In bread making, he commented, in addition to eggs and milk, "even butter has been used by races enjoying peace, when attention can be devoted to the varieties of pastry-making." [77] Perhaps the Romans did not have long enough periods of peace, for there is no indication they took up butter as food, and no recipe in the Apicius cookbook mentions it.

For centuries butter continued to be little used in countries producing olive oil and was generally limited to medical purposes. Through at least the midseventeenth century, it was sold only in apothecary shops in Mediterranean countries. In 1665, one of the men accompanying the Elector Palatine, Frederick II, in his travels through Spain, wrote of the Elector's search for butter to take on his journey along with other necessaries. "After much inquiry concerning butter, he was directed to an apothecary's shop were the people were much astonished at the largeness of the quantity he asked for, and shewed him a little, entirely rancid, which was kept in a bladder for external use." [78]

In the north, butter had been an important food for some time. By the twelfth century, it was exported in quantity from Scandinavia. It was so popular in Rouen that one of the towers of the cathedral became known as the Butter Tower, because it was built at the end of the fifteenth century with money paid for indulgences permitting the use of butter during Lent. There was so much butter in Iceland in the early seventeenth century that, each year, fir chests thirty feet long were constructed, filled with salt butter, and buried in the ground.

Bread, butter, and cheese were staples of the lower classes in England and northern France through the seventeenth century. Butter came into use in cooking only later. The sole use the rich had for it in the Middle Ages was to serve it before or after meals, especially on fish days. In his fifteenth-century *Boke of Nurture*, John Russell cites butter as one of the "fruits" served along with plums, damsons, grapes, and cherries before a meal "to make men merry."

In the seventeenth century, the rich began using more and more butter, almost exclusively for cooking. Eighteenth-century recipes called for butter in large amounts: green-pea soup, for example, took a pound of it. In the seventeenth century, the rich left uncooked butter to the working class. Perhaps the condition in which it reached towns made it too unappetizing to use raw; the ready availability of nonrancid, firm, solid butter in towns is as recent a development as refrigeration and rapid transport.

CABBAGE

... by cabbages swear I.
—fragment from Eupolis
(fifth century B.C.)

Eaten in various forms by the Egyptians, Greeks, and Romans, cabbage is one of the oldest known vegetables. The original plant, called sea cabbage, grew wild along Mediterranean rivers and northern seacoasts. Of the many varieties of cabbage, most are native to Europe. Theophrastus, who classified plants twenty-four centuries ago, mentions three kinds of cabbage in his *Inquiry into Plants*: curly-leaved, smooth-leaved, and wild. Four centuries later, Pliny the Elder named seven cultivated varieties in addition to wild cabbage. It is not certain that any of these is identical with our green cabbage of today, and our red cabbage was definitely unknown to the Greeks and Romans. Kale and collards are believed similar to the ancient varieties.

The Greeks, according to Pliny, held cabbage in poor repute while the Romans put it high on the epicure's list. The ancients did not pickle cabbage for sauerkraut though they prepared it in many ways used today. Roman epigrammatist Martial speaks of cabbage sprouts boiled green in water with a dash of soda. The Apicius cookbook gives seven recipes for cabbage including one with caraway seed, a combination popular in parts of northern Europe today.

In addition to being a common vegetable on the Roman table, cabbage had special uses. Theophrastus claimed the growing vine loathes even the smell of cabbage. Another early source said wine produced from a vineyard where cabbage grows is always darker. Because it repelled the vine, cabbage was believed to prevent intoxication. Egyptians opened a banquet with cabbage for this purpose. Cato remarked a man could eat and drink all he liked with no ill effect if he ate raw cabbage seasoned with vinegar before dinner and a half dozen leaves after dinner. If it was overlooked at dinner, cabbage was called on to cure the hangover the following day. Alexis, an Athenian playwright of the fourth century B.C., recommended a nap followed by boiled cabbage to dispel a hangover. Cabbage also served to swear by; the oath, "So help me, Cabbage!" was not uncommon in Greek plays of the sixth and fifth centuries B.C.

Roman agronomist Columella mentioned various uses of cabbage in veterinary medicine. The Greeks gave cabbage to women in childbed. Belief in the benefits of cabbage persisted through the sixteenth and seventeenth centuries when a variety of curative powers were attributed to it. Among others, it was said to give milk to wet nurses and to keep hair from falling out.

The cabbage family is a very large one, including kale, collards, Brussels sprouts, head cabbage, cauliflower, broccoli, and kohlrabi. Head cabbage, the tightly wrapped kind popular today, was developed in northern Europe in the Middle Ages. Though the Greeks and Romans wrote of eating cabbage sprouts, Brussels sprouts in

the form we know them were first grown in Belgium in or before the fifteenth century, and the first written description of the vegetable dates from 1587. Boiled Brussels sprouts seem an arch-English dish, but the vegetable only crossed the Channel in the nineteenth century.

Kohlrabi, like Brussels sprouts, is first mentioned in the sixteenth century, at the same time that broccoli, a native of southern Europe, began to be known in the north. Although cauliflower is named in translations of Greek and Roman literature, it is not certain that the plant has been properly identified. If the Greeks and Romans ate cauliflower, the vegetable must have fallen into such complete disuse thereafter that it was taken for an entirely new and unknown vegetable when it was brought from the Near East to Italy in the sixteenth century. Cauliflower became known in Europe only very slowly; it was introduced to Germany at the end of the seventeenth century, and remained little known in England as late as the nineteenth.

CACAO, COCOA, CHOCOLATE

All three are related and not to be confused with coca, a native plant of the Andes that yields cocaine. Cacao is a small tropical tree known to botanists as the *Theobroma cacao*, popularly and commercially called cocoa. The plant's name is derived from the Nahuatl Indian word for "seed," *cacahuatl*. Chocolate (a name also derived from the Nahuatl, *chocólatl*) refers to the ground and roasted cacao bean or to a beverage or candy made from it. The word "cocoa" is often used to mean chocolate that has been pulverized after the removal of part of its fat.

Chocolate was discovered by the Spaniards in Mexico. There is an unconfirmed legend that Columbus was the first to see it in use and to bring back specimens, but Cortes is usually credited with discovering it in Mexico in 1519. The Aztecs had a passion for chocolate, though it was not a common drink. Cultivated only in the lower, warmer parts of Mexico, the bean was rare enough to be reserved for chiefs and warriors; the townspeople drank cacao mixed with corn flour and seasoned with hot pepper. The pure cacao of Montezuma and his court was kept in gold jars and drunk well beaten and flavored with wild honey, vanilla, maguey, and sometimes chilies and other hot spices. In Bernal Diaz's eyewitness account of his journey with Cortes, chocolate was always served Montezuma with great reverence in cups of pure gold.

The Spanish tried cacao, liked it, and spread the cultivation of the tree and the drinking of the beverage through the Antilles. *Chocolaterías*, chocolate shops where the prepared beverage was sold, began to open in the Spanish New World. The ladies of the colony of Chiapa became so fond of it that they even had it brought to them in church and changed churches when the local bishop forbade the practice. Spanish chocolate was flavored with various tropical plants: cinnamon, cloves, pepper, vanilla, and, eventually, sugar.

In Europe, the Spanish quickly became addicted to chocolate, and chocolate shops opened throughout the country. For many years, chocolate was brought to Spain already prepared from the bean. It was later made in Spain too, but the Spanish guarded the secret of its manufacture and held a monopoly on cacao until the eighteenth century. Though immediately popular with the Spanish populace, chocolate encountered opposition. The Church and authorities disapproved of the new beverage. After analyzing the new substance, the medical corps concluded it was the "coldest" in the world. To counteract its coldness, they felt it necessary to add "warm" spices such as cinnamon, nutmeg, pepper, ginger, etc. (which was exactly what the Mexicans had been doing). Even with these additions, doctors were uncertain whether chocolate was a panacea or a poison. Playwright Molina satirized the abuse of chocolate in one of his comedies. In 1644, the Spanish government passed a law forbidding the sale of chocolate beverages in Madrid. As in the case of most laws for the control of food, ways were immediately found to circumvent it.

Chocolate as a beverage was introduced to Italy in 1600 and to France by Anne of Austria, daughter of Philip III of Spain and wife of Louis XIII. She made it fashionable in France before it reached England in the midseventeenth century. Part of its popularity can be traced to Pope Pius V's decision that drinking chocolate did not break Lenten fasting rules. However the use of chocolate did not become widespread in France until the royal chocolatery was established in 1776. When the Spanish monopoly ended, chocolate improved in quality and dropped in price with a corresponding growth in consumption, which increased almost tenfold in Europe between 1806 and 1860.

Chocolate was considered a cure-all in the nineteenth century. In 1830, Louis Philippe's royal chocolateer (who was also a pharmacist) served special preparations of chocolate to combat various ills: chocolate with salep for people who were too thin, "antispasmodic" chocolate for those who were too nervous, etc.

The French perfected the manufacture of chocolate in the nineteenth century. It was probably not until then that solid, edible chocolate was sold in England. Chocolate was introduced to cooking in about 1800; chocolate cakes and pies were not made before then. It was used in main dishes as well as desserts as it still is in some Spanish dishes, particularly those of strong flavor such as hare or snails. Contrary to what one might think, the addition does not make the dish sweet or repellent; it is undetectable as chocolate, but gives the sauce a dark rich flavor rather like the flavor imparted by a rich meat glaze. In a recipe Alexandre Dumas includes in his *Dictionnaire*, coot with chocolate calls for a full cup of the prepared beverage to get rid of the "wild marine flavor" of coot.

CANDY

The earliest record of candy was found in Egyptian papyruses in Theban tombs dating back to before 2000 B.C. Drawings on the tombs show how candy was mixed, poured into molds, and baked in ovens. Egyptian candies were often cast in the shape of bulls or geese, probably for offerings to the gods. They were flavored with spices, herbs, and fruits, thickened with flour and starch, and sweetened with honey, sugar being unknown in ancient Egypt. The Romans and Greeks enjoyed candy too; ruins of candy shops have been identified in excavations.

There was a vogue for candied nuts, fruits, and seeds, called comfits, in France and England of the sixteenth and seventeenth centuries, and much earlier in Spain. The ordinances of Pedro III, thirteenth-century king of Aragon, declared his court must always include a good and faithful principal apothecary whose main job was to be making comfits, and whose secondary occupation would be the less important one of giving medical care and advice.

From the Middle Ages on, candy-making spread as sugar became increasingly available. There is little reference to sugar candy until the fourteenth century, though the word candy may come from the Sanskrit *khanda,* the name given to pieces of crystallized sugar. Medieval candy was a royal treat. When sugar dropped to a price bourgeois households could afford, in the sixteenth and seventeenth centuries, cookbooks for the housewife began to include many recipes for making candy at home.

The birth of the modern confectionery industry, in which England took the lead, occurred only in the nineteenth century. It was at Prince Albert's Great Exhibition in London of 1851 that foreign confectioners first tasted bonbons, chocolate creams, hard candies, and caramels. England is particularly addicted to sweets still, consuming half a pound weekly per person. Americans, eating an average of almost 20 pounds a head each year, are not far behind.

CARP

Carp is native to eastern Asia. Various authorities have assured us the Greeks and Romans ate carp, and the word appears in some translations of ancient literature. John Beckmann, in a detailed study of all pertinent references in early writings, concludes the descriptions are too vague to determine whether the fish in question is carp or not. According to Beckmann, carp were first positively identified in southern Europe and the name *carpa* was first used by the sixth-century Latin writer Cassiodorus, who mentioned it as a delicate, expensive fish eaten by princes.

Ten more centuries went by before carp was introduced to northern Europe, where it became very popular because it reproduces abundantly (female carp can produce 700,000 young a year) and is one of the easiest fish to breed in reservoirs. Carp were imported to the United States in 1876, installed in fish ponds in

Washington, D.C., and within three years, distributed to twenty-five American states and territories.

In early nineteenth-century France, "to serve a Carpe, one must begin by cutting the head, which one sends to the most distinguished guest." [79] So wrote Grimod de la Reynière, adding that the head was the choicest morsel because of the tongue. Beauvilliers included in his cookbook a recipe for ragout of carp tongues—a hundred of them stewed in *sauce Italienne*.

CARROT

The Greeks and Romans were familiar with both wild and cultivated carrots. The Greeks considered them an aphrodisiac. Diphilus of Siphnos, physician of the third century B.C., noted the carrot was sometimes called a love philter. Neither Greeks nor Romans used carrots as much in cooking as we do, and like so many vegetables they fell into disuse for centuries after the fall of Rome. Wild carrot is mentioned by Louis XIII's childhood physician Héroard, who writes of the Dauphin trying a little wild-carrot compote. Carrots grew wild in England, but cultivated ones were unknown until introduced by the Flemish in the sixteenth century. In the early seventeenth century, the vegetable was still so rare in England that ladies wore carrot tops in their hats and on their sleeves in place of feathers.

CAVIAR
(see also STURGEON)

Almost all caviar comes from the rivers of the Caspian and Black Seas and the Sea of Azov, though sturgeon was once so plentiful in the United States that quantities of American caviar were exported to Europe. Caviar was given away free with nickel beer in America when beer was a nickel. Caviar is no longer commercially exploited in America because there are few sturgeon left; the American, in any case, was never the best quality.

The salted roe of various species of sturgeon, caviar is by no means all the same. The quality depends on the kind of sturgeon, the way of refining and preparing the roe, and the amount of salt used to preserve it. The best and most difficult to prepare and transport has very little salt (whence the term *malosol*, which means "little salt" in Russian). The best caviar is rather soft and liquid, while the coarser varieties are hard pressed.

In *La bonne table*, Ludwig Bemelmans tells of a great Parisian gourmet who used to test caviar with a small gold ball he had made by Cartier and wore on the end of his watch chain. In a restaurant he would drop this ball from a height of one foot through the caviar heaped on his plate. If it fell through the caviar effortlessly, all was well; if it stuck, the caviar was sent back to the kitchen.

Caviar was brought to Western Europe by the Hanseatic League as early as the fifteenth century but remained virtually unknown for another three hundred years. Though mentioned by Rabelais and by Shakespeare, it was just beginning to be sought in France in 1741 according to the *Dictionnaire du commerce* of that date, and its name was still unknown to the French in general.

In the late nineteenth century, caviar and sturgeon were so plentiful that a literary gourmet wrote in 1877:

> If it were not a pleasure, it would be an imperative duty to eat caviare. . . . It is said that when sturgeon are in season, no less than two-thirds of the female consists of roe. It is certainly odd to think of a fish weighing perhaps 1,000 pounds being two-thirds made up of eggs. . . . At such a rate of reproduction, the world would soon become the abode of sturgeons alone, were it not that the roe is exceedingly good. . . .[80]

CELERY

Theophrastus wrote of several varieties of celery, with white, red, or parti-colored stems and close, curly, or rough leaves. Celery was much used by the Romans who sometimes ate it with bread as we might eat jam or cheese. Celery seed was called for as a seasoning in the Apicius cookbook.

Throughout the Middle Ages and Renaissance, the alexander, a kind of cross between parsley and celery which Theophrastus called horse celery, was used as a potherb and in salads while celery remained unknown in most of Europe. When celery began to be widely cultivated in the seventeenth century after it was introduced from Italy, the alexander fell from favor.

Grimod de la Reynière found it necessary to warn the timid in his 1803 *Almanach* that celery is eminently aphrodisiac. In the Middle Ages, it was recommended for calming irritated states of mind.

CEREALS
(see also *BEER AND BREAD*)

Cereals are man's oldest, most basic food. All staple grains were domesticated in Neolithic times, though exactly when and in what order, no one is certain. The cultivation of grains is what made the first settled communities possible because, unlike most other foods, grains could be stored to keep the community alive over the winter and through lean years.

The term cereal is derived from Ceres, Roman goddess of grain. Aside from being a generic term for grain crops, cereal means a porridge, the meal of a grain stirred into milk or water and cooked until thick. Porridge, not bread, was the staff of life of early civilizations, and of many peoples through the Middle Ages or later. Though it has been made for at least five millennia, bread, and particularly wheat bread, remained something of a luxury until a few centuries ago.

The normal Greek meal was composed of a cooked cereal, called *sitos*, with a little olive oil on top (used as we use butter) and accompanied by diluted wine. Anything available might be added as a side dish: figs or olives or dates, an onion or a turnip, a dried or pickled vegetable, or, more exceptionally, salt fish or pork. The porridge might also be seasoned with a gravy according to a recipe given in Anacharsis' travelogue of the fourth century B.C.:

> Take some peeled barley. Pound it in a mortar and put the flour in a vessel. Pour oil on it. Keep stirring this mixture whilst it heats gently on the fire. Feed it now and then with pullet, kid, or lamb gravy, taking special care not to let it boil over, and when stewed to the exact point of perfection, serve it up.*

Barley, which grows wild over a large area of Asia Minor, probably rivals wheat as the oldest cultivated cereal, though today it is used more for feeding farm animals and in malting than as a table food. Remains of barley have been found in the sites of Neolithic pile dwellings in Switzerland as well as in early tombs and dwellings of Babylon. Aside from being useful in porridge, it was valued as a medicine (Hippocrates devoted a book to the praise of barley water) and made into alcohol. The oldest known recipe for barley wine is an inscription on a Babylonian library brick dating back to 2800 B.C.

The ordinary Roman's diet consisted mainly of a gruel known as *puls*, often made from barley, sometimes from millet or wheat, and, only if nothing else was available, from oats. Oats were native to Tartary, and brought to Arabia and Egypt about 2000 B.C. with the domesticated horse. The Romans thought little of oats, but imported them to the British Isles, where they became a staple of Scotland and Ireland. On the whole, oats are not much used for human consumption today. Only five percent of the world's crop reaches man's table, mainly in the form of rolled oats or oatmeal, and as a preservative in ice cream and other dairy products.

Wheat is known to have been cultivated in the Nile Valley as early as 5000 B.C. It is hard to grow on poor land, which accounts for its remaining a luxury in many areas until the eighteenth century. On the other hand, it grew wild on good land in Asia from

---

* Anacharsis, *Travels of Anacharsis the Younger in Greece*, Vol. II, p. 57.

the earliest times. By the first century, there was a thriving Mediterranean trade in wheat with ships going to and from Egypt, Italy, Sicily, Sardinia, and Gaul. Writing at that time, Columella spoke of seven varieties, including a kind of hard-grained wheat the Romans called *far*, after which the popular national dish of Brittany was named. The Romans also knew of wheat starch, which they used to thicken sauces. Pliny gives a recipe for making it in his *Natural History*. A hulled wheat porridge called *frumenty* (from *frumentum*, Latin for grain) was a common European dish until three hundred years ago. Not native to the New World, wheat was planted there by the early settlers.

After wheat, rye is the most important European cereal. Its cultivation may have started later than that of the previously mentioned grains. In any case, there are no traces of it in Egyptian ruins or Swiss lake dwellings of the Neolithic age. Rye is particularly important in central and northern Europe because it will flourish where poor soil or too cold a climate prevent the growing of wheat. Buckwheat, another sturdy grain that will grow in northern climates on poor soil, is the favorite staple of Russia in the form of *kasha*, a buckwheat porridge.

Maize, or Indian corn, was first seen in Europe when Columbus brought some back from America. No one knows how long the

Indians had been cultivating corn. Shriveled ears of corn have been found in pre-Incan tombs and graves, but its origins have been lost in history. It is assumed the grain was first cultivated in Peru and gradually spread over a period of centuries to other parts of the Americas. Because corn, unlike most plants, does not grow wild and cannot survive and spread without cultivation, the Indians regarded it as a divine gift.

Before the first explorers arrived in the New World, the Indians were preparing the many corn dishes we rightly consider native American foods: corn meal mush, hominy and grits, corn bread, roast and stewed corn, and popcorn. Corn is an important crop in Europe and the Americas today, but most of it is used for feeding and fattening livestock. Even in the United States, where corn is a common table food, four-fifths of the crop never leaves the farms, but is reserved for the animals. There are few regions of Europe where corn is served at the table, though a kind of corn meal mush is a staple in parts of Italy and Roumania.

CHEESE

Cheese has been made in Europe and the Near East for at least 4,000 years. Vases with draining holes for making cheese were found in prehistoric lake dwellings in Switzerland. The earliest dairy product, made long before butter, cheese was a standard ingredient in ancient pastries. Along with milk and honey it was a staple food for the Athenian army in early campaigns. Cheesecake was a Greek and Roman favorite. Athenaeus, writing in the early third century, devoted an entire section of his work on gastronomy to cheesecake.

Cheese has been made out of the milk of over a dozen mammals, from asses to zebus. Cows' milk cheese only became common about 200 B.C. One of the earliest descriptions of cheese making is Homer's passage depicting the Cyclops milking ewes and goats in his cave, curdling half the white milk and storing it in wicker baskets. In the fourth century B.C., playwright Antiphanes speaks of "green cheese, dry cheese, crushed cheese, grated cheese, sliced cheese, and cream cheese." The preferred cheese in Greece, however, was the Sicilian, available in many parts of the country from the fifth century B.C.

The Romans curdled their cheese with rennet, wild thistle flowers, or safflower seeds, or stirred it with a green branch from a fig tree as the early Greeks had done. They flavored it with thyme, green pine nuts, garlic, or pepper, or hardened it in brine, or basted it with new wine, or smoked it with apple-tree wood. One cheese which sounds particularly good was flavored with marjoram, mint, coriander, and onion before being sprinkled with chives and salted. Columella spoke of cheese as the basic food of tribes that did not grow grain, and of economic importance in settlements too remote to permit carrying the milk to market to sell.

The largest and most famous was the Po Valley cheese, Luna, named after the port from which it was shipped to Rome. Luna cheeses, stamped with the sign of the moon, weighed as much as a thousand pounds each. As Martial said, they "will afford your slaves a thousand lunches." Martial also mentions Venetian cheese, a Roman breakfast favorite, smoked cheese from Velabrum, and cheese from Trebula, which he recommended toasted or put in water, whatever that may have meant.

In their invasions of northern Europe, the Romans discovered new cheeses, importing the ones they preferred from various parts of the spreading empire. Two of these are still among the world's favorites: Roquefort from southern France and Cheshire from England.

Centuries later, Roquefort was singled out by Emperor Charlemagne, who first ate it in the company of the monks of Saint-Gall. It was they who taught him not to remove the green mold. He found it good enough, mold and all, to order two cases a year. The name "Roquefort" has been protected since the fourteenth century and limited to the produce of the town of the same name whose 2,000 inhabitants are all engaged in the manufacture of the famous cheese. (The town's 500 cats are also engaged as guards in the twenty-five caves in which Roquefort ripens for the market.)

Brie was also known to Charlemagne and singled out by him, as it was by the rulers of France for centuries to come. Talleyrand called Brie the king of cheese, but it might well have been known as the cheese of kings, for it enjoyed high royal favor in France from Charlemagne to the twelfth-century king, Philippe II, who used to give presents of Brie to distinguished visitors, through

Louis XVI, who was overcome by a sudden craving for red wine and Brie immediately after his arrest.

Among other cheeses of long pedigree are Gorgonzola, made in Italy since the ninth century, Parmesan, known by at least the thirteenth century, and Pont-l'Évêque, also known since the thirteenth century. Camembert, whose invention is sometimes credited to a Norman peasant, Marie Harel, in the late eighteenth century, is mentioned by name in two earlier French dictionaries according to André Simon, who traces the cheese to the twelfth century in his *Cheeses of the World*. Nevertheless a statue to Marie Harel stands in the village of Camembert to perpetuate the legend.

As the only dairy product that could be successfully shipped prior to rapid transport and refrigeration, cheese was a standard item of trade throughout Europe for centuries. There are hundreds of known, named varieties. Exactly how many there are depends on the system of classification; the French alone claim three to four hundred.

One of the curious notes in cheese history is the making of outsize cheeses to celebrate historic occasions. In 1801, the village of Cheshire, Massachusetts, made a mammoth cheese to present to President Jefferson. When Van Buren became President, he too was given a mammoth cheese, and after Jackson's inauguration, a huge cheese sent by New Englanders was exhibited for a week in a hall of the White House where it was gradually eaten away by the victorious Democrats. A less natural end befell a 1,200-pound Cheddar presented to Queen Victoria on her wedding by the inhabitants of a town in the Cheddar district. After the Queen had accepted the gift, the farmers asked permission to exhibit it, which she graciously granted. After the exhibition she did not want it back. The farmers began quarreling over the cheese, which disappeared into the fog of chancery like Dickens's Jarndyce and Jarndyce case, never to be heard of again. An even larger Cheddar, weighing no less than six tons, was exhibited at the New York State Fair in Syracuse in 1937.

The manufacture of cheese has given rise to the curious profession of cheese taster. Cheese tasters, in the case of the Dutch, are cheese rappers. By rapping his knuckles on the outside, an Edam cheese taster can tell how mature the interior is. In Roquefort, it is the chief taster who decides which cheeses are to be exported and to which countries they should be sent to accommodate the various regional tastes. There are amateurs who pride themselves on their ability to taste cheeses too. One Parisian cheese club is said to require aspiring members to identify, blindfolded, a large number of cheeses.

Although the French always serve cheese during a proper meal, they are not the greatest per-capita consumers, ranking only fourth. Italy leads, with the French and Swiss in second and third place, and the U. S. trailing in tenth at an average of only 10.6 pounds per year per person. In production, the U. S. leads with almost a quarter of the world total, while France places second with about 10 percent.

As every American knows, most American cheese comes from Wisconsin. To promote it, Wisconsin once passed a short-lived law requiring hotels and restaurants to serve at least two-thirds ounce of Wisconsin cheese with any meal costing over twenty-five cents. Many European cheeses are imitated in the U. S., but there are also a few native contributions: Liederkranz, pineapple, and brick. Cheddar is by far the most popular, accounting for 80 percent of the cheese sold in the U. S.

Only a hundred years ago, most cheese on the market, even in the U. S. A., was farm made. It consequently varied greatly in quality even when made by the same farmer. Modern cheeses, produced commercially in mass, are standardized in taste, presentation, and size. Like modern fruits, they are of a generally acceptable, little changing quality, instead of being either inedible or superb. But they are what we shall have from now on. André Simon's *Cheeses of the World* contains sad news for turophiles. He points out that it is a delusion to think the cheese market may ultimately bow to the wishes of the more discriminating consumers. It could not, because the farmer earns more by selling liquid milk than by making good cheese; furthermore, in order to have the greatest possible quantity of milk to sell, he sacrifices quality by replacing the Guernsey or Gloucestershire breeds with others that produce more, though more watery milk. What is left over is what goes into the making of cheese.

CHERRY

Cherry trees grew wild in Persia, Armenia, Greece, Italy, England, and North America. Lucullus, Roman general and epicure, is sometimes credited with having brought the cherry to Rome from the Black Sea kingdom of Pontus in Asia Minor in the first century B.C. He is also said to have named it *cerasus* after a city of that name in Pontus.

It has been fairly well established that what Lucullus brought back was a new type of cherry, the *Prunus cerasus*, which had been cultivated in the Near East for centuries. Before Lucullus returned from Asia, the Romans knew only an acid, black, wild cherry they called "corna," that has been identified as *Prunus avium*.

By the first century A.D., cherries were common in Roman orchards and had been taken from Rome to Egypt (where Pliny reports they did badly) and to Britain (where they did much better). A few hundred years later, their culture was so advanced that the agricultural expert Palladius could discourse on ways to breed pitless cherries.

CHICKEN

Primitive people have raised chickens in many parts of the New World and the Old since history began. Most Incan families had chickens; chicken raising was common in pre-Roman Gaul, England, and Germany. The Greeks learned of chickens from the Asians in the sixth century B.C., and for a long time the fowl were known as "birds of Persia." Cocks were a common sacrificial offering for people who could not afford an ox or a sow.

The Romans kept chickens in the fourth century B.C. and quickly came to appreciate the delicacy of capons. According to one story, when a Roman consul, unable to sleep because of the noise from everyone's chickens, passed a law forbidding the cries of birds from households in the city, the Romans castrated the cocks, turning them into capons.

Chicken has been alternately prized and despised as a food. Caesar notes the Britons were forbidden by their religion to eat hen or goose, but bred them for pleasure. In the Middle Ages, when every country dweller had a few chickens and most people lived in the country, chicken was common food—so common that it came to be looked down on as food for the poor. *Poule-au-pot*, a thick chicken soup that makes a meal, was popular in late sixteenth-century France when Henri IV is said to have promised everyone a chicken every Sunday, anticipating by several centuries the 1932 Republican slogan. In the seventeenth century, chickens were growing scarce and expensive in England. To serve poultry became a sign of having arrived in the world. Chicken was then a rare holiday dish for the lower classes and a Sunday treat for the bourgeois. Thus it remained up to the very recent development of the poultry industry with its commercially prepared feed, rapid forcing of growth, and assembly line preparation, packaging, and distribution.

CHICORY

Chicory, endive, and Belgian endive are sometimes confused. Chicory, or *Cichorium intybus*, is a perennial whose roasted root is sometimes added to coffee and whose curly leaves are used in salad. The endive *(Cichorium endivia)* is an annual or biennial plant closely related to chicory and also used in salad. To add to the confusion, it is sometimes referred to as escarole. The blanched crown of chicory is also called endive, or sometimes Belgian endive, because it was in Belgium that the blanching process was developed.

The Belgian endive was discovered in 1850 by the chief gardener of the Belgian Horticultural Society, who had some chicory plants in a dark basement and noticed that, if earth was pressed around them, the leaves folded to form a hard, white salad cone. The growing of endives has remained a fairly exclusive Belgian process.

Belgian endives were unknown in ancient times, but the curly-leaved salad was cultivated in early Egypt where, Pliny tells us, it grew wild. Several varieties of chicorylike plants were listed by Theophrastus in the third century B.C. The Romans were also familiar with several varieties which they ate both raw and cooked. In Spain, the plant reaches its peak of whiteness and sweetness in February, and a dish featuring chicory with a very peppery sauce is a specialty of the Catalan coast in that month. A recipe given by Alexandre Dumas presents an interesting contrast; he mixes chicory leaves with violet petals and sprinkles them with two or three pinches of a Florentine iris used in sachets.

COFFEE

Coffee is important in the history of food because it transformed the first meal of the day. Before coffee became popular, people drank beer for breakfast, accompanied, if they could afford it, by cold meats, fish, cheese, and salt or dried herring. Only after coffee and chocolate became breakfast beverages did breads, eggs, and marmalade become common breakfast fare.

When and where coffee was first drunk is not certain. The place most often cited is Yemen, though some sources say it was Abyssinia or the Sudan. The often repeated and probably apocryphal story of the discovery of coffee goes as follows: Once upon a time, somewhere between the sixth and thirteenth centuries, a Muslim priest in Yemen noticed that goats were gayer and livelier after eating the berries of a certain plant. The priest roasted the berries, infused them, and discovered coffee.

By the fourteenth century, coffee was very popular in the Middle East. Many Muslim authorities frowned on it and even proscribed it in the sixteenth century in a series of edicts, some of which were promptly revoked and all of which were ignored. Aroused religious fanatics (Muhammad had not drunk coffee; why should his followers?) persecuted coffee lovers. Sultans and sheikhs, who found cafés and coffee drinking stimulated an undesirable intellectual ferment, tried for three decades to eliminate the new beverage. Despite opposition, coffee gained public favor steadily. By the seventeenth century, a wife not provided her fair share of coffee had grounds for divorce in Turkey.

In Europe, coffee aroused similar opposition on the part of the authorities and a similar, immediate, and passionate attachment on the part of addicts, particularly among the upper classes and intellectuals. (Madame de Sévigné was an exception; she predicted with equal inaccuracy that both coffee and Racine would go out of fashion.) As late as the beginning of the nineteenth century, Grimod de la Reynière wrote that coffee was harmful for women, who risked losing their health, freshness, and lovers by indulging in it. On the other hand, an early advertisement publicized coffee as protection against everything from eyesores to "the king's Evil." Rossini believed it stimulated the mind, though for a limited time. "Coffee," he once remarked to Balzac, "is a matter of 15 or 20 days, which is luckily time enough to write an opera." [81]

The Italians were the first Europeans to try coffee, some time early in the sixteenth century. Coffee had a number of counts against it from the start. It was new, it was a stimulant, and it came from the land of infidels. The medical profession predicted dire consequences. The Council of Leipzig forbade its sale. Poets wrote satires on coffee; Bach wrote an amusing *Coffee Cantata*. Catholic priests in Italy claimed the devil had given coffee to the infidels and that anyone who drank it endangered his soul. They proposed condemning it, but Pope Clement VIII put it to the test by trying it, and liked it. He is reported to have said, "Why, this Satan's drink is so delicious that it would be a pity to let the infidels have exclusive use of it. We shall fool Satan by baptizing it, and making it a truly Christian beverage." [82]

Coffee reached France and England later, about the middle of the seventeenth century. After the first coffee house opened in England in 1650, coffee houses multiplied so rapidly that by 1789 there were over 2,000 in London alone. Perhaps one of the reasons for their popularity was that coffee cost less than ale, wine, or other alcohol. (Some doctors and social reformers welcomed coffee as an antidote to alcoholism.) Whatever the reason for their rapid success, coffee houses became centers of literary meetings, intellectual discussions, and political unrest. Charles II felt cafés were so politically dangerous that he tried (unsuccessfully) to close them in 1675. Trade as well as politics drew people to coffee houses. Each trade or profession had its own favorite house, where business was often transacted. Lloyds of London began as a coffee house, patronized mainly by ship underwriters and named after the man who ran it, Edward Lloyd. For a time the clientele of Lloyd's coffee house was the only body issuing marine insurance.

In Germany, Frederick the Great regarded coffee as a noble drink and tried to limit it to the court. To emphasize its aristocratic nature, he used to brew it with champagne. In France, coffee was first made fashionable by the Turkish Ambassador Soliman Aga, who served it at his receptions. Louis XIV liked to brew his own coffee over an alcohol lamp for his intimate guests.

The beverage became popular with the general public when it was offered at the fair of Saint-Germain in 1672 by an enterprising Armenian. Thereafter, cafés with the mirrored walls and marble-topped tables still seen in France began to open. One of these, Procope, which opened in Paris in 1675, still exists on the rue de l'Ancienne-Comédie with its old décor, but not its old habitués: Rousseau, Danton, Marat, Robespierre, Bonaparte, Verlaine, Jules Ferry, Anatole France and Gambetta. In France as in England, cafés were political hotbeds. French historian Michelet wrote of 1789 that there was no doubt the outbreak of revolution could be traced in part to the change in people's habits and temperaments wrought by the advent of the café.

In 1723, the French government charged Captain de Clieu with taking the first coffee plant to the Americas. The voyage was very long, so long, and accompanied by such shortages, that in order to keep the plant alive, the captain shared his water ration with it, half and half. It lived to grow in Martinique and became the ancestor of most American coffee plants and the founder of the Latin American plantations that were of world importance by the early nineteenth century. While most of the world's very limited coffee supply came from Yemen until the end of the seventeenth century, the Western Hemisphere now produces 75 percent of the world's total.

Coffee syrups were invented in the late seventeenth century, coffee comfits in the eighteenth. It was in the eighteenth, and above all nineteenth, century that coffee began to be used in recipes. Its popularity as a beverage declined in England in favor of tea while rising steadily in France. Paris had only 700 cafés in 1789; by 1843, it had 3,000. Coffee drinking survived the continental blockade of 1807–1811, though the French had to resort to putting chicory in their coffee (as they still do) and substituting beet sugar for cane. Napoleon made coffee the soldiers' drink because he thought it a less dangerous stimulant than alcohol.

The colonies followed England in adopting tea. Though coffee could be had in some seventeenth-century American taverns, it was not common until after the Boston Tea Party, when drinking coffee became an act of patriotism. Today, despite a steady decline in the 1960's, the United States consumes about half the world's supply of coffee, averaging 2.4 cups per day per person—man, woman, and child. Yet it does not have the highest consumption per capita; Sweden does.

The coffee industry has given rise to the highly specialized profession of coffee tasting. According to the Coffee Brewing Center of New York, new coffee tasters are trained by the old timers over a period of about three years. No special talents are required for the job, but nonsmokers are preferred. Contrary to popular belief, the tasters could not take a can of blended coffee off a grocery shelf and identify the source of the ingredients, and it is not their job to do so. Their task is to decide whether certain growths will blend well together. The country, plantation, and hillside from which coffee comes can only be identified in unblended coffee. The man who identifies it is not the coffee taster, but a registered coffee grader, who does it not by taste but by looking at the green bean.

CUCUMBERS

Cucumbers originated in northwest India, where they have been cultivated for over 3,000 years. The Greeks knew three varieties by the third century B.C. In first-century Rome, according to Columella, Tiberius managed to have a supply of fresh cucumbers almost all year by having them forced in baskets covered with slabs of transparent stone that were put in the sun in a sheltered spot from midwinter through spring. The most convenient system, Columella added, was to put the baskets of plants in large containers mounted on wheels so that they could be brought in and out of the sun easily. Columella also suggested soaking cucumber seeds in milk or mead before sowing to make the vegetable sweeter.

The Apicius cookbook gives three recipes for cucumber, including a kind of stew. Pliny, who recommended the cucumber for a number of ills such as gout, toothache, deafness, and impetigo, preferred cucumber peeled and cooked in oil, vinegar, and honey.

Though enjoyed in the kingdom of Aragon and in France in the thirteenth century, the cucumber was only introduced to England in the late sixteenth. It was then considered unhealthy. Unhealthy or not, in the form of dill pickles, cucumbers became very popular in the seventeenth century. In the eighteenth, cucumbers were constantly in use: stuffed, as garnishes, and in stews, sauces, and salads. All English books of that time included at least one recipe for cucumber sauce.

CURRANT

There are two entirely different fruits known as currants. One, a small acid berry, is used fresh. The other, used dried, is a small, highly flavored grape grown almost exclusively in Greece. Unknown until the fourteenth century, currants are now a chief commercial export from Greek vineyards. Their golden age, however, was in the fifteenth, sixteenth, and seventeenth centuries when they were so freely used in stews, stuffings, breads, pastries, and puddings that in 1640, William Lithgow wrote of England, "Where some liquorous lips forsooth can now hardly digest Bread, Pastries, Broth and bag puddings without these currants." [83]

The name "currant" is a corruption of Corinth derived from the medieval "raisins de corauntz," as the dried grapes were then called.

DATE

Dates were cultivated in ancient Egypt, where a potent date wine was popular. As early as 2600 B.C. there is a reference to the extraction of sweet juice from date palms. The Greeks and Romans imported dates, first mentioned in Greece in the fifth century B.C. By the first century, forty-nine kinds were known in Rome.

The date palm was never cultivated for fruit in Europe because it thrives only in the latitude of the Canary Islands and North Africa. Dates grown along the European shores of the Mediterranean are ornamentals. The date palm grew well, however, in the warmer climates of the Americas, to which Spanish missionaries brought it in the eighteenth and early nineteenth centuries.

DOG

Hippocrates recommended dog meat as strengthening and digestible. The Romans favored puppies. Suckling puppies were thought to be such pure food that they took the place of sacrificial victims to placate the divinities and were often served at inaugural banquets in the early days, according to Pliny, who adds that even in his times (the first century A.D.), puppy flesh was presented at dinners held in honor of the gods.

North American Indians also ate dogs. Young dogs were sold in the marketplace in Aztec Mexico. In Europe, since the fall of Rome, dogs have been eaten only in times of shortage.

DONKEY

The Romans liked donkey meat, particularly in sausage stuffing, but generally preferred the imported wild asses Persians considered royal food. When the Roman statesman Maecenas, who was rich enough to afford whatever he wanted, offered stewed marinated donkey meat to his guests in the first century B.C., it was the first time domestic ass had been served in Rome. Donkey enjoyed a brief vogue thereafter.

Much later, in sixteenth-century France, Chancellor Duprat bred and fattened donkeys for his table, according to Alexandre Dumas. *Larousse gastronomique* assures us that when the English besieged Malta and drove the inhabitants to eating dogs, cats, rats, and donkeys, they became so fond of the latter that they preferred it to beef and veal. Donkey meat was served again during the siege of Paris in the Franco-Prussian war of 1871, but has since sunk into disuse, though, according to *Larousse gastronomique*, it is tasty and much superior in flavor to the horsemeat sold in France today.

DORMOUSE

The dormouse is one of many foods once prized and no longer in favor. Little known in Greece, dormice were sought after in Rome.

From the beginning of the first century, when one Q. Fulvius Lupinus noticed the animals put on weight in winter when hibernating in hollow trees, the Romans fattened them in the dark in special jars called *gliraria*. These were vases with ramps inside for the dormouse to walk on and holes in which his favorite nuts were stored. Dormice were valued according to their weight. To be certain his guests appreciated the dish at its true value, the Roman host sometimes had dormice weighed at the table.

Dormice were proscribed by the sumptuary law of 115 B.C., but the Romans continued to enjoy them nevertheless. The Apicius cookbook gives a recipe for roast dormouse stuffed with ground pork, pepper, nuts, and silphium. At Trimalchio's luxurious dinner in *The Satyricon*, dormice were served with honey and poppy seed.

Dormice were mentioned as food by Rabelais, and a recipe for preparing them was included in a sixteenth-century Italian cookbook.

EGG

When we think of eggs, we think of hens' eggs, but many other kinds have been eaten. The Romans ate eggs from hens, ducks, geese, partridge, pigeons, pheasants, ostriches, and peacocks; the latter were the most esteemed. Lapwing, plover, and, particularly, turtle eggs are prized by gourmets. Duck eggs are still popular in parts of western Europe. Ostrich and flamingo eggs were for sale in France in the nineteenth century, according to Alexandre Dumas who included a recipe for Arabian omelet (made of ostrich and flamingo eggs, of course) in his *Grand dictionnaire de cuisine*. "Thanks to the zoos that have been established even in secondary cities," he wrote, "ostrich and flamingo eggs are now available almost everywhere. They sell at one franc each today, and each ostrich egg is good for ten hens' eggs."

Eggs have been used much as they are now since Greek and Roman times: fried, in omelets, pancakes, and in sauces. Eggs in pastry hoods were one of the delicacies of a dinner described in Petronius' *Satyricon*. One difference in the use of eggs today lies in the quantity recipes require. One fifteenth-century recipe calls for an even one thousand eggs. Through the Middle Ages and up to very recent times, an astonishing number, sometimes several dozen, were normally used in cake baking in order to make cakes rise; baking powder was only invented in the midnineteenth century. Another discarded custom is the serving of hard-boiled eggs after dessert; Louis XIV used to end his meals this way. He had classic examples to follow; eggs were often served as part of the last course in ancient Greece, along with nuts and pastries.

For centuries man has been looking for a good way to preserve eggs. Until the invention of refrigeration, the methods were varied and the results not very satisfactory. Eggs were put in water, oil, sand, ashes, salt, or sawdust, or were coated with suet. An early mention of powdered eggs can be found in the fourteenth-century *Chronicles* of Jean Froissart, who listed powdered egg yolks among the provisions for Charles VI's army.

Diodorus, a historian of the first century B.C., claims eggs were artificially hatched in Egypt in the heat produced by manure. But the forced mass production of eggs, the egg industry, as it were, developed much later. As E. Parmalee Prentice wrote in *Hunger and History*, "It is a striking phenomenon of history that though the egg is one of the oldest human foods, the business of producing eggs on a large scale is hardly older than the manufacture of motor cars and radios."

Eggs have long had a mystical and religious significance connected with birth and rebirth. Decorated eggs only became part of the popular customs of Christian Easter celebrations in about the sixteenth century, but egg decoration is believed to have been practiced in the Ukraine several thousand years before Christ.

Outsized eggs seem to have held a special fascination. Through the late Middle Ages and the Renaissance, a favorite recipe combined quantities of yolks, then quantities of whites, to make a kind of monster egg, sometimes the size of twenty normal ones.* These giant eggs were used for "grand sallets." The fascination has not died. According to a news item, a 13,000-egg omelet was displayed as a work of art in a Swiss department store in April, 1969.

EGGPLANT

The eggplant, or *Solanum melongena*, is, like the potato, a member of the nightshade family. A native of southeastern Asia, it is

---

* For recipe, see page 318.

one of the more recent European vegetables, having been introduced to France and England only in the sixteenth and seventeenth centuries, though it was eaten in Catalonia three to four hundred years earlier.

Once known as *Mala insana* (mad apple) because of its supposed resemblance to mandrake, eggplant was slow to find acceptance. In 1596, English herbalist Gerard recommended growing the plant for decoration instead of food: "I rather wish Englishmen to content themselves with the meate and sauce of our own countrey than with fruite and sauce eaten with such perill: for, doubtless, these apples have a mischeevious quality; the use thereof is utterly to be forsaken." Gerard's words apparently echoed popular sentiment, for though the eggplant found its way to England at the end of the sixteenth century, it spent 220 years in the garden before it reached the table.

ELEPHANT

Dumas wrote in 1869, "Cochin China is probably the only country where elephants are eaten today and considered a great delicacy. When the king has one killed for his table, he sends pieces to grandees as a mark of special favor." [84] The trunk and feet were particularly appreciated in ancient times and again, during the siege of Paris in the Franco-Prussian War, when the city zoo sold all its animals, including the two famous elephants Castor and Pollux, because it could no longer feed them. It was during the siege that the famous restaurant Voisin became known for its preparation of elephant trunk, appropriately seasoned with *sauce chasseur*.

FIG

. . . And peck at fodder whereon slaves are fed,
A modicum of figs and barley bread.
                    —Phoenix (*ca.* 280 B.C.)

The fig is one of the oldest Mediterranean foods. One of the speakers at the banquet in Athenaeus' gastronomical work of the early third century called it the first cultivated fruit, "made to be the guide of men to civilization." Grown in early Egypt, it was a Greek and Roman staple. Even a generation ago it was a staple food in peasant Spain where a piece of bread and a few figs sometimes made a meal.

According to a story told by classical authors, figs were once so important in the part of present-day Greece then known as Attica that their export was forbidden. Like other similar laws, this one gave rise to smuggling, and smuggling gave rise to informers. The latter came to be called "fig detectives" or, in Greek, *sycophants*, from the Greek word for fig *(sykon)* and the verb to show *(phainein)*. Sycophant later came to mean false accuser or false adviser and thence progressed to its present meaning of flatterer, particularly flatterer of the great.

The story may not be true. Plutarch expressed doubt that the export of figs from Attica was ever actually forbidden. Athenaeus, who gives a version of the story of fig detectives, also quotes another authority who claimed the term "sycophant" was first given to trustworthy citizens in charge of collecting fines and taxes, consisting of figs, wine, and oils, for public expenditures.

The Romans were familiar with a variety of figs. Columella mentions a total of nine in the first century; Macrobius, writing four centuries later, cites two dozen. Besides eating them with bread, the Romans made them into vinegar and wine and preserved them in various ways. Preserved figs were found in jars in Pompeii, and Columella gives several recipes for preparing them. Some are simply dried and stored in vessels with fennel; others are split and formed into loaves or pressed into the shape of flowers or stars. Columella's recipe for fig balls is particularly appetizing:

> Remove stems, spread figs in sun. When slightly dry but not hard, heap in stone or earthenware basin. Wash feet and tread with toasted sesame seeds, Egyptian anise, fennel, and cumin. Wrap up medium-sized balls in fig leaves. Put on racks, dry, and store in pitch-treated vessels. Sometimes baked before storing.[85]

The Spanish took the fig tree to the New World, but almost all figs still come from the areas where they have always been grown.

FISH
(see also *CARP, CAVIAR, HERRING, STURGEON*)

The Belly, miracle of ingenuity,
Brings the parrot-wrasse,
Submerged in Sicilian water,
Alive to the table;
Pulls oysters from the Lucrine Lake
To make a sale to the palate
The high price most of the flavour.
    —Petronius, *The Satyricon*, No. 119

One of the oldest foods, fish is one of the most neglected today. For the world as a whole, fish represents only 2 percent of foods consumed. It has been alternately despised and prized throughout history. In Mesopotamia, fresh and smoked fish were eaten but were scarce enough to be served only at the banquets of the rich. The ancient Egyptians liked fish, and the Hebrews around the Sea of Galilee lived on it. Yet, if we are to judge from one of the earliest written records of Western civilization, fish was unpopular food in Homerian times. Homer shows familiarity with fishing; he mentions long rods, casting, ox-horn lures, and barbed hooks. However he mentions them only to write of men driven to fish for lack of other food. To Homer's heroes, fish was preferable to starvation, nothing more.

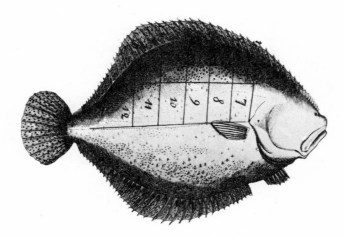

This attitude soon changed. Athenaeus' gastronomical anthology devotes 175 pages to references to fish in Greek and Roman sources. As early as the eighth century B.C., Hesiod called sturgeon the best pickled or salted food to be had. Epicharmus wrote in the sixth century B.C. that sturgeon was worth its weight in bronze. Two centuries later, the wealthy were enjoying a vast variety of fresh fish while the masses had salt or dried fish to accompany their inevitable porridge. Athenaeus identifies between 60 and 65 kinds of fish mentioned in sources of the fourth century B.C., in addition to dozens of varieties of shellfish.

Because fish were plentiful around Athens, only rare or imported ones were prized by the rich. They ate tuna from Byzantium, eels from Boeotia (in central Greece), crayfish from an island in the western Aegean, sprats and bream from an island off the east coast, black perch from the Nile, huge tuna hearts packed in jars from Cadiz (Spain) or Tarentum (Italy), and mussels from Pontus (Asia Minor). Rare fish brought exorbitant prices. A character in a play of about 300 B.C. by Diphilus of Sinope boasts of buying a conger eel for its weight in gold. Antiphanes, in a play written in the first half of the fourth century B.C., has a character say: "I used to think that the Gorgons were a fiction, but whenever I go to market, I am strong in my belief in them; for one glance at the fishmongers and I am straight away turned to stone. Therefore I must necessarily talk to them with my face turned away, for if I see what a small-sized fish it is for which they charge such a high price, I am then and there frozen solid." [86]

Efforts were made to control fishmongers at a very early date. About 400 B.C., Xenarchus comments that they were no longer allowed to rinse their wares to freshen them. A half century later, Alexis wrote in a play of a legislator proposing a law requiring fishmongers to sell their fish standing, not seated at their ease.

Like the early Greeks, the early Romans ate small quantities of fish. As Rome prospered, fish became a luxury. By the second century B.C., Cato the Elder had reason to exclaim he "wondered how a city could continue to exist unscathed in which a fish sold for more than an ox!" [87] Fish aroused the interest of gourmets more than any other food, and fortunes were paid for favorites. Athenaeus comments that fishmongers of first-century Rome were equal to those in Antiphanes' play of five centuries earlier. Juvenal tells of a mullet going for 6,000 sesterces, a good price for a fish that weighed no more than two pounds. Pliny told of a man paying 8,000 sesterces for a mullet, and Suetonius surpassed them both with a story of three mullets sold for 30,000 sesterces in the reign of Tiberius.

There were changes of fashion in fishes. According to Pliny, the early Romans considered sturgeon or sterlet the best, though by Pliny's time, the first century, while still as rare, it was held in no esteem. Later the sea wolf came into vogue along with a fish known as *asellus*, believed to be cod. Pliny's contemporaries put the liver of parrot-wrasse first. Next ranked lamprey, followed by mullet, which was very expensive indeed, as we have seen. Mullet was particularly appreciated because it changed color in dying. Seneca described dying mullet enclosed in globes of glass through which the variety of colors and the red scales gradually growing paler and paler would be watched by those about to eat it.

The particular place where a fish was caught made a great deal of difference to Roman gourmets. The discriminating Roman demanded pike caught between two specific bridges in the Tiber. Gourmets prided themselves on pinpointing an oyster bed by the taste of the oyster, as wine lovers identify the vineyard. Juvenal wrote of one of these gourmets in his Fourth Satire:

> No man in my day was a greater
> Gourmet: he knew, at the very first bite, what bed
> An oyster came from, Circeii, Lake Lucrinus
> Or Richborough: sea-urchins he placed with a single glance.

The transport of fish from afar posed a problem, yet the Romans ate fresh fish from the Rhine and the Danube, and, as Juvenal's satire shows, oysters from England. Many fish were dried, salted, or preserved in honey. For fresh fish, water tanks may have been used on ships. Athenaeus cites the example of King Hieron of Syracuse, who equipped a wheat-transport ship with a fish tank filled with seawater in the third century B.C.

The difficulties of transporting fresh fish and the difficulty of obtaining it when the weather was bad led Romans to establish reservoirs in which to keep and, in some cases, fatten fish for use on the table. The idea was not original. Egyptian pharaohs had royal fish ponds; so did the Sumerian King Gudea in 2340 B.C.

The Greeks built reservoirs for their beloved eels. Sicily was far more advanced in pisciculture. About the beginning of the fifth century B.C., the inhabitants of Agrigentum built a pool fourteen hundred yards in circumference and ten yards deep, into which they conducted water from neighboring rivers to keep large numbers of fish for the table.

From the day in about 90 B.C. when Licinius Murena established the first Roman seawater preserve for fish breeding and stocking, he was copied by other Roman aristocrats, the Philippi, the Hortensii, Lucullus, and C. Hirtius. The Romans had tried stocking fish in inland lakes a century earlier, but from the first century B.C., freshwater fish were left to the poor.

Roman nobles rivaled each other in spending money and effort on sea reservoirs, which were costly to build, costly to stock, and costly to maintain. The reservoirs had to have fresh supplies of water daily, yet be constructed to keep the fish from escaping. They had to be designed for the algae and type of bottom (mud, sand, or rock) the particular species favored. In addition, the fish had to be fed, usually on bread, figs, cheese, berries, and scraps from the fish market. Quintus Hortensius kept an army of fishermen to catch minnows for feed, and C. Hirtius spent two million sesterces just on bait for his eels. Despite the expense, fish reservoirs multiplied. By the first century A.D., they were common throughout Italy and to be found as far from Rome as Phoenicia and Narbonne.

Eels were a particular favorite. Hirtius, the first to breed them in a separate preserve, stocked enough to be able to give Caesar 6,000 for his triumphal banquets in 45 and 46 B.C. Hortensius became so attached to one eel that he is said to have wept when it died, and one Roman socialite adorned her favorite with earrings. Vedius Pollio, a Roman knight, fed slaves who displeased him to his eels, though this was unusual enough to arouse wide comment and the censure of Emperor Augustus.* The Romans also stocked fish in open waters. Parrot wrasse was imported live from the Carpathian Sea on Tiberius' orders and successfully established near the mouth of the Tiber.

---

* Pliny the Elder, *Natural History*, Book IX: 39. According to versions given by other Roman authors, there was only one slave in question, and Emperor Augustus intervened to save him and reprimand Pollio.

The building of artificial ponds in which to keep fish fresh was continued in many countries after the Roman Empire fell. An abundant supply of fish regardless of weather or distance from the sea was very important in Catholic Europe. The breaking of a religious fast without special permission was a serious offense, punishable by death in certain epochs (under Charlemagne, for example). Meat eating on a fast day denoted the heretic, and heretics risked being burned at the stake. Only after the Reformation did fish consumption and respect for fast days begin to fall.

Many fish we eat today and others we no longer eat were popular in the Middle Ages. The porpoise was served whole at dinners of the rich throughout the sixteenth century; porpoise pudding was a favorite. Whale was a royal dish in fifteenth-century England, and lamprey a favorite at the medieval English court.

In the latter half of the sixteenth century, fish days were of great importance, first because of the need to encourage the building of ships and training of sailors for the navy; secondly because of the scarcity and high price of meat. A proclamation of 1563 establishing a second fish day per week stated the measure was "necessary for the restoring of the navy of England." Enforcing two fish days per week, particularly when the second was not a religious day of abstinence, proved so difficult that the attempt was soon abandoned.

Fish remained an expensive luxury except at the sea coast until the invention of the railroad. Chronicles and letters of seventeenth- and eighteenth-century France pass in silence over the meats served at banquets while going into ecstasies over an abundance of fish. It is difficult to conceive, but fresh fish from the Mediterranean simply was not available in Paris, even to the king. Louis XV offered a handsome reward to anyone able to bring a fresh gilt-head to Paris, but no one stepped forward to claim it.

FLOWERS
(see also ROSE)

Flowers have always been used in cooking and still are. Cauliflower is a true flower. Many of our spices are flowers. The caper is a pickled flower bud, the clove is a dried flower bud, and saffron the stigma of a type of crocus. However, from Greek times through the nineteenth century, flowers and flower essences were used in far greater variety than today. Iris, violets, roses, marigolds, pop-pies, cornflowers, and cowslips were once used like spices and herbs. The ancients ate them in salads, as vegetables, and made them into wine and vinegar. Later they were used for coloring and in fritters, syrups, conserves, pastes, pastries, ices, custards, candies, and decorations for sweets. Sometimes it was the unopened buds and young shoots that were eaten, or the leaves, sometimes the petals of the whole flower, sometimes the roots, as in the case of iris bulbs and dahlia roots.

Violets, which were planted in Roman gardens, were a standard item on the medieval menu, often served chopped with lettuce and onions for salad or put in a broth. Cowslips and violets were made into coloring syrups and cooked in custards and omelets. Violets pounded in a mortar with marigolds, cowslips, primroses, bugloss, and sugar were made into a paste with tragacanth gum and water in Tudor England, while the French liked a pudding of boiled pounded violets, milk, honey, and flour. A salad recipe from a seventeenth-century English cookbook calls for buds of cowslips, violets, and primroses mixed with strawberries.

Sunflower seeds are still important in parts of the world, the leaves of young nasturtiums are still recommended as a happy addition to salads by contemporary gourmets, dandelion greens are a not uncommon vegetable, and candied flowers still top a few pastries. There is rose-hip jam too. Otherwise few flowers other than spices and cauliflower are used in foods today.

FRUIT
(see also individual entries)

Fruits were picked and eaten by primitive man wherever they grew wild. They were planted very early in history. The ancient Egyptians cultivated apples, dates, figs, sycamore figs, grapes, melons, and pomegranates. The apple, olive, and pomegranate were introduced between the eighteenth and sixteenth centuries B.C. The Greeks knew pears, medlars, and myrtle berries as well, and added peaches and apricots after Alexander the Great's eastern expeditions of the fourth century B.C. The chief Mediterranean fruit, however, was that old staple, the fig, fresh or dried.

Though both Greeks and Romans ate fruit, Galen, the second-century physician whose influence on diet and medicine persisted through the Renaissance, regarded fruit with suspicion, pointing out that his father had lived to the age of one hundred by virtue of never eating it. The Romans ate fruit in quantity nevertheless. After the Empire was established, they sought special varieties of fruit everywhere. They ate almonds, apples, apricots, blackberries, blueberries, cherries, cornel berries, citrons, figs, gooseberries, melons, mulberries, myrtle, quince, peaches, pears, plums, pomegranates, raspberries, sorb apples, strawberries, and watermelon. Berries came from northern Italy, pomegranates from Africa, large cherries from Pontus, peaches from Persia, pears and plums from Armenia and Greece, citrons from Media (now Iran), and so on. Wherever they found new foods, they imported both plant and produce. They exported plants too. It is the Romans who brought apples, cherries, chestnuts, figs, mulberries, plums, quince, and walnuts to England, almonds, peaches, and pears to Egypt, and more extensive vineyards to Gaul.

The Romans gave a great deal of importance to the preserving of fruit and had many ingenious methods, so effective that when Gallienus was Emperor in the middle of the third century, he was served melons in the depth of winter, green figs and apples out of season, and grapes preserved for three years. Cato the Elder, writing of the proper housekeeper, said she "must have a large store of dried pears, [dried] sorbs, figs, raisins, sorbs in must, preserved pears and grapes and quinces. She must also keep preserved grapes in grape pulp and pots buried in the ground, as well as fresh Praenestine nuts kept in the same way, and Scantian quinces in jars, and other fruit that are usually preserved as well as wild fruits. All these she must store away diligently every year." [88]

Fruit fell from favor at the end of the Roman Empire. Many fruits once popular were consigned to oblivion, to be rediscovered and brought back to Europe by the Crusaders. Though fruit was plentiful in summer during the Middle Ages, with the exception of Spain, little was eaten, and most of it was viewed with suspicion and distrust. It only returned to favor very gradually in the fifteenth, sixteenth, and seventeenth centuries, during which many new fruits were discovered or rediscovered in Europe, Asia, and the New World.

Dried fruits—figs, raisins, prunes, pears, cherries, and nuts— were the first to appear on medieval tables. Dried fruits were imported from the Levant and Portugal to England as early as the thirteenth century and were common in great houses in the sixteenth. Candied fruits made with sugar or honey were very fashionable, as were berries preserved in sugar, known as sukets. These delicacies, and the oranges that were sought after from the sixteenth century on, were limited to the upper classes.

Oranges were almost the only fresh fruit eaten by the aristocracy, who clung to the belief that raw fruit was generally dangerous. The poor undoubtedly ate more fruit than the rich. The populace ate fruit in the street and at places of amusement at any time of day in sixteenth- and seventeenth-century England.

After 1800, when the usefulness of lemons and limes in preventing scurvy had been established, every English ship leaving port for foreign lands was required by law to carry a supply of lemon or lime juice. This use of limes gave British seamen the nickname of "Limey." Many new fruits were cultivated in France and England in the sixteenth and seventeenth centuries, among them apricots, currants, gooseberries, peaches, raspberries, strawberries, muskmelons, and watermelons. It became fashionable to plant orchards around great country houses. The new gentry of England, who established many new estates, were particularly enterprising in the cultivation of fruit. Nevertheless many scorned fruit as tasteless, perhaps in contrast to the highly spiced dishes then popular. In 1655, Dr. Thomas Muffet wrote in *Health's Improvement* that he found melons, pears, apples, and plums insipid —"tasting just of nothing."

Botanically, fruit includes nuts, beans, the squash-cucumber-pumpkin-watermelon family, tomatoes, wheat, and a few other odd items, but the popular application of the term, so much closer to the use of fruit in cooking and serving, seemed preferable here.

GAME

La Chasse est un plaisir noble, et
qui n'appartient qu'a la Noblesse.
—Louis Liger, *Le Ménage de la ville et des champs* (1712) *

Game was man's meat from primitive to feudal times. The early Greeks hunted and ate every wild animal in Greece, which then

* "Hunting is a noble pleasure, and one that belongs only to the nobility."

boasted of lions and panthers. The Romans, who were particularly fond of wild boar and wild sow, bred game by planting fruits attractive to wild animals on their estates. What the game ate made a great deal of difference to the Roman epicure, who would only eat fox during the season of ripe grapes, when the foxes fed on them.

The first Roman to establish a large park for big game was Q. Fulvius Lippinus, who made an enclosure of about twenty-five acres for boar, deer, and wild sheep on his estate in the first century B.C. The Romans had previously had warrens for rabbits, and the idea of enclosures for larger game was not original with them. More than twenty centuries earlier, the Egyptians of the Old Kingdom had domesticated oryx, gazelles, hyenas, and antelope in parks. They had even force-fed wild animals. The Persians, too, had game parks; so did the Mesopotamians, at least from the time of Tilgath Pileser I (*ca.* 1100 B.C.).

Lucullus and other rich Romans quickly copied Fulvius Lippinus. One Roman had a thirty-acre wooded game park with a dining pavilion in the center from which guests, while eating, could watch a huntsman summon the wild animals with a horn and feed them. In some parks, animals were raised for the owner's table, in some,

Venison

for sale, and in others, simply for show. One factor contributing to the rapid development of *vivaria* (as the game parks were called) was the custom of hunts as spectacles. Organizers of these public games felt it necessary to have plenty of wild animals on hand. A third-century list shows 239 exotic beasts in Emperor Gordianus' menagerie.

In feudal France and much of Europe, hunting became the exclusive privilege of the aristocrats, who jealously guarded what wild land remained for their sport. Game was the gentleman's meat and an important part of his menu. Butchers' meat was not considered fit food for noble banquets until the late sixteenth century.

From the Norman Conquest on, hunting in England was limited to royalty and nobility. William the Conqueror set aside large sections of forest where no one could hunt without his permission even if he owned the land; the penalty was loss of an ear. Under Henry I, the penalty was death, and in the eighteenth century, poachers were not infrequently deported for life. In the reign of Charles II, hunting was limited to the aristocracy, down to and including squires and their eldest sons; no one else could hunt even if invited by the landowner. Proprietors of game parks callously usurped common grazing lands. When it was protested that they thereby deprived the people of a livelihood, they replied there were too many people in England already. It was because being able to hunt conferred status that the tombs of medieval nobles so often depict their hounds, hawks, and falcons. The medieval lord used to go everywhere, even to church, with his hounds at his heels and his hawk on his fist.

GARLIC

The orgins of garlic fade into prehistory, though it is believed to be native to the Asian Himalayas. Pliny the Elder claims garlic was sworn by as a deity in ancient Egypt. The Pyramid builders ate it. The Hebrews learned of it during their stay in Egypt and therefore said it originated in that country, but no one knows whether it did.

The Greeks generally detested garlic. However, Homer mentions it, and two early Greek physicians, Hippocrates and Dioscorides, considered it of medicinal value (though Hippocrates warned it was bad for the eyes). In classic Greece, athletes used to eat garlic before games in the stadium in order to be at their best, and people fed it to fighting cocks before putting them in the ring.

Garlic was indispensable to the Romans, who used it in quantity and introduced it to France and Spain. It was in Roman times that the famous Mediterranean garlic sauce, *allioli,* was first made. Garlic was appreciated not only for its flavor, but for all sorts of preventive and curative powers. A Roman physician of the second century B.C., Celsius, said it cured fever. Pliny listed 25 medicinal uses of garlic for ills from toothache to madness. Virgil recommended it as a tonic and said it prevented wasp bites.

Garlic was much appreciated in Paris from the fourteenth century on. In the sixteenth century, it was again extolled as a tonic. Parisians used to eat garlic with fresh butter every day in May in order to gain strength for the rest of the year.

Through the eighteenth century, garlic was recommended as protection against epidemics, particularly the plague. Doctors of those days were in the habit of carrying cloves of garlic in their pockets to avoid contracting or spreading diseases. Garlic continued to be valued by doctors until very recently and still enjoys high regard in folk medicine in Europe. As late as World War II, tons of garlic were used as a disinfectant for battle wounds.

GOOSE and FOIE GRAS

The Egyptians, Greeks, and Romans raised geese, and so did the Britons prior to Roman occupation, though forbidden to eat them by their religion. The Romans also refrained from eating geese until Caesar captured Gaul, because geese were previously held sacred for having given warning when the Gauls were scaling the walls of the Capitol in 390 B.C. With Gaul conquered and no longer a threat, the Romans ate so many geese that their supplies had to be augmented by geese driven to Rome from Picardy.

The Romans enjoyed goose liver without resorting to the cruel methods of the Alsatian specialists who, according to Alexandre Dumas, blinded the geese, nailed their feet to the floor, and stuffed them with nuts while refusing them anything to drink. Livers ten to twelve times normal size were obtained by these methods. In Rome, geese were merely fattened on ripe figs in confined space and darkness. To enlarge livers further, an aristocratic Roman gastronome conceived the idea of soaking the still-warm livers of fresh-killed geese in milk and honey for several hours. Goose liver was so sought after in Rome that Pliny commented geese were valued solely for their livers.

In oblivion for centuries after the fall of Rome, goose liver came back into favor in sixteenth-century France. By the eighteenth century, the Alsatians were fattening geese artificially to obtain unusually large livers (the average weigh a pound, but some reach two to three). *Foie gras* was brought to perfection in the eighteenth century. First a cook in the employ of the military commander of Alsace thought of saucing and baking it, then a pastry cook inserted the superior Périgord truffle, and today's *foie gras* was launched to the delight of epicures around the world.

GRAPE
(see also *WINE*)

We know grapes were grown and wine was made over 4,000 years ago, because there is a record of these activities in Egyptian hieroglyphics dating back to about 2400 B.C. In Greece and Rome, many kinds of grapes were cultivated for the table. First-century agriculturalist Columella names ten. Grapes drying into raisins hung from the rafters in humble Roman dwellings. Sometimes the grapes were sun dried or dried before a fire first. Other methods were designed to keep the grapes firm and intact. They were stored in jars in grape pulp, boiled wine, or must, or simply hung on their branches inside large vessels treated with pitch and sealed with plaster. Grapes were also coated with potter's chalk and sun dried. Sometimes the fruit was buried in a layer of sand or covered with barley, bran, sawdust, or wood shavings (bran, barley, and sawdust are used to preserve grapes today). However successful they were at keeping grapes in storage, the Romans had not solved the problem of keeping them in transit. Columella recommended growing grapes for the table only if the vineyard was close enough to the city to warrant selling raw grapes to marketers along with other fruit.

HERBS
(see also individual entries)

Better is a dinner of herbs where love is
than a fatted ox and hatred with it.
—Proverbs: 15:17

The curative power of herbs was recorded by Hippocrates in the fifth century B.C., and herbs were gathered, cultivated, and used in both cooking and medicine long before that. They were important in Egypt, Greece, and Rome as perfumes, for purifying, for preserving, as liniments, as salads, and in cooked dishes. The Syrians anointed themselves with saffron oil, fenugreek, marjoram, and orris, the Greeks with mint and thyme. Herbs raw or cooked and seasoned with garum and vinegar were a common Roman salad. Among the herbs popular in the Roman cuisine were various mints, mustard, anise, dill, fennel, coriander, caraway, capers, origanum, thyme, sage, rue, parsley, chervil, smallage, basil, and cress. The Romans spread their favorite herbs throughout the Roman Empire, where they were neglected during the Dark Ages except for the herb gardens of monasteries, which grew herbs mainly for medicinal uses.

The Crusades brought a renewed interest in spices and herbs. A culinary and medicinal herb garden became part of every manor house. Salads of herbs returned to favor, and people in the country ate porridges of herbs combined with starches. Herb conserves were much in use in the sixteenth century; Queen Elizabeth I always had lavender conserve on the table. The old French dressing ravigote, once made of just mixed herbs, derives its name from the French verb *ravigoter*, "to cheer or strengthen."

In the seventeenth century, herbs reached the peak of popularity in England. People not only grew them but scoured the countryside for them. Every country house of any size had its still room where the mistress of the house prepared aromatic waters, medicines, perfumes, and beauty and household aids from herbs.

Among the many herbs no longer in general use but popular in Europe from the thirteenth through the sixteenth century or later are hyssop, alecost or costmary, blite, plantain, rue, tansy, galingale, burnet, lovage, orach, purslane, rampion, rocket, skirret,

237

corn flag, and cuckoopint. It would be impossible to list them all. William Harrison claimed in his sixteenth century *Description of England* that there were 300 to 400 herbs in use.

Until the early nineteenth century, when herbs again fell into neglect, 80 percent of medicines were derived from plants.[89] As one writer on plants commented in 1827, medicinal herbs disappeared from private gardens when doctors began to be available in every part of England.[90] Pills were replacing potions. Medicinal herbs became important again in England for a brief period during World War I when the British Board of Agriculture and Fisheries issued propaganda to encourage people to grow them. There is a current revival of interest in culinary herbs. Herb cookbooks are on the market again, and herb cooking continues to grow in popularity.

HERRING

The original red herring was salted and hung for weeks in kilns over smoldering sawdust fires. The expression "dragging a red herring" may date back to the sixteenth-century shenanigans of the canons of the cathedral of Rheims. As recounted by Alexandre Dumas, on Maundy Thursday, each canon dragged a herring behind him on a string, and each tried to step on the other's herring and keep his own from being stepped on.

Herring is a prolific fish, perhaps the world's most plentiful, but it has not always been appreciated. In the Middle Ages, when decimating famines struck and herring was plentiful, starving people refused to eat it. The attitude toward herring was reversed in in the first half of the fifteenth century when a Dutch fisherman named William Beukels (also spelled Bruckels, Buckelfz, and Bachelen) devised the art of drawing, emptying, and preparing it in a special brine. It was thenceforth possible to keep herring longer than the few days salting and smoking it had previously permitted. By the sixteenth century, herring was the fish most in demand by all classes in England. The new Dutch herring industry contributed to the growth of Dutch power in the Hanseatic League and made the fortune of Amsterdam. James Solas Dodd wrote in 1752 in his *Essay Towards a Natural History of the Herring*, that it was almost entirely on the basis of their herring fisheries that the Dutch were able to raise themselves to plenty, wealth, and power. In recognition of Beukels, Emperor Charles V is said to have eaten a herring on his grave in Bier Uliet in 1536, but the story may be apocryphal.

HONEY, HYDROMEL, and MEAD

The land of milk and honey is an ancient land; those were the staple foods of the Greek army in peacetime centuries before Christ. A drawing in a Neolithic cave near Valencia depicts a man robbing a store of wild honey. The Babylonians, Assyrians, and ancient Egyptians appreciated honey. Egyptians of the thirteenth and twelfth centuries B.C. raised honeybees in their gardens in addition to collecting wild honey from the desert.

In early times, honey was considered divine. Not knowing what made it, men concluded it was of heavenly origin. When bees became associated with its manufacture, honey did not lose its halo; bees, instead, acquired one and were considered supernaturally endowed. Honey was used in libations and as a sacramental food. It was the food of the gods in Greek myths, along with nectar and ambrosia.

In early times, honey was used as a preservative for food and also for the dead. Both Emperor Justin II and Alexander the Great are said to have been embalmed in honey. Fish was imported to Rome in pots of honey; fish, fruits, and meats were stored in honey. Honey was the main sweetening until sugar became generally available in the eighteenth century. Honey was used in early Middle Eastern pastries (as it is today) and was the basis of a number of fermented drinks through the Renaissance. Hydromel, much appreciated by the Egyptians and served through the eighteenth century, is one of the oldest fermented drinks. The recipe was very simple: mix one part honey to three parts warm water and let it ferment. The Romans sometimes left the mixture in the sun for forty days, after which they stored it in a loft where smoke from the fireplace would reach it and add to its flavor. Mead was a combination of honey with must or malt, sealed in a jar for a month and then strained. It was a popular aperitif at Roman banquets and was common in pre-Roman Gaul.

Honey was important as medicine as well as food. Indeed, we still use it for coughs and it is recognized to have slight antiseptic powers.

Early agriculturalists had a great deal to say about the herbs that should be available in the bees' feeding grounds for honey to be at its best. The most famous honey in Greece has borne the name of Mount Hymettus near Athens for over 2,000 years.

HORSEMEAT

Horsemeat is eaten in many countries today and is regarded as extremely healthful. Special butcher shops deal exclusively in horsemeat in France. It is bought by rich as well as poor (though not served to guests). Horsemeat has fallen in and out of favor throughout history. Hippocrates mentioned horsemeat as food, proof the Greeks did not share the Roman taboo against eating it. One source claims many Saxon nobles ate horse. In the Elizabethan era, a French general served horsemeat to English officers, and horse was mentioned as a food by the chronicler to Charles V, Holy Roman Emperor.

In the midnineteenth century, a meat shortage led to an effort to popularize horsemeat in France. Two hundred prominent men were invited to eat horsemeat at the Grand Hotel in Paris. Flaubert, Alexandre Dumas, and Sainte-Beuve were among the guests dining on truffled horsemeat, fillets of horsemeat, and horsemeat à la mode, with rum and horsemarrow cake for dessert. Despite the publicity and the opening of a few butcher shops selling horse in the poorer districts, the new food did not become popular. It was so unpopular, in fact, that an eyewitness wrote that, though there was hardly a dog or cat left alive in Paris at the end of the Prussian siege of 1871, there were 30,000 horses. Even the rat market did a better business.

ICE

> He is the first to discover whether
> snow may be had in the market. . . .
> —Euthycles,
> *The Wastrels* (early fourth century B.C.)

In the Athenian marketplace of the fifth century B.C., along with fish, vegetables, and meat, you could buy snow for cooling your wine. Cool drinks in hot weather were so common among the rich that both Hippocrates and Aristotle felt it necessary to warn people that drinking melted snow and ice was harmful. From the fifth century B.C., the rich in southern Europe and the Middle East used large amounts of snow and a lesser amount of ice. No one wanted to drink warm wine or warm water in summer if he could avoid it. Nero even had his bath water cooled with snow. That extraordinary Roman emperor Heliogabalus had a mountain of snow carted to the pleasure garden near his house one summer. Various refinements were introduced by the Romans. Nero had the idea of boiling water and then cooling it in a glass container buried in the snow, a method Pliny agreed was much more wholesome than drinking melted snow. Roman poet Martial described what may be the earliest thermos: a flask enclosed in light wickerwork that kept water iced or boiling hot.

The Greeks and Romans kept snow and ice through the summer in caves or in pits and trenches dug for the purpose. Even armies at war took the trouble of preparing a place to store snow. When Alexander the Great besieged Petra, he had thirty pits dug, filled with snow, and covered with oak branches. Chaff and coarse cloth or sod and sheep dung were also used to cover snow buried in the ground. Wine cooled with snow was often passed through a linen strainer to remove the dirt. Methods of keeping snow and ice changed little until the invention of the insulated icebox in the early nineteenth century.

Ice and snow for cooling came into use in northern Europe much later than in the Mediterranean. When François Ier of France visited the Pope in Nice in the midsixteenth century, his physician wrote of his astonishment at being served wine cooled with ice from the neighboring mountains. The physician dismissed the custom as unhealthy, but later that century, snow was used by the rich in France, though many considered it an effeminate luxury. From the seventeenth century on, ice houses were a standard feature of the European country estate. Natural ice became an important item of trade; it was cut, shipped, and sold in quantity. For a time, New England led the market; 156,540 tons were exported from Boston in 1845 alone. Ice was used to preserve the catch on fishing boats from the midnineteenth century; before that, ships usually had to return to port daily to ensure the freshness of the fish. Natural ice went off the market only at the very end of the nineteenth century when artificial methods of making ice were developed and automatic refrigerators came into use.

ICES and ICE CREAM

The antecedents of ice cream are very old, though it remained a luxury until forty or fifty years ago. Roman ladies liked to chew on ice; Nero enjoyed snow flavored with honey, and a frozen cream called *melca* is mentioned in second-century Roman sources. Our present-day ices and ice creams were probably developed from the flavored ices the Middle Easterners and Chinese have made for a very long time—how long, no one knows. Marco Polo is said to have brought back a recipe for ice from China. "Sherbet" is a Middle Eastern word, and our present-day sherbets can be traced to the ices flavored with lemon, orange, rose petals, pomegranate, and coffee that were made in Turkey, Persia, and Arabia at the time of the Crusades. These sherbets were first made in Europe by the Italians, who traded so extensively with the Middle East in the thirteenth and fourteenth centuries.

In the midsixteenth century, when Catherine de Médicis married Henri II of France, she brought with her an army of Florentine cooks who made what were probably the first ices in France. The new dish was immediately popular, but the cooks guarded the secret so that only the court could enjoy it. By the following century, the secret had leaked out, and the public was able to eat ices and sherbets too. About 1660, an Italian called Procopio opened the Café Procope where he sold ices; he had instant success and many imitators. By 1676, there were 250 dealers in ices in Paris. After physicians announced that ices were good for various ills, they sold all year instead of only in summer. By 1700, a book of recipes for ice cream was printed, but its great popularity did not come until the development of the hand freezer about 1860 and the simultaneous rise of an ice-cream industry. Ice cream is immensely popular today, with 300 flavors on record. The Americans, who eat far more ice cream than all the rest of the world put together, are responsible for the invention of the ice-cream soda, the ice-cream cone, and the Eskimo Pie, all of which met great and instant success. The Eskimo Pie, for example, invented by a midwestern baker in 1921, was sold in thousands of retail stores within two months.

LEEK

The leek remains unappreciated and expensive in America, though it is easy to grow, and there is nothing better for soups and stews, not to mention the delight of cooked-leek salad. In France, leek salad is called the asparagus of the poor.

The leek was popular in Mesopotamia in 2000 B.C. and was eaten by the ancient Jews, Egyptians, Greeks, and Romans. The earliest Roman cookbook contains five recipes for leeks: in stuffings and chicken stews, and wrapped in cabbage leaves and baked.

The leek has been the national emblem of Wales since the day in the sixth century when a victorious Welsh king had his troops wear leeks in their headgear in battle in order to distinguish them from the enemy Saxons.

MEAT
(see also *BEEF, DOG, DONKEY, DORMOUSE, ELEPHANT,*
GAME, HORSE, and *PORK*)

Domesticated animals were eaten by the third millennium B.C. However, in Mesopotamia of 2000 B.C., in the Egyptian Old Kingdom, in Homeric days in Greece, and for several centuries in Rome, there were no butchers; no retail meat was sold. The animal was killed in the household, usually as a religious sacrifice. Because there was no satisfactory way of keeping or disposing of leftovers, the only people who could afford to slaughter a large animal were those who could afford to eat it within a few days: large proprietors with great staffs, rich people giving banquets, and temple priests.

243

Mutten

The number of animals that could be killed for meat was in any case severely limited by lack of pastureland, lack of fodder, and the need to reserve animals for work or breeding.

Even after butchers and meat markets were introduced to Greece and Rome, the rich did not often buy market meat. Though controlled by laws and an inspection force, its quality was somewhat dubious. Furthermore, people hesitated to eat meat that had not been sacrificed. The separate, spacious forum containing the slaughterhouse and butcher shops was a place in which no respectable Roman matron would be seen. The lower classes, on the other hand, must have bought meat in quantity because they protested the price of beef and pork in the third century, an indication these were items they were used to buying.

By 1355, there were three butchers' companies in London as well as a market outside the city. Nevertheless, little butchers' meat was eaten by rich or poor through the sixteenth century because of the impossibility of keeping livestock through the winter and the difficulty of preserving and transporting raw meat. Cattle arrived in London on the hoof, toughened and emaciated. The meat had to be sold at once or salted after slaughter, and because salt was expensive, salt meat was not always properly cured. Much of the little meat sold was rotten. In his early sixteenth-century colloquies, Erasmus described people holding their noses on passing a

butcher's shop. Rabbits, birds, larger game, and home-raised poultry and pigs—these were the substitutes for butchers' meat, in
addition to the pigeons every manor house kept in lofts for winter.

People were not so badly off in the Middle Ages, when even the
poor kept a few chickens and pigs in the country and towns were
small enough to be supplied by the surrounding countryside. As
towns grew and more and more land was enclosed, meat became
poorer, scarcer, and dearer. After the introduction of root crops
made it possible to keep cattle over the winter and selective breeding improved the quality of meat, the rich began to serve it. There
was an abrupt change between the early sixteenth century, when
butchers' meat did not appear on a fashionable table, and the
seventeenth and eighteenth centuries, when several menus are on
record of all-beef meals consisting of dozens of dishes from beef
soup through ox-tongue salad to beef-brain fritters in orange juice.
Still, short supply and lack of both transport and storage facilities
kept it generally out of the question for the poor. The quality remained dubious until a hundred years ago. As late as 1863, an
official English report advised that over a fifth of the meat sold in
the market came from diseased cattle. Indeed, it was only at that
late date that doctors came to realize people could get fatal diseases from eating diseased meat.

Every part of meat animals was appreciated in ancient times: the
salivary glands, thymus, lymphatic ganglions, testicles, udders,
intestines, spinal marrow, and blood. Greeks and Romans were

Veal.

particularly fond of sow's matrix, preferably one from a sow that had just miscarried. As recently as 1808, one of the fashionable dishes cited by gourmet Grimod de la Reynière in his *Manuel des amphitryons* was calf's head served in its hide. The most distinguished morsels of calf's head were the eyes,* followed by the jowls, temples, ears, and tongue in that order. Each portion of ear, eye, etc., should be served, according to Grimod de la Reynière, with a portion of the brain, which the carver scoops out of the top of the head.

The ancients raised a great many animals for meat that we no longer eat or no longer domesticate. Oryx, gazelles, antelope, hyenas, and dormice were fattened for the table. There are recipes in cookbooks of the fourteenth to seventeenth centuries for hedgehogs, dormice, and other unusual meats. Hedgehog was a princely dish when stuffed with pork maws, ground pork, spices, and sugar, roasted on a spit, glazed in various colors, and decorated with fried split almonds to simulate quills. Butchers' meat was supplemented by any sort of game that could be gotten. A writer of the early seventeenth century commented that in the dearth of other food, people were eating bears, badgers, foxes, cats (both domestic and wood), wolves, dogs, mice, porcupines, hedgehogs, and field rats. During acute shortages, such as the siege of Paris by the Prussians in 1870–1871, every animal in the zoo ended on the table, and elegant restaurants vied with each other in composing menus of dishes such as *rat goût de mouton, gigots de chien flanqués de ratons,* and *émincé de râble de chat.* Today a number of animals are enjoyed regionally that are not generally eaten. Opossum and squirrel are still cooked in the American rural South, and gourmet stores in the North import boned, canned muskrat from Canada.

From time to time, writers on food have proposed the introduction of new animals to offset a shortage of the usual meats. In 1936, chef Joseph Vehling wrote that reindeer from Lapland were being acclimatized in North America to augment the supply of meat. In 1869, Alexandre Dumas wrote enthusiastically of the leporide, a cross between hare and rabbit but larger than either (thirteen to fourteen pounds), which he predicted would shortly appear on the market and enjoy the greatest favor. Dumas recommended raising

---

* An eighteenth-century recipe for calves' eyes is to be found on page 319.

kangaroos for meat because they are delicious and grow rapidly to a good height. However, what has led to an increase in meat supplies so far is not the introduction of new animals, but new methods of feeding for rapid growth and new ways of preserving and shipping meat.

Tanzania recently licensed a company to shoot and market game animals for meat. The plan, which is calculated to ensure the preservation of each species, may produce several thousand tons of game meat per year, some of which will be exported. The species selected are zebra, hartebeeste, eland, impala, buffalo, giraffe, Grant's and Thomson's gazelles, and gnu. Tiger meat is already on sale in America, according to a spokesman for Tanzania's College of African Wild Life Management.

The greatest meat-eating country the world has known is America of the frontier days. It has been established that, outside the Eastern seaboard, the average man and woman ate more than three hundred pounds a year, but the meat consisted of wild game. Much less is eaten now (173.7 pounds per capita in 1967), though the United States leads world production of beef, veal, and pork.

MILK

Many early civilizations lived on meat, cheese, and milk. (The Aztecs, who had no cattle, are a conspicuous exception.) Homer writes of a meat, cheese, and milk diet among the Libyans; Caesar tells us the Germans lived mainly on it. The first settlers of Rome, who were shepherds, offered milk, not wine, to the gods. The Latin word for money, *pecunia*, comes from *pecus*, meaning large cattle, because in those early days wealth was based on the number of cattle owned.

The Greeks and Romans used goat and ewe milk for cheese, in cooking, and as a beverage, saving cows' milk for the rearing of calves. They also drank asses' and mares' milk, but mainly as medicine. At the height of the Roman Empire, gourmets liked camels' milk mixed with three parts water.

Little milk was sold in the Middle Ages because it could not be transported without spoiling. The milk trade began only in the seventeenth century, and it was only then that cookbooks started to include milk and cream in recipes. Even at that time, little milk was drunk. It was regarded as full of vapors, liable to cause convulsions, cramps, headaches, and sore eyes, and salutary only for the very young and very old. It was often sour or watered unless bought as in India today from a cow driven to the customer's door and milked before the watchful eye of the household. It was only in the latter nineteenth century that people realized milk could be made safe by boiling. Pasteur's discovery was first put to use in the dairy industry at about that time, but with the object of preserving milk rather than killing germs. Dried and condensed milk, also introduced in the nineteenth century, made cheap milk available to the poor in cities for the first time.

MINT

Mint sauce is a very old idea; the Romans made it. They thought mint aroused the appetite and liked to rub tables with it, strew it on the floor, or use it to stuff cushions used at banquets.

Brought to Britain by the Romans, mint was used in the Middle Ages to whiten teeth. It is still put in toothpaste.

The mint family is a very large one, including catmint, peppermint, pennyroyal, marjoram, and oregano. The latter, ubiquitous in Greece, is becoming more and more popular in the United States. Consumption of oregano increased 5,200 percent between 1948 and 1956.

MUSHROOMS

I would here also give some general directions for the cooking of mushrooms, as this is the only article of food that the voluptuaries of the present day are in the habit of dressing with their own hands, and so feeding upon it in anticipation, being provided with amber handled knives and silver plates and dishes for the purpose.

—Pliny, *Natural History*, XXII

The Egyptians thought mushrooms too good for the common man. The Greeks and Romans enjoyed them raw, grilled, and boiled, and they were a food first-century Roman gourmets liked to prepare themselves. Mushrooms were rare and expensive in Italy (many were imported from Asia Minor). They were regarded as a delicacy, but also looked upon with suspicion. Emperor Claudius died after eating a dish of mushrooms, one of his favorite foods, though it is generally believed that his wife put poison in them. Be that as it may, Claudius was not the only one to die after eating mushrooms. Pliny wrote, "Recently they have carried off whole households and all the guests at banquets; Annaeus Serenus, for instance, Captain of Nero's Guards, with the tribunes and centurions. What pleasure can there be in such risky food?" For those who insist on eating mushrooms despite fair warning, Pliny advised making them safer by boiling them with meat or pear stocks or mixing them with vinegar. Vinegar, thought to have an "opposite" nature, was supposed to neutralize the dangers lurking in mushrooms. A physician of the third century B.C. recommended a sauce of honey and vinegar for mushrooms to "remove the choking element," and as late as 1702, Louis XIV's physician proposed honey and anise as antidotes.

In addition to the death of Claudius, mushrooms have been held responsible for the deaths of Tiberius, Pope Clement VII, Charles V of France, and Czar Alexis of Russia.[91] When mushrooms returned to favor in the sixteenth century after a thousand years of almost total neglect, physicians and herbalists expressed their alarm. As late as the nineteenth century, Alexandre Dumas wrote that even edible mushrooms could prove toxic if overindulged.

The Greeks and Romans thought thunder caused mushrooms to grow, possibly because mushrooms often sprang up after thundershowers. They, of course, knew only wild mushrooms. Experiments in growing mushrooms were first made in Louis XIV's reign. By the eighteenth century, there were extensive underground caves in which mushrooms were commercially grown in France. France is still a champion mushroom grower, with over twenty varieties. The most common species, and the one constantly seen in the United States and Great Britain, is the *Agaricus campestris*. It is a pity that a greater variety of commercially grown mushrooms is not available on the market.

It may be of some interest that one pound of mushrooms contains only 90 calories.

NUTS
(see also *ACORN, ALMOND*)

The Romans used almonds, chestnuts, filberts, hazelnuts, pine nuts, pistachios, Tarentine nuts, and walnuts. In the early days and in times of famine, they also used acorns. By no means all these were native to Italy. The almond reached Rome from Greece in the second century B.C. The filbert came from the shores of the Black Sea, the walnut from Persia via Greece, and the pistachio from Persia through Syria. Pine nuts, still used in Italian and Spanish dishes, went out of fashion in northern Europe in the eighteenth century.

Technically a legume, the peanut was discovered in Peru where it was a native plant cultivated by the Incas. It traveled a long distance before being planted in North America. The seeds the Spaniards took to Spain and Africa from South America produced the African peanut that was carried on America-bound slave ships as food for the Negro slaves. As a result, the Negroes hated peanuts, and the whites despised them. For centuries the peanut was grown in southern gardens as a curiosity until George W. Carver (1864–1943) pioneered the growing of peanuts as a commercial crop. The principal peanut producers today are India, China, West Africa, and the United States.

OLIVE

The olive is an Oriental tree that spread to the Western world long ago. Olive pits have been discovered in Neolithic sites in Spain and Pliocene beds near Bologna. The olive is often mentioned in the Old Testament and may have reached Greece in prehistoric times. The Phoenicians brought olive trees to Marseilles; the Greeks introduced them to the Romans, who developed new varieties. Cato mentioned seven varieties in the second century B.C.; Macrobius, writing in the fifth century A.D., named sixteen. Still, demand outran supply. By the second century, Romans had so neglected agriculture that they were obliged to import olives and eventually to forbid their export outside the Empire. By the ninth century, olive oil was so scarce in Europe that the Council of Aix-la-Chapelle authorized priests to make anointing oil from bacon.

Olive oil, made in Egypt as early as the fourth millenium B.C., was used both for cooking and as an ointment in Greece and Rome. Such quantities were dispensed in Greek gymnasiums that Pliny reported the governors of these establishments sold the scrapings of the oil used there for the equivalent of $2,400. Olives preserved with various herbs were popular at banquets, where they were presented at the end of the meal to encourage thirst and drinking, a custom revived in nineteenth-century England. "At the more sumptuous repasts," Columella wrote in the first century, "olives are served as a preserve. They are removed from the brine, crushed, mixed with minced chives, rue, parsley, and mint, mixed with pepper, vinegar, and a little honey or mead, sprinkled with green olive oil, and covered with a bunch of green parsley." [92]

Introduced to the New World by the Spanish, the olive grows in South America and California. Olive trees planted by the conquistadors still line the streets of the capital of Peru. Almost all olive oil comes from the Mediterranean basin, however, and all but five percent of that production is consumed there.

ONION

A vegetable that has always been popular even when the rest were despised, the onion is also one of the oldest. The Sumerians planted onions in the Euphrates Valley in 3500 B.C. Egyptian laborers lived on bread and onions. Onions were eaten raw, dry, cooked, and in preserves by the Greeks and Romans. Homer mentioned onions as adding relish to a drink. Hippocrates believed they were good for eyesight, though bad for the body in general. His warning did not keep the Greeks from eating onions of various kinds. In the third century B.C., Theophrastus named a total of six varieties, one of which is probably the shallot.

The onion maintained its popularity through the Dark Ages, Middle Ages, and Renaissance to the present. A seventeenth-century book on agriculture claimed that, if a man ate onions with honey for breakfast every day, he would stay healthy. Today onions are probably the most indispensable vegetable in cooking.

American Indians ate wild onions, but the cultivated onion was brought to the New World by the Spanish.

ORANGE

Neither the Egyptians nor the Greeks had oranges, which are of Far Eastern origin. Oranges were cultivated in Rome by the first century and later taken to Spain and Portugal by the Arabs. It was the Crusaders who brought the orange to northern Europe, where it became a much-sought luxury and an essential of the *haute cuisine* of the fifteenth, sixteenth, and seventeenth centuries. Often called for in sauces, orange juice partially replaced the previously ubiquitous vinegar and verjuice. It was considered very royal to have oranges in your hothouse in the seventeeth and eighteenth centuries. The Elector Palatine built the first greenhouse in the world for his oranges, and Louis XIII built a kind of cloister for orange trees in the Tuileries gardens.

In 1493, Columbus planted orange seeds from the Canary Islands in the New World. By the middle of the sixteenth century there were oranges in Latin America and Florida. Today the United States produces two to three times as many oranges and tangerines as any other country.

After the orange ceased to be important in cooking, it became a dessert fruit. Drinking orange juice is a fairly new idea too. The popularity of orange juice after 1920 greatly increased the consumption of oranges. Forty percent of the American crop is made into frozen, concentrated orange juice.

OYSTER

"Blessed if I don't think that ven a man's wery
poor, he rushes out of his lodgings and eats
oysters in reg'lar desperation."
—Sam Weller in Dickens' *Pickwick Papers*

Oysters existed on earth long before man, who has been eating them for at least four thousand years and cultivating them for two thousand. The first to lay out oyster beds was a Roman named Sergius Orata, who did so sometime prior to 91 B.C., not out of gluttony, but avarice. He succeeded in making a pile of money out of his innovation and established the supremacy of the Lucrine Lake for oysters. References to oysters from Lake Lucrine are scattered through the essays and poems of imperial Rome. Raw oysters served on ice are an old Roman idea too. Pliny described it lyrically: "Luxury has added coolness by burying them [oysters] in snow, thus wedding the tops of the mountains to the bottom of the sea. . . ." [93]

Various kinds of oysters were distinguished by the Romans, who imported them from as far away as England. Shells of these oysters, so little changed as to be clearly identified as coming from a particular English site, have been found in Roman ruins. How oysters could arrive fresh from so far is not clear, though the Roman gourmet Apicius is reputed to have invented a way of keeping them fresh in transport. He used to send fresh oysters to Emperor Trajan when the latter was many days' journey from the sea.

After the Roman Empire fell, oysters were eaten by rich and poor alike. In a book called *Diets Dry Dinner*, printed in 1599, oysters are dismissed as "passing toothsome" though "engendered of mere mire." Only gradually did they acquire the high reputation they enjoy today, and only after supplies became short and prices rose.

In the sixteenth century, oyster lovers could afford to indulge immoderately. Montaigne wrote of seeing a valet eat over a hundred at a time. Henry IV of France is reported to have eaten hundreds at one sitting. There were an estimated 4,000 oystermongers in seventeenth-century Paris to serve the appetites of oyster fans. Casanova is said to have eaten fifty every evening, doubtless sharing the popular view that they were aphrodisiac.

Oysters and wine made a seventeenth-century breakfast in England, where they remained inexpensive until the midnineteenth century, so inexpensive that Dr. Samuel Johnson used to feed them to his cat. The shellfish were sold from wheelbarrows or street stalls, which were particularly numerous in the poorer sections of London. Oysters and poverty went together. As Sam Weller pointed out to Mr. Pickwick, you know you are in the slums when you see an oyster stall to every half dozen houses. In seventeenth-century Maryland, one of the settlers' grievances was that their provisions were so short they were forced to eat oysters from the Maryland shore to keep from starving.

In the early nineteenth century, Brillat-Savarin noted that every dinner of importance began with oysters, and that many guests never stopped before eating a gross of them. Grimod de la Reynière deplored the practice, commenting that experience proves oysters in excess of five or six dozen cease to be a pleasure. Nevertheless, some men's capacity for oysters seem to have been limitless. One impoverished government employee complained to Brillat-Savarin he had never had his fill of them. Brillat-Savarin invited the man to be his guest at dinner and eat all the oysters he wanted. When the man reached his thirty-second dozen, Brillat-Savarin, losing patience, suggested they renew the invitation another day because it was time to get on with the meal. At dinner, the author commented, the man "behaved as vigorously as a man who had been fasting." [94]

Oysters are still sold at street stalls in Paris, but they are no longer inexpensive, alas. The heedless exhaustion of natural oyster banks has made them too scarce. Most people now have to be satisfied with a first course of six or twelve oysters, and few would think of making Alexandre Dumas' oyster sauce for roast chicken which starts casually, "Take 72 oysters. . . ."

PARSLEY

Phyllis! a cask I have of Alban wine
Now more than nine years old; my garden shows
Fresh parsley, chaplets for the feast to twine.
—Horace, Book IV, 11

The Greeks bordered gardens with parsley and rue and wove it into chaplets for banquets. Pliny termed it a universal favorite, an herb that enjoyed a popularity all its own in sauces. The Romans used it to take the tang of vinegar out of dishes and to rid wine of bad odors. Dumas called it "the obligatory condiment of every sauce" and said it must be put in "every sauce and every stew."

Though the Romans took it to England, it reached France from Italy in the Middle Ages. It became popular in England in the mid-sixteenth century, when it was cultivated again for the first time since Roman days.

Parsley is unfortunately often reduced to a kind of green decoration. Freshly chopped and used in quantity, it is a delightful seasoning; the Catalans make an omelet with nothing but eggs and parsley, quantities of parsley.

PARTRIDGE

The partridge, raised domestically by the Romans, has been a favorite of gourmets for 2,000 years, particularly wild partridge, still served frequently in Europe. Brillat-Savarin claimed some gourmets could distinguish by its superior flavor the thigh on which the partridge usually stands while sleeping. Grimod de la Reynière said a variety of partridge called *bartavelle* deserved such deep respect that it should be eaten kneeling.

PASTA

Noodles, spaghetti, and all similar Italian specialties are not originally Italian but Chinese (or, some claim, Japanese). Marco

Polo is said to have brought back a recipe for pasta from China to Venice. However, Artemas Ward, author of *The Encyclopedia of Food*, is one of several authorities who say the Germans learned about pasta first; the Italians were merely the first to appreciate it. They began to appreciate it in the fourteenth century. Within a few decades, it had transformed their eating habits.

Macaroni became known in France in the latter fifteenth century, probably through the wars Charles VIII waged in Italy. Macaroni then meant a ball of the soft part of bread moistened with bouillon and sprinkled with cheese. Macaroni in the form we know it today was invented in southern Italy in the sixteenth century. The Italians kept devising new forms and varieties of pasta until they reached the present total of over 150. For the first few centuries there was no tomato sauce on pasta because there was no tomato. Wine alone sometimes served as spaghetti sauce in the seventeenth century.

Italy remained the country most appreciative of pasta. Even after Catherine de Médicis put it on court menus in sixteenth-century France, the dish was not very successful there. Its failure to find favor is understandable if it was made according to the recipe given by Dumas in which a casserole of macaroni, meat, onion, and cheese is doused with a glass of ice water just before being served. In Naples, the glass of ice water is obligatory, Dumas asserted.

PEA

Peas are an ancient vegetable, first appearing in middle Asia in prehistory. Remains of peas were found in the sites of Neolithic pile dwellings in Switzerland. Pea soup and "pease porridge, beautiful and brown" are mentioned in Greek plays of the fifth century B.C. Five centuries later, Roman agriculturalist Columella included the pea on his list of "most useful and pleasing vegetables." But at no time was the pea so sought after as in the age of Louis XIV, after the sweet wrinkled pea was discovered by cross-fertilization. Throughout the Middle Ages and the early years of the Renaissance, green peas along with most other fresh vegetables had been regarded as useless if not dangerous. When Louis XIV ate the first pea directly off the vine, his courtiers were convinced he might die. When he not only lived but pronounced it delicious, early green peas became a sought-after luxury commanding astronomical prices in France and England.

"We are still on the chapter of peas," Madame de Maintenon wrote from Marly in May of 1696; "impatience to eat them, the pleasure of having eaten them, and the anticipation of eating them again are the three subjects I have heard discussed for the last four days. Some women, after having supped, and supped well, at the King's table, have peas in their rooms to eat before going to bed." [95]

Later, when the bourgeois were richer and kings poorer in France, the earliest peas were priced beyond the royal purse. Brillat-Savarin notes that "the first plate of green peas, of which the price was invariably eight hundred francs, or thirty-two pounds, was not eaten by the king, but by the farmers-general." [96]

PEACH

The peach was unknown in Greece until Alexander the Great brought it from Persia. The Roman general and gourmet Lucullus is credited with bringing the peach to Rome from Asia Minor. It was called *persica*, or Persian apple, after the country of its origin. In the first century, peaches commanded the highest price of any fruit, up to thirty sesterces each (or the equivalent of over thirty pounds of bread).

The peach is one of the fruits the Romans took to England. The Spanish brought it to Florida in the sixteenth century. It enjoys the distinction of being the only fruit the English writer Sir Thomas Elyot recommended as not harmful to man in his *Castel of Helth* (1539).

PEACOCK

A native of India, the peacock was raised domestically as early as the third century B.C. by Ptolemy II, king of Egypt. Alexander the Great brought the peacock to Greece. It was introduced to Rome in the first century B.C. by the famous orator Hortensius and was thenceforth domesticated and served with great pomp by the rich. A certain Marcus Aufidius Lurco made a handsome profit in about 60 B.C. by being the first to fatten peacocks for the table. In the Middle Ages, peacock was a barnyard animal and an essential feature at every banquet. Peacock remained the festive bird par excellence until replaced by the turkey in the midsixteenth century.

The preparation of the bird was elaborate. The skin was removed—tail, feathers, and all—and put aside. Before being roasted, the body was sprinkled with cumin and the head wrapped in a damp cloth so that it would not singe. After being allowed to cool, the roasted bird was sewn back into its plumage. The comb was gilded, the tail feathers spread out, and a lighted wad of wool dipped in alcohol was placed in the beak. Sometimes the bird was served without feathers, its body overlaid with gold leaf. The preparation was mainly for eye appeal, for the flesh was tough and not noted for its flavor, except in a young bird. Roasted peacocks must have been a spectacular sight, particularly in numbers. No fewer than 104 of them were served at the enthronement of Archbishop Neville in 1467.

PEAR

Pears grew wild in Greece and Italy. The Greeks served them in water at their symposia. Many varieties were cultivated by the Romans—thirty-six according to Pliny. The Romans ate pears raw, dried, or preserved in honey; they also made pear wine.

Though pears of one kind or another are native to Europe, Asia, and North Africa, there were none in the Americas until introduced by the Spaniards and early colonists of New England. The pear is now the world's second most important deciduous fruit tree, outstripped only by the apple. There are several thousand named varieties of pears, though a handful dominate the market.

PEPPER, CHILI, PAPRIKA

Our common black pepper was not always common; it used to be worth its weight in gold. When Alaric the Visigoth extorted a ransom from the besieged city of Rome in A.D. 409, one of the things he demanded was three thousand pounds of pepper. Pepper has since been used to pay taxes, rents, dowries, and bribes. It was such a tempting valuable in Elizabethan times that dockmen unloading it were required to wear pocketless uniforms.

Black pepper comes from an Indian plant known botanically as *Piper nigrum*. (White pepper is the same berry with the outer coat removed.) The word "pepper" itself is of Indian origin, derived from the Sanskrit *pippali*. The Greeks learned of pepper through the Phoenicians. Hippocrates discoursed on its medical uses, Alexander the Great's men saw it in India, and various Greeks mentioned it before and after that, but it was little used in Greece until the Romans came.

Before pepper was used in Rome, myrtle berries served instead. Pepper is first mentioned by Roman writers of the first century and seems to have come into fashion only then. It was much sought after in imperial Rome. Pepper wine, pepper vinegar, and peppery olives were very popular. Ground pepper is called for constantly in Roman cooking, often in dishes where it seems highly inappropriate—quince marmalade, for example.

Pepper used to be brought to Rome from India by a laborious route. It was carried overland to the tip of the Red Sea, then by ship to the Egyptian shore, by camel caravan from there to Alexandria, and thence by ship to Ostia and overland to Rome, where it was kept under guard in special depots for spices, particularly pepper. Such a lucrative trade led to a great deal of fraud. Weights were falsified and pepper was adulterated with black mustard seeds or juniper berries.

The will of the historian the Venerable Bede shows how much pepper was esteemed in the Dark Ages. A bag of pepper was among the treasures to be distributed to his fellow monks at his death in 735. Pepper to impart or disguise flavor was vital to medieval food, which was apt to be tough and flavorless or rancid. Pepperers were organized in England by the eleventh century and within a few hundred years became powerful, with privileges of inspecting, testing, and receiving fees on certain imported drugs and spices.

The monopoly the Venetians and Genoese held on the vital spice was a strong motive in the search for a sea route to the Far East. After the Italian spice trade monopoly was broken by the Portuguese discovery of a sea route, the Portuguese monopoly was broken by the Dutch, and the Dutch monopoly by the English.

However, the English still lacked colonies with pepper vines. Their attempts to plant pepper along with other spices on their plantations failed consistently. Pepper was the one spice they were unable to grow. The dried seeds refused to sprout, and traders in pepper refused to tell them where the plant could be found. That discovery was made at the end of the eighteenth century, but by the Americans, not the English. One day an American ship captain heard in a chance conversation that wild pepper grew freely in parts of Sumatra. In two decades, America led the world's pepper trade.

A number of plants we call pepper have little in common with *Piper nigrum* other than a sharp taste, and some do not even have that. Most of these belong to the *Capsicum* genus, discovered by Columbus. The chili pepper, native to the Andes and Mexico, is a *Capsicum*. The name "chili" (after the Nahuatl term *chilli*) covers many kinds of hot peppers. Chili powder, a Texan innovation, is a mixture of various Mexican peppers, herbs, and spices. Cayenne pepper was named after the Cayenne Island of French Guiana; it, too, is made from hot peppers of the *Capsicum* group. Hot peppers were valued in the eighteenth and nineteenth centuries as cures for flu, sore throats, and yellow fever. Hot relishes and sauces were highly favored in England in the eighteenth century. The number of recipes calling for a bit of cayenne in cookbooks of that era is nothing less than astonishing.

PINEAPPLE

The pineapple, growing wild through the warmer areas of Latin America from Mexico to Brazil, is an American contribution. The Indians baked pineapple with meat as we do with ham today.

Cortes sent a pineapple to Emperor Charles in Spain which the Emperor is said not to have even tasted, but it probably did not arrive in good condition. At first it proved impossible either to ship or transplant the pineapple. Oviedo, governor of Santo Domingo in the early sixteenth century, tried to get the fruit to Europe unspoiled by picking it before it was ripe, but it always rotted on the way. The plant refused to grow from the seeds he sent; the slips and shoots died en route. Only the introduction of the steamship brought a permanent solution by shortening the voyage.

In the eighteenth century, the pineapple was successfully grown in a few European hothouses. It was first served for dessert in France in 1694. The Duchess of Northumberland wrote in her diary of being given one as a very special rarity by Voltaire in 1772. In 1805, Grimod de la Reynière called it the most distinguished fruit on the French dinner table and one that appeared only at the most sumptuous.

After the steamship came into use, pineapples were exported from plantations established in Hawaii, the East Indies, and Asia. Singapore was the major exporter at the end of the nineteenth century, but Hawaii leads today, exporting 45 percent of the world's supply.

POMEGRANATE

The emblem of Granada, the pomegranate, is an old Semitic symbol of life, fertility, and abundance. Pomegranates originated in Africa, from where they traveled east to Asia Minor and beyond, and north to Spain with the Moors. It is probably the Spanish who brought them to America.

Dried and fresh pomegranates were eaten in Mesopotamia 4,000 years ago; they were eaten by the ancient Jews and by the ancient Egyptians, who used the root for medicine. Pomegranates were one of the chief Greek fruits. The seeds were used for seasoning in Greece, and later in sixteenth- and seventeenth-century Europe, as they are today in the Caucasus.

PORK

Everything in a pig is good. What ingratitude has permitted his name to become a term of opprobrium?

—Grimod de la Reynière

The pig, raised in India in the third millennium b.c., is one of the oldest domesticated animals. It was to be found in almost every early civilization where it was not forbidden as food. The Egyptians and Hebrews thought it impure. On the contrary, the Greeks, who began raising pigs in the Homeric era, made it a favorite for sacrifices.

Pigs were fattened for the Greek table on chestnuts and mast; unfattened pigs were fed to slaves. Suckling pig was the delight of the fifth century B.C., as was ham. There was one taboo about pigs in that era: the eating of pig brains was proscribed on the grounds that it would be like eating the heads of one's parents. Almost every other part of the animal was enjoyed. Pig's feet, or trotters, were a favorite in ancient Greece. Other delicacies enjoyed were the ears, sweetbreads, entrails, and, above all, the paunch, often served in vinegar and silphium. A playwright of the fourth century B.C. ridiculed a notorious gourmet by saying that while almost any man was willing to die for his country, Callimedon would undoubtedly give his life for a boiled sow's paunch. Another gourmet delight was the matrix, stewed in a sauce of brine and vinegar or boiled and served with rue.

In Rome, pork became the favorite butchers' meat after butchers were established. The demand was so great that hams were imported from various parts of the Empire, from Asia Minor to what is now Belgium. There was a separate market for pork in imperial Rome, the Forum Suarium. Offering meat of so many different flavors adaptable to so many ends, the pig was of enormous interest to Roman gourmets. Sows' udders were a rare and expensive delicacy, especially appreciated at the time of lactation. Apicius discovered that pig's liver increased greatly in size if the pig was force-fed with figs and then surfeited with wine and honey just before slaughter. The Romans ate the paunch, kernels, testicles, womb, cheeks, ears, snout, feet, entrails, and cracklings. Sumptuary laws forbidding the serving of many of these delicacies at banquets

Pork

failed to check enthusiastic gourmets. The main dish at an important banquet in imperial Rome was usually a wild boar or a stuffed pig. The stuffing might be small birds, such as figpeckers and thrushes, mixed with oysters.

Pork fat was used a great deal for cooking by rich and poor, and the poor also ate quantities of pork. It was distributed free by Emperor Aurelius, but that was when Rome, impoverished by the neglect of agriculture, was threatened with starvation.

In medieval times, pork was the favorite meat of the populace, who had Saint Peter to thank for a revelation allowing Christians to incorporate pork in their diet. Because lard was considered fasting fare, large numbers of pigs were consumed by monasteries. So long as there were forests in which pigs could forage for themselves, poor people in the country could afford to keep them. Bacon and hams were stored away in the lowliest house until, in the sixteenth and seventeenth centuries, fields were enclosed and laws passed to keep pigs from foraging on their own. That pigs were previously free to forage had caused France to lose a prince to a pig. Prince Philippe, son of Louis le Gros, was killed in 1131 when a pig running loose in the streets of Paris bumped into his horse. Raising pigs in town was forbidden by François Ier in 1539, but the law was generally evaded. An exception was made for members of the order of the Antonins, whose patron saint is usually portrayed with a pig at his side, and who, in consequence, kept the right to let their pigs roam freely in Paris.

POTATO

The potato, which now appears on the tables of the Western world almost daily, was treated with suspicion by most of Europe for almost three centuries after its discovery.

The Spanish discovered the potato in 1534 in the Andes, the only place it was then cultivated. Not long afterward, they brought it back to Spain where people paid up to a thousand dollars a pound for it in the belief it made the impotent potent. From Spain, the potato was sent to the Pope. Toward the end of the sixteenth century, the papal legate sent on specimens which eventually reached a Belgian botanist, Charles de l'Escluse, who drew a botanical sketch with a Latin caption in which the potato was designated *taratoufli,* or little truffle. It is because of the name used in that sketch that the vegetable known as *papa* to the Peruvians became known as *kartofel* to the Germans.

The potato was first eaten in Spain, next in Italy, and thirdly in the Lowlands, then Spanish possessions. Elsewhere in Europe it was grown as an exotic garden plant. Stylish gentlemen wore potato flowers in their buttonholes.

The potato was brought to England in the latter half of the sixteenth century, whether by Sir John Hawkins, Sir Francis Drake, or Sir Walter Raleigh experts disagree. Some hold it was washed ashore from ships of the Spanish Armada sunk off the British coast. The new vegetable was suspected of being poisonous and a possible carrier of leprosy and dysentery. A sixteenth-century banquet the English government gave to popularize the new vegetable backfired when, through ignorance, the mildly poisonous leaves and stems were served instead of the tubers.

The famished Irish accepted the new plant out of desperation. By the seventeenth century they had adopted potatoes to the exclusion of almost all other crops, an expedient that led to the disastrous famines of the 1840's. It was the Irish who brought the potato to North America in the early eighteenth century. Scotland remained unreceptive. It is, in fact, of the nightshade family, but so are tomatoes and a number of other useful plants.

In England, the potato had enjoyed a very brief period of interest as an expensive and curious exotic food when first introduced. This interest quickly died, and despite propaganda such as John Forster's book of 1663 entitled *England's Happiness Increased*, which was devoted entirely to the potato, the new vegetable was considered fit only for the poor and ignorant—in particular, the Irish. The English workman, who despised the Irish, would go to any length to avoid imitating him in anything, and therefore resisted all propaganda in favor of the potato. In the early eighteenth century, a number of important books on gardening and agriculture published in England failed to mention the potato at all, but by the end of the century it was a standard dish at every meal except breakfast in the northern part of the country.

France was the last European country to adopt the potato. In 1749, a French agriculturalist called the potato the worst of all vegetables. In Burgundy, its cultivation was forbidden by law. As late as 1771, the French government was forced to appeal to the Medical Faculty of Paris for an opinion on whether the potato was safe to eat.

The man who finally made potatoes accepted in France was an apothecary named Parmentier (the culinary term "parmentier" today means prepared or served with potatoes). After living almost exclusively on potatoes for a year while a prisoner in Prussia during the Seven Years' War, Parmentier decided the potato would improve the French diet. He met savage opposition. Accused of trying to force his "pig fodder" on the pensioners, he was forced to resign from the post of pharmacist at the Hôtel des Invalides. Parmentier's opportunity came in 1769, when the town of Besançon held a contest for the plant that would make the best substitute for grain cereals in time of famine. The jury gave Parmentier's potato first prize. Parmentier was asked to travel through France to study the poor quality of bread and recommend changes. Like most Europeans, he thought of the potato as a source of flour rather than a vegetable. In it he saw the possibility of cheap, nutritious bread for everyone. Parmentier was the first to work out a recipe for making bread from potatoes without the addition of cereal flour, but his idea was never adopted.

Undiscouraged, Parmentier continued to believe in the usefulness and versatility of the potato. He invited some prominent friends, including Benjamin Franklin, to a dinner composed entirely of potatoes prepared in twenty different ways. He began growing potatoes on sixty-odd acres of poor land the French government let him use to prove the new vegetable would grow in bad soil. To arouse public curiosity, he arranged to have the field conspicuously guarded by soldiers by day but not by night, when, as he anticipated, the field was systematically robbed by people eager to try so valuable a food. On August 25, 1785, Parmentier brought a potato-flower bouquet to Louis XVI on the occasion of the royal birthday and had the satisfaction of hearing the King announce that thanks to the potato there would be no more famine. Marie Antoinette pinned on a potato flower, Louis XVI put one in his buttonhole, Parmentier did likewise, and the courtiers were so eager to follow suit that some paid as much as ten louis for a single flower. Nevertheless it took the hard times of the French Revolution and the famine of 1816 for the potato to be generally accepted. In the First Republic, restaurants vied with each other in inventing ways of serving it.

One of the major reasons for the slow acceptance of the potato was the stubbornness with which people tried to make it into bread.* When starch or flour was first extracted from the potato after great effort in the late eighteenth century, French social historian Legrand d'Aussy commented the result was probably not worth the effort. He added that the "pasty taste, natural insipidity, and unhealthy quality" of the potato made it fit only for the "coarser palate and stronger stomachs of the populace." [97] No doubt the potato struck tastes corrupted by heavily spiced food as unbearably bland. It is a curious twist that in Mexico, when the potato was imported from Spain, it was considered food for the bourgeois.

The sweet potato, unlike the white potato, was native to Mexico as well as Peru. Columbus is credited with bringing it to Spain in 1493 and Sir John Hawkins with bringing it from Santa Cruz to England in 1553. It enjoyed brief popularity as a conserve, roasted, or made into comfits. It is often confused with the yam, which is native to both hemispheres. Neither sweet potatoes nor yams are often used in northern Europe, though the former was made fashionable for a short time by Empress Josephine, who grew the popular Creole vegetable at Malmaison.

PRESERVING

The techniques of refrigeration and canning were developed less than two hundred years ago, but people have been preserving food for at least four thousand years. The earliest and most common methods—salting, drying, and pickling in brine—are still used today, though we no longer depend on them for winter food. In early Mediterranean civilizations, the only vegetables available in winter were dried (peas, beans, chick-peas, lupines, and lentils) or pickled (pickled turnips were particularly popular in Rome). Fruit was dried or pickled, preserved in honey, or made into jams. Today we still

---

* Contemporary recipes for potato bread usually call for mashed potato with an equal or greater amount of flour from wheat or some other grain.

266

have raisins, dried prunes, apricots, dates, figs, and sometimes apples and pears. We also have pickled peaches, watermelon rind, and other fruit pickles, both sweet and sour. The Romans sometimes buried fruit and vegetables in underground pits, perhaps not unlike the root cellars still described in cookbooks of the early twentieth century. Herbs were dried for seasoning in Greece and Rome as they are today. All meat and fish that was not consumed immediately was treated for preserving by salting, drying, pickling, or smoking. Our salt cod, herring in brine, hams, smoked fish, and chipped beef undergo the same age-old processes.

Roman methods, with perhaps a little less variety and ingenuity, were used throughout Europe until the nineteenth century when canned, refrigerated, and, finally, frozen foods gradually became available to most of the Western world. There were a few timid innovations before 1800. Vegetables were cooked and stored in stoppered jars in cool rooms. Recipes for dehydrated soup cakes appeared in eighteenth-century cookbooks as conveniences for the traveler, along with dried vinegar. And as long ago as Elizabethan days, Francis Bacon made a few incomplete experiments with preserving meat in snow.

Be that as it may, modern methods of preserving food began with canning, discovered in 1795 by a Frenchman named François Appert, who had the inspiration of destroying bacteria-causing fermentation in food by subjecting it to high heat and sealing the containers hermetically. He used glass, which was heavy and fragile, but the invention sounded practical enough to Napoleon for him to make Appert official purveyor to the French Army. For the first time an army could move without trainloads of raw provisions and cattle on the hoof! During the Napoleonic wars, glass bottles from Appert's new factory came into the hands of the English, who thought of sealing the food in tin cans and took out a patent on canning in 1814.

Refrigeration is more recent. Icehouses were common among the wealthy in the seventeenth century. In the nineteenth, there was a large market for ice cut by the thousands of tons from frozen rivers, ponds, and flooded fields and used to pack fish on railroads and ships. By 1890, artificial ice was produced in large amounts. The first household refrigerator, an insulated cabinet cooled by a block

267

of ice, was introduced early in the nineteenth century, but mechanical domestic refrigerators were widely sold only after 1918.

It was automatic refrigeration that made possible the development of frozen foods. Patents had been taken out for freezing processes as early as 1842. The frozen-food industry was born about forty years later. It happened in 1880, when meat was first shipped from Australia to Great Britain on a refrigerated ship and, quite by accident, froze on board. The meat kept so well that the accident became the method. Preserving by freezing has grown steadily in importance ever since.

There have been many changes in preparation, packaging, and distributing, including the recent development of freeze-drying, a form of vacuum drying without heat that produces a product that need not be kept under refrigeration.

Every facet of our food has been profoundly and permanently affected by modern methods of preserving. There has even been a change in the kinds of plants grown and animals bred as agriculturalists seek products that lend themselves better to freezing. The character of food in the future may be determined more than anything else by future developments in the field of food preservation and processing.

RICE

Staple for half the world today, rice is believed to have been first cultivated in India, whence it spread to China and Mesopotamia about 2000 B.C. The Romans knew of rice from their travels, but it was not cultivated in Europe until much later: in Italy and Spain in the Middle Ages, in southern France in the sixteenth century. Rice cultivation began in the United States at the end of the seventeenth century when the captain of a trading ship from Madagascar, who had put into port at Charleston by chance, sold a bag of seed rice to a local merchant. Today, though cultivation is widely distributed, Asia produces more than nine tenths of the world's rice.

In the eighteenth century, the English government promoted the use of rice to offset the growing cost of food for the populace. Rice was cheap, filling, and available when local grain crops failed. For a number of years during the reign of George III, England admitted rice free of duty to encourage consumption. Arthur Young, eighteenth-century agricultural propagandist, took up the cause in the following words:

> Rice is known by all to be the most nourishing of grain, and sold so cheap in all the shores of England as 2 d. a pound. Four penny-worth of bread are easily eat in a day; but boil a pound of rice, in a penny-worth of milk, and you will not so soon find a man that can eat it.[98]

However practical rice may have been as a substitute for bread and other cereals, it did not become a basic food in Europe with the exception of Spain. However, many rice recipes appeared in cookbooks by the end of the eighteenth century.

ROSE

The cultivation of roses spread from Persia to the eastern Mediterranean, Greece, and then Italy very early in our history. The rose is one of the oldest cultivated flowers and the one most constantly used in cooking. The Greeks imported roses by the shipload from Egypt, wore roses at banquets in the belief they prevented drunkenness, and drank rose wine. The Romans grew roses in nurseries heated by hot waterpipes. A rose above the Roman banquet table meant those present would hold anything said in confidence, hence the expression *sub rosa*.

Rose water was frequently called for in recipes from the thirteenth century on. Whole fish were sometimes cooked in it. It was put in stews and soups. Rose petals were added to salads. Stewed roses and primroses were a delicate dessert. Using roses in cooking was a fortunate custom, because the flower is a source of vitamin C, in short supply in those scurvy-ridden days. Rose hips are still used as a source of vitamin C today as well as for making jam.

SAFFRON

Saffron is the most expensive flavoring agent in the world, worth more than its weight in gold. It is also one of the oldest, mentioned in the Song of Solomon. Seventy-five thousand blossoms of a fall-

269

blooming crocus native to the eastern Mediterranean are needed to make a single pound of saffron, which consists of the stigma of this flower.

Among the ancient Egyptians, Greeks, and Romans, saffron was used as dye, perfume, and flavoring and coloring agent in foods, and was fed to bees to give flavor to honey. Royal Persian robes were dyed with saffron. On important occasions, public buildings and streets in Rome and Greece were sprinkled with saffron water. It was used to scent theaters and baths; it was made into salves. Emperor Heliogabalus swam in a pool perfumed with saffron.

Large amounts of saffron were used in European cooking for centuries. One of the courtiers at the Hungarian court in the midfifteenth century remarked that people's fingers were stained with saffron from picking up sauced meat in their fingers. Europeans, who had to import saffron from the Middle East, were anxious to cultivate it locally, but the Arabs forbade the export of plants from the country. According to an old story, a pilgrim to the Holy Land at last managed to bring the first saffron bulb to England in the fourteenth century by concealing it in the hollow of his staff. Had he been discovered in the Levant, he would have paid the death penalty.

By the fifteenth and sixteenth centuries, every writer on agriculture included instructions on the cultivation of saffron, which continued to be a very profitable item of trade. It remained popular until effaced by turmeric and curry in the late eighteenth and early nineteenth centuries, though continuing in use in Spain.

Throughout the centuries of its popularity, saffron was valued as a medicine as well as a flavoring. Before the smallpox vaccination was discovered, saffron was suspended around the necks of victims of the disease. The benefits ascribed to the golden spice would make a very long list. Not only did it help in shortness of breath and diseases of the lung, liver, and bladder, it was a remedy for drunkenness and an effective moth killer. An overdose was reputed to kill people as well as moths. Taken in quantity, it was said to be exhilarating, to cause involuntary laughter, and, in excessive amounts, death in a fit of laughter. A small amount, on the other hand, led to light spirits. In 1623, Francis Bacon noted "the English are rendered sprightly by a liberal use of saffron in sweetmeats and broths."[99]

SALT

Salt has been used for over 3,000 years; through most of that time, it has been expensive and scarce. The Egyptians of the thirteenth and twelfth centuries B.C. used salt in medicines, special diets, and for preserving food, but we have no evidence it was in general use in cooking. In Greece, Rome, and pre-Roman Gaul, salt was taken from the sea and nearby salt marshes. Particularly important for preserving foods, it was economized where possible. Many Roman recipes call for seawater rather than salt, though Pliny believed that bread made of flour and seawater was extremely unhealthy. Plato spoke of salt as a relish, along with olives and cheese. Salt with bread seems to have been for Romans what butter with bread is today.

Though it was used with economy in Rome, even the poor had salt. In poems about his impoverished life in exile, the poet Leonidas, writing in the third century B.C., tells of mixing barley meal with herbs and coarse rock salt for food. Every Roman household had salt on the table in a special container. Those of the rich were of silver, those of the poor of terra-cotta. Under the most severe sumptuary laws, Romans were allowed two pieces of silver: a small dish used in sacrifices and the salt container. Salt played a part in early Greek and Roman sacrifices. It was considered so necessary and valuable that the first compensation the Roman government issued its soldiers was salt. The word "salary" (*salarium* in Latin) comes from this payment in salt, as do expressions such as "worth his salt."

The salt cellar remained an important item in the Middle Ages. It served as a division between lords and commoners when the master and his vassals all ate at one long table. To sit below the salt was to be with the plebians, on the wrong side of the salt cellar. Small individual salt dishes, one of the many signs of the breakdown of feudalism, came in style in the seventeenth century.

From early times, salt mining and trade have been controlled, aided, and taxed by governments. Salt was expensive in France until 1789 because of taxes the government imposed on it, but the government also assisted in its exploitation. As early as 1100, the French government built nine roads for salt transport in the vicinity of Poitou, the region considered to have the best salt. The roads had

271

to be maintained on penalty of fines, and the salt wagons, drawn by five, six, or seven horses, had to adhere to a strict schedule. Special meadows were reserved for the horses of salt convoys and special shelters for their drivers. In the fifteenth century, a tunnel was driven through a mountain in order to speed salt transport. To attack salt dealers was a heinous crime in the Middle Ages.

SESAME

Sesame, only popular as a seasoning in the United States in the past dozen years, is one of the oldest seeds grown by man for oil. It was cultivated in the third millennium B.C. in Harrapā, India, and is still widely used in India both for cooking and for anointing. In about 3000 B.C., the Assyrians used it for oil, wine, and as a food. Sesame was grown in Greece and Roman Italy too, where it was put in perfumes and on breads.

Prior to the discovery of cheaper oils (mainly soy bean and cotton), sesame seed oil was the standard vegetable oil in the United States. From 50 to 60 million pounds of seeds were imported yearly for oil in the 1930's. After cheaper oils were introduced, the import of sesame seeds dropped to a few million pounds a year, but has since risen to 35 million, now that sesame has become popular.

Part of its popularity is due to recognition that it is a rich source of protein, calcium, phosphorus, and the vitamin niacin. Once credited with magical powers, it is now praised as a health food. Health food stores carry an increasing number of sesame seed products such as candy bars and tahini, the sesame seed paste used extensively in Near and Far Eastern cooking.

SHELLFISH
(see also OYSTER)

And best of dainties is the prawn
that peeps from green fig leaves. . . .
—Ananius (third century B.C.)

Since fishing and hunting for food preceded cultivation, it is not surprising that a great variety of shellfish were eaten in early history. Records dating from the fifth century B.C. show that the early Greeks and Romans ate barnacles, clams, cockles, conchs, several varieties of river and sea crabs, crayfish, cuttlefish, limpets, two kinds of lobster, mussels, octopuses, periwinkles, pinnas, purple

272

shells, scallops, sea snails of various kinds, sea urchins, squid, and whelks. The shellfish were eaten raw, boiled, fried, baked on coals, or cooked with a sauce or a vegetable such as sorrel. Shrimp were eaten with bread, scallops with cumin and pepper. Oysters were sometimes accompanied by garum; sea urchins were eaten raw or pickled with parsley and mint.

Shellfish were considered superior in spring and summer, particularly if caught when the moon was waxing. Certain waters were preferred for specific shellfish. Horace noted Tarentum produced the biggest scallops, the Lucrine Lake the best mussels, Misenum the best sea urchins, etc.

Not content with looking afar for their shellfish, the Romans grew two species in artificial beds. Preserves for sea snails were established in the middle of the first century B.C. The Roman responsible for this gastronomic innovation, Fulvius Lippinus, used to import his sea snails from Africa, Greece, and other parts of the Roman Empire and fatten them on a mixture of wheat and boiled wine. Artificial oyster beds, established sometime prior to 91 B.C., were an instant and lucrative success.

Shellfish were not much appreciated in Europe after Roman times until the end of the sixteenth and seventeenth centuries, when oysters, crayfish, and, lastly, lobsters became fashionable. Through the nineteenth century, recipes used crayfish and oysters in staggering quantities and often bizarre combinations. Two hundred crayfish went into a single soup in Charles Carter's mideighteenth century *London and Country Cook,* while another cookbook, *The Whole Duty of a Woman,* suggested two dozen to one hundred as a suitable garnish for soup.

America contributed the round American quahog and the softshell clam as well as the New England clambake made with softshell clams steamed in a pit with seaweed. Some of the shellfish the early Greeks and Romans ate have never become popular in the United States. Cockles, mussels, winkles, limpets, whelks, and sea urchins and other small shellfish are appreciated in Europe, but are

found only occasionally on the American market. Mussels are one of the best and cheapest sources of nourishment: an acre of productive mussel beds will produce approximately ten thousand pounds of flesh a year. The French, who eat 140 million pounds of shellfish every year, have been cultivating mussels for centuries, but almost the only extensive commercial use they are put to in America is the manufacture of buttons and the feeding of hogs and chickens.

SPICES

The history of the spice trade is the history of the rise and fall of empires. How early it began we do not know, but it was at least 4,000 years ago. Spices were important in Assyria, Babylon, and ancient Egypt. In Babylon, they were mentioned as items of commerce along with gold, silver, and gems. The Phoenicians were trading spices in 2000 B.C., about the time Joseph was sold to spice merchants traveling by camel to Egypt. Thebes, Memphis, and Coptos were early trading centers for spices; Alexandria later became the major center, a position it held until the sixteenth century. Romans and Greeks imported spices, which they found essential for many purposes besides flavoring food. Spices were used in dyes, ointments, incense, perfumes, medicines, religious ceremonies, fumigation, and preserving. Egyptian embalmers filled body cavities with spices to preserve them. Rooms were purified with spices, baths perfumed with them, people anointed with them. Spices were also valued for stimulating thirst. Alexandre Dumas believed they stimulated the intellect as well, commenting that he was tempted to believe we owe Titian's masterpieces to the influence of spices.

After the Romans spread a taste for spices through Europe, the latter continued to be prized through the Dark Ages although so scarce they were used very sparingly. Spices were valued as part of royal dowries and magistrates' pay. They were listed in inventories of the possessions of important people. They were gifts for a king, inspiration for a poet. Despite exorbitant prices, more spice by far was consumed per capita in the Middle Ages than today, according to French historian Pierre Gaxotte. Because the majority were too poor to afford such a luxury, the rich must have eaten huge amounts. Old cookbooks and historical accounts indicate that they did. Perhaps necessary to disguise tainted fish and meat or to give character to insipid desalted foods, spices were used in greater and greater quantities as palates became used to them. In a royal household, the grinding of spices was a full-time job carrying the title of yeoman powder beater. Frederick the Great used to add a spoonful of ginger and another of nutmeg to a heavily spiced soup. Plates of spices were served after dinner in rich households. People carried spices around in their pockets and ate them like candy.

At the beginning of the tenth century, Venice monopolized the import of spices, which thenceforth constituted the bulk of her trade and the foundation of her fortune. The Medicis grew rich on spices, carried to Europe on Venetian or Genoese vessels from centers such as Alexandria or Aleppo, to which they were brought by caravan. To discover a new route to the Spice Islands that would circumvent the Italian states' monopoly became the major preoccupation of the rest of Europe. To find a route, Vasco da Gama set out eastward around the Cape of Good Hope in 1498 and actually opened a route to the Spice Islands, thereby accomplishing what Columbus had failed to do on his journey six years earlier.

Lisbon became the center of the spice trade for the next century, until the Dutch built a battle fleet, invaded the Indian Ocean, and drove out the Portuguese. By the end of the seventeenth century, the Eastern spice trade was the monopoly of the Dutch who went to great lengths to keep it. At a time when other nations were trying to plant Oriental spices in the West Indies, the Dutch soaked nutmegs in limewater to make them infertile before exporting them, and imposed severe penalties on anyone in Ceylon who had cinnamon in his possession without authorization.

A Frenchman with the appropriate name of Poivre is credited with making spices available to France without paying large sums to the Dutch. He managed to smuggle out cloves and nutmegs and plant them successfully on French tropical islands. After the English stopped seeking a northeast or northwest passage (efforts that led to discoveries in North America but no spices), they challenged the Dutch directly. There was a struggle for power in the Far East until the Dutch monopoly was broken in 1795, leaving the British in control of all the Dutch spice islands except Java. Dutch trade would have been diminished in any case by the great increase in the production and export of spices from tropical America, particularly the West Indies.

With the increase in availability and decrease in price, spices became less fashionable. Since World War II, however, there has been a sharp rise in the demand for spices; consumption in the United States has approximately doubled.

SPINACH

It is not certain where spinach came from or when. Though the Greeks and Romans cooked and ate a great number of leafy green vegetables, spinach is first identified about 1250, when it was enjoyed by the kings of Aragon. Because the old botanists called it *olus hispanicum* and the Moors called it *hispanach*, it was assumed to have been first discovered or developed in Spain. It is now known to be native to southwestern Asia.

The vegetable was little known in France and England of the fourteenth century, when "spynoches yfried" or fried spinach was mentioned in *Forme of Cury*, and something called "espinar" or "spinoches" was described with care in *Le Ménagier de Paris* as a dish to be eaten at the beginning of Lent. By the sixteenth century, spinach was cultivated in France and England, where it was particularly popular during Lent because it ripened when few vegetables were available. From that century on, cookbooks included a great many spinach recipes, most of them calling for cinnamon and sugar.

In the 1920's, when the relatively high content of iron and vitamins A and C in spinach was publicized, the vegetable came into the forefront again. The comic strip "Popeye" helped parents induce their children to eat it.

STRAWBERRY

The Greeks and Romans ate strawberries, but only the small, wild variety. As early as the fourteenth century, these small berries were planted in great quantities in the gardens of the Louvre. From the sixteenth century, strawberries with cream were popular in

France and England. The larger variety of strawberry was not known until brought back from Chile in the early eighteenth century by a naturalist commissioned by Louis XIV to survey the natural wealth of the New World to determine what might be acclimatized in the Old. Strawberries became one of the most fashionable eighteenth-century fruits.

STURGEON

Sturgeon is a once-royal fish that has almost gone out of favor except when smoked. Unfortunately the fish is in danger of going out of existence as well because of its wanton slaughter for caviar.

Sturgeon used to be both more plentiful and more widely appreciated. It was favored salted or pickled in Greece in the eighth century B.C. The Romans, who preferred caviar sturgeon from the Caspian, had it brought to the banquet table to a chorus of trumpets and flutes in the heyday of the Empire. It was not always popular in Rome, however. Pliny comments with wonder that, though still rare in the first century A.D., it was no longer sought after.

The finest caviar sturgeon has always come from the rivers of the Caspian, the Black Sea, and the Sea of Azov, but sturgeon was once common in other parts of the world. In the sixteenth century, it was so plentiful in the estuary of the Rhone that it was the cheapest fish in southern France. As late as the nineteenth century, it was sometimes caught in the Seine. Once caught, sturgeon provides plenty of food. According to old accounts, the beluga sturgeon sometimes weighed as much as 3,000 pounds.

European cookbooks of the seventeenth century used to devote whole chapters to sturgeon, and in England, a law no longer observed but still valid as late as the 1920's, according to Artemas Ward, declared the fish could be eaten only at the king's table or with royal permission. While Americans and most Europeans only eat sturgeon smoked today, the Russians, as always, consider sturgeon the finest fresh fish, and sturgeon recipes still dominate fish chapters in Russian cookbooks. *Vesiga*, spinal marrow from the sturgeon, is essential in certain Russian dishes. It is a curious fact that when fresh sturgeon can be found in the U. S. markets, it is relatively inexpensive; once smoked, however, it soars into the luxury class.

SUGAR

Until the beginning of the sixteenth century, sugar was limited to royalty and nobility in Europe and was used as a seasoning like cinnamon or saffron, or as a medicine. Just as expensive as spices, which were very expensive indeed, sugar was sold by spice merchants or pharmacists. It is still treated as a seasoning in the Orient today. In Russia, a pinch of sugar is used in almost everything to heighten flavors just as monosodium glutamate is in Japan. Before the wide-scale cultivation of cane sugar in the West Indies, Europeans who could afford it at all used it in sauces for dishes such as pork, rabbit, and eels. Pastries requiring sweetening in large amounts were made with honey as they had been since the earliest Egyptian dynasty.

The first recorded large shipment of sugar to England arrived in 1319. By the sixteenth century, the English upper classes kept it on the dining table in a special box with a special spoon. Sugar was not there to sprinkle on cereal or strawberries, however, but to put in wine; Elizabethans thought it made wine less intoxicating. Sugar was still hardly known by name to most Frenchmen in the first half of the seventeenth century and only came into common use at the end of the eighteenth.

Though general consumption of sugar is relatively recent, sugarcane has been grown for a long time—no one is quite certain how long. The earliest mention of sugarcane that can be positively identified goes back to the seventh century, when it was described by two Byzantine chroniclers. Some experts believe sugar originated in India, reached Persia by the third century, Arabia two hundred years later, and Egypt shortly afterward. Its name, derived from the Sanskrit *sarkarā*, supports the theory of Indian origin.

There are a number of descriptions in early Greek and Roman literature of a sweet juice obtained from a cane in India. Nearchus, who was with Alexander the Great's army in India in the fourth century B.C., was the first to speak of this sweet liquid. Later descriptions by geographer Strabo and naturalist Theophrastus are based on Nearchus' account. Pliny also spoke of a sweet juice, and Dioscorides, Greek physician of the first century, wrote of a sweet substance of saltlike consistency. Most authorities believe the canes described in these early sources are sweet flag or some other reed containing sweet juice rather than sugarcane, and that whatever Dioscorides' saltlike grains were, they could not have been sugar because it was not refined until at least two hundred years later. In the unlikely possibility that Greeks and Romans ever saw sugar, it was certainly not available to them in the same form as today's, nor did they make use of it.

Until sugar could be refined and crystallized from the juice of the cane, it was difficult to transport or store it. Refining first took place sometime between the third and eighth centuries. Sugar was commercially manufactured in Egypt in the ninth or tenth century. The Moorish conquest brought sugarcane to Spain while the rest of Europe acquired a taste for it in the Middle East during the Crusades. It was a royal gift in the eleventh century and still so scarce in the thirteenth that we read of Henry III of England asking someone to try to get him three pounds of it if possible. For centuries, Venice kept a monopoly on sugar refining and import from the East. When Columbus took sugarcane plants with him on his second voyage to America, he established a breach in the Venetian hold on sugar trade. The Spanish planted sugar plantations throughout their tropical colonies; the French and English followed suit. Refineries were set up in many parts of Europe to process sugar from the New World. Gradually sugar became available to everyone —available, but still a luxury. Only in the nineteenth century did it become a basic part of everyone's diet.

Today's high consumption is of even more recent date. In the United States it has soared from less than nine pounds per head in 1823 to 93 to 94 pounds in 1923, and over 100 in the late 1960's, a consumption topped by the United Kingdom's 110 plus. The development of the beet-sugar industry is largely responsible for the change, and Napoleon can take much of the credit for that.

Refining sugar from beets was not a new idea in the Napoleonic era. The Chinese had done it in a crude form many centuries before, but Europeans had assumed that only plants grown in tropical heat contained sugar. In the middle of the eighteenth century, a

German chemist proved otherwise, signaling the beet as a particularly rich source. Another German completed plans for the commercial extraction of sugar from the beet, and a French industrialist reaped the benefit of these discoveries in 1812.

By that date, sugar was looked upon as a daily necessity, partly because of the recent addiction to coffee and tea. The continental blockade having cut off France's sugar supply, Napoleon looked for other sources and offered a million-franc prize to the man who would demonstrate the best commercial method of extracting sugar from the beet. Using the German inventor's plan, Benjamin Delessert had established a factory for the manufacture of beet sugar, which Napoleon was persuaded to visit in 1812. The Emperor was sufficiently impressed to make Delessert a baron and to set aside land for beet farming in northern France. When the Empire fell, the price of cane sugar, no longer blockaded, fell with it, and most of the new factories went bankrupt. The beet-sugar industry came back into its own again with a rise in sugar consumption. By 1900, the world consumed two pounds of beet sugar to every pound of cane.

SWAN

From Roman times through the Middle Ages, swan was a festive dish, often presented regally with flutes and trumpets. Fifty swans were served at a feast for King Richard II in 1387.

Roast cygnets from the Thames are still served at an annual banquet in Vintners' Hall in London, presided over by the Swan Warden. The Vintners give five cheers instead of the usual three at this banquet in memory of an occasion in the Middle Ages when they were host to five kings, the kings of England, Scotland, France, Denmark, and Cyprus.

TEA

That excellent and by all physicians approved China drink . . .
—advertisement in *Mercurius Politicus*, September 30, 1658

Two pounds two ounces of tea was a gift for a king, presented to Charles II by the East India Company in 1660. Muhammadan travelers of the ninth century described tea drinking in China, but

it was first mentioned in Europe by an Italian in 1590 and first imported by the Dutch twenty years after. Tea reached England and France only in the midseventeenth century, coming into common use half a century later.

When introduced to France about 1660, tea aroused as lively an opposition as coffee had. The eighteenth-century French historian Legrand d'Aussy repeated a rumor that, in order to sell it, the Dutch East India Company had bribed two physicians to extoll its benefits. Balzac said women who drink tea are pale, sickly, talkative, boring, and preachy.

While Frenchmen preferred coffee, Englishmen preferred tea. By 1860, every inhabitant of England consumed 2.67 pounds of tea per year; by 1908, six pounds. By the midtwentieth century, the English were drinking five times as much tea as coffee. The United States, which had started as a tea-drinking country and switched to coffee after the Boston Tea Party, drinks twenty-five times as much coffee as tea.

TOMATO

The tomato, without which we cannot imagine Italian or Spanish food today, was not discovered until the sixteenth century and took another three hundred years to become generally accepted. Brought back by the Spaniards from Mexico and Peru, tomatoes, like most new foods, were first regarded with suspicion and fear. Called tomatoes after the Aztec word *tomatl*, they were also known as love apples, probably because they were believed to be aphrodisiac. For two and a half centuries, they were grown chiefly as a curiosity.

Tomatoes became part of the Spanish cuisine only in the late eighteenth century. From Spain, the tomato habit spread to southern France and Italy. It was the men of the Marseilles Legion, eating their tomatoes in Paris during the Revolution, who are credited with convincing the Parisians that the new vegetable was safe and even good to eat.

The Americans, now the world's greatest consumers, were among the last to be convinced. According to the *Encyclopaedia Britannica*, there is no record of anyone growing tomatoes in the United States until Thomas Jefferson did so in 1781. The northeastern states continued to shun the new plant until the midnineteenth century. As late as 1900, tomatoes were little used except in purees and were considered inedible raw. Many people still believed the tomato was poisonous, possibly because it belongs to the same family as deadly nightshade, the *Solanaceae*.

TRUFFLE

Penser qu'on ne sait pas le nom du premier
cochon qui a trouvé une truffe!
　　—Edmond and Jules de Goncourt, *Journal* *

This fungus has been appreciated by gourmets since early history. The Romans and Greeks imported truffles from Africa and other parts, but probably did not know the best of truffles, the black ones found today only in a small region of France, the Périgord. Even in the early nineteenth century, when Brillat-Savarin wrote his book on gastronomy, he confessed that no one knew how truffles were produced or how they grew; all that was known was that they could not be planted. Knowledge of the truffle had not advanced much since Pliny wrote that truffles are "lumps of earthy substance bundled together and cannot be grown by seed."

* "To think one does not know the name of the first pig to have found a truffle!"

By the nineteenth century, no one believed anymore that truffles were created by lightning or out of the spit of witches. The scientific explanation, which we now have, is almost as mysterious. It seems that, when truffles are eaten by small animals in the forests, the spores of the truffle pass through the animal's digestive system intact to start new truffles in a new place.

Growing truffles is a slow business. First the farmer plants oak or beech trees. When these mature, he puts truffles in the ground around the trees. Then he has only to wait another six to ten years, and he can harvest truffles. Despite the discouragingly long process, some truffle farms exist in France. Once established, the fungi may not stay. Truffle beds have been known to move about eighty miles in two or three generations.

Since no part of the truffle is ever exposed to daylight, finding it presents a challenge. The truffle hunter takes advantage of the keen nose and fondness for truffles of a variety of animals. Whatever is at hand is used in the hunt. The Russians use bear cubs, the Sardinians goats, the French pigs, and the Italians dogs. Champion truffle dogs sniff out the delectable fungi at long distances.

After the fall of Rome, the truffle became lost to gastronomy until the fourteenth century. Today some gourmets cannot imagine a great meal without truffles, which are consequently an important industry in France.

Each area where truffles are found produces a distinct type and quality. Unfortunately, truffles are both rare and inferior in North America (where they are confined largely to Oregon and California). France is blessed with many truffles, among them the best in the world. Since canned truffles have little resemblance to fresh ones, nature has given French gastronomes a gustatory monopoly.

TURKEY

A dispute has raged for centuries as to whether the ancient Greeks and Romans knew the turkey or not, and whether it was new to Europe when brought by the Spaniards from the New World. Our name for the turkey family, Meleagridae, comes from the Latin word *meleagris*. On the basis of detailed descriptions of the fowl and its habits, it seems almost certain the bird the Romans called *meleagris* was guinea fowl. Confusion deepens with the appearance of the word "turkey" in England prior to the appearance of our American bird. However it has been established that guinea fowl were known as turkeys in fifteenth-century England in the mistaken belief that they came from Turkey. When Shakespeare speaks of a turkey in *Henry IV*, he is referring to guinea fowl. After the American bird was introduced and became popular under the name "turkey," the original meaning of the word was forgotten.

The theory has been advanced that Jacques Coeur, Charles VII's treasurer, brought turkeys to Europe from the Middle East in the midfifteenth century, but there is no proof. Other writers concluded that because turkeys are now found in Asia and Africa, they did not originate in North America. This conclusion is countered by the argument that Asian and African turkeys were introduced by European settlers.

It is certain that when Gonzalo Hernandez de Oviedo, governor of Santo Domingo, wrote of seeing the bird in America in 1525, he regarded it as a totally new and unknown species. Having no name for it, he called it a kind of peacock. The name stuck in Spain where turkeys are *pavos* and peacocks royal *pavos*, or *pavos reales*. The Portuguese more logically dubbed the bird *peru*. The French, who saw their first turkey in the late fifteenth or early sixteenth century called it bird of India; the "of India," or *d'Inde*, was later contracted into the current French word for turkey, *dinde*. The name is not illogical if you bear in mind that America was spoken of as India for some time after its discovery.

The Spaniards brought the turkey to Spain in 1530 from Mexico, where the bird was already domesticated. It reached England about the same time. English colonists soon after introduced the Mexican turkey to New England, where wild turkeys already existed. Turkeys were immediately fashionable in Europe and, at first, a royal gift. When Charles IX passed through Amiens in 1566, a dozen turkeys were among the presents given him by the city. Turkeys soon replaced peacocks and swans as birds to serve at a feast. When they became more common, they could no longer appear at a banquet, at least not whole. Brillat-Savarin wrote of a dinner in Connecticut in 1789 at which twenty turkeys were prepared for twenty guests, but all that was served was the oyster of the turkey.

Since the first Thanksgiving in 1621, Americans have eaten more and more turkey, and the turkey population has grown. There is now one turkey for every two people in the United States.

TURNIP

The Roman scholar Pliny, who expressed his opinion about almost everything, called the turnip the most useful vegetable after cereals and beans. Turnip tops and bottoms were used in Greece and Rome. They were pickled for winter use and for appetizers; in spring and summer, they were served in salad with mustard dressing. Turnip roots were boiled or roasted, whole or sliced. In Gaul, turnips were used as winter fodder for animals.

The turnip was a common vegetable. When a riot broke out against Emperor Vespasian, the crowd threw turnips at him (tomatoes were then unknown). Healthful and satisfying, they were not highly esteemed food, though often a staple in the country. Various authors tell the story of a Roman leader who defeated the luxury-loving Samnites in battle. After their defeat, the Samnites sought out the Roman leader to try to bribe him. When they arrived at his country house, they found him cooking turnips—just turnips—for his supper. The Samnites left at once, realizing anyone satisfied with just turnips for supper could not be bribed.

Useful as the turnip was in the ancient world, it was unknown in much of Europe for centuries after the Roman Empire collapsed. By the early sixteenth century, it was a popular French stew vegetable, but only reached England in the midseventeenth century. It was about that time that it was adopted as fodder for livestock in the winter.

VANILLA

Vanilla is a native American spice—if it is a spice at all; experts disagree on that point. The vanilla bean is the seed pod of a kind of orchid native to Mexico that has been planted in the tropics from Java to Martinique to Madagascar. The Mexican is still the most sought after.

Probably the most popular dessert flavoring today, vanilla was first tasted by Cortes when he drank chocolate at Montezuma's court. Vanilla was often used to flavor chocolate in the early Spanish colonies. It had barely begun to be used as a flavoring in France and England at the end of the seventeenth century.

VEGETABLES

Vegetables were more important in early history than they are today, though they fell into ill repute for many centuries in between. Cereals, milk products, and vegetables—fresh in season, pickled, dried, or smoked in winter—made up the daily diet of the first Greeks and Romans. Legumes such as lentils, beans, and chickpeas were basic foods. Among vegetables, garlic and onion were staples for rich and poor alike, followed in popularity by cabbage, beets, turnips, and horseradish. Some vegetables were limited to the rich—asparagus, for example.

Modern botanists are unable to identify with certainty all vegetables and varieties of which the Greeks and Romans wrote. Many, including cabbage, probably did not exist in their present form. It is certain the Greeks and Romans knew the vegetables mentioned above. It is fairly well established that they also had carrots, chicory, cress, cucumbers, lettuce, a kind of kale, a squash or pumpkin, parsnips, some plants of the thistle family related to the present-day artichoke and cardoon, broccoli, celery, fennel, and leek. They may or may not have had cauliflower and shallots. In addition they ate a number of plants no longer common fare today: acanthus, alexander, asphodel, cuckoopint, lupine, sea and land nettles, a variety of bulbs, and some unidentified plants such as silphium that may have vanished from the earth. They did not have any of our common green beans or lima beans, sugar peas, eggplant, maize, tomatoes, potatoes, or sweet potatoes. Except for sugar peas, all these became known in Europe only after the discovery of America.

Some ancient physicians issued warnings against vegetables. Hippocrates thought it advisable to eat few of them in winter. Diphilus of Siphnos wrote about 150 years later that "broadly speaking, all green vegetables give little nourishment, produce no fat, are poor in flavour, remain on the surface of the stomach, and are hard to assimilate." [100] Among the risks run by people indulging in certain vegetables were impotence, chills, weakness, dull sight, and indigestion. Nevertheless, many vegetables were eaten, and great care was given their preparation in houses of the rich. The Apicius cookbook devotes a whole chapter to vegetable dishes with a total of fifty-eight recipes. Vegetables appear elsewhere in the book in combinations as well: jellied salads with cheese or chicken, for example, or asparagus with figpeckers.

Charlemagne encouraged the cultivation of vegetables. His capitularies mention the onion family, cress, chicory, lettuce, leeks, beets, parsnips, carrots, cabbages, radishes, cardoons, and various legumes. Otherwise vegetables slid into oblivion for a long period of time. Only the onion, leek, and garlic resisted the wave of unpopularity from the end of the Roman Empire until some time in the seventeenth century. Garlic, in particular, was thought to ward off the plague, enough alone to make it popular.

Generally speaking vegetables were considered harmful in the Middle Ages, though good enough for the poor who could not afford meat. Besides engendering wind and melancholy, vegetables were believed to have little food value. The gardens of large monasteries consisted almost entirely of herbs, many for medical purposes. The few vegetable gardens in existence grew cabbages and the onion family, all primarily for soups. Vegetables do not seem to

have been served at table in their own right, at least not by the rich. Menus or purchase lists of fifteenth- and sixteenth-century feasts are extraordinarily long and varied, but almost never include a single vegetable.

The only European country in which vegetables were extensively grown during the Dark Ages was Spain. The kings of Aragon were enjoying a sophisticated cuisine in the early Middle Ages with asparagus, broad beans, carrots, cucumbers, eggplant, and other vegetables. It seems probable that Spanish influence led the Flemish and Dutch to plant vegetable gardens long before their neighbors. In any case, it was from the Dutch that first the French, then the English learned to grow vegetables.

"Introduced to England from the Netherlands in the sixteenth century" is a tag you can attach to many vegetables. The very idea of growing them, whether in cottage gardens or on extensive estates, reached England from Flanders in the latter part of the sixteenth century. Root vegetables like turnips, carrots, and parsnips were planted in English soil for the first time. In France, too, the sixteenth century was a time of change, first under the influence of Catherine de Médicis, who brought advanced ideas on food from Italy, and next under the impact of the French agriculturalist Olivier de Serres, whose experimental farm served as an example for market gardeners throughout Europe. He worked on selective breeding to obtain earlier and later vegetables and improved varieties. His discoveries led to the establishment of kitchen gardens on many estates and to a change in the character of food, which became more varied and less spiced in order to preserve the subtle flavors of vegetables. During the reign of Louis XIV (1643–1715), dishes of rare or out-of-season vegetables were served between meat courses to whet the appetite.

Under the stimulus of the age of exploration, governments and individuals studied plant life everywhere. Plants were taken to the New World and acclimatized there. Plants from the New World were taken to the Old where they were studied, grown, and sometimes adopted in the cuisine, instantly or after centuries. Some could not be acclimatized; others simply never found favor. There are many common vegetables of Central and South America seldom or never seen in northern markets. The vegetable was beginning to take its place in the nineteenth century, though botanist Henry

Phillips could still write in 1820 that "the middle or lower class of English families . . . have yet to learn the art of improving their dishes with vegetables." [101] At that time, the rich were eating rare or out-of-season vegetables as delicacies while urging the coarser ones on the poor as a way of making meat go farther. (The awakened social conscience of the time often took the form of telling the poor how to manage their budget better.) At last, with the reversal of medical opinion and the development of a bourgeois cuisine in a more egalitarian age, the vegetable came into its own. There was even a brief fashion for vegetarianism in the late nineteenth century in reaction to the richness of the table.

VINEGAR

The Romans and Greeks had a variety of vinegars made from grapes, figs, dates, betony, and squill. They used it often in cooking and even more in preserving.

Vinegar sellers of medieval and Renaissance France offered an even greater variety of flavored vinegars, which the French used widely in sauces and sprinkled liberally on game dishes. Pepper vinegar was common, partly because there was no tax on wine brought into Paris with pepper in it. Aside from pepper, vinegars were flavored with cloves, carnations, chicory, mustard, fennel, ginger, pistachio, roses, bugloss, truffles, raspberries, etc. In the eighteenth century, French vinegarers offered for sale 92 kinds of toilet vinegar and 55 for the table. Cookbooks included recipes for drying vinegar into balls that could be carried in a traveler's pocket and dissolved in water or wine for use.

The word "vinegar" is derived from *vin aigre*, "sour wine." What made wine turn into vinegar remained a mystery until Pasteur's studies of fermentation in the 1850's. As often happens, someone had made the fundamental discovery earlier but had been pushed aside. When a Dutch chemist suggested in 1732 that living organisms transformed wine into vinegar, the idea was rejected as both ridiculous and disgusting.

Vinegar had a long medical history. It was prescribed by Hippocrates in the fifth century B.C. and used to combat scurvy in the U. S. Civil War. Rabelais observed it was supposed to ward off quinsy and was useful for cleaning teeth.

WHALE

The whale was a popular and princely dish in the fifteenth century. Four centuries later, Dumas praised it heartily, comparing the flavor to beef and noting it was so healthful fishermen attributed their excellent constitutions to eating it.

Whales make very definite seasonal migrations over distances up to 3,000 miles. In the thirteenth century, they were found close to the French coast, thereby providing an easy and copious supply of fish for Lent and fast days. Whale was one of the staples of the poor in sixteenth-century France, while whale's tongue prepared with peas or spit-roasted was a bourgeois delicacy. When a method of converting whale fat to a valuable oil was discovered, the whale lost its importance as food.

WINE
(see also GRAPE)

Wine may not be a food, but it is used in cooking and has had a profound influence on cuisine. It is rare to find a worthy culinary tradition where wine is not the habitual drink.

Wine is a very old drink indeed. Grapes were gathered and fermented in Switzerland and Italy before vines were cultivated; Noah made wine. Wine was drunk in ancient Egypt, though it made an appearance much later than beer. It was also drunk in pre-Homerian Greece, though water and milk were the usual beverages. Wine was scarce in early Rome. To make certain it went around, women were forbidden it. There is a story that Romulus absolved a man who killed his wife for having secretly drunk wine from a vat in the house. Wine does not seem to have been forbidden women on religious grounds because Roman women were allowed to drink wine that had turned bad, cooked wine, and the wine made from dry raisins. The women of Marseilles fared less well; they were forbidden to drink anything but water. Similar restrictions were imposed on soldiers, who were issued *posca*, soured wine or water mixed with vinegar, until the beginning of the Empire. Emperor Pescennius Niger forbade soldiers to drink wine at all during campaigns, though otherwise men and women drank wine freely from the first century on.

There have been many kinds and classes of wine and many prices for it since antiquity. Seals on wine drunk by Pharaoh Ikhnaton (who reigned from 1379 to 1362 B.C.) mark it as belonging to one of three categories: good, very good, and very, very good. Homerian wine was a thick, heavy one made by harvesting the grapes late, when already a bit wilted, and leaving them in the sun for six days before putting them to ferment. Greek wine was cloudy, contained impurities, and was filtered before serving. It was often cooked, honeyed, or infused with spices—bay leaf, pepper, mastic, crushed roasted dates, pennyroyal, roses, and wormwood (which made a kind of vermouth). The Greeks were particularly fond of sweet and aromatic wines. An Athenian quoted in Anacharsis' travelogue of the fourth century B.C. describes sweetening wine by adding flour kneaded with honey to the cask and infusing wine with aromatics, fruits, and flowers. "My pleasure," he remarked, "is, on opening one of my barrels, to have the odour of violets and roses instantly exhale and fill my cellar." Seasonings served to flavor wine and preserve it longer. Yet there was also pure wine, which Columella, writing in the first century, praised as the best: wine that had nothing added to preserve it and nothing to obscure its natural quality.

Though the Egyptians, Greeks, and Romans used glass for other purposes, glass bottles are not mentioned until the fifteenth century, and storing wine in them became common only in the seventeenth. In the old days, wine was kept in casks, jars (amphorae), or skins (it is still kept in skins in parts of Spain). Rich Romans took pride in keeping wine in cellars and in serving a great wine from a great year. Athenaeus' third-century gastronomical summary contains a discourse on 34 kinds of wines, their qualities and optimum

ages (from five to twenty-five years). One Roman cellar mentioned contained 199 distinct wines. Wealthy Sybarites used to have cellars near the seashore to which wines were piped in from their country estates.

Wine was almost always drunk diluted. Apparently in ancient times it was strong, bitter, or otherwise disagreeable in its pure state, if not actually dangerous. There are tales of people who died from drinking straight wine. Solon forbade the drinking of pure wine, and in one region, according to Athenaeus, drinking unmixed wine without a medical prescription was punishable by death. Hippocrates recommended drinking wine "as undiluted as possible" in winter as if this would be a bitter pill. In his work "On Drunkenness," Theophrastus mentions the custom of offering a small amount of unmixed wine at the end of the dinner as a reminder of the "strength in the god's generous gift."

In winter, wine was warmed. In summer, it was cooled if possible, whether in a well, a cold stream, or a bowl of ice water or snow, or by being mixed directly with snow or ice. Wine was mixed, for dilution, in a special bowl and in proportions hotly disputed by experts in arguments that sound like those of martini mixers: should it be five parts water to two parts wine, or three parts water to one part wine? Sometimes wine was mixed with seawater, which Athenaeus claimed made wine sweet. Anacharsis said seawater rendered wine more digestible and less heady. It is interesting that wine barrels are scrubbed out with seawater in preparation for the new harvest by European peasants near the sea today; inland, salt water is sometimes used.

Wine, like all other beverages and foods, was the subject of intense debate by physicians. In the Middle Ages, they argued the pros and cons of a custom then current whereby otherwise sober people deliberately got drunk once a month for their health. After champagne was developed in the late seventeenth century, the Paris Medical Faculty was fiercely divided over the relative merits of burgundy and champagne.

Wine was made from many plants other than grapes. Date wine was the most common in early Middle Eastern and Egyptian civilizations. Greeks and Romans made wine from dates, pomegranates, figs, quince, cornel berries, medlars, sorb apples, mulberries, pine nuts, pears, and squill. They also extracted a liquor from turnips, horseradishes, and asparagus, and from laurel leaves, juniper, cypress, myrtle, and various herbs.

The Romans planted vineyards in France, in the Rhine Valley, and possibly also in England. Some wine was drunk in England from Anglo-Saxon times through the sixteenth century, though the bulk of the people drank mead and ale. Everywhere the amount of wine available depended on the harvest, and the harvest not only on the climate but on the maintenance of a certain degree of peace in the country. As a consequence, through the turbulent Dark Ages, little wine was drunk outside monasteries, where monks needed wine for Christian liturgy. In the sixteenth century, the French again lost the habit of drinking wine because the vineyards were more or less abandoned during a prolonged series of wars. Wine drinking revived under Louis XIII, but because wine was both poor and expensive, people spiced and diluted it. In winter it was drunk warm, heated with a bar of hot metal or mixed with boiling water. The most common spiced wine, hippocras, remained popular until the seventeenth century. Wine was normally diluted until the nineteenth.

It was impossible for wine to mature fully until the cork and bottle came into use, barrels being suitable for maturing for a limited number of years only. Therefore, until the eighteenth century, wine was drunk young. By the time it was a year and a half old, it was usually fit only for vinegar. Not until the nineteenth century were wines included on menus, served in individual glasses on the table, and presented in regulated order.

France, with a consumption of 32 gallons per capita, outstripped all other countries in 1964. The United States has a per-capita consumption of less than a gallon per year.

WORT

Old books on cooking and agriculture often speak of worts, usually in compound names such as spoonwort. The word "wort" means plant or herb, particularly a potherb. Most of the many worts cultivated in ancient, medieval, and Renaissance days are no longer used in cooking today. Some of the common ones were bruisewort, colewort, glasswort, heartwort, liverwort, mugwort, pepperwort, skirwort (skirret), and spoonwort.

293

MENUS and RECIPES
from EVERY ERA

❖❖❖

ANCIENT GREECE

Phyloxenus of Cythera, who lived in the late fifth and early fourth centuries B.C., was as famous for his gourmandise as for his dithyrambic poetry. He combined both talents in a long poem called "The Banquet," excerpts of which were preserved by Athenaeus. The poem gives a detailed picture of a Greek feast of about 400 B.C. After describing tables glistening in the rays of high-swinging lamps and loaded with delectable condiments, snowy-topped barley cakes, and wheat bread, Phyloxenus itemizes the lengthy menu as follows: [1]

a glistening dish of eels
a soused ray of perfect roundness
a pot of shark meat *

a pot of sting ray
a rich dish of squid and sepia
gray mullet
breaded squid
browned prawns

flower-leaved cakes
spiced fresh confections
large frosted puff-cakes of wheat

a huge slice of imported tuna
hot entrails
the intestines, chine, and rump of a pig with hot dumplings

[1] Athenaeus, *The Deipnosophists*, Book IV: 146–47.
* Recipe follows.

boiled milk-fed kid, split in two
boiled meat, ribs, snouts, heads, and feet
tenderloin spiced with silphium
boiled and roast kid and lamb with mixed minced entrails
jugged hare
young cockerels
partridges and ringdoves
bread
honey and curds *
cheese

GREEK RECIPES

Pickled Turnip

. . . the turnip roots, you cut in thin slices, gently cleaning away the un-dried outer skin, and after drying them in the sun a little, either dip a quantity of them in boiling water and soak them in strong brine; or again, put equal parts of white must and vinegar in a jar together, then plunge the the slices in it, having dried them off with salt. Often, too, you may pound raisins and biting mustard-seeds with a pestle and add it to them. When cream of tartar forms, and the top grows more and more bitter, then 'tis time to draw off the pickle for those who seek their dinner.

—Nicander of Colophon,
Georgics, Book II (second century B.C.) [2]

Stuffed Squid

As for the squids, I chopped up their fins, mixed in a little lard, sprinkled them with seasoning and stuffed them with finely-chopped greens.

—Alexis,
speech of a cook in *The Eretrian* (fourth century B.C.) [3]

Fish Baked in the Ashes

No cheese, no nonsense! Just place it tenderly in figleaves and tie them on top with a string; then push it under hot ashes, bethinking thee wisely of the time when it is done, and burn it not up.

—Archestratus,
Gastrology (fourth century B.C.) [4]

---

* Recipe follows.
[2] Athenaeus, *The Deipnosophists*, Book IV: 133.
[3] *Ibid.*, Book VII: 326.
[4] *Ibid.*, Book VII: 278.

Dog-shark with Caraway

In this city of Toronê you should buy the belly-slices of the dog-shark, cut from the hollow parts below. Then sprinkle them with caraway-seed and a little salt, and bake. Put nothing else, my friend, upon it, unless it be yellow oil. But after it is baked, you may then fetch a sauce and all those condiments which go with it. But whatsoever you stew within the ribs of the hollow casserole, mix no water from a sacred spring, nor wine-vinegar, but simply pour over it oil and dry caraway and some fragrant leaves all together. Cook it over the hot embers without letting the flame touch it and stir it diligently lest you unwittingly scorch it.

—Archestratus [5]

Gastris

In Crete, they make a small cake called gastris. It consists of the following: walnuts, filberts, almonds, poppy-seed; roast them, tending them well, then mash them carefully in a clean mortar; having mixed the fruit with it soften with boiled honey, adding considerable pepper, and soften; it becomes dark with the poppy-seed. Flattening it all out make it into a square. Then mash some white sesame, soften it with boiled honey, and draw it out into two thin slabs, placing one below, the other on top of it in such a manner that the dark part comes in the middle, and shape it nicely.

—Chrysippus of Tyana
Bread-Making (*ca.* A.D. 50) [6]

Curds

Pour honey into some milk, squeeze it out and placing it in a bowl allow it to stiffen. If you have small sieves handy turn the bowl over into them and allow the whey to run out. When you think it has become stiff enough, lift the bowl and shift the curds on to a silver platter. Thus the moulded pattern will be seen on top. If, however, you have no sieves, use new fans such as are used for fanning the fire; they are just as useful for that.

—Chrysippus of Tyana [7]

ANCIENT ROME

The following menu, cited by Macrobius in his early fifth-century work,[8] is taken from the fourth book of the annals of the *pontifex maximus* Metellus, who

---

[5] Athenaeus, *The Deipnosophists*, Book VII: 310.
[6] Athenaeus, *The Deipnosophists*, Book XIV, 647–48.
[7] *Ibid.*, Book XIV, 647.
[8] Macrobius, *Oeuvres de Macrobe*, Book II, *Saturnales*, pp. 458–59.

was given this dinner by his quaestor and friends on his return to Spain after a year's absence. The dinner is a particularly luxurious one with many imported foods. Macrobius chose it to prove that his own epoch was no more indulgent than that of earlier Romans, in this case the first century B.C.

sea urchins
raw oysters
clams
spondyls (spiny oysters)
thrushes
asparagus

fattened hen
a basin of oysters
a basin of clams
black and white barnacles

more spondyls
glycymeridae (dog cockles)
sea nettles
figpeckers

deer kidneys and wild boar kidneys
fattened fowl sprinkled with flour
murices (mollusks)

sow's udders *
rack of wild boar
a basin of fish
a basin of wild-boar testicles
ducks
boiled teal
fattened hare
roasted fowl
breads of Picenum

Poet Martial offered friends much simpler menus in invitations to dinner at the end of the first century B.C.

---

* Recipe follows.

I [9]

lettuce and leeks
tuna garnished with eggs and rue
eggs roasted in the embers
Velabran cheese
olives

II [10]

mallows, lettuce, leek, mint, and herbs
lizard-fish garnished with sliced eggs and rue
paunch of tuna
kid
meat-balls
beans
young sprouts
cold chicken and ham
ripe apples

Trimalchio's banquet in the *Satyricon* of Petronius is a satire of a *nouveau riche's* dinner, ostentatiously served with ludicrous entertainment. Petronius gives the menu in detail: [11]

Gustatio (hors d'oeuvres)

black and white olives
dormice * sprinkled with honey and poppy seed
hot sausages on a silver gridiron with damson plums
and pomegranate seeds underneath to represent a fire
rich pastry eggs, each containing a figpecker coated
with egg yolk and seasoned with pepper
mead
a circular tray with the signs of the Zodiac containing dainties
symbolic of the signs: butter beans, a beef steak, testicles and kidneys,
an African fig, a young sow's udder, a tart, a cake, a lobster, a bull's eye,
a horned fish, a goose, and two mullets, with a honey-comb as centerpiece.
The tray was presented, then removed to reveal underneath plump fowl,
sow's udders, a hare, and fish in pepper sauce.
Falernian wine

------

[9] Martial, *Epigrams*, Book XI. LII.
[10] *Ibid.*, Book X. XLVIII
[11] Petronius, *The Satyricon*, pp. 48–84.
* Recipe follows.

Mensae primae (main course)

a wild boar stuffed with wild thrushes, served with piglets of cake
and dried Theban and fresh Syrian dates
grapes
pigs stuffed with sausages * and blood puddings
boiled calf
tray of cakes and apples filled with powdered saffron

Mensae secundae (last course)

pastry thrushes stuffed with raisins and nuts
quinces stuck with thorns to resemble sea urchins
pork meat molded in the form of a goose surrounded by fish and game
oysters, scallops, snails

After finishing the last course, the guests bathed, then proceeded to another dining room where another spread awaited them.

ROMAN RECIPES

Columella's Salad

Put into a mortar savory, mint, rue, coriander, parsley, chives, or, if you have no chives, a green onion, leaves of lettuce and of colewort, green thyme or cat-mint. Also green flea-bane and fresh and salted cheese: pound them all together and mix a little peppered vinegar with them. When you have put this mixture in a bowl, pour oil over it.

—*De Re Rustica*, Book XII

TWO ROMAN CHEESECAKES

Libum [12]

Bray 2 lbs. of cheese thoroughly in a mortar; when it is thoroughly macerated, add 1 pound of wheat flour, or, if you wish the cake to be more dainty, ½ lb. of fine flour, and mix thoroughly with the cheese. Add 1 egg, and work the whole well. Pat out a loaf, place on leaves, and bake slowly on a warm hearth under a crock.

—Cato,
De Agricultura, Book LXXV

---

* Recipe for pigs stuffed with sausages follows.
[12] *Libum* was used in Roman religious festivals.

Savillum

½ lb. flour, 2½ lbs. cheese—mix as for libum; add ¼ lb. honey and 1 egg. Grease earthenware dish with oil. Pour in and cover with crock. Be sure center bakes. When done remove dish, cover with honey, sprinkle with poppyseed, and put back under crock for a while. Serve in the dish with a spoon.

—*Ibid.*, Book LXXXIV

Asparagus Patina (Omelet)

Put in the mortar asparagus tips, pound, add wine, pass through the sieve. Pound pepper, lovage, fresh coriander, savory, onion, wine, *liquamen*,[13] and oil. Put puree and spices into a greased shallow pan, and if you wish break eggs over it when it is on the fire, so that the mixture sets. Sprinkle finely ground pepper over it and serve.

—*Apicius De Re Coquinaria*, Book IV [14]

Hot or Cold Patina of Elderberries

Take elderberries, clean them, and boil in water. Dry slightly and arrange in a greased shallow pan with a small stick. Add 6 *scruples* (¼ oz.) of pepper, moisten with *liquamen*, then add 1 *cyathus* (1/12 pint) each of *liquamen*, wine, and *passum*,[15] mix well; finally put in the pan 4 oz. of oil, place in the hot ashes, and bring to the boil. When the mixture is boiling break 6 eggs over it, stir well, and so bind it. When it has set sprinkle with pepper and serve [hot or cold].

—*Ibid.*, Book IV

Chicken in the Numidian Way

Prepare the chicken, boil, take out [of the water], sprinkle with asafoetida and pepper, and roast. Pound pepper, cumin, coriander seed, asafoetida root, rue, Jericho date, pine-kernels; moisten with vinegar, honey, *liquamen*, and oil. Mix well. When it boils thicken with cornflour, pour over the chicken, sprinkle with pepper, and serve.

—*Ibid.*, Book VI

Sucking Pig Boiled and Stuffed

Disembowel the pig; brown. Pound pepper, lovage, origan, moisten with *liquamen*, add sufficient cooked brains, also break eggs, blend with *liquamen*, add cut-up sausages that have been cooked whole. First wash the browned

---

[13] The translators equate *liquamen* with garum and suggest salt as a substitute.

[14] Barbara Flower and Elisabeth Rosenbaum, *The Roman Cookery Book*. (London: George G. Harrap, 1958).

[15] A specially prepared cooking wine; the translators suggest substituting a very sweet Spanish wine.

pig with *liquamen*, then stuff, skewer, and hang it in a basket in a boiling cauldron. When it is cooked sponge and serve without pepper.

—*Ibid.*, Book VIII

Dormice

Stuff the dormice with minced pork, the minced meat of whole dormice, pounded with pepper, pine-kernels, asafoetida, and *liquamen*. Sew up, place on a tile, put in the oven, or cook, stuffed, in a small oven [*clibanus*].[16]

—*Ibid.*, Book VIII

Sow's Udder

Boil the udder, bind together with reed, sprinkle with pepper, and put in the oven or on the gridiron. Half roast. Pound pepper, lovage, *liquamen*, blend with wine and *passum*, thicken with cornflour, and pour over the udder.

—*Ibid.*, Book VII

Mustard

Carefully cleanse and sift mustard-seed, then wash it in cold water and, when it has been well cleaned, leave it in the water for two hours. Next take it out and, after it has been squeezed in the hands, throw it into a new or thoroughly cleaned mortar and pound it with pestles. When it has been pounded, collect the whole mash in the middle of the mortar and compress it with the flat of the hand. After you have compressed it, scarify it and, after placing a few live coals upon it, pour water mixed with nitre on it in order to eliminate any bitterness and paleness from it. Then immediately lift up the mortar, so that all moisture may be drained away, and after this add sharp white vinegar and mix it with the pestle and strain it. This liquid serves very well for preserving turnips. If, however, you should wish to prepare mustard for the use of your guests, when you have squeezed out the mustard, add pine-kernels which should be as fresh as possible, and almonds, and carefully crush them together after pouring in vinegar. Finish the process in the manner I have described above. You will find this mustard not only suitable as a sauce but also pleasing to the eye; for, if it is carefully made, it is of an exquisite brilliance.

—Columella
De Re Rustica, Book XII

Rose-Dish

This dish was presented at the fictional Roman banquet of Athenaeus' *Deipnosophists*. In the following speech, the cook explains the recipe (which is very similar to one called "Patina of Roses" in the Apicius cookbook):

I give the name of "rose-dish" to this casserole; it is prepared in such a fashion that when you get it you may have not merely a sauce fit to wreathe

---

[16] *Clibanus:* an oven or vessel for baking bread, according to Pliny.

the head, but even inside of you, you may feast your little body with a complete dinner. I crushed the most fragrant roses in a mortar, then laid on carefully boiled brains of fowls and pigs, from which the stringy fibres had been removed, also the yolks of eggs; then olive-oil, garum-sauce, pepper, and wine. All this I stirred thoroughly and placed in a new casserole, giving it a fire that was gentle and steady.

With these words [the narration continues], he opened the casserole and produced for the company such a delicious odour that one of the company truly said: "If it were but shaken, in the bronze-floored mansion of Zeus, its fragrance went forth even to earth and to heaven." So great was the fragrance diffused from the roses.

—Athenaeus,
The Deipnosophists, Book IX: 406.

THE DARK AND MIDDLE AGES

Coronation Feast of Henry IV of England, 1399

Menu as given in the original document: [17]	Explanation of dish:
I	
Braun en peverade *	Cured pork or boar in a sauce of pepper and pungent spices mixed with wine, vinegar, and bread.
Viaund Ryal *	Wine and honey, highly spiced and thickened with rice flour.
Teste de senglere enarmez	Boar's head and tusks.
Graund chare	Meats such as beef and mutton. Usually served with mustard.
Syngettys	Cygnets. These were usually prepared by the carver in chawdron sauce, a mixture of chopped liver and entrails, blood, bread, wine, vinegar, and spices.
Fesaunte	Pheasant. Ordinarily served with verjuice or with ginger and salt.
Heroun	Heron. Normally eaten with ginger and salt.
Crustade Lumbarde *	Small birds baked in a pie crust in a custard of milk and eggs with spices, currants, pine nuts, dates, and raisins.
Storieoun, graunt luces	Large pike.
A Sotelte	Sotelty: a symbolic device in pastry.

_____

[17] Menu taken from *Two Fifteenth Century Cookery Books* (London: Early English Text Society, 1888).
* Recipe follows.

II

Venyson en furmenty	Venison with a porridge of wheat, milk, and egg yolks, often colored with saffron.
Gely	A jelly.
Porcelle farce enforce *	Stuffed sucking pig. A common stuffing consisted of tripe, cooked pork meat, hard-boiled egg yolks, cooked, peeled chestnuts, and spices. The pig was basted with vinegar while roasting, and eaten with *poivre jaunet,** a sauce of vinegar, bread, saffron, and ginger.
Pokokkys	Peacocks.
Cranys	Cranes.
Venyson Roste	Venison, possibly stewed; "roste" merely indicated a relatively dry sauce.
Conyng	Fattened rabbit. Sometimes served with vinegar and ginger.
Byttore	Bittern. Served with salt alone.
Pulle endore	Boned roast hen, glazed with egg yolk and cumin.
Graunt tartez	Large tarts.
Braun fryez	Fried brawn (cured boar).
Leche lumbarde *	Ground pork mixed with egg yolks, spices, dates, currants, and raisins, boiled in a bladder, then sliced and served with a sauce of ground raisins, red wine, almond milk, cinnamon, ginger, pepper, cloves, sandalwood, and saffron.
A Sotelte	

III

Blaundesorye	Ground capon flesh made into a thick pudding with almond milk, rice flour, and sugar or honey.
Quyncys in comfyte	Quince comfits.
Curlewys	Curlews.
Pertyche *	Partridge, often roasted, then minced and served warmed in a sauce of wine, ginger, and salt.
Pyionys	Probably pigeons.
Quaylys	Quail. Usually served with just salt.

---

* Recipe follows.

Snytys	Snipe. Served with just salt.
Smal byrdys	Small birds. Usually eaten with cinnamon and salt.
Rabettys	Wild rabbits.
Pome doreng	Pork-liver balls colored with saffron or sandalwood.
Braun blanke leche	Cured pork or boar diced, cooked in sweetened, thick almond milk, cooled, and sliced.
Eyroun en gele	Eggs in jelly.
Doucettys *	Minced pork in a custard of milk and eggs flavored with honey and pepper and baked in a pie crust.
Pety perneux	Marrow, ginger, minced dates, currants, and egg yolks cooked in a rich pie crust.
Payn puff	Like pety perneux but with a more tender crust.
Egle	Eagle.
Pottys of lyle	Pottage of ?
A Sotelte	

A FEAST FOR A FRANKLIN [18]
A menu of *ca.* 1460

I

Brawn with mustard
Bacon and peas
Beef or stewed mutton
Boiled chicken or capon
Roast goose and pig
Capon
Bakemetes or custade if eggs and cream to be had [19]

II

Mortrewes or Iusselle [20] *
Veal, lamb, kid, or cony (fattened rabbit)
Roast chicken or pegeon
Bakemetes or dowcettes [21] *

---

[18] Taken from John Russell, *The Boke of Nurture* (Bungay, Suff.: Roxburghe Club, 1867).
[19] Bakemetes: oven-cooked dishes including custards.
[20] Mortrewes: mashed, boiled meat cooked with bread, egg yolks, and spices, or with rice flour, milk and almonds. Iusselle: eggs, saffron, and broth.
[21] Dowcettes: custard pies of meat, eggs, milk, and honey.
* Recipe follows.

The fritturs, leche [22]
Apples and pears, spiced
Bread and cheese
Spiced cakes
Bragot (ale, honey, spices), mead

BANCQUET DE MONSEIGNEUR DE FOYES

Menu as given in the
original document: [23]

Explanation of dish:

Es Premiers Mets

I

Poussins au sucre, levras ou
laperaux à la cresme
d'amandes, froide saulce,
vinaigre, venoison à souppes.

Young chickens with sugar, hare or
young rabbit with almond cream,
cold sauce, vinegar, venison on
crusts of bread.

Second Mestz

II

Espaules de chevreau farcis,
poulettes de mer, panneaulx
tous armés, cailles au sucre.

Stuffed shoulder of kid, chicken of
the sea, young peacocks served
with head and tail feathers, quail
with sugar.

Tiers Mestz

III

Daulphins de cresme, lashes
lombardes,* poires, orenges
frictes, gelée, pasties de
levratz.

Pudding, leche lumbard,* pears,
oranges, jelly, hare pastries.

Fruicterie

Dessert

Cresme blanches, et fraises,
jonchée, et almandes.

Pudding, strawberries, cheese(?),
and almonds.

MEDIEVAL RECIPES

Boor in Peverade or Braune in Peverade
(boar or cured boar's meat in hot sauce)

Take for a boor in peverade the ribbes of a boore while thai [they] be fresshe, and parboyle hom, and half roste hom, and then chop hom, and cast hom in the brothe of beef, and alay hit [dilute it] with wyne, and put in therto clowes [cloves], maces, pynes [pine nuts], raisyns of corance [currants], powdor of pepur [ground pepper], onyons mynced gret [coarsely

---

[22] A preparation that can be sliced.
[23] A fifteenth-century manuscript included in Guillaume Tirel, *Le Viandier* (Paris: Techener, 1892), p. 99.
* Recipe follows.

minced], and draw up a liour [make a mixture] of chippes of bred [bits of bread], and put in therto, and saunders [sandalwood] and saffron, ande honey, and in the settlynge downe take a lytel vynegur [a little vinegar], medelet [mixed] with pouder of canel [ground cinnamon], and cast therto [and add it]; and then take braune lechet of twoe ynches length [sliced brawn two inches long], and cast into the same pot, and dresse hit up the t'one with the t'other: and serve hit forthe.

— from a fifteenth century copy of a manuscript of ancient cookery of much earlier date [24]

Vyaund Ryal

Take wyne greke, other rynysshe wyne [take Greek or Rhine wine], and hony, clarified therewith [and honey clarified with it]. Take floer of rys [rice flour], powdor of gynger [ground ginger] other [or] of peper and canel [cinnamon], other [or] floer of canel [cinnamon flour?], powdor of clowes [ground cloves], saffron, sugar, cypre [?], mylberyes [mulberries], other sandres [or sandalwood], and medle [mix] alle these to gider [together]. Boile it, and salt it, and loke that it be stondying [stiff].

—*Forme of Cury.* No. 99

Crustade Lumbarde

To mak custad lombard mak a large coffyn [pie crust] then tak dates from the stones [stone dates] tak gobettes of mary [small pieces of marrow] and smalle birdes and parboile them in salt brothe and couche ther in [and put them in] then tak clowes [cloves] mace and raisins of corans [currants] and pynes [pine nuts] fryed and strawe ther on [strew them on top] and sett hem in the oven to bak and luk [look to it that] ye have a coup of cowes creme [cup of cow's cream] yolks of eggs good pouderes [spices] saffron sanderes [sandalwood] and salt then fill the coffins ther with.

—*A Noble Boke of Cookry ffor a Prynce Houssolde*

Pourcel Farci
(stuffed sucking pig)

Let it be scalded, and well washed, and roasted, and the stuffing is the tripe of the sucking pig and pork flesh cooked with cooked yolks of eggs, cheese, cooked and peeled chestnuts, a good mixture of ground spices, all put in the stomach of the pig; then roasted and basted with vinegar and boiling lard; eat with *poivre jaunet.**

—Guillaume Tirel,
Le Viandier

---

[24] Printed in *A Collection of Ordinances.*
* Recipe follows.

Poivre Jaunet

Mix ginger, saffron, and bread crumbs, dilute with vinegar and boil. Some put in grains of paradise and cloves with verjuice.

—Ibid.

Leche Lumbard

Take rawe pork, and pulle off the skyn; and pyke [pick] out the skyn, synewes, and bray [crush] the pork in a mortar with ayern rawe [raw eggs]. Do [add] thereto sugar, salt, raysons, corance [currants], dates mynced, and powdor of peper [ground pepper], powdor gylofre [ground cloves]; and do it in a bladder [put it in a bladder], and lat it seeth [let it boil] till it be ynowgh [enough: done]; and whan it is ynowh, kerf [carve it], leshe [slice] it in likeness of a peskodde [pea pod], and take grete raysons [large raisins] and grynde hem in a mortar; drawe hem up [mix it] with rede wyne [red wine]; do [add] thereto mylke of almandes [almond milk]; color it with sanders [sandalwood] and safron, and do [add] thereto powdor of peper, and of gilofre [cloves], and boile it. And whan it is boiled, take powdor of canel [ground cinnamon] and gynger, and temper it up [dilute it] with wyne; and do [mix] all thyse thinges togyder, and loke [look] that it be rennyns [thin?]; and lat it not seeth after that it is cast togyder [do not let it boil after mixing]; and serve it forth.

—Forme of Cury. No. 65

Pertuche Rost
(roast partridge)

A pertuche tak a fedir [feather] and put it in to his hed and let hym dye and pulle hym dry and drawe hym [remove entrails] and rost hym as ye wold raise the legges and wingys of an henne and mynce hym sauce hym with wyne pouder of guinger [ground ginger] and salt and warme it on the fyere and serve it.

—A Noble Boke of Cookry ffor a Prynce Houssolde

Doucettys
(doucettes)

Take Porke and hakke [chop] it smal, & Eyroun [eggs] y-melled to-gedrys [mixed together], & a lytel milke, & melle hem to-gederys with Hony [honey] & Peper, & bake hem in a cofyn [pie crust], & serve forth.

—from a manuscript of cookery of ca. 1430–40

Souppe en Moustarde
(mustard soup on toast strips)

Take oil in which you have poached your eggs, wine, water, and boil it all in an iron pot: then take the crusts of bread and put them to toast on the grill, then make square pieces out of them, and put them to boil; then take the toasts out and put them in a dish: and put mustard in the bouillon and let it boil. Then put your toasts in layers and pour your bouillon on top.

—*Le Ménagier de Paris*

Caboche in Potage

Take caboches [cabbages] & quarter hem, & seeth [boil] hem in gode broth, with oynonns y mynced, & the whyte of lekes y slyt [probably slit lengthwise], & corve smale [chopped in small pieces], & do thereto [add] safronn and salt and force [season] it with powdor douce [a mixture of mild spices].

—*Forme of Cury*, No. 3

A ROUTINE MENU FOR DINNER IN 16TH CENTURY ITALY [25]

Antipasto

Prepared melon and sugar, sweetbread patties, peahen dressed like pheasant, veal and ham pie.

Boiled Meats

Chicken, pigeon with peas and spices *seccaticcia*, stewed kid, almond sauce and fennel.

Dessert

Wild cherry tart, marzolino cheese, muscat pears, and fennel.

A SIMPLE ENGLISH SUPPER MENU OF 1587 [26]

The First Course

A Salet. A Pigges Petitoe. Powdered Beefe [dried beef] Slised. A Shoulder of Mutton or a Breast. Veale. Lambe. Custard.

The Second Course

Capons roasted. Connies [fattened rabbits] roasted. Chickins rosted. Pigeons rosted. Larkes rosted. A pye of Pigions or Chickens. Baked Venison Tart.

Note: The third course, usually not specified in menus, consisted of cheeses, creams, jellies, and sometimes also sweetmeats. Clouted cream and cream cheeses were particularly popular.

---

[25] Nesca A. Robb, "The Fare of Princes. A Renaissance Manual of Domestic Economy," in *Italian Studies*, Vol. VII (1952), p. 51.
[26] Thomas Dawson, *The Good Huswifes Jewell* (London: John Wolfe, 1587).

THE AGE OF EXPLORATION

DINNER FOR KING WILLIAM AND QUEEN MARY, 1689 [27]

A Declaration of their Majesties Diett of Ten Dishes of Meate and three plates at Dinner, and Eight Dishes and three plates at supper, to be divided, viz. Five Dishes at Dinner, and four at Supper, together with the plates each meale to the Groome of the Stoole to the Queen, and the remayning five Dishes at Dinner, and four at Supper, to the Grooms of his Majesties Bed-Chamber.

Dinner

Pottage of Capons i, or Pulletts ii, or Chickens iiii, or
Partridges iii.
or Beef boiled, 24 lb.
Mutton rosted,
Turky or Goose large, or Capons fatt ii.
Chickens fatt vi. or
Pidgeons tame, viii. or
Pheasants ii. or Partridges vi. or
Cocks vi, or Quails viii, or
Buck baked quarter or Hen Pye,
Tarts of Sorts,

Desert Plates.

Morelles or Trouffles,
Jelly, or
Asparagus,

Instead of boiled beef.
On Sundays a Chine.
On Thursdays a Surloyn.

DINNER GIVEN BY THE MARQUIS D'ARCI, FRENCH AMBASSADOR TO TURIN, APRIL 10, 1690 [28]

Menu as given in the original document	Translation
Premier Service	*First Course*
Potages	Stews or thick soups
2 Potages: Une Bisque de Pigeons; et un Potage de Santé avec Poularde	2 stews: a pigeon stew and *potage de santé* [29] with a fat pullet
Entrées	Dishes with sauce or garnish
Un Quartier de mouton farci	Stuffed quarter of mutton
Une Poularde en ragoût	A fat pullet in a thick sauce

---

[27] Printed in *A Collection of Ordinances.*
[28] François Massialot, *Le Cuisinier roial et bourgeois* (Paris, 1691), pp. 16–17.
[29] *Potage de santé:* a thick stew of meat, fowl, bacon, and vegetables.

Une Poitrine de Veau farcie	Stuffed breast of veal
Des Pigeons au Basilic avec une Petite Farce	Pigeons with basil and a stuffing
Et la grande pièce de Boeuf au milieu	And a large cut of beef for the center of the table

Second Service	*Second Course*
Pour le Rôt	*The unsauced meats*
Un grand plat de Rôt, composé de diverses Volailles suivant la saison; et deux Salades	A large platter of fowl in season; and two salads
L'Entremets	*Side-dishes*
Un Pain au Jambon	Probably a bread hollowed out and stuffed with ham
De la Crême brulée	A rich custard with caramel glaze
Un Ragoût de Ris-de-Veau et Foies-gras	A stew of sweet breads and *foie gras*
Un plat d'Asperges, Sausse au jus lié	A dish of asparagus with a sauce of thickened asparagus juice

The dessert, being the responsibility not of the chef but of another household officer, is not mentioned. For an important meal there were puddings, jellies of various colors, dried, fresh, and candied fruits, comfits, marchpanes, and a variety of sweetmeats.

The Marquis d'Arci's menu is a modest one. For a great feast, Massialot cited a menu of 16 potages, 4 large and 12 medium entrées, plus 32 hors d'oeuvres (smaller side-dishes) for the first course alone, followed by a second course of 16 meat dishes, 10 small salads, 4 large entremets (side-dishes), and 12 medium ones, with 22 hors d'oeuvres. The preparation required 36 kitchen officers (*officiers de cuisine*), 60 small casseroles, 40 miscellaneous casseroles, and 30 spits.

SIXTEENTH AND SEVENTEENTH CENTURY RECIPES

Potch'd Eggs with Anchovy Sauce

First Potch your Eggs in Water, then melt your Anchovies in Butter, then strain it through a Strainer with some Flower browned in a searcing Pan, juice of Lemons, Capers, Salt, and Nutmeg. This done, pour it all over your Eggs.

—*L'Escole parfaite des officiers de bouche,*
translated into English by Giles Rose in 1682

To Make White Meat of the Flesh of Capons

2 lbs. blanched almonds, ground, diluted with a little water
capon breast pounded
white loaf crummed into capon broth

312

a little verjuice

½ oz. ginger and ½ lb. sugar in broth

Strain through cloth. Boil ½ hour while stirring, then put in 3 oz. rosewater. Pour over capon or other bird flesh and for better shew strew pomegranate grains over it. If you want meat of two colors use yolk and saffron for one; if you have 2 capons, make one white and the other yellow.

> —Giovanni de' Roselli
> *Epulario, or The Italian Banquet*, sixteenth-century Italian cookbook

To Make Olives of Veal

Take thin slices of a Leg of Veal, and have ready some Suet finely shred, some Currans, beaten Spice, sweet Herbs, and hard yolks of Eggs, and a little Salt mixed well together, then strew it on the insides of your slices of Meat, and roul them up hard, and make them fast with a scure [skewer], so spit them and roast them, baste them with Butter, and serve them in with Vinegar, Butter and Sugar.

> —Hannah Wooley,
> *The Queen-like Closet*

To Make a Frycace of Colde Mutton or Veale

Chop fleshe small and frye it in sweet Butter. And then put thereto a little white Wine, Salt, and Ginger and serve it forth in faire dishes.

> —*A Book of Cookyre*, gathered by A. W.

To Boyle Meates for Supper

Take veale and put it into a posnet [small porringer] with carret roots cut in long pieces then boile it and put thereto a handfull of prunes and crummes of Bread. Then season it with pepper, salt and vinegar.

> —Thomas Dawson,
> *The Good Huswifes Jewell*

Langue de Mouton en Ragoust
(stewed mutton tongue)

After cleaning well, cut in two, then flour it, fry briefly in a frying pan, and put it to stew with vinegar, verjuice, salt, pepper, orange juice, and mashed capers. Simmer until it is well cooked and the sauce is of the right consistency, then serve.

> —La Varenne,
> *Le Cuisinier françois*, No. 89

Pastel de Caracoles
(snail pasty)

You can cook these snails as explained; then take them out of their shells, and remove the white part, which is the intestines, and moisten them with a little fat and season them with all sorts of spices and a little minced green herbs and a little salt; and you can make a pasty of them, and you can put in the pasty some precooked asparagus or some rampion first cooked in water and salt: and you will thicken and enrich it with egg yolks, a little broth of chick-peas, and lemon juice or a little vinegar. These pasties are very good.

—Francisco Martínez Montiño,
Arte de Cocina

Tortelleti of Green Pease, French Beans, or Any Kind of Pulse, Green or Dry

Take pease green or dry, French beans, or garden beans green or dry, boil them tender, and stamp them; strain them through a strainer, and put to them some fried onions chopped small, sugar, cinamon, cloves, pepper, and nutmeg, some grated parmesan, or fat cheese, and some cheese curds stamped [ground to a paste].

Then make paste, and make little pasties, boil them in broth, or as before said [in strong broth, cream, milk, or almond milk], and serve them with sugar, cinamon, and grated cheese in a fine clean dish.

—Robert May
The Accomplish't Cook

A Tart of Cream of Artichokes

When your artichoke bottoms are well boil'd, beat them in a Mortar, and strain them through a Cullendar, with Butter, or melted Lard, the Yolks of two Eggs raw, season this with Salt and Nutmeg, and put it into fine Paste, but let it be very thin, and bake it and serve it away with Gravy and juice of Lemons.

—*L'Escole parfaite des officiers de bouche*

To Make Bisket of Potato-Roots or Parsneps

Take their Roots boil'd very tender, and beat them in a Mortar with their weight of searced [sifted] Sugar, then put in a little Gum-dragon, beat them to a Paste, and mould them up with Sugar searced [sifted], and make them up in what shape you please, and dry them.

—Hannah Wooley,
The Queen-like Closet, No. 243

Tourte de Melon en Marmellade (melon marmalade pie)

Boil the flesh of a melon with a glass of white wine; when it is thick, crush it in a mortar with two macaroons, a little sugar and cinnamon, and make a pie shell of fine pastry without a cover. Add sugar and orange flower water on serving or glaze it.

—Sieur Pierre de Lune,
Le nouveau et parfaict cuisinier

To Make Gingerbread

Take three stale Manchets [wheat loaves of the finest flour], and grate them: dry them and sift them thorow a fine sieve: then adde unto them one ounce of Ginger being beaten [ground], and as much Cinamon, one ounce of Liquorice and Anniseeds beeing beaten together and searced [sifted], halfe a pound of Sugar; then boil all these together in a posnet [small porringer] with a quart of claret wine, till they come to a stiff paste with often stirring of it, and when it is stiffe, mould it on a table, and so drive it thin, and put it in your moulds: dust your moulds with Cinamon, Ginger, and Liquorice, beeing mixed together in fine powder. This is your Ginger-bread used at the Court, and in all Gentlemens houses at festival times. It is otherwise called dry leach.

—Sir Hugh Plat,
Delightes for Ladies, No. 22

THE CLASSICAL CENTURY

QUEEN ANNE'S DINNER, FEBRUARY 6, 1704 [30]

The diagrams indicate the presentation of dishes on the table for each course.

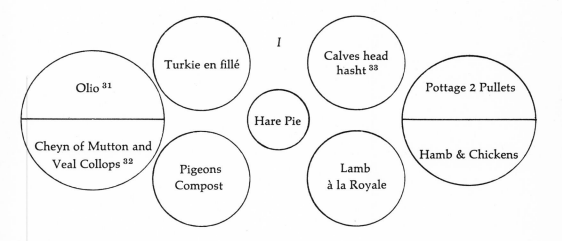

[30] Patrick Lamb, *Royal Cookery*, 3d ed. (London: E. and R. Nutt and A. Roper, 1726). Lamb was Master-Cook to King Charles II, King James II, King William and Queen Mary, and Queen Anne.
[31] Olio: an elaborate dish of twenty-five to thirty-five ingredients such as 6 pigeons, 6 chickens, a few rabbits, oysters, sausages, vegetables, etc. The divided circle indicates that the top dish occupied this position when the course was served, but was removed during the course to be replaced by another, in this case the mutton and veal.
[32] Cheyn: chine; *collops:* the antecedent of veal scallopini.
[33] With oysters, anchovies, marrow, almonds, bacon, etc.

II

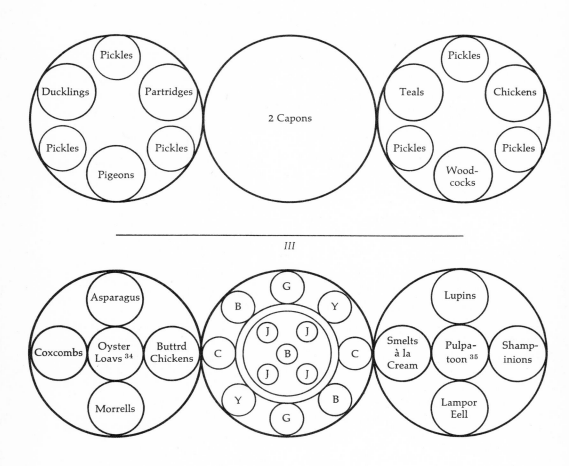

III

2 Blamange [36] (B)
2 Yellow jellies (Y)
2 Crystal jellies (C)
2 Green jellies (G)

---

[34] Stewed oysters in a crust of bread.
[35] Pulpatoon: possibly identical with *poupeton*, for which La Varenne gives a recipe calling for veal, fat, and eggs made into a hash which serves as bed for pigeons, sweetbreads, asparagus, mushrooms, egg yolks, kidneys, cock's combs, and other delicacies, covered with more meat and baked.
[36] Blancmange: now a white sweet dish with no meat. The inner circle, not explained in the original diagram, probably contained an additional blancmange and four plain jellies.

FAMILY DINNER OF FIVE DISHES [37]

Haricot of Mutton *

Apple Sauce   Marrow Pudding   Stewed Cucumbers

Roast Goose

The dessert for such a simple meal would consist of five dishes of nuts and fruits, placed on the table in the same way as the first course. A more elaborate dessert menu, suggested by the same author, is as follows: [38]

Oranges

Pears   Olives   Cakes

Syllabubs *

Sweetmeats   Olives   Apples

Chestnuts

THE AMBIGU

The ambigu was an eighteenth-century invention, a one-course meal of hot or cold dishes or both, all placed on the table at once. Normally there were no soups, no vegetables, and few sauces. The following menu for an ambigu was composed by Sieur Louis Liger in 1710 and intended to serve as a model: [39]

A large platter of meat, such as a whole lamb surrounded by *fricandeaux*.[40]
A large basket of fruit in season or of oranges.
Another large basket filled with the same.
A compote of pears.
A compote of apples.
A compote of quince.
A compote of green apricots.
A middle-sized entrée of braised capon.
A middle-sized entrée of beignets of artichoke bottoms.
A plate of candied apricots.
A platter of four roast partridge.
A middle-sized entrée of marinated calf's liver.

---

[37] Charlotte Mason, *The Ladies' Assistant*, p. 5.
[38] *Ibid.*, p. 81.
[39] Louis Liger, *Le Ménage de la ville et des champs.* (Jean Léonard, 1712)
[40] Stuffed, rolled slices of meat; see La Varenne's recipe, p. 313.
* Recipe follows.

A plate of verjuice conserves.
A frangipane [almond cream] tart.
A platter of four roast rabbits.
A platter of stewed mushrooms.
A platter of *blanc manger* [a white, jellied sweet].
One of stuffed tongues.
One of sliced ham.
A platter of pigeons with basil.
One of sweetbreads and stuffed cock's combs.
One of *gâteau feuilleté* [flaky pastry].
One of *poupelain* [a pastry].
A plate of chestnuts.
A plate of cheese.

EIGHTEENTH CENTURY RECIPES

To Make an Egg as Big as Twenty

Part the yolks from the whites, strain them both separate through a sieve, tie the yolks up in a bladder in the form of a ball. Boil them hard, then put this ball into another bladder, and the whites round it; tie it up oval fashion, and boil it. These are used for grand sallads.

—Hannah Glasse,
The Art of Cookery Made Plain and Easy

Pastelillo de Sollo
(fritters of sole)

Mince the fish raw, and when it is well minced, put in a half dozen eggs, the number varying in proportion to the quantity of sole, season it with all sorts of spices and a little verjuice, and put in salt and oil; when it is all well mixed, make a dough of it with flour, ground and sifted sugar, a little oil or lard, a few egg yolks, and salt; moisten with a little white wine: from this dough, make small fritters and fry them in a frying pan: sprinkle a little sugar on top and serve them hot; very good.

—Juan Altamiras,
Nuevo Arte de Cocina

To Roast a Pound of Butter

Lay it in salt and water two or three hours, then spit it, and rub it all over with crumbs of bread, with a little grated nutmeg, lay it to the fire, and, as it roasts, baste it with the yolks of two eggs and then with crumbs of bread all the time it is a roasting; but have ready a pint of oysters stewed in their own liquor, and lay in the dish under the butter; the bread has soaked up all the butter; brown the outside, and lay it on your oysters.

—*The House-keeper's Pocket Book*

Salmogundy

Mince very fine two boiled or roasted Chickens or Veal, which you like best: Mince also very small the Yolk & the White of hard Eggs by themselves. Shred also the Pulp of lemon very small; then lay in the Dish a Layer of the Whites of Eggs, over which a Layer of Anchovies, and on them a Layer of the shred Pulp of Lemon, next a Layer of Pickles, then a Layer of Sorrel, and last of all a Layer of Spinach and Cloves, or of Shalots Shred small: Having thus filled the Dish, set an Orange or Lemon on the Top, and garnish with Scrap'd Horse-Radish, Barberries, and Slices of Lemon; let the Sauce be Oil, beat up thick with the juices of Lemons, Salt, and Mustard. We serve this Dish in the Second Course, or for a Side-Dish, or a Middle Dish for Supper.

—The Whole Duty of a Woman

Queue de Boeuf à la Sainte-Menehould
(oxtail à la Sainte-Menehould)

Cut an oxtail in three pieces, cutting it first in the middle, and then cutting the thick end with a butcher's chopper; put it to cook in a casserole for cooking beef; when it is cooked, let it cool, then marinate it for an hour with a little oil, salt, coarse pepper, parsley, chives, two shallots, and the tip of a garlic clove, all minced fine; make the marinade stick to the ox tail by coating it with bread crumbs; grill until it takes on a good color while basting it with the rest of the marinade. Serve without sauce.

—Menon,
La Cuisinière bourgeoise

Calf's Eyes

After having removed what is not good, blanch them and cook them in a braise made with white wine, bouillon, bouquet garni, salt, pepper; when they are cooked, you can dress them in various fashions; if you make them *à la Sainte Menehould*, bread them, grill them and serve with a pepper sauce [*sauce à la poivrade*]; cooked in a braise as above, they may be served with various ragouts [stewed garnishes] such as cucumbers, little onions, or a salpicon [a garnish combining truffles, mushrooms, and other ingredients].

—Menon,
La Cuisinière bourgeoise

Côtelettes en Haricot
(haricot of mutton chops)

Cut the chops in two, brown them in melted lard, add a pinch of flour, and put turnips in at the same time; both must take on a good color.

Then put in a little bouillon, salt, pepper, and clove, let it all cook gently; when it is half cooked, put in about a glass of wine; when it is cooked, take it out and serve it hot. You can add chestnuts in cooking it.

—Louis Liger,
Le Ménage de la ville et des champs

319

Stuffed Chickens

Make a good stuffing of fillet of veal, beef marrow, mushrooms, salt, pepper, parsley, and a raw egg yolk, chop it all well together, and stuff your chickens, brown them with lard, let them take on a good color, cook them in good bouillon, well seasoned, and with the fat removed, add mushrooms, some sweetbreads and artichokes; when it is all well cooked, enrich the sauce with egg yolks first diluted with some verjuice.

To tenderize the chickens quickly, throw them in the coolest water available as soon as they have been killed; others bury them for a while; these expedients are convenient, particularly in the country when someone arrives unexpectedly and one does not know what to give him to eat.

—Louis Liger,
Le Ménage de la ville et des champs

Petits Pois à la Demi-Bourgeoise
(young peas)

Take a quart and a half of young peas, wash and put in a pot with a piece of butter, a bouquet of parsley and chives, a head lettuce cut in quarters; cook them in their own juice over a very low fire.

When they are cooked and there is almost no sauce left, put in a liaison of two eggs with cream, blend it over the heat, and serve.

—Menon,
La Cuisinière bourgeoise

Zanahorias
(carrots)

They are a simple food and a crude one. If you like carrots, you can put them to cook with water and salt; cut them in strips; put them in a casserole with fried onion and season them with all sorts of spices and salt. Add hot water to cover; make them sweet with sugar or honey, and [add] vinegar; let them be either sweet or sour; then brown a little flour, and when it is well browned, mix in a little of the water from the cooking of the carrots, thicken it by boiling, and with that, the crude aliment will be transformed into a reasonable food, [though] still unrewarding and of little nourishment.

—Juan Altamiras,
Nuevo Arte de Cocina

To Fry Potatoes

Cut them into thin slices, as big as a crown-piece, fry them brown, lay them in the plate or dish, pour melted butter and sack and sugar over them. These are a pretty corner-plate.

—Hannah Glasse,
The Art of Cookery Made Plain and Easy

To Make an Amlet of Asparagus

Having blanch'd and cut the Asparagus in small Pieces, fry them in fresh Butter, with a little Parsley and Chibbols [spring onions]; then pour some

Cream upon them, and having season'd them well, boil them on a gentle Fire; Mean while make an Amlet with new-laid Eggs, Cream and Salt: When it is enough [done], dress it on a Dish, and having thicken'd the Asparagus with one or two Yolks of Eggs, pour it on the Amlet, and serve it up hot.

—Patrick Lamb,
Royal Cookery

Selleri Sauce
(celery sauce)

One takes two–three big celery roots, boils same whole in salt water, cuts them up with a handful of tender cured celery, browns a small spoonful of flour and blends it with a small piece of butter, adds the celery, good meat broth, nutmeg, and a little pepper. When the sauce has cooked enough, add whatever meat is called for.

—Friederike Löffler,
Neues Koch Buch

To Make Cucumber Sawce (Lady Rawleigh)

Take 3 or 4 cucumbers, pare them and wipe out the seeds, and take a pretty quantity of gravy, and sum claret, 1 or 2 anchovie according to your tast, some baten [ground] peper and salt, a onion. It must stew allmost 2 hours. Then put in a bitt of butter. Remember and put some water in the boyling with the gravy. Serve it in the same dish with the mutten.

—*Diana Astry's Recipe Book*, No. 9

Walnut Catsup

Take two hundred walnuts when quite tender, put them into a gallon of salt and water for a week; drain and dry them, mash them to a pulp in a marble mortar, with a pound of salt; let it rest three or four days, and press all the juice from it, to each gallon of liquor put a quarter of a pound of minced shallots, half an ounce of bruised cloves, some of mace and black pepper, one teaspoonful of Cayenne, and a quarter of a pound of salt; give it a boil up, and strain it through a flannel bag.

By adding a glass of brandy to each quart, it will keep all the better.

—William Kitchiner,
Apicius Redivivus, No. 438

Everlasting Syllabub

Take 3 pints of the thickest and sweetest cream you can get, a pint of rhennish [Rhine wine], half a pint of sack, 3 lemons, near a pound of double-refined sugar, beat [grind] and sift the sugar and put it to your cream, grate off the yellow rind of three lemons, put that in, and squeeze the juice of three lemons into your wine; put that to your cream, beat all together with a whisk just half an hour, then take it up all together with a spoon and fill your glasses.

—Mrs. Hannah Glasse,
The Compleat Confectioner

To Make Sack-Posset or Sack-Cream

Take 12 Eggs (the Whites of but six) beat 'em, and put to 'em a Pint of Sack and half a Pound of Sugar; set 'em on a Fire, keeping 'em stirring 'till they turn white, and just begin to thick; at the same Time on another Fire have a Quart of Cream, boil and pour it into the Eggs and Sack, give it a Stir round, and cover it a Quarter of an Hour before you eat it: The Eggs and Sack must be heated in the Bason you use it in, and the Cream must boil before you set on the Eggs.

—Mary Eales (confectioner to Queen Anne),
Mrs. Mary Eales's Receipts

To Sugar All Sorts of Small Fruit

Beat the White of an Egg, and dip the Fruit in it; let it lye on a Cloth that it may not wet; then take fine sifted Sugar, and rowl the Fruit in it 'till 'tis quite cover'd with Sugar; lay it on a Sieve in a Stove, or before a Fire, to dry it well; it will keep well a Week.

—*Ibid.*

THE AGE OF REVOLUTION

A Nineteenth Century Picnic

The following is Grimod de la Reynière's plan for a picnic for six ladies and six gentlemen in 1806.[41] All the food was to be prepared by a caterer. The author anticipated a meal lasting about four hours.

A fricassee of some nice fat chickens, put in a loaf of bread.
2 large galantines, one of beef tongue, the other of a nice hare.
A very nice roast young turkey, cold.
A good Mayence or Bayonne ham, well cooked and trimmed.
A nice pâté of boned pullets, accompanied by either quail or larks
according to the season.
A covered pastry of partridge, well garnished.
A nice almond cream tart.
A very fine *biscuit de Savoie* [a light cake].
A well-cleaned salad with oil and vinegar in bottles and a napkin
to toss it when it has been seasoned.
Coffee, sugar, mustard.
Fruit in season, some plates of petits fours, cookies, macaroons, comfits,
and, for the men, Gruyère or Roquefort.
6 bottles of ordinary wine, 2 bottles of Jurançon, 2 of Champagne,
1 bottle of Malaga, 1 of Frontignan, and 2 of liqueur.

---

[41] *Almanach des gourmands*, Vol. IV, pp. 69–71.

A DINNER FOR TWENTY-FOUR GIVEN ON NOVEMBER 28, 1809, AT THE FAMOUS PARISIAN RESTAURANT ROCHER DE CANCALE [42]

First Course

Four Potages [43]
Crayfish Bisque
Potage à la Reine made with almond milk, served with *biscottes* [oven-dried bread]
Four Removes [44] *for the Potages*
Pike *à la Chambord* [garnished with truffles, shrimp, mushrooms]
Truffled turkey

Twelve Entrées
Aspic of small fillets of partridge

Mixed vegetables

Pullet fillets, larded with truffles

Red partridges *au fumet* [45]

Sautéed fillets of larks
Scallops of fattened pullet with velouté sauce

Julienne soup with asparagus tips
Chicken consommé

Turbot

Rump of beef with Madeira, vegetable garnish

Fillets of young rabbit dressed in a ring
Vol au vent à la financière [a patty shell filled with truffles, cockscombs, kidneys, mushrooms, and olives in a sauce]
Larded wing tips with chicory garnish
Two fattened chickens with crayfish butter
Scallops of salmon *à l'espagnole*
Filets mignons larded with truffles

Second Course

Four large platters
A trout
A pâté of foie gras

Crayfish
Glazed ham

Four dishes of roast [46]
A pheasant
Smelts

Snipe
Sole

Eight Entremets [47]
A bowl of *blanc-manger* [white jelly]
Stewed apples
Asparagus
Truffles *à la serviette* [cooked in Madeira and meat glaze]

A bowl of orange jelly

Vanilla soufflé
Cardoons with marrow
Truffles *à la serviette*

---

[42] Quoted in G. H. Ellwanger, *The Pleasures of the Table.*
[43] Potage: now a soup.
[44] Remove: a dish brought in to replace another during a course.
[45] Fumet: a concentrated flavoring.
[46] Roast: still game, meat, or fish with little or no sauce.
[47] Entremet: still a side dish.

PENNY COOKERY MENUS

The poor were not neglected by cookbook authors. Mrs. Isabella Beeton devoted an entire book to menus and recipes for the lowest budget, because she recognized, as she put it, that "to make a little go a great way is the want, the necessity of toiling millions." [48] Her menus are designed for a man with a wife and four children and a weekly salary of ten shillings and up. The following bill of fare is for a weekly salary of fifteen shillings, of which eight shilings nine pence are to be spent on food.

Breakfast	Dinner	Supper
Sunday..Tea & bread, &c.	Stewed tripe for 2 and porridge (for 4)	Turkish rice & bread
Monday..Coffee & bread, &c.	Stew, soup No. 2, potatoes	Cabbage & dumplings
Tuesday..Oatmeal porridge, &c.	Sheep's head and dumplings	Potato rice
Wednesday..Tea & bread, &c.	Sheep's head and rice	Crowdie * & bread
Thursday..Coffee & bread, &c.	Sheep's head and dumplings	Remains of crowdie & bread
Friday..Oatmeal porridge	Carrot soup and dumplings	Rice porridge
Saturday..Coffee & bread, &c.	Bacon & potatoes, broken-bread pudding	Suet dumplings

ESCOFFIER'S MENU FOR A MAY SUPPER [49]

Menu	Explanation of dish
Melon Cocktail	Melon cocktail, flavored with a liqueur or champagne
Velouté léger de Poulet en Tasse	Light cream of chicken soup in a cup
Filets de Sole glacés sur mousse de Crevettes	Cold jellied fillets of sole served on a bed of shrimp mousse
Côtelettes de volaille Pojarski	Fried patties of ground chicken or other fowl
Petits pois à la Française	Peas cooked in butter with onions and flavoring

---

[48] Isabella Beeton, *Beeton's Penny Cookery Book*, p. 8. The weekly menu is from p. 9.
[49] Auguste Escoffier, *Ma Cuisine.*
* Recipe follows.

Terrine de Canard au Porto	Pâté of duck with port wine
Salade Saint-Jean	Salad
Mousse aux fraises parfumées au Curaçao	Strawberry mousse flavored with curaçao
Langues de chat	Cookies

NINETEENTH CENTURY RECIPES

Omelette au Thon
(tuna omelette)

For six people, take the milt of two carp, well cleaned, and blanch by putting in boiling, lightly salted water for five minutes.

You will also need a piece of fresh tuna the size of an egg, to which you will add 1 small minced shallot. Chop the milt and tuna together so that they are well mixed, and put the mixture in a casserole with a lump of very good butter. Sauté it until the butter is melted. Therein lies the secret of the omelette.

Take another lump of butter, blend it with some parsley and chives, and put it on a fish-shaped platter on which the omelette will be served. Sprinkle the parsley, chive, and butter mixture with lemon juice and place the platter on hot coals.

Then beat twelve eggs (the freshest are best), add the sauté of milt and tuna and blend well.

Cook the omelette in the usual way; try to make it longish, thick, and juicy. Spread it on the prepared platter with care and serve it. To be eaten at once.

This dish should be reserved for choice lunches, gatherings of informed devotees who take time to eat. Above all, accompany it with a good old wine and you will have something to remember.

—Brillat-Savarin,
Physiologie du goût

Ragoût de Crêtes et de Rognons de Coqs en Financière
(cock's combs and kidneys financière)

After blanching and cooking the cock's combs in a *blanc* [seasoned white stock], drain them along with the kidneys; put the necessary amount of reduced velouté sauce in the pot if you want a white ragout; if you want it to be brown, use reduced *sauce espagnole*, adding a little consommé if it is too thick. Simmer your cock's combs a quarter of an hour; add, a moment before serving, your kidneys, some mushrooms, precooked, some artichoke bottoms and truffles as you see fit. If your ragout is white, enrich it as indicated in the recipe for Ragout of sweetbreads; if brown, follow the procedure explained in the same recipe.*

—Antoine Beauvilliers,
L'Art du cuisinier

---

* The only liaison given in the recipe for Ragout of sweetbreads is one of egg yolks diluted in bouillon or water and flavored with parsley. A bit of lemon juice or verjuice is added at the last.

Salmis de Perdreaux à la D'Artois
(salmi of partridge à la d'Artois)

Take three partridge roasted on the spit without having been larded; cut off the limbs, trim them and discard the skin; arrange the limbs in a small saucepan and heat them with a little consommé without allowing it to boil; put the kidneys and trimmings of the partridge in a mortar; crush them; put a good glass of madeira in a saucepan with three chopped shallots, three sprigs of parsley, and a little peel from a bigarade [sour orange]; let it boil, then add five skimming spoons of *sauce espagnole*; let it boil on a good fire for ten minutes; remove the casserole from the fire, mix the crushed carcasses with the sauce, add a little liquid and strain; scrape up everything on the outside of the sieve; put this puree or salmi in a small double boiler; drain the partridge limbs, arrange them on a serving platter, sprinkling among them some croutons sautéed in butter (you will have already made a border of small croutons sautéed in oil for your platter); remove your sauce from the double boiler, add the juice of a bigarade or two, a little coarsely ground pepper and half a butter roll; strain it and pour the sauce on your salmi.

—*Ibid.*

New and Economical Lobster Sauce

Break up a fresh lobster, use the solid flesh for salad or any other purpose, pound the soft part and shell together (in a mortar) very fine, place the whole in a stewpan, cover with a pint of boiling water, place over the fire, and let simmer ten minutes, when pass the liquor through a hair sieve into a basin, and use for making melted butter, to which add a little cayenne pepper and a piece of anchovy butter the size of a walnut; if any red spawn in the lobster, pound and mix it with a small piece of fresh butter, and add to the sauce with a little lemon-juice when upon the point of serving; an anchovy pounded with the shells of the lobster would be an improvement; some of the flesh may be served in the sauce.

MELTED BUTTER: Put 2 oz. of butter into a stewpan, with which mix a good teaspoonful of flour, using a wooden spoon, add a salt-spoonful of salt, half a one of pepper, a little grated nutmeg, and half a pint of water, stir over the fire until just upon the point of boiling, when take off, add two ounces more butter, and half a tb of vinegar, keep it stirred until quite smooth, and the butter well melted, when pass through a hair sieve or tammie if required (you can also use milk instead of water for the above); it is then ready for use. In making melted butter great attention ought to be paid to the above directions, it being almost in daily use.

ANCHOVY BUTTER: Take the bones from ten anchovies, wash the fillets; dry them upon a cloth, and pound them well in a mortar; then add a quarter of a pound of fresh butter; mix well together, and proceed as in the last.

—Alexis Soyer,
The Gastronomic Regenerator, No. 78, 137, 138

Ortolans and Truffles

Alexis Soyer was unable to make this dish for an elegant dinner at the Reform Club in London because weather prevented the arrival of the two dozen ortolans ordered from Paris. He consoled himself by describing it:

. . . having already procured 12 of the largest and finest truffles I could obtain, it was my intention to have dug a hole in each, into which I should have placed one of the birds, and covered each with a piece of lamb's or calf's caul, then to have braised them half an hour in good stock made from fowl and veal, with half a pint of Lachryma Christi added; then to have drained them upon a cloth, placed a border of poached forcemeat upon the dish, built the truffles in pyramid, made a puree with the truffle dug from the interior, using the stock reduced to a demi-glace and poured over, roasted the 12 remaining ortolans before a sharp fire, with which I should have garnished the whole round, and served very hot.

—Ibid.

Soupe aux Cerises
(cherry soup)

This is a good sweet entremet. Sauté black cherries whole with their pits along with cubes of the white part of bread, previously sautéed in butter. Moisten it, sprinkle it with sugar, douse it with kirsch, and serve it with the syrup and croutons.

—Alexandre Dumas,
Grand dictionnaire de cuisine

Crowdie (A Capital Scotch Broth)

Things wanted—The liquor in which a leg of mutton or piece of beef has been boiled, ½ pint of oatmeal, salt, and pepper.
How to use them—Make the oatmeal into a paste with a little of the liquor over the fire; stir it well into the remainder, and serve hot, with bread, potatoes, or boiled rice.

Cost for 6 persons, not 6 d.

—Beeton's Penny Cookery Book, No. 16

Onion Porridge (supper dish)

Things wanted—2 or 3 large Spanish onions; to each pint of water a small piece of butter, salt, and pepper.
How to use them—Peel the onions, and split them into quarters; put them into a stewpan with the other things, and let them simmer gently for an hour.

A cheap supper for six persons with bread.

—Ibid., No. 119

NOTES

✦✦✦

1 Athenaeus, *The Deipnosophists*, Book IV: 130.
2 Antiphanes, quoted in *ibid.*, Book IV: 170.
3 Carystius of Pergamum, cited in *ibid.*, Book XII: 542.
4 *Ibid.*, Book VII: 293.
5 This and the following three quotes are taken from *Travels of Anacharsis the Younger in Greece*, Vol. II, Chapter XXV.
6 Livy, *The History of Rome*, Vol. XXXIX: VI.
7 Athenaeus, *The Deipnosophists*, Book VI: 274.
8 Varro, *Res Rusticae*, Book III: IV.
9 Martial, *Epigrams*, Book VII: XX.
10 Juvenal, *The Sixteen Satires*, Satire V.
11 Suetonius, *The Lives of the Twelve Caesars*, p. 198.
12 Robert Étienne, *La Vie quotidienne à Pompéi*, p. 230.
13 Horace, "The Simple Life," Book II: 2, *The Complete Works of Horace.*
14 Martial, *Epigrams*, V: LXXVIII.
15 Julius Capitolinus, "Life of Pertinax," XII, *Scriptores Historiae Augustae.*
16 Suetonius, *The Lives of the Twelve Caesars*, p. 80.
17 *Ibid.*, p. 247.
18 *Ibid.*, p. 233.
19 Flavius Vopiscus, "The Life of Probus," XIX, *Scriptores Historiae Augustae.*
20 "Ordinances made at Eltham in the 17th Year of Henry VIII," in *A Collection of the Ordinances and Regulations for the Government of the Royal Household made in Divers Reigns.*
21 "Close Roll of 9 Edw. II," in *A Collection of Ordinances.*
22 Recipes for mawmenee and monchelet are from *Forme of Cury.*
23 *A Noble Boke of Cookry ffor a Prynce Houssolde*, p. 121.
24 "Articles ordained by King Henry VII for the regulation of his household, 31 December, 1494," in *A Collection of Ordinances.*
25 Edward Hall, *Hall's Chronicle*, pp. 804–05.
26 Paul Hentzner, *A Journey into England* (1598), p. 20.
27 Richard Hakluyt, *The Principal Navigations, Voyages, Traffiques, and Discoveries of the English Nation*, Vol. I, p. 282.
28 The detailed list of provisions is given in Richard Warner's *Antiquitates Culinariae* (1791) and taken from a 1770 reprint from an ancient paper roll whose original was then in the Bodleian library, Lel. Collect. A slightly different list plus the information on the number of cooks and assistants is given in Alexis Soyer's *Gastronomic Regenerator* and Humelbergius' *Apician Anecdotes*, both of which cite a manuscript found in the Tower of London.
29 Condensed from a listing quoted in Paul Van Brunt Jones, *The Household of a Tudor Nobleman, University of Illinois Studies in*

the Social Sciences, Vol. 6, no. 4 (Dec., 1917), pp. 78–9, taken from Lord North's household book.

30 Thomas Tusser, *Five Hundred Points of Good Husbandry*, p. 73.

31 Susanna Avery, *A Plain Plantain*, p. 32.

32 "Liber Niger Domus Regis Edward IV," in *A Collection of Ordinances*.

33 "Ordinances of King James I, 1604," prologue, in *A Collection of Ordinances*

34 Quoted in Mary Bateson, "Social Life, 1509–1558," in *Social England*, Vol. III, Sect. I, p. 234.

35 Quoted from "Maison du roi," in Edmond et Jules Goncourt, *Histoire de la société française pendant la révolution*, pp. 31–32.

36 Richard Brathwait, *Household of an Earle*, in *Miscellanea Antiqua Anglicana*, p. 33.

37 *A Perfect School of Instructions for Officers of the Mouth*, pp. 18–19.

38 Antoine de Courtin, *Nouveau traité de la civilité*, p. 17.

39 Thomas Coryat, *Coryat's Crudities*, Vol. I, p. 236.

40 The Princess Palatine, Charlotte Elizabeth of Bavaria, *Correspondance*, Vol. V, pp. 149–150 (Paris, 1904).

41 From "Procès de Louis XVI, 1798," in Alfred Franklin, *La Vie privée d'autrefois*, Vol. III, p. 212.

42 François Marin, *Les Dons de Comus ou Délices de la table*, quoted in Franklin, *La Vie privée d'autrefois*, Vol. III, pp. 206–07.

43 *Kettner's Book of the Table*, p. 288

44 Louis-Sébastien Mercier, *Tableau de Paris*, Vol. V, p. 47.

45 Hannah Glasse, *The Art of Cookery Made Plain and Easy*, p. iv.

46 Karl P. Moritz, *Travels Through Various Parts of England, 1782*, Vol. IV of William F. Mavor, *The British Tourists*, p. 14.

47 Quoted in Wilmarth S. Lewis, *Three Tours*, note 49, p. 63.

48 Alexis Soyer, *The Gastronomic Regenerator*, pp. 84–85.

49 Quoted in J. C. Drummond, *The Englishman's Food*, p. 211.

50 Excerpt dated April 4, 1762, from *The Diaries of a Duchess*.

51 *The Works of Horatio Walpole*, Vol. I, pp. 148–50 (London: G. G. & J. Robinson, 1798).

52 Dr. John Trusler, *The Honours of the Table*, p. 7.

53 Louis-Sébastien Mercier, *Paris pendant la révolution*, Vol. II, p. 132.

54 Theodore Child, *Delicate Feasting*, pp. 205–06.

55 William Makepeace Thackeray, *Works*, Vol. XXV, pp. 378–79.

56 Theodore Child, *Delicate Feasting*, p. 212.

57 Quotes in this paragraph are from Grimod de la Reynière, *Almanach des gourmands*, Vol. I, pp. 221–25.

58 Julian Street, *Table Topics*, p. 237.

59 From "Notice sur Carême" by Frédéric Fayot in the 1854 edition of Carême's *Pâtissier royal parisien*.

60 Abraham Hayward, *The Art of Dining*, p. 24.

61 Julian Street, *Table Topics*, p. 95.

62 John Cordy Jeaffreson, *A Book About The Table*, pp. 292–93.

[63] Abraham Hayward, *The Art of Dining*, pp. 22–23.

[64] Lady Morgan, *France in 1829–1830*, pp. 410–15.

[65] *Our English Home*, p. 70.

[66] *Encyclopaedia Britannica*, 9th ed., "Johnson," Vol. XIII, pp. 719–21.

[67] W. H. Lewis, *The Splendid Century*, p. 209.

[68] George Dodd, *The Food of London*, p. 289.

[69] From *Wine and Food*, No. XXII, quoted in André Simon, *Food*, p. 66.

[70] Bernal Diaz, *The Conquest of New Spain*, pp. 225–227.

[71] Maud Howe Elliott, *Uncle Sam Ward and His Circle*, pp. 558–59.

[72] *Ibid.*, p. 559.

[73] Lucy Kavaler, *Mushrooms, Molds, and Miracles*, p. 61.

[74] Marcus Terentius Varro, *Res Rusticae*, III: V.

[75] Robert May, *The Accomplish't Cook*, p. 231.

[76] Anacharsis, *Travels of Anacharsis the Younger in Greece*, Vol. II, p. 57.

[77] Pliny the Elder, *Natural History*, Book XVIII: xxvii.

[78] Quoted in John Beckmann, *A History of Inventions and Discoveries*, Vol. II, p. 389.

[79] Grimod de la Reynière, *Manuel des amphitryons*, p. 112.

[80] *Kettner's Book of the Table*, pp. 450–51.

[81] Honoré de Balzac, "Traité des excitans modernes," appendix to 1839 edition of Brillat-Savarin's *Physiologie du goût*, pp. 460–61.

[82] William H. Ukers, *All About Coffee*, p. 22.

[83] Quoted in *Food and Drink Through the Ages, 2500 b.c. to 1937*, p. 55.

[84] Alexandre Dumas, *Grand dictionnaire de cuisine*, p. 532.

[85] Columella, *De Re Rustica*, XII: xv.

[86] Athenaeus, *The Deipnosophists*, Book IV: 224.

[87] Plutarch, *Moralia*, "Sayings of Romans," 198.

[88] Cato, *De Agricultura*, CXLIII.

[89] Richard Lucas, *Nature's Medicines*, p. 28.

[90] Henry Phillips, *History of Cultivated Vegetables*, Vol. II, p. 147.

[91] G. H. Ellwanger, *The Pleasures of the Table*, p. 399.

[92] Columella, *De Re Rustica*, Book XII: xlix, 4.

[93] Pliny the Elder, *Natural History*, Book XXXII: xxi.

[94] Brillat-Savarin, *Physiologie du goût*, No. 40.

[95] Letter of May 10, 1696, from Madame de Maintenon to Mgr. l'Archevesque de Paris, *Lettres*, Vol. V, pp. 60–61 (Paris: Letouzey et Ané, 1939).

[96] Brillat-Savarin, *Physiologie du goût*, No. 62.

[97] Legrand d'Aussy, *Histoire de la vie privée des Français*, Vol. I, p. 145.

[98] Arthur Young, *Farmer's Letters to the People of England*, p. 204.

[99] Quoted in Henry Phillips, *History of Cultivated Vegetables*, Vol. II, p. 196.

[100] Quoted in Athenaeus, *The Deipnosophists*, Book II: 70.

[101] Henry Phillips, *Pomarium Britannicum*, p. 227.

BIBLIOGRAPHY

❧❧❧

PART ONE

I General

ARESTY, ESTHER B., *Delectable Past*. New York: Simon and Schuster, 1964.

BABEAU, ALBERT, *La Vie rurale dans l'ancienne France*. Paris: Émile Perrin, 1885.

DRUMMOND, J. C., and WILBRAHAM, ANNE, *The Englishman's Food: A History of Five Centuries of English Diet*. London: Jonathan Cape, 1939.

DUMAS, ALEXANDRE, *Grand dictionnaire de cuisine*. Paris: Alphonse Lemerre, 1873.

ELLWANGER, G. H., *The Pleasures of the Table*. New York: Doubleday, Page, 1902.

ÉLUARD-VALETTE, CÉCILE, *Les grandes heures de la cuisine française*. Paris: Les Libraires Associés, 1964.

Food and Drink Through the Ages 2500 B.C. to 1937 A.D. London: Magg Bros., 1937.

FRANKLIN, ALFRED, *La Vie privée d'autrefois*, Vol. III, *La Cuisine*, Vol. VI, *Les Repas*. Paris: E. Plon, 1887–1902.

Gastronomy in Fine Arts, A loan exhibit held by the Cultural Division of the French Embassy in New York, November 29, 1951, to January 30, 1952.

HALLIWELL-PHILLIPS, JAMES ORCHARD, *A Dictionary of Archaic and Provincial Words*. London: G. Routledge & Sons, New York: E. P. Dutton, 1924.

HARTLEY, DOROTHY, *Food in England*. London: MacDonald, 1954.

HAZLITT, W. CAREW, *Old Cookery Books and Ancient Cuisine*. London: Elliot Stock, 1886.

HUMELBERGIUS SECUNDUS, DICK, *Apician Anecdotes*. New York: J. D. Strong, 1836.

331

JEAFFRESON, JOHN CORDY, *A Book About the Table*, 2 vols. London: Hurst & Blackett, 1875.

Kettner's Book of the Table. London: Dulau, 1877.

KIRWAN, A. V., *Host and Guest*. London: Bell & Daldy, 1864.

LEGRAND D'AUSSY, PIERRE JEAN BAPTISTE, *Histoire de la vie privée des Français*, 3 vols. Paris: Laurent-Beaupré, 1815 (original 1782).

MESTAYER DE ECHAGÜE, MARIA (Marquesa de Parabere), *Historia de la Gastronomía*. Madrid: Espasa-Calpe, 1943.

MONTAGNÉ, PROSPER, *Larousse gastronomique*. Paris: Larousse, 1938.

OLIVER, RAYMOND, *Gastronomy of France*, trans. by Claude Durrell. Cleveland, Ohio: The Wine & Food Society in association with World Publishing Co., 1967.

Our English Home: Its Early History and Progress. Oxford and London: J. H. and Jas. Parker, 1861.

PRENTICE, E. PARMALEE, *Hunger and History*. Caldwell, Idaho: Caxton Printers, 1951.

PYNE, W. H., *The History of the Royal Residences*, 3 vols. London: A. Dry, 1819.

SIMON, ANDRE L., *A Concise Encyclopedia of Gastronomy*. New York: Bramhall House, 1942.

———— *Food*. London: Burke, 1949.

Social England, vols. I–III; articles by Mary Bateson, C. Creighton, A. H. Mann, D. J. Medley, and George Saintsbury. New York: G. P. Putnam's; London: Cassell, 1909.

SOYER, ALEXIS, *The Pantropheon*. Boston: Ticknor, Reed, & Fields (original, 1853).

STREET, JULIAN, *Table Topics*. New York: Alfred A. Knopf, 1959.

WARD, ARTEMAS, *The Encyclopedia of Food*. New York: Ward, 1923.

WARNER, REVEREND RICHARD, *Antiquitates Culinariae*. London: R. Blamire, 1791.

II ANTIQUITY: MESOPOTAMIA, EGYPT, AND GREECE

General, Near East, and Egypt

Archives royales de Mari, Vol. XII, Textes administratifs de la salle 5 du palais, 2ᵉ Partie, Maurice Birot, Paris: Direction Générale des Affaires Culturelles, Ministère des Affaires Étrangères, 1964.

ATHENAEUS, *The Deipnosophists*. The Loeb Classical Library. 7 vols., trans. by Charles Burton Gulick. London: William Heinemann, 1927.

CONTENEAU, DR. G., *La Civilisation d'Assur et de Babylone*. Paris: Payot, 1937.

DANIEL-ROPS, HENRY, *La vie quotidienne en Palestine au temps de Jésus*. Paris: Hachette, 1961.

DAREMBERG, CH., et SAGLIO, EDM., *Dictionnaire des antiquités grècques et romaines*, 5 vols. Paris: Hachette, 1877–1919.

MARTYN, CHARLES, *Foods and Culinary Utensils of the Ancients*. New York: Caterer, 1906.

MONTET, PIERRE, *Les Scènes de la vie privée dans les tombeaux égyptiens de l'ancien empire.* Strasbourg, France: Istra, 1925.

———— *La Vie quotidienne en Égypte au temps des Ramsès.* Paris: Hachette, 1946.

PARROT, ANDRE, *Mari; une ville perdue.* Paris: Éditions "Je sers," 1936.

PIGGOTT, STUART, *Prehistoric India.* Harmondsworth, M'sex.: Penguin Books, 1950.

PRITCHARD, JAMES B., *Ancient Near Eastern Texts Relating to the Old Testament.* Princeton, N.J.: Princeton University Press, 1950.

RANSOM, CAROLINE L., *Couches and Beds of the Greeks, Etruscans, and Romans.* Chicago: University of Chicago Press, 1905.

RICHTER, GISELA, *Ancient Furniture.* London: Oxford University Press, 1926.

XENOPHON, *The Persian Expedition,* trans. by Rex Warner, Harmondsworth, M'sex.: Penguin Books, 1949.

Additional sources specifically pertinent to Greece

ANACHARSIS, *Travels of Anacharsis the Younger in Greece,* 7 vols., trans. by Abbé Jean-Jacques Barthélemy. London: G. G. J. and J. Robinson, 1791.

ARISTOPHANES, *Collected Works,* 3 vols., trans. by Benjamin Bickley Rogers. The Loeb Classical Library. London: William Heinemann, 1960–1963.

BOECKH, AUGUSTUS, *The Public Economy of the Athenians.* Boston: Little, Brown, London: Sampson Low, 1857.

GELLIUS, AULUS, *The Attic Nights,* 3 vols., trans. by John C. Rolfe. The Loeb Classical Library. London: William Heinemann, 1927.

HERODOTUS, *History,* 4 vols., trans. by A. D. Godley, The Loeb Classical Library. London: William Heinemann, 1946.

HIPPOCRATES, *Hippocrates and the Fragments of Heracleitus,* 4 vols., trans. by W. H. S. Jones. The Loeb Classical Library. London: William Heinemann, 1943.

HOMER, *The Iliad of Homer,* trans. by Ennis Rees. New York: Random House, 1963.

———— *The Odyssey,* trans. by E. V. Rieu. Harmondsworth, M'sex.: Penguin Books, 1946.

JEANMAIRE, M. H., "La Cryptie lacédémonienne," *Revue des Études Grècques,* Vol. XXVI (1913).

MIREAUX, ÉMILE, *La Vie quotidienne au temps d'Homère.* Paris: Hachette, 1954.

STRABO, *Geography,* 8 vols., trans. by H. L. Jones and J. R. S. Sterrett. The Loeb Classical Library. London: William Heinemann, 1923–1932.

XENOPHON, *Hellenica, Anabasis, Apology,* and *Symposium,* 3 vols., trans. by Carleton L. Brownson. The Loeb Classical Library. London: William Heinemann, 1947.

ZIMMERN, ALFRED, *The Greek Commonwealth.* New York: Modern Library, n.d.

III ANTIQUITY: ROME

In addition to the references given below, the following works listed in the preceding section were useful sources of material for this chapter: Athenaeus, *The Deipnosophists;* Daremberg-Saglio, *Dictionnaire des antiquités grècques et romaines;* Martyn, *Foods and Culinary Utensils of the Ancients;* Ransom, *Couches and Beds of the Greeks, Etruscans, and Romans;* and Richter, *Ancient Furniture.*

APICIUS, *Cookery and Dining in Imperial Rome,* trans. and ed. by Joseph Dommers Vehling. Chicago: Walter M. Hill, 1936.

———— *The Roman Cookery Book,* trans. by Barbara Flower and Elisabeth Rosenbaum. London: George G. Harrap, 1958.

CAESAR, JULIUS, *The Gallic War and Other Writings,* trans. by Moses Hadas. New York: Modern Library, 1957.

CARCOPINO, JÉRÔME, *Daily Life in Ancient Rome.* Harmondsworth, M'sex.: Penguin Books, 1941.

CATO, MARCUS PORCIUS, *De Agricultura,* trans. by W. D. Hooper and H. B. Ash. The Loeb Classical Library. London: William Heinemann, 1934.

COLUMELLA, LUCIUS JUNIUS MODERATUS, *De Re Rustica,* trans. by H. B. Ash, E. E. Forster, and E. H. Heffner. The Loeb Classical Library. London: William Heinemann, 1941.

DUCKWORTH, GEORGE, *The Complete Roman Drama,* 2 vols. New York: Random House [1942].

ÉTIENNE, ROBERT, *La Vie quotidienne à Pompéi.* Paris: Hachette, 1966.

HARCUM, CORNELIA GASKINS, *Roman Cooks,* Baltimore, Md.: J. H. Furst, 1914.

HORACE, *The Complete Works of Horace,* trans. by Casper J. Kraemer, Jr. New York: Modern Library, 1936.

JUVENAL, *The Sixteen Satires,* trans. by Peter Green. Baltimore, Md.: Penguin Books, 1967.

LIVY, *History of Rome,* trans. by B. O. Foster. The Loeb Classical Library. London: William Heinemann, 1936.

MACROBIUS, *Oeuvres de Macrobe,* 2 vols. Paris: Firmin-Didot, 1827.

MARTIAL, *Epigrams,* 2 vols., trans. by Walter C. A. Ker. The Loeb Classical Library. London: William Heinemann, 1961.

PALLADIUS, *On Husbondrie.* London: Early English Text Society, 1873 and 1879.

PETRONIUS, *The Satyricon,* trans. by John Sullivan. Baltimore, Md.: Penguin Books, 1965.

PLATNER, SAMUEL BALL, *A Topographical Dictionary of Ancient Rome.* London: Oxford University Press, 1929.

PLATO, "Symposium," "Gorgias," *Collected Works,* Vol. 5. The Loeb Classical Library. London: William Heinemann, 1925.

PLINY THE ELDER, *Natural History,* 10 vols., trans. by H. Rackham, W. S. Jones, and D. E. Eichholz. The Loeb Classical Library. London: William Heinemann, 1950.

PLINY THE YOUNGER, *Letters,* 2 vols., trans. by W. M. L. Hutchinson. The Loeb Classical Library. London: William Heinemann, 1961.

PLUTARCH, *The Parallel Lives*, various editions.

—— *Moralia*, 15 vols., trans. by F. C. Babbitt. The Loeb Classical Library. London: William Heinemann, 1936.

Scriptores Historiae Augustae, 3 vols., trans. by David Magie. Biographies of thirty Roman Emperors attributed to six Roman authors: Julius Capitolinus, Vulcacius Gallicanus, Aelius Lampridius, Trebellius Pollio, Aelius Spartianus, and Flavius Vopiscus. The Loeb Classical Library. London: William Heinemann, 1922.

SUETONIUS, *The Lives of the Twelve Caesars*, trans. by Joseph Gavorse. New York: Modern Library, 1931.

TACITUS, *The Annals*. New York: Washington Square Press, 1964.

—— *Agricola, Germania*, trans. by Maurice Hutton. The Loeb Classical Library. London: William Heinemann, 1946.

THEOPHRASTUS, *The Characters of Theophrastus*, trans. by J. M. Edmonds. The Loeb Classical Library. London: William Heinemann, 1929.

—— *An Inquiry into Plants; Concerning Odours*, 2 vols., trans. by Sir Arthur Hort. The Loeb Classical Library. London: William Heinemann, 1916.

VARRO, MARCUS TERENTIUS, *Res Rusticae*, trans. by Ronald G. Kent. The Loeb Classical Library. London: William Heinemann, 1934.

IV THE DARK AND MIDDLE AGES

AGRIPPA VON NETTERHEIM, HENRY CORNELIUS, *The Vanity of Arts and Sciences*. London: R. Everingham for R. Bentley, 1694 (original, 1569).

"Ancient Cookery, A.D. 1381," *Forme of Cury*, q.v.

"Ancient Cookery," *A Collection of Ordinances*, q.v.

The Babee's Book. London: Chatto and Windus; New York: Duffield, 1908.

BARCLAY, ALEXANDER, *Eclogues*. London: Early English Text Society, 1928 (original probably 1513–1514).

Beowulf, a heroic poem of the eighth century. Various editions.

Daz Büch von güter Spise. Berlin: Erich Schmidt, 1958 (written late Middle Ages).

Caxton's Book of Curtesye, ed. by Frederick J. Furnivall. London: Early English Text Society, 1868 (original, 1477–1478).

COKE, JOHN, *A Debate Between the Heralds of England and France*. 1550 (original earlier).

COMBE, WILLIAM, *A History of the University of Oxford*, 2 vols. London: R. Ackermann, 1814.

ERASMUS, *The Colloquies of Erasmus*, trans. by Craig R. Thompson. Chicago and London: University of Chicago Press, 1965 (original 1522?).

—— *De Civilitate Morum Puerilium*, trans. by R. Whytyngton, J. Wallye, 1554 (original 1530).

The Forme of Cury, ed. by Reverend Samuel Pegge. London: J. Nichols, 1780 (presumably written ca. 1390 by the master cook of King Richard II).

FRANKLIN, ALFRED, *Les Rues et les cris de Paris au XIIIe siècle.* Paris: Léon Willem & Paul Daffes, 1874.

FROISSART, JEAN, *Oeuvres de Froissart,* various editions. (Original written in fourteenth century.)

GROSSETESTE, ROBERT, "Rules" (written *ca.* 1240), *Walter of Henley's Husbandry.* New York & London: Longmans, Green, 1890.

HALL, EDWARD, *Hall's Chronicle.* London: J. Johnson, 1809.

HARTLEY, DOROTHY, *The Old Book.* London: Alfred A. Knopf, 1930.

HOLMES, URBAN TIGNER, JR., *Daily Living in the Twelfth Century.* Madison, Wis.: University of Wisconsin Press, 1952.

"Libre de Totes Maneres de Confits," Boletín de la Real Academia de Buenas Letras de Barcelona, no. 18. Barcelona: 1945–1946.

MACHYN, HENRY, *Diary of a Resident in London 1550–1563.* London: J. B. Nichols & Son, 1848.

MARTÍNEZ, J. ERNESTO MARTINEZ FERRANDO, *Jaime II de Aragón, su Vida Familiar,* Vol. II. Barcelona: Escuela de Estudios Medievales, 1948.

MEAD, WILLIAM EDWARD, *The English Medieval Feast.* London: George Allen and Unwin, 1967.

Le Ménagier de Paris, 2 vols. Paris: Jérôme Pichon, 1846 (original written *ca.* 1393 by an anonymous Parisian bourgeois).

MONTIÑO, FRANCISCO MARTÍNEZ, *Arte de Cocina.* Barcelona: C. Sapèra y J. Ossèt, 17?? (original, 1617).

A Noble Boke of Cookry ffor a Prynce Houssolde. London: Elliot Stock, 1882 (original probably written shortly after 1467).

"Old English Cookery," *The Quarterly Review,* vol. 178, no. 355 (January, 1894), pp. 82–104.

Paris à travers les âges. Paris: Firmin-Didot, 1875–1882.

PROCOPIUS, *The Secret History,* trans. by G. A. Williamson. Baltimore, Md.: Penguin Books, 1966.

RHODES, HUGH, *Boke of Nurture,* bound with Roxburghe Club edition of John Russell's *The Boke of Nurture, q.v.* (originally published 1577).

ROSELLI, GIOVANNI DE', *Epulario, or, The Italian banquet.* London: William Barley, 1598 (original probably 1516).

RUNCIMAN, STEVEN, *Byzantine Civilization.* New York: Meridian Books, 1956.

RUSSELL, JOHN, *The Boke of Nurture.* Bungay, Suff.: Roxburghe Club, 1867 (original 1460–1470).

SERJEANTSON, M. S., "The Vocabulary of Cookery in the Fifteenth Century," *Essays and Studies* by members of the English Association, Oxford, vol. 23 (1938), pp. 25–37.

SOLDEVILA, FERRÁN, *Pere el Gran, Primera Part: l'Infant.* Barcelona: Institut d'Estudis Catalans, 1952.

TIREL, GUILLAUME *dit* TAILLEVENT, *Le Viandier,* ed. by Baron Jérôme Pichon and Georges Vicaire. Paris: Techener, 1892 (original *ca.* 1375).

Traité de cuisine écrit vers 1300, from ms. in Bibliothèque Nationale, in Pichon edition of Tirel's *Le Viandier.*

Two Fifteenth Century Cookery Books, ed. by Thomas Austin. London: Early English Text Society, 1888.

TUSSER, THOMAS, *Five Hundred Points of Good Husbandry*. Lackington, Allen, 1812. (This 1573 edition is an enlargement of the original, *A Hundred Good Pointes of Husbandrie*, printed in 1557.)

VILLENA, MARQUES DE, *Arte Cisoria*. Madrid: Oficina de Antonio Marin, 1766 (original 1423).

WALTER OF HENLEY, *Le Dite de Hosebondrie*, trans. by Elizabeth Lamond, in *Walter of Henley's Husbandry*, New York & London: Longmans, Green, 1890.

DE WORDE, WYNKYN, *The Boke of Kervynge*, bound with Roxburghe Club edition of John Russell's *The Boke of Nurture*, *q.v.* (original, 1513).

WRIGHT, THOMAS, *A History of Domestic Manners and Sentiments in England During the Middle Ages*. London: Chapman & Hall, 1862.

V THE AGE OF EXPLORATION

ASTRY, DIANA, *Diana Astry's Recipe Book*, *ca.* 1700, Bedfordshire Historical Record Society, Vol. XXXVII (1957).

A small collection of recipes for the preservation of particular fruits, *ca.* 1630, from the Antiquarian Repertory, Vol. IV, p. 95, included in *A Collection of Ordinances*, *q.v.*

AVERY, SUSANNA, *A Plain Plantain*. Ditchling, Sus.: S. Dominic's Press, 1922 (original seventeenth century).

BELON, PIERRE, *Observations des plusieurs singularités et choses mémorables*. Anvers, France: Christofle Plantin, 1555.

BLUNT, WILFRID, *Sebastiano, The Adventures of an Italian Priest*. London: James Barrie, 1956.

BOILEAU-DESPRÉAUX, NICOLAS, *Oeuvres*, Satire III, Vol. I. Paris: J. J. Blaise, 1821 (original date, 1667).

A Book of Cookyre, gathered by A. W. London: Edward Allde, 1587.

BONNEROT, JEAN, "Esquisse de la vie des routes au XVIe siècle," *Revue des Questions Historiques* Année 60, 3e série, tome XIX (1931), pp. 5–88.

BOORDE, ANDREW, *A Dyetary of Helth*. London: Early English Text Society, 1870 (original edition, 1542).

BRATHWAIT, R., "Household of an Earle," *Miscellanea Antiqua Anglicana*. London: Robert Triphook, 1816 (from a manuscript of the early seventeenth century).

A Collection of Ordinances and Regulations for the Government of the Royal Household, made in Divers Reigns, from King Edward III to King William and Queen Mary. London: Society of Antiquaries, 1790.

CORYAT, THOMAS, *Coryat's Crudities*, 2 vols. Glasgow: University Press, 1905 (original, 1611).

COURTIN, ANTOINE DE, *Nouveau traité de la civilité*. Paris: Josset, 1679.

CULPEPER, NICHOLAS, *The English Physician Enlarged*. Taunton: Samuel W. Mortimer, 1826 (original, 1653).

DALLINGTON, ROBERT, *The View of Fraunce*. London: Oxford University Press, 1936 (original, 1604).

DAWSON, THOMAS, *The Good Huswifes Jewell*. London: John Wolfe, 1587.

DIGBY, SIR KENELM, *The Closet of the Eminently Learned Sir Kenelme Digbie Kt. Opened*. London: 1669.

ELYOT, SIR THOMAS, *The Castel of Helth*. Scholars' Facsimiles and Reprints (original, 1541).

ERLANGER, PHILIPPE, *La Vie quotidienne sous Henri IV*. Paris: Hachette, 1958.

L'Escole parfaite des officiers de bouche, trans. by Giles Rose. London: 1682.

L'ESTOILE, PIERRE, *Journal pour le règne d'Henri III*. Paris: Gallimard, 1943.

FOURIER DE BACOURT, COMTE E., "Menu d'un dîner d'amis offert par Antoine Morel, Prévôt de Bar-Le-Duc," *Mémoires de la Société des Lettres, Sciences, et Arts de Bar-Le-Duc*, 3e série, tome VI, pp. 259–65.

GOURVILLE, JEAN HÉRAULT DE, *Mémoires*, 2 vols. Renouard, 1894.

HAKLUYT, RICHARD, *The Principall Navigations, Voyages, Traffiques and Discoveries of the English Nation*, 8 vols. New York: E. P. Dutton; London: J. M. Dent, 1907–1910 (original, 1599).

HARRISON, G. B., *The Elizabethan Journals*, 2 vols. Garden City, N.Y.: Doubleday, 1965.

HARRISON, WILLIAM, *The Description of England* (1577), part of *Holinshed's Chronicle*, q.v.

HENTZNER, PAUL, *A Journey into England, 1598*. Reading, Berks.: T. E. Williams, 1807.

HOLINSHED, RAPHAEL, *Holinshed's Chronicle of England, Scotland, and Ireland*, 6 vols. London: J. Johnson, etc., 1808 (original, 1577).

I. M., *A Health to the Gentlemanly Profession of Serving Men*. Oxford University Press, 1931 (original, 1598).

Introduction to England. New Shakespear Society Publications, ser. 6, nos. 5 and 8. London: N. Trübner, 1877.

JONES, PAUL VAN BRUNT, *The Household of a Tudor Nobleman*. University of Illinois Studies in the Social Sciences, vol. 6, no. 4 (December, 1917).

LAUDER, SIR JOHN, "Journal de voyage," *Mémoires de la société des antiquaires de l'ouest*, 3e série, tome 12 (1935). Poitiers: Société Française d'Imprimerie et de Librairie.

LA VARENNE, FRANÇOIS PIERRE DE, *Le Cuisinier françois*. Rouen: Richard L'allemant, 1683 (original, 1651).

LÉMERY, LOUIS, *A Treatise of All Sorts of Foods*. London, 1704/1745.

LEWIS, W. H., *The Splendid Century*. Garden City, N.Y.: Doubleday, 1957.

LOCATELLI, SÉBASTIEN, *Voyage de France, 1664–1665*, Paris: Alphonse Picard, 1905.

LUNE, SIEUR PIERRE DE, *Le nouveau et parfaict cuisinier*. Estienne Loyson, 1668 (original, 1656).

MASSIALOT, FRANÇOIS, *Le Cuisinier roial et bourgeois*. Paris: Charles de Sercy, 1698 (original, 1691).

MAY, ROBERT, *The Accomplish't Cook*. London: 1671 (original, 1660).

NEWMAN, L. F., "Some Notes on Food and Dietetics in the 16th and 17th Centuries," *Journal of the Royal Anthropological Institute of Great Britain and Ireland*, vol. 76, pt. 1 (1946), pp. 39–49.

NICHOLS, JOHN, *The Progresses and Public Processions of Queen Elizabeth*, 3 vols. London: John Nichols, 1823.

PAPIN, DENYS, *A New Digester or Engine for Softening Bones*. London: Bonwicke, 1681.

PEPYS, SAMUEL, *Diary*, various editions.

PERCY, HENRY ALGERNON, 5th Earl of Northumberland, *The Regulations and Establishment of the Household of Henry Algernon Percy*. London: 1770 (original, 1512).

PLAT, SIR HUGH, *Delightes for Ladies*. Herrin, Ill.: Trovillion Private Press, 1942 (original 1593 or 1594).

The Queens Closet Opened, transcribed from her Majesties' own receipt books by W. M. Cornhill, England: Nathaniel Brook, 1655.

ROBB, NESCA A., "The Fare of Princes. A Renaissance Manual of Domestic Economy," *Italian Studies*, Vol. VII (1952), pp. 36–63.

SAINCTOT, NICOLAS DE, *Le Cérémonial de France à la cour de Louis XIV*. Paris: P. Lethielleux, 1936 (original seventeenth century).

SAINT-SIMON, DUC DE, *Mémoires*, various editions.

SALMON, WILLIAM, *The Family Dictionary*. London: 1696.

SCAPPI, BARTOLOMEO, *Dell' Arte del Cuoco del Trinciante, e Mastro di Casa*. 1643 (original, 1570).

SERRES, OLIVIER DE, *Théâtre d'agriculture et ménage des champs*, 2 vols. Paris: Société d'Agriculture, 1804 (original, 1600).

SPANHEIM, ÉZÉCHIEL, *Relation de la cour de France* [1629–1710]. Paris, 1900.

The Star Chamber Dinner Accounts, 1567–1605. London: Wine and Food Society, 1959.

VOLTAIRE, *Le Siècle de Louis XIV*, 2 vols. Paris: A. Hatier.

WOOLEY, HANNAH, *The Queen-like Closet*. London, 1684 (original, 1670).

VI THE CLASSICAL CENTURY

ALTAMIRAS, JUAN, *Nuevo Arte de Cocina*. Barcelona: M. A. Martí Viuda (1767).

BOSWELL, JAMES, *London Journal, 1762–1763*. New York, Toronto, London: McGraw-Hill, 1950.

BOTSFORD, JAY BARRETT, *English Society in the Eigthteenth Century*. New York: Octagon Books, 1965.

CARTER, CHARLES, *The London and Country Cook*. London: Charles Hitch, 1747 (original, 1732).

A Collection of Receipts in Cookery, Physick and Surgery. London: Richard Wilkin, 1719.

CORRADO, VINCENZO, *Il Cuoco Galante*. Naples: Nella Stamperia Raimondiana, 1786.

EALES, MARY, *Mrs. Mary Eales's Receipts*. London: H. Meere, 1718.

FAIRFAX, ARABELLA, *The Family's Best Friend*. London: 1753.

GLASSE, HANNAH, *The Art of Cookery Made Plain and Easy*. London: W. Strahan, 1774 (original, 1747).

——— *The Compleat Confectioner*, London: 1772.

GOLDSMITH, OLIVER, "The Haunch of Venison," *Miscellaneous Works*, vol. 4. London: John Murray, 1837 (written 1771).

GONCOURT, EDMOND and JULES DE, *La Duchesse de Châteauroux et ses soeurs*. Paris: G. Charpentier, 1879.

——— *Histoire de la société française pendant la révolution*. Paris: G. Charpentier, 1880.

HANBURY, REV. WILLIAM, *A Complete Body of Planting and Gardening*, 2 vols. London: 1770.

HÉROARD, JEAN, *Journal de Jean Héroard sur l'enfance et la jeunesse de Louis XIII*, 2 vols. Paris: Firmin-Didot, 1868.

The House-keeper's Pocket Book, and Compleat Family Cook (London? 1785?).

HOWARD, HENRY, *England's Newest Way in All Sorts of Cookery*. London: Chr. Conings, 1717 (original, 1703).

JOHNSON, SAMUEL, *Journey to the Western Islands of Scotland* (1773). *British Tourists*, Vol. II, q.v.

LAMB, PATRICK, *Royal Cookery*. London: E. and R. Nutt and A. Roper, 1726 (original, 1710).

LEWIS, WILMARTH S., *Three Tours Through London in the Years 1748, 1776, 1797*. New Haven, Conn.: Yale University Press, 1941.

LIGER, LOUIS, SIEUR D'AUXERRE, *Le Ménage de la ville et des champs et le jardinier françois*. Brussels: Jean Léonard, 1712.

LÖFFLER, FRIEDERIKE LUISE, *Neues Koch Buch*, Stuttgart, Germany: Johann Cristoph Betulius, 1791.

MAISON DU ROY, LOUIS XV, *L'État et menu général de la maison du roy*. London: Maggs Bros.

MAVOR, WILLIAM F., ed., *The British Tourists*, 6 vols. London: E. Newbery, 1800.

MASON, CHARLOTTE, *The Ladies' Assistant*. London: J. Walter, 1787.

MAXWELL, CONSTANTIA, *The English Traveller in France*, 1698–1815. London: George Routledge & Sons, 1932.

MENON, *La Cuisinière bourgeoise*. Lyon, France: A. Leroy, 1805 (original, 1746).

MERCIER, LOUIS SÉBASTIEN, *Paris pendant la révolution*, 2 vols. Paris: Poulet-Malassis, 1862.

——— *Tableau de Paris*, 12 vols. Amsterdam: 1782–1788.

MORITZ, KARL P., *Travels Through Various Parts of England*, 1782, *British Tourists*, Vol. IV, q.v.

NORTHUMBERLAND, DUCHESS OF, *The Diaries of a Duchess* (1716–1776). London: Hodder & Stoughton, 1926.

PENNANT, THOMAS, *First Tour in Scotland* (1769), *Second Tour in Scotland* (1772), *British Tourists*, Vol. I, q.v. *Tour of London* in Vol. VI of Mavor's *British Tourists*.

RAFFALD, MRS. ELIZABETH WHITAKER, *The Experienced English House-keeper*. London: R. Baldwin, 1773.

SULLIVAN, RICHARD JOSEPH, *Tour Through Different Parts of England, Scotland, and Wales* (1778), *British Tourists*, Vol. III, *q.v.*

TRUSLER, DR. JOHN, *The Honours of the Table*, 2d ed. London: Literary Press, 1791.

TWISS, RICHARD, *Tour in Ireland* (1775), *British Tourists*, Vol. II, *q.v.*

The Whole Duty of a Woman: or, An Infallible Guide to the Fair Sex. London: T. Read, 1737.

YOUNG, ARTHUR, *The Farmer's Letters to the People of England*. London: W. Nicoll, n.d. (original, 1767).

—— *Tour in Ireland, 1776–1779*, *British Travelers*, Vol. III, *q.v.*

VII THE AGE OF REVOLUTION

ACCUM, FREDERICK, *A Treatise on Adulterations of Food and Culinary Poisons*. Philadelphia: Ab'm Small, 1820.

ACTON, ELIZA, *Modern Cookery*. London: Longmans, Green, 1887 (original, 1845).

ANDRIEU, PIERRE, "Les Sociétés gastronomiques françaises à travers les âges," *Les Éditions de la Journée Vinicole*, November 12, 1952.

AUDOT, LOUIS EUSTACHE, *Bréviare du gastronome*. Paris: Audot, 186?.

—— *La Cuisinière de la campagne et de la ville*. Paris, Audot, 1872.

BALZAC, HONORÉ DE, "Traité des excitans modernes," appendix to 1839 edition of Brillat-Savarin's *Physiologie du goût*.

BEAUVILLIERS, ANTOINE B., *L'Art du cuisinier*. London: Longman, Rees, Orme, Brown, and Green, 1827 (original, 1814).

BEETON, ISABELLA, *Beeton's Penny Cookery Book*. London: Ward, Lock & Tyler, 187?.

—— *Dictionary of Every-Day Cookery*. London: S. O. Beeton, 1865.

BERCHOUX, JOSEPH, *La Gastronomie ou l'homme des champs à table*. Paris: Giguet et Michaud, 1803.

BLAGDON, FRANCIS?, *Paris as It Was and As It Is*, Vol. II. London: C. & R. Baldwin, 1803.

BRIFFAULT, EUGENE, "Paris à table," *Romans du Jour Illustrés*. Paris: Gustave Havard, 1851.

BRILLAT-SAVARIN, ANTHELME, *Physiologie du goût*, various editions.

BRISSE, BARON ILDEFONSE-LÉON, *365 Menus and 1200 Recipes*. London: Sampson Low, 1882 (original, 1867).

CARÊME DE PARIS, M[ARIE] ANTONIN, *L'Art de la cuisine française au XIXe siècle*, 5 vols. Paris: au dépôt de la librairie, 1854 (original, 1828).

—— *Le Maître d'hôtel français*, 2 vols. Paris: Firmin-Didot, 1822.

—— *Le Pâtissier royal parisien*, 2 vols. Paris: 1854 (original, 1815).

CHILD, THEODORE, *Delicate Feasting*. New York: Harper, 1890.

CONIL, JEAN, *Haute cuisine*. London: Faber & Faber, 1953.

CURNONSKY and ANDRIEU, PIERRE, *Les fines gueules de France*. Paris: J. A. Quereuil, 1935.

DODD, GEORGE, *The Food of London*. London: Longman, Brown, Green, and Longmans, 1856.

ELLIOTT, MRS. MAUD HOWE, *Uncle Sam Ward and His Circle*. New York: Macmillan, 1938

ESCOFFIER, AUGUSTE, *Le Livre des menus*. Paris: Ernest Flammarion, 1927.
——— *Ma cuisine*, Paris: Flammarion, 1934.

GONCOURT, EDMOND and JULES DE, *Histoire de la société française pendant le directoire*, Paris: G. Charpentier, 1879.

GRIMOD DE LA REYNIERE, ALEXANDRE BALTHASAR LAURENT, *Almanach des gourmands*, 8 vols. Paris: Maradan, 1803–1812.
——— *Manuel des amphitryons*, Paris: Capelle et Renand, 1808.

HAYWARD, ABRAHAM, *The Art of Dining*. London: John Murray, 1899 (original, 1852).

KITCHINER, WILLIAM, *Apicius Redivivus. The Cook's Oracle*. London: John Hatchard, 1818.

LABOUCHÈRE, HENRI DU PRÉ, *Diary of the Besieged Resident in Paris*. New York: Harper, 1871.

LAMB, CHARLES, "Dissertation on Roast Pig," *Essays of Elia,* various editions.

McCOLLUM, ELMER VERNER, *A History of Nutrition*. Boston: Houghton Mifflin, 1957.

MONSELET, CHARLES, *Gastronomie*. Paris: G. Charpentier, 1874.

MORGAN, LADY, *France in 1829–1830*, 2 vols. London: Saunders and Otley, 1830.

PELLAPRAT, HENRI-PAUL, *L'Art culinaire moderne*. Paris: Comptoir Français du Livre, 1960.

RUNDELL, MARIA ELIZA, *A New System of Domestic Cookery*. New York: Robert M'Dermut, 1817.

SOYER, ALEXIS, *Culinary Campaign*. London: G. Routledge, 1857.
——— *The Gastronomic Regeneration*. London: Simpkin, Marshall, 1852.

THACKERAY, WILLIAM MAKEPEACE, "Barmecide Banquets," "Memorials of Gourmandizing," *The Works of William Makepeace Thackeray,* Vol. 25. London: Smith, Elder, 1885.

UDE, LOUIS EUSTACHE, *The French Cook*. London: Ebers, 1841 (original, 1814).

VANDAM, ALBERT DRESDEN, *An Englishman in Paris*, 2 vols. New York: D. Appleton, 1892.

WALKER, JOHN, *The Art of Dining*. New York: Robert M. De Witt, 1874.

WECHSBERG, JOSEPH, *Dining at the Pavillon*. Boston & Toronto: Little, Brown, 1962.

The New World

DIAZ, BERNAL, *The Conquest of New Spain*, trans. by J. M. Cohen. Baltimore, Md.: Penguin Books, 1963.

MASON, J. ALDEN, *The Ancient Civilizations of Peru*. Harmondsworth, M'sex.: Penguin Books, 1957.

VON HAGEN, VICTOR W., *The Aztec: Man and Tribe*. New York: New American Library, 1958.

PART TWO:

AN HISTORICAL INDEX TO SOME COMMON FOODS

In addition to the sources listed above, the following works were useful in reference to specific subjects covered in the historical index.

ASHTON, JOHN, *The History of Bread*. London: The Religious Tract Society, 1904.

BECKMANN, JOHN, *A History of Inventions and Discoveries*, 4 vols. London: J. Walker, etc., 1814 (original 1782).

Cheese Varieties and Descriptions. U.S. Department of Agriculture Handbook No. 54, 1953.

Cocoa and Chocolate; a Short History of Their Production and Use. Dorchester, Mass.: Walter Baker, 1910.

DODD, JAMES SOLAS, *Essay Towards a Natural History of the Herring*. London: T. Vincent, 1752.

ECKLES, CHARLES HENRY, *Milk and Milk Products*. New York: McGraw-Hill, 1936.

ELLIS, AYTOUN, *The Penny Universities: a History of the Coffee-Houses*. London: Secker & Warburg, 1956.

A Glossary of Spices. New York: American Spice Trade Association, 1966.

GOTHEIN, MARIE LUISE, *A History of Garden Art*, 2 vols. London: J. M. Dent & Sons, 1928.

HAZLITT, W. CAREW, *Gleanings in Old Garden Literature*. London: E. Stock, 1904.

A History of Spices. New York: American Spice Trade Association, 1966.

KAVALER, LUCY, *Mushrooms, Molds, and Miracles*. New York: John Day, 1965.

LEHNER, ERNST and JOHANN, *Folklore and Odysseys of Food and Medicinal Plants*. New York: Tudor Publishing Co., 1962.

LERY, FRANÇOIS, *Le Cacao*. Paris: Presses Universitaires de France, 1954.

Let's Talk Turkey. Chicago: The Poultry and Egg National Board in cooperation with the National Turkey Federation, 1968.

LUCAS, RICHARD, *Nature's Medicines*. New York: Parker, 1966.

Memoirs of the Literary and Philosophical Society of Manchester, Vol. IV, Part II, Falconer's account of the history of sugar, 1796.

MERRIAM, C. HART, "The Acorn, A Possibly Neglected Source of Food," *National Geographic Magazine*, Vol. 34 (August, 1918).

MOYNIER, M. M., *De la truffe*. Paris: Legrand et Bergougnioux, 1836.

PERRY, JOHN W., *The Story of Spices*. New York: Chemical Publishing, 1953.

PHILLIPS, HENRY, *History of Cultivated Vegetables*, 2 vols. London: Henry Colburn, 1827.

———— *Pomarium Britannicum.* London: Henry Colburn, 1827.

RENNER, H. D., *The Origin of Food Habits.* London: Faber & Faber, [1944?].

SALAMAN, REDCLIFFE N., *The History and Social Influence of the Potato.* London: Cambridge University Press, 1949.

SIMON, ANDRÉ L., *Cheeses of the World.* London: Faber & Faber, [1956].

STRONG, L. A. G., *The Story of Sugar,* London: Georg Weidenfeld & Nicolson, 1954.

TRAZ, GEORGES DE, *Histoire des cafés de Paris par François Fosca* (pseud). Paris: Firmin-Didot, [1935].

UKERS, WILLIAM H., *All About Coffee.* New York: Tea and Coffee Trade Journal Company, 1935.

WRIGHT, RICHARDSON, *The Story of Gardening.* New York: Dodd, Mead, 1934.